Basudara Stories of Peace from Maluku

Basudara Stories of Peace from Maluku

Working Together for Reconciliation

Editorial Team

Jacky Manuputty • Zairin Salampessy
Ihsan Ali-Fauzi • Irsyad Rafsadi

Translated by Hilary Syaranamual

© Copyright 2017
Copyright of this publication in its entirety is held by the editors and the translator.
Copyright of the individual chapters is held by the respective authors and the translator.
All rights reserved. Apart from any uses permitted by Australia's Copyright Act 1968, no part
of this book may be reproduced by any process without prior written permission from the
copyright owners. Inquiries should be directed to the publisher.

Monash University Publishing
Matheson Library and Information Services Building
40 Exhibition Walk
Monash University
Clayton, Victoria 3800, Australia
www.publishing.monash.edu

Monash University Publishing brings to the world publications which advance the best
traditions of humane and enlightened thought. Monash University Publishing titles pass
through a rigorous process of independent peer review.

www.publishing.monash.edu/books/bspm-9781925495140.html

Series: Herb Feith Translation Series
Series Editor: Jemma Purdey

Harmonisation of Manuscript: Hanna M.W. Parera, Husni Mubarok, Siswo Mulyartono

Design: Les Thomas

Cover image: Traditional wooden harbour in Masohi town, Central Maluku District, 2012.
Photo by Agus Lopuhaa.

National Library of Australia Cataloguing-in-Publication entry:
Title: Basudara stories of peace from Maluku : working together for
                  reconciliation / editors: Jacky Manuputty, Zairin Salampessy, Ihsan
                  Ali-Fauzi and Irsyad Rafsadi; translated by Hilary Syaranamual.
ISBN: 9781925495140 (paperback)
Series: Herb Feith translation series.
Subjects: Peace-building--Indonesia--Maluku.
                  Ethnic conflict--Indonesia--Maluku.
                  Conflict management--Indonesia--Maluku.
                  Religious tolerance--Indonesia--Maluku.
                  Maluku (Indonesia)--Religious life and customs.
Other Creators/Contributors:
                  Manuputty, Jacky, editor.
                  Salampessy, Zairin, 1968- editor.
                  Ali-Fauzi, Ihsan, 1965- editor.
                  Rafsadi, Irsyad, editor.
                  Syaranamual, Hilary, translator.
Dewey Number: 303.60959852

First published by
  Inter-Faith Organisation in Maluku (LAIM)
  Jl. Christina Martha Tiahahu No.17, RT. 003 RW. 01 Kelurahan Amantelu, Kecamatan
  Sirimau - Ambon 97122
In cooperation with
  The Centre for the Study of Religion & Democracy (PUSAD)
  Paramadina Foundation
  Bona Indah Plaza Blok A2 NO. D12, Jl. Karang Tengah Raya, Jakarta 12440
  Ph. (021) 765 5253   http://paramadina-pusad.or.id
1st Edition: January 2014

Printed in Australia by Griffin Press an Accredited ISO AS/NZS 14001:2004 Environmental
Management System printer.

The paper this book is printed on is certified against the Forest
Stewardship Council ® Standards. Griffin Press holds FSC chain of
custody certification SGS-COC-005088. FSC promotes environmentally
responsible, socially beneficial and economically viable management of
the world's forests.

CONTENTS

Editors' Foreword x
Translator's Note xiii
Acknowledgements xiv
Preface xv
    Gerry van Klinken

PART I.   Ale Rasa Beta Rasa: What You Feel, I Feel 1

Chapter 1
Thousands of Headlines without Deadlines 3
    Rudi Fofid

Chapter 2
Sticking to Principles 25
    Zairin Salampessy

Chapter 3
I Covered a Story, I Told the Story, I Wept 42
    Novi Pinontoan

Chapter 4
A Lesson for Peace in Maluku 59
    Dian Pesiwarissa

Chapter 5
Holding onto Beliefs 66
    Dino Umahuk

Chapter 6
Traces of Encounters 86
    M. Azis Tunny

PART II. Ain Ni Ain: We Come from the Same Egg 101

Chapter 7
When the Church Speaks Out 103
I.W.J. Hendriks

Chapter 8
The Turning Point on the Road of Basudara Relationships 112
Jacky Manuputty

Chapter 9
A Sermon on Peace from the Pulpit of the Al-Fatah Mosque 121
Hasbollah Toisuta

Chapter 10
Footsteps Leading to Encounters 131
Weslly Johannes

Chapter 11
Two of Abraham's Children: A Snippet from the Fajar Hidup
Vicarage. 146
Elifax Tomix Maspaitella

Chapter 12
Meeting Point on a Different Corner: Notes on Encounters
in Makassar. 154
Zainal Arifin Sandia

Chapter 13
Developing Peace when Dialogue became Dead-locked 161
Abidin Wakano

CONTENTS

PART III. Hena Masa Waya: Village above the Water 171

Chapter 14
A Policy of Restoring Peace of Mind 173
    M.J. Papilaja

Chapter 15
When the Conscience Speaks................................ 185
    M. Noor Tawainela

Chapter 16
Maluku Ashamed 194
    Steve Gaspersz

Chapter 17
When the Nation is Silent 200
    Theofransus Litaay

Chapter 18
Tragedy at the Crossroads of Transition 205
    Almudatsir Z. Sangadji

Chapter 19
When Politics Speaks 218
    Thamrin Ely

Part IV. Hiti Hiti Hala Hala: Enjoying the Good Things Together and Facing Difficulties Together 223

Chapter 20
We are All Brothers and Sisters 225
    Hilary Syaranamual

Chapter 21
Peace Is Just One Breath Away.............................. 233
    Sandra Lakembe

Chapter 22
The Story of a Little Campaigner for Peace in Maluku 242
    Inggrid Silitonga

Chapter 23
Why Must Religion Divide Us? 259
    Tiara Melinda A.S.

Chapter 24
Sleeping with the Enemy 269
    Helena M. Rijoly

Chapter 25
A Letter to a Dear Friend 288
    Nancy Souisa

Chapter 26
Gandong'ee, Let's Sing! 292
    Jacky Manuputty

Conclusion
Positive Avoidance, Segregation and Communal Cooperation
in Maluku 297
    Rizal Panggabean

Epilogue
Stories with a Million Dimensions 302
    Aholiab Watloly

Glossary 323
Acronyms and Abbreviations 328
About the Contributors 332
About the Herb Feith Translation Series 341

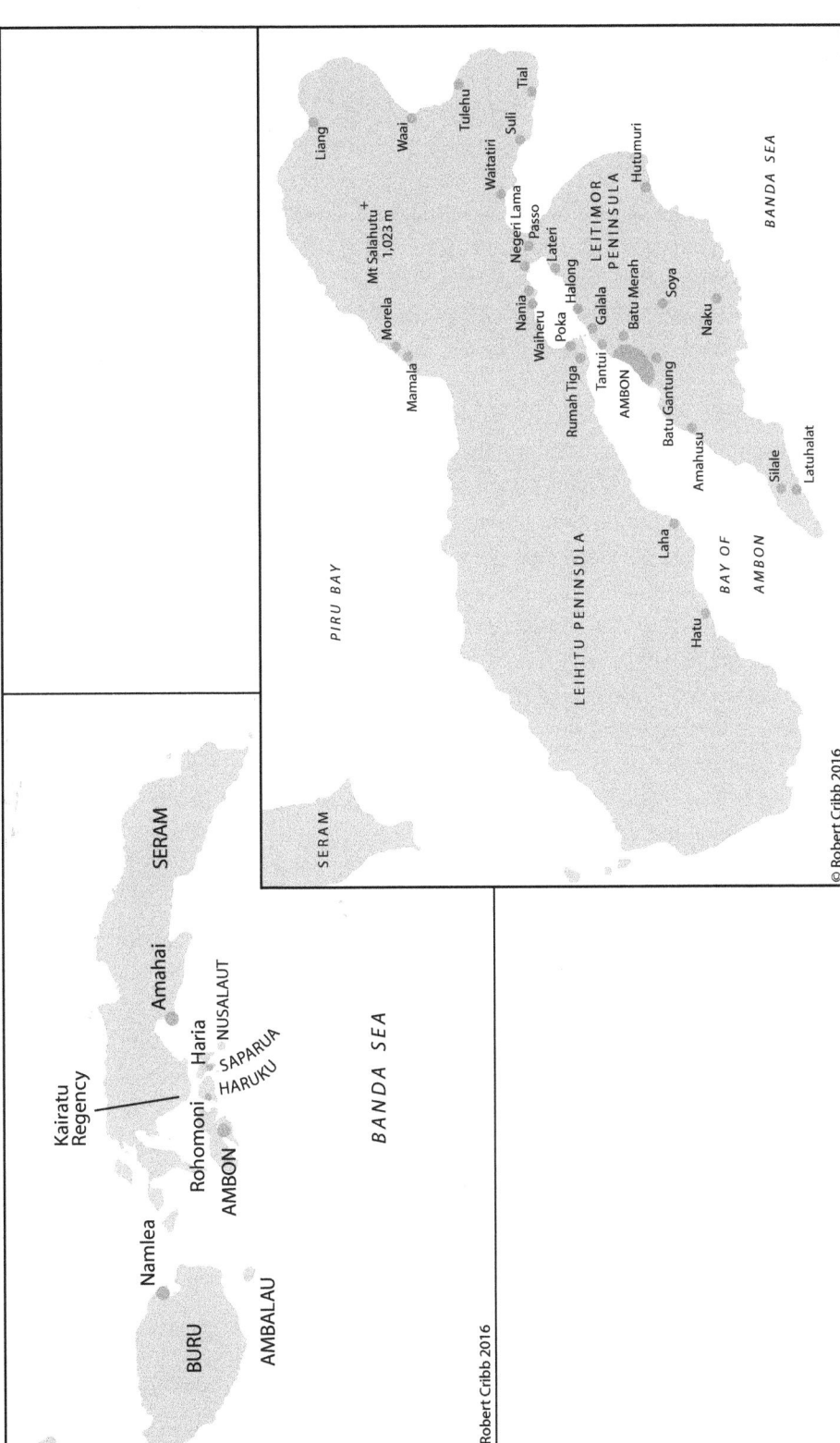

EDITORS' FOREWORD

Carita (story) or *bercerita* (storytelling) is a form of verbal communication told by a narrator to his/her listeners. Usually it is the mother who tells bedtime stories to her children. A story could be a fairytale, fable or fantasy, but it could also contain descriptions of the mother or other people's life experiences. As well as sending someone to sleep, a story can also contain deeper meaning. Even when told in simple language, it can be full of metaphors, analogies and examples.

'Orang basudara' is a phrase that is rich in meaning. The phrase does not just technically define the relationships between blood relatives. It also conveys feelings including love and solidarity; sharing the same fate; and being willing to help one another. The phrase orang basudara cannot be separated from other phrases or sayings in the same way that the following also cannot: '*sagu salempeng dipata dua*' (*sagu salempeng* broken in two),[1] '*ale rasa beta rasa*' (what you feel I feel), '*potong di kuku rasa di daging*' (if your nail is ripped you'll feel it in your body), '*katong samua satu gandong*' (we all come from the same womb).

This is why we have chosen *Basudara Stories of Peace from Maluku* as the title of this book.[2] Here, the 'Basudara's Stories of Peace' refers to communication, using writing, to give eyewitness accounts, experiences and reflections about life by a number of local people before, during and after the conflict that took place in 1999.

To mark 15 years after the end of the conflict, the stories we offer in this book are ones that bring new hope, comfort and optimism. All the contributions in this book were written in the spirit of orang basudara.

We need to remember that, in the middle of the conflict that brought distress and suffering, when many people were trapped and 'forced', directly or indirectly, to be involved in the raging conflict, some people found their own distinctive ways to maintain their distance and be critical of the conflict and also to strive for peace. Although they were not many in number, the steps they took and their contributions need to be described, to support the rebuilding of a civilised community for the people of Maluku.

---

1   Translator's note: *Sagu salempeng* is a biscuit made from sagu flour and baked in a mould. It is only edible when dunked in tea or coffee.

2   Translator's note: The original title of this book is *Carita Orang Basudara*, literally 'Stories of the Basudara'.

This book aims to record and document their experiences, so they don't just disappear into thin air. More than that, we are also sure that not just the community concerned, but all humankind, can learn many valuable lessons, now and in the future, from the experiences of the human conflict in Maluku.

The First from Maluku[3]

When we started this book in 2007, we were very idealistic. We used a number of methods for collecting the material, such as the inductive method, bottom-up approach, and proposed a variety of writers or sources who were part of, or who worked at, ground level, such as imam or da'I, ministers, priests, activists, researchers, journalists and others. We also tried a reflective approach by delving into the experiences of practical encounters in the field before, during and after the conflict. We also tried the contextual approach, by looking critically at the problems of religious conflict from a contextual (theological) point of view.

But we couldn't carry out our idealistic plans for a number of reasons. In the end we chose to invite a number of individuals to tell their stories. This became *Basudara Stories of Peace from Maluku*.

Unfortunately, at the time of publication of the original Indonesian version, a number of potential authors, who had originally said they were willing to write failed to meet the deadline due to other commitments or other reasons. This book, therefore, does not claim that only these authors served to bring about peace in Maluku. We hope that the experiences of people whose stories could not be included here can be read on another occasion, because those very valuable experiences also need to be recorded.

Apart from Gerry van Klinken and Rizal Panggabean, the writers in this book were directly involved in the dynamics of the conflict from 1999 to 2002. To the best of our knowledge, this is the first book that has recorded their eyewitness accounts directly, written by themselves, in their own words.

The writers' backgrounds are varied and include journalists, ulama, politicians, a former mayor, social activists, lecturers, photographers, women activists, artists and students. Their ages are also varied, and this is reflected here: from an author who describes her involvement when she was only eight or nine years old, to an author who recorded his experiences of the conflict and the peace process when he was in his sixties. Their involvement in the

---

3   Translator's note: Maluku is the official Indonesian name for the province that, in the past, was known in English as 'the Moluccas'.

conflict was also varied: many of the authors were deeply involved at each stage of the conflict and the peace process, but other authors were not in Ambon for the whole of the conflict. This variety makes *Basudara Stories of Peace from Maluku* an interesting mosaic and helps the reader understand the events of the conflict and peace process from different points of view.

From Maluku to the World

Why were we interested and prepared to work hard to publish this book? As an organisation that cares about the inter-faith humanitarian problems, the Inter-Faith Organisation in Maluku (Lembaga Antar Iman Maluku or LAIM) felt called to mediate by providing a space to record and document the variety of experiences of working for peace and upholding humanitarian values in Maluku. We believe that the experiences recorded here will be very useful for the community, at the least as alternative reading to the many documents that have covered the conflict so far. For us, this book is a type of historical document from those who till now feel they haven't had a voice (voice of the voiceless).

Apart from this, we also believe that the experience in Maluku can become a mirror into which we can look for lessons in preventing violent conflict or strengthen endeavours for peace in other parts of the world. This is why the Centre for Study of Religion and Democracy (PUSAD), Paramadina Foundation became involved in this writing project and the publication of this book.

This is also the the context within which we invited Gerry and Rizal to write the preface and the conclusion of this book. Besides being known as scholars who are familiar with cases of conflict, they are also known as passionate supporters of reconciliation and peace building. Their writings show that Maluku can learn from the world, and the world can learn from Maluku!

It is now time for good stories, filled with voices for peace (not violent conflict), to be heard more from Maluku and other places in Indonesia. If we really want to see peace, why don't we start with more frequently reading and writing about it or discussing it?

Editorial Team
Ambon and Jakarta, 25 December 2013

TRANSLATOR'S NOTE

Living in Ambon and understanding the local dialect and the meaning behind many of the local sayings has influenced the way I have approached the translation of these stories. Large sections of the original text assume that the reader understands the local dialect and the Ambonese world view. It is important that the reader can catch something of the Ambonese way of life but not be bogged down with too many unfamiliar terms. I have tried to keep a balance between the use of Ambonese terms and making things clear in English. I have not translated the section titles because they were already in the glossary. I have removed some terms from the glossary which were in everyday Ambonese because they have not been used in the English version. I have had to add various Muslim terms to the glossary because they are not necessarily known widely to the non-Muslim reader. The original text was aimed at Indonesian readers who would be familiar with the terms. I have tried to be very careful in order to avoid misunderstanding in some of the more sensitive sections. Some sentences were checked with the original authors to make sure that my understanding was correct.

ACKNOWLEDGEMENTS

Before it was published in its current form, *Basudara Stories of Peace from Maluku* went through a long, time-consuming process. The most difficult part of the process was gathering a number of contributors from different backgrounds and asking them to write about their experiences and involvement in the violent conflict or in the peace.

In the beginning a number of the prospective authors rejected our invitation, because writing their stories would bring them face-to-face once more with their experiences of the violent conflict in the bitter and traumatic past. Several prospective female authors sharply rejected our endeavours. They said that the traumatic conditions experienced by women and children were far worse than the men's traumatic experiences.

All this is understandable, remembering that so far there has been no serious attempt at trauma counselling for people after the conflict in Maluku. Approaches used in the post-conflict recovery in Maluku have tended to urge people to forget the darkness of the past conflict, rather than coming to terms with it.

Therefore, in publishing this book, we are primarily very grateful to the contributors who were prepared to share their stories here. May their contributions become a flaming torch to shed light on future peace endeavours.

Besides that, we would like to thank activists from the peace network in Maluku for their support and help. Finally, we would like to convey our gratitude to *Kerk in Actie* (the Netherlands) and The Asia Foundation (Jakarta) for their financial support for the writing and publishing of this book.

LAIM and PUSAD Paramadina
Ambon and Jakarta, 25 December 2013

PREFACE

Ale Rasa Beta Rasa – What You Feel, I Feel: Compiling History Together in Ambon

Gerry van Klinken[1]

Ambon is still beautiful, full of laughter, full of chattering. But there is an amazing silence in Ambon about the community unrest, or better called the local civil war, that started on 19 January 1999. This silence has come to an end today! We started with an experiment, to talk about things that are not usually talked about.

Ambon has undergone reconciliation – but without talking in public about the incidents that really took place during the civil war: 'reconciliation without truth'. This was the term used by John Braithwaite, a researcher from the Australian National University, to explain the atmosphere after several incidents of communal violence that occurred in Indonesia after *Reformasi*,[2] including acts of communal violence in Ambon and the surrounding areas, North Maluku, Poso and the anti-Madurese violence that occurred in Kalimantan.

In fact, the Malino II Agreement in February 2002 included a point about endeavouring to find out the truth of what happened. This has, however, never been done. People are afraid that the truth will 'open up old wounds'.

The same explanation is also often heard in other historical tragedies that have taken place in Indonesia; for example, the massacres that took place after G30S in 1965, the Darul Islam violence in the 1950s, even the Republic of South Maluku (RMS) rebellion in 1950.[3] These incidents are

---

1   Revised from a paper that was delivered during activities held by the Inter-Faith Foundation in Maluku, 'Dialogue and Reflection together 10 Years on from the Conflict in Maluku', Ambon, 19 January 2010.
2   Translator's note: *Reformasi*, literally 'reformation', is the period after President Soeharto stepped down in 1998.
3   Translator's note: G30S refers to the attempted military coup in 1965, after which thousands suspected Communists were massacred. This was in the first years of President Soeharto's rule (the period under Soeharto was known as the 'New Order').

mentioned in school textbooks, but only in an abstract manner. The reader is never given real explanations about what happened to people, such as Mr Albert, Mrs Bachtiar, or Sus Lies.

Only a part of the National Revolution of 1945-1949 has been written to date – the heroic opposition against the colonialists. There is nothing written about the murders of *Indo* (mixed race), Chinese or other Indonesians, who were regarded as having a Dutch mindset (the amazing novel *Burung-Burung Manyar*, written by Mangunwijaya in 1981, is an exception). So many old wounds have been bandaged in silence. In Ambon, the community unrest in 1999-2002, more than a decade ago, still leaves painful, old, open wounds.

I am an historian. Like the German philosopher from the 19th century, Hegel, I believe that truth is always historical in nature. We become 'we' because of our past. Our convictions, feelings, personalities, our private relationships – all are the fruit of our fertile past. Our civilisation is rooted in the soil of our past. We do not create our future from nothing. The future is an extension of past times. We learn from experience, and then we try to find a new direction, with a starting point in the past. We can only build a good future after understanding the past – whether our own personal past, or the collective past as a people, as a society. Thus compiling history is a sacred burden for humankind.

Each generation must rewrite its own history, according to its own interpretation. This sacred burden doesn't originate from the president, it doesn't originate from the nation of Indonesia, nor does it originate from religion. The sacred burden of continually reinterpreting history comes from us, as human beings. In reflecting on history we become more glorious human beings, more civilised, more humane. We become more open to other people who live together on this one earth. We become more understanding towards others people of different cultures, especially our neighbours.

Of course such history is not usually taught in school. It's a pity, everywhere history is ruined in school. It is the same in Australia; history becomes a state propaganda tool. History is no longer the property of the people. What I want to talk about here is not the textbook history taught in schools. No! The history that I like to read is far more alive, far more populist, more like literature (like the books of Mangunwijaya or Pramoedya Ananta Toer), more like poetry, or music, more of a reflection

---

Darul Islam (literally, The House of Islam) was an Islamist movement, founded in 1942 and lasting until about 1962, which aimed for Indonesia to become an Islamic state. The RMS (Republik Maluku Selatan or Republic of South Maluku) was an independence movement, formed in 1950, which declared an independent state.

on meaning than just facts. Reflecting on history that is flesh and blood is not a bitter task, rather a pleasure.

In my opinion, the stories of the civil war in Ambon need to be expressed, especially in public. The next generation will want to know, and should know, what happened over a decade ago. The younger generation must understand about the victims – about the Butonese who have become refugees, about the young warriors who were slain in A.Y. Patty Street. The people who died should be respected, not because of anything, but because they were also human beings, who should not be forgotten.

A people can be rich materially, they have McDonald's and the internet, but if they do not know history, whether it be positive or negative, the society is poor. In Berlin, Germany, I once visited a museum that was built to remember the massacre of six million Jews by the German Nazis during World War II. This Museum is always full of visitors. Every German child studies about the Holocaust in school, the events of the massacre. School children also visit Auschwitz, the concentration camp where the Jews were massacred in Poland which is still preserved as a monument. After experiencing the atmosphere in Auschwitz, they are invited to reflect on themselves and their present environment. 'Are their negative feelings towards the Turkish newcomers who are Muslims the same or dissimilar to the negative feelings shown towards the Jews 70 years ago? If they are similar, then what is to be done to change this situation?'

Thus, things that happened decades ago still make people think. World War II has become the biggest theme in European literature until now, although the generation that witnessed it almost no longer exists. Such is the history of the Jews in Germany and the history of the Aborigines in Australia.

Australian children are beginning to learn in high school about the genocide that took place against the Aborigines in the 19th century. Indeed, it is painful because, for decades these matters were never mentioned in Germany and Australia. Every society has to face their demons.

The civil war in Ambon perhaps was far more painful, because it involved two parties who were almost the same.

Indeed, it is not easy to tell stories, because there are deep feelings of hurt, and strong taboos. But there are different ways to tell a story. It may be that certain methods are more feasible than others.

Allow me first of all to discuss a few reasons that are often mentioned to discourage the commemoration of the incidents that occurred during the Ambonese civil war, 1999-2002. I will try to give an answer to each of these reasons. After that, allow me to suggest three ways to attempt public storytelling.

In Ambon, I felt there is a taboo, a strong prohibition about telling stories about the community unrest. Why is this prohibition so strong? I think that the reasons can be divided into three groups. All of these objections are meant to ensure that the damage doesn't occur again. The first concerns social harmony, the second concerns respect for important institutions, and the third concerns personal trauma.

The first reason that makes it taboo to talk in public about the community unrest in Ambon is the fear that to talk about it, will damage the fragile social harmony. Christians will accuse Muslims, Muslims will accuse Christians. There will not be an agreement about what occurred. Each person regards their own version as right.

This reason makes a lot of sense. We all want peace, not a return of violence. However, there are two problems with this reason. First, it demonstrates an erroneous concept of history, and second, it can too easily become a pretext for people whose hands are covered in blood, so their crimes will not become public.

This reason is based on an erroneous concept of history because it assumes that only 'my' experiences can be said to be history, while 'your' experiences cannot. This is definitely not history. History is learning about the lives of others. For humankind to become whole, we have to learn to feel what other people feel. *'Ale rasa beta rasa'* – is not wrong, it is actually in the spirit of compiling history.

This reason can too easily become the excuse used by war criminals, and indeed is often used in that manner. That is the reason the perpetrators of the massacres that took place in 1965–1966 have never been publicly revealed even to this present day. The murderers were members of various organisations that worked together with the military.

In the Ambonese civil war, I also believe that members of problem organisations, including religious and political institutions – church, mosque, political parties – were involved. At the end of the 1990s, it was the era of reformation, democratisation, with intensive mobilisation in the political and religious spheres. The rules of the game weren't clear; security forces were divided and weak. Some churches in Ambon were involved in the violence; some mosques in Ambon were involved. They should be the first to break the taboo and say, 'We are guilty'.

What will happen if the reason of social harmony continues to block these stories? I am concerned that the results will, on the contrary, be even worse, creating a hypocritical society. People will remain silent in public, while behind closed doors many one-sided stories are recalled. 'I am a victim, they are the ones who were in the wrong, and we only defended ourselves'. Children will grow up being suspicious of other people. That is the way to maintain divisions in society. That is not what we all hope for.

The second reason that has been used for maintaining the taboo on storytelling is that important institutions in the community will be shamed. People will lose their respect for government and religion. The community unrest of 1999-2002 is regarded as something that makes Ambon ashamed, something shameful for religion. The feeling of shame is regarded as negative. People cannot lose face; we cannot make people feel ashamed.

It is the same as the first reason; this reason has many positive aspects. We will only feel ashamed about what we do ourselves. This reason is a disguised confession that the Ambonese themselves were at war. This war wasn't introduced from Jakarta but emerged in Ambon by itself. Indeed, war is a disaster – no Ambonese wants to start a war. But not all disasters are like a tsunami which occurs without people being responsible for it. Instead of putting a stop to war, there are those who fan the flames to make the situation worse. Instead of looking for justice, there are those who deliberately make false accusations. At least part of the responsibility lies in Ambon itself, not on the marginalised people in Ambon, but respected people, important people, businessmen, politicians, religious leaders and public figures. Indeed, there are people who should feel ashamed. Feeling ashamed is the first step towards change. When we feel ashamed, we are saying, 'It is indeed wrong, don't let it happen again.' There is truth, therefore, in the reason that telling stories of the community unrest will make people ashamed.

While shame is painful, 'sorry' is the most difficult word to say. Institutions that have power – including church institutions, Ulama institutions, political parties, the Governor's office, the regent's office, the military command or police – are often reluctant to apologise. This is because they are frightened of being regarded as weak and that they will no longer be respected.

Therefore, attempts to uncover history must be democratic. I am sure that change lies in the new generation, including the generation that is represented here. The new generation will ask the older generation, 'Why did you do it?' The younger generation will ask the questions that need to be asked. They will ask the church, 'Why did you stay silent?' They will ask the police, 'Why did you take sides?' They will ask the Ulama, 'Why did you spread hatred?' Only in this way, religious life and the life of the country will enter a new, improved era.

The third reason for maintaining the taboo on storytelling, perhaps, is the concern that these stories will revive old psychological traumas. Those who used to suffer nightmares, don't wish to have them return. This reason, as with the previous two reasons, contains a lot of truth. For some people historical truth is liberation and healing, but for others it triggers nightmares. It could be that the uncovering of the history of community unrest is not beneficial for all. We must be really sensitive about this matter.

At the same time, we can't assume that historical truth itself kills. Sometimes, when we repeat a bad experience, this can break the emotional bondages. Suddenly we feel that the experience has become distant. On the contrary, people suddenly say with surprise: 'Oh, that's how I felt at that time. I was so full of hatred. But the times have changed.'

Again, not all aspects of this story cause trauma, not all of it destroys humankind. There are some aspects that bring hope, even make us laugh, because they are so funny. The civil war in Ambon also produced many stories that are truly heroic. For example, the female peddler from Wisma Atlit, who reopened trading between the people of Mardika and Batu Merah. Or the health worker who distributed aid to refugees from all types of religious backgrounds. Or the Ambonese whose mother was Christian and whose father was Muslim, who became confused and didn't know who to view as the enemy. These stories should not be forgotten, including the story of the history of LAIM itself.

I would therefore like to suggest three ways to re-tell the incidents of the past. All of them are practical in nature. This process doesn't need a doctorate in history. There are no teachers in this process, just students. History is not a result but a process. The process of compiling of history is a process that brings about renewal, liberation and openness.

It is better if this type of compilation of history is worked on together, not individually or too academically. It should become a joint aspiration. This could be through a truth and reconciliation commission, established by the Peoples' Consultative Assembly at provincial level, or through an inter-faith commission, or an NGO commission, or by LAIM itself, perhaps aided by several professional historians.

Firstly, look for the right words. History is primarily about words. It has to be a true story. We all want to know what happened. Listen to the words of those who experienced it first-hand, record and discuss. Is there anyone who kept a diary? Is there anyone who wrote a letter at that time, who is willing for the contents of the letter to be made available to the general public? Start by listening.

The listener should cross the boundaries. Christians have to ask Muslims to tell their stories and record them. Muslims have to ask Christians to tell their stories, record them and discuss them together. People from Tulehu should ask people from Waai to tell the stories of their experiences. People from Mardika should ask people from Batu Merah to tell their stories. They can tell their stories individually or in a group. Ask what the experience was like living in a refugee camp, knowing that their houses were only one kilometre away but were out of reach because someone from another religion was living in them. Ask how neighbours suddenly became enemies. Ask someone what he taught his own children during the community unrest. Ask someone who fought on the front line to tell what he felt the first time he saw blood sticking to a corpse. Ask, where they buried their eldest child, who died in a battle and go to visit his grave.

Make a recording for posterity – on paper, or in a video, or just a voice is enough. True stories, complete with photographs if needed. These words have to be kept for the next generation. The main aim is they will become really revolted by what is called a civil war.

Who should be asked to tell their stories? Listening to stories also needs to be democratic. It is not the stories of important people that should be given priority, but the stories of ordinary people. Especially listen to the stories of the weak. Search for women's stories, how they provided for their families. Jeroen Adam wrote his dissertation about this in Ghent, Belgium. Search for stories about sexual crimes. This often happens during the clashes. Listen to the experiences of the children, especially the child fighters called 'agas' or 'linggis'.

Special efforts must be made to listen to the stories of peacemakers. Tonny Pariela in 2008 wrote a good dissertation about this. We need many more stories of this type. There are still many new things which have not yet been disclosed.

In addition to stories of ordinary people, there must be comprehensive and precise information about many things, because at that time much of the information which circulated was inaccurate. Make a map that shows all the villages that were burnt to the ground or partially burnt down, don't forget the small villages such as Larat and Ngat in Kei Besar. Make other maps that show the locations and dates of the biggest clashes; other maps that show the locations of the boundaries between red areas and white areas from one time to another. Make other maps that show the new trade routes that developed at the height of the clashes – there were many efforts to find new routes.

Second, purify the emotions. History does not only contain words. Commemorations full of ritual can also play an important part. Commemorations are opportunities to allow the emotions to run freely – feelings of sadness, feelings of nostalgia, feelings of thankfulness, feelings of shame, even good feelings. Humans are creatures of tradition. Old traditions can be restored and given new meanings. The Ambonese are clever in their use of tradition. It can be with a song, with music, or even without any sound being made – only with a minute's silence in front of several photographs, with flowers.

19 January is an important date. We commemorate this date by discussing what happened 15 years ago. Does this date need to be commemorated each year? Is that possible? The objective must be clear – 19 January can become a moment to say: 'This happened. Don't let it be repeated.' The commemoration carried out with unadulterated emotions like this has amazing potential. It can create a new future for religion in Ambon. No longer being defensive, no longer being defiant, no longer linked to the structure of power, but open, humane and full of liberty.

Third, note the place. The commemoration has to be down to earth; it has to have a specific place, just like human life. The war 15 years ago was basically a battle to take hold of important places – traditional land, houses, mosques, churches, even shops. Is there a simple monument in A.Y. Patty Street to commemorate the deaths of men and women who fought there? Is there a small plaque at the crossing point between the red and white areas, the place where the soldiers were on guard? It doesn't need to be large, a brief description – this used to be the demarcation line that separated enemies, now it is a meeting place.

Places of worship often became special targets. They are monuments of identity. Do the places of worship that have been re-built, look different from what they used to? Do the visitors to this place of worship know that this place used to be a symbol of war not a symbol of peace? How have the mosques and churches become part of the sacred burden to compile history?

Finally, I would like to suggest an idea, or more precisely ask a question. Does Ambon need a museum of peace and reconciliation? Or does it need just a room that contains a permanent exhibition?

The World Peace Gong was inaugurated in Ambon, on 25 November 2009. This is very good. Photographs of the community unrest, photographs of the security forces trying to stop the unrest, photographs of the signing of the peace declaration. The monument is grandiose, inaugurated by the president, with floodlights, in a location that stands in front of the Governor's office. If on World Peace Day this year the local elite gather at this monument, then it will become an important symbol of the good intent to preserve social harmony in the future.

But I also think that Ambon is still open to a museum in a different form. A museum that belongs to the people and that becomes a place where people can easily mix with each other. With its emphasis on the experiences of the ordinary people, this museum can exhibit maps, photographs, videos, songs, posters, and other material about the 1999-2002 community unrest. More importantly, a museum of peace and reconciliation can be a lively place. A place where there are encounters between Christians and Muslims, who can reflect, remember, and discuss together, where the dead are respected and a place which can inspire new hope, where people consider the past and also the future, a place for reconciliation through truth.

Such a museum, if it was built, must be bold. It should have a very strong commitment to the people, but with a sacred burden to develop dialogue based on an understanding of history, a sacred burden to create a better future through knowledge about the past. A museum like this must fight pressure from institutions that are not yet ready to say 'sorry'. It should not be afraid, and should not compromise with what is called 'biased truth' as was often heard during the community unrest. A museum like this would become like the Holocaust Museum in Berlin, or the Vietnam War Memorial in Washington, which wants to say, 'This is what happened; see our good intentions to prevent it happening again.'

This book, first suggested in 2007, has become a reality. The silence about the community unrest of 1999-2002 has begun to be broken. Something, which in the past would have been impossible, has proved to be possible. All of the personal stories in this book have been conveyed with amazing honesty. It was not easy to display deep personal feelings in public. More amazingly, all the contributors come from the communities that used to face each other with angry scowls. This is sufficient to make this book an historic monument.

The contents also cannot be taken lightly. I find it interesting to note how both *Salam* (Muslim) and *Sarane* (Christian) writers use similar language.[4] At the most critical times, when carrying personal burdens – houses burnt down, being threatened with machetes, ears pounded by sharp words – they

---

4   *Salam* is a local Moluccan term for a Muslim, while a Christian is usually called *Sarane*. So far there has never been any special study related the use of these terms in the close Muslim-Christian relationship in Maluku, however by using these terms *Salam* and *Sarane*, in general the local Moluccan Muslims and Christians feel close to each other within the culltural frame.

all tried to open themselves to others. As Abidin Wakano says, he 'tried to become a bridge and an oasis for all people in the midst of that situation.' Such attempts made the contributors reflect on their own religion. Thamrin Ely even hoped that people would emulate Bertrand Russell; study to be civilised with a shrewdness that doesn't need religion. At least, the majority of the contributors hope that religious practice will include more dialogue, and be more pluralistic. Jacky Manuputty wrote: 'I believe that a Christian can never become Sarane without continuing to mix with Muslim brothers and sisters who are Salam, and vice versa.' Hasbollah Toisuta dreamed about people who have regained the humanitarian heritage of the basudara, which had been swallowed by the vicious appetite of unfeeling ruthlessness.

Part I

Ale Rasa Beta Rasa: What You Feel, I Feel

Chapter 1

THOUSANDS OF HEADLINES WITHOUT DEADLINES

Rudi Fofid

The *Tujuh Lumut* or 'Seven Mosses'

Seven students from the Faculty of Law of Pattimura University Ambon, were on placement at the Baileo Maluku Foundation. They were Samson Atapary, Julius Lawalata, Daniel Utra, Joseph Renleew, Paulus Lakaneny, Hans Syaranamual and Tenny Letekay. The leading lights of the NGO, Roem Topatimasang, Nus Ukru and Rony Titaheluw were training them in the various processes of organising the community, study, field surveys and other NGO activities. Samson and friends called themselves 'The Tujuh Lumut' (seven mosses).

In 1996, the Tujuh Lumut met at Paparisa Manuala Beach, on the Leihitu peninsula of the island of Ambon. Paparisa was founded by husband and wife, Ramly and Waty Soulissa. On a wooden pier stretching out to the sea, there was a sort of floating gazebo. There, Zairin Salampessy and I were speakers, training in investigations about the environment. We discussed methods of investigation and introduced the working principles of investigative journalism.

Outside of this topic, we also talked about the traditional village of Kaitetu with its old church that stands next to the old Mapauwe mosque. Truly amazing. On the Leihitu peninsula which has a Salam (Muslim) majority, there was also the small village of Kaitetu with its Sarane (Christian) congregation. Thus, the Salam-Sarane basudara had lived there in harmony and peace. What's more, there no longer appeared to be a boundary between the villages of Hila and Kaitetu.

'This is a real monument of religious harmony. What is the point of building a monument to demonstrate religious harmony? Aren't the villages of Hila-Kaitetu a living monument?' That was our conclusion.

We even thought about writing a full description of the harmonious life demonstrated between the people of Hila-Kaitetu, as a feature in a newspaper. At the very least, that feature would put on record the pattern of harmonious living that took place there. The students did not have the opportunity to carry out this idea because the Tujuh Lumut took half-day's leave from the training area. They went to pay their last respects to a prominent figure that they greatly respected, Bert Ririmasse. Bert Ririmasse, the traditional leader of Haruku had passed away in Batu Gantung, Ambon.

The Tujuh Lumut then carried out an investigative survey of the forests of Seram. This was incredible, because they discovered that permit holders of logging concessions were carrying out random felling of trees. For example, one logging firm had even cut down trees in the lands belonging to the Manusela National Park. This discovery was published in the media; however the holders of logging concessions kept quiet, and the manager of the Manusela National Park also seemed to shut his eyes and ears.

I was impressed with the Tujuh Lumut, because through the many processes they were becoming more mature in their leadership, group work, financial management, time management, mastering of media technology, personal and public communication skills, and intelligent use of language. They were more and more capable of working closely with and motivating the people. In discussion and debate, they were like the devil's logic, as in the song by Iwan Fals.[1]

Nus Ukru from the Baileo Foundation was the person who introduced the Tujuh Lumut to me. This relationship continued, especially after community unrest broke out in Maluku. The Tujuh Lumut and I worked together in a team of volunteers. But we were also embarrassed when we recalled our idea to record the harmonious way of life displayed between Hila-Kaitetu. This is because when the conflict in Ambon broke out, this monument to harmonious living was the first to come crashing down.

---

[1] Translator's note: The song is '*Aku Sayang Mu*' (I Love You) by Iwan Fals: ' … *Bila engkau bicara … setan logika, Sedikit keras kepala … ah dasar betina …* ' [' … If you speak … devil of logic, You are a bit stubborn … Oh, that's because you are female …']

Tujuh Jaga, the Seven Guardians

It was Sunday, 17 January 1999. The sun was beating down on the highest peak. Its rays were shimmering on the waters of Baguala Bay. The sand of Natsepa beach also blinded the eyes. Fortunately, a bintanggur tree (*Calophyllum inophyllum*) provided shelter for about 30 nature lovers from the campuses and schools in Ambon. For two days, I had been a speaker there, providing training in basic journalism from an environmental perspective. The tale of the Tujuh Jaga (Seven Guardians) emerged because I asked the participants to describe an experience from an environmental perspective.

Senior High School students Ridolf Latumahina and student Hasbullah Assel coincidentally wrote about the same incident. Tujuh Jaga is the name of one of the famous peaks on the spine of Mount Salahutu. Young Ambonese, who have been to Tujuh Jaga, always want to return there. This peak is not only romantic, but is also full of mystical tales. Climbers believe that invisible guardians live there. If the climbers are not polite, a guardian will be angry. As a result, one or more of the climbers will be possessed.

The tales of spirit possession on Tujuh Jaga were told in a dramatic manner. Ridolf and Hasbullah told the story of a female climber, who became possessed by the spirit of the guardian of the mountain and spoke with a fellow climber. She listed all the wrong doings of the young people and demanded the enactment of the procedure for the returning of the spirit. The climbers also had to promise not to repeat their wrongdoings.

The tale of possession by spirits meant the participants weren't bothered by the scorching heat of the sun. For a while they forgot their feelings of hunger during the fasting month. In addition to Ridolf and Hasbullah, others present included Dino Umahuk, Hanafi Holle, Yayat Hidayat, Dur Kaplale and Linda Holle. Although the majority of the participants were fasting, they still prepared breakfast and lunch for the Sarane participants who were not fasting. Dewi Tuasikal was very busy preparing wrapped rice meals and cakes for her Sarane friends.

Before going their separate ways, they were determined to be true protectors of the environment, including defending human beings as an important element of the environment. Defending human beings means not taking into account the tribal or religious backgrounds of the people they are defending. This resolve was expressed in the Natsepa Declaration:

'We resolve to defend the one and only earth that we love'.

When they arrived at the seminar, they were in distinct groups but the atmosphere of the leave-taking was happy. The Salam participants enthusiastically invited their Sarane friends to their houses at the end of Ramadan. We all agreed to meet in my home on the second day at the end of Ramadan, to formulate the idea that we had called 'An Academy for Environmental Journalism'.

'The main thing is to have rice cakes and goat stew ready. Don't forget, 20 January, we'll all meet up at Rudi's home in Batu Gantung,' said Ridolf.

The First Signs of Smoke

The meeting in Batu Gantung never took place. This is because on Tuesday, 19 January 1999, the infamous community unrest erupted. At that time, I was deputy editor-in-chief of the tabloid *Tabaos*. The office of this tabloid was on the ground floor of the Pemuda Building on Said Perintah Street. My friends and I had planned to go and visit a few of our Muslim friends in their homes. While waiting for some of my friends to turn up I had edited some news articles for the second edition of *Tabaos* for January 1999. Previously, the edition of *Tabaos* was published with the cover theme, 'Salam – Sarane Unite'. We quoted an interview with Bishop Emeritus Mgr. Andreas Sol MSC. In essence, the bishop emphasised that in the 30 years that he had been bishop, there had never been a war between Salam and Sarane.

That afternoon, after Eid Al Fitr[2] prayers in Merdeka Square were over, at around 3 o'clock, I was still in the editor's office when I was interrupted by the phone ringing. Zairin Salampessy, who lived on the boundary between Mardika and Batu Merah, teased me. He said that the goats had run away because they had to wait such a long time. What he meant was that the goat stew, which had been prepared by his mother, was still waiting for someone to come and eat it. I promised that I would be there as soon as all our friends had met up together.

I phoned a reporter from the *Suara Maluku* newspaper, Nevy Hetharia, who lived in Amahusu. I asked Nevy to come quickly and not to forget to bring Alfin, his first-born son who was not yet two years old. Nevy agreed. Five minutes later, Zairin phoned again. He asked me not to forget to bring a camera when I came to his house. This was because in front of his house there were clashes between people from Mardika with people from Batu Merah. This sort of thing had happened many times in the past. But when I put the phone down, Nevy phoned again.

---

2   Eid Al Fitr marks the end of the fasting month for Muslims.

'Rud, I'm not going to bring Alfin with me. People are saying that there is chaos in Batu Merah. They say that Nehemiah Church in Batu Merah has been burnt down. Is it true?' he asked.

I phoned Zairin and passed on what Nevy had said. Zairin checked from his house. It turned out that there was no smoke coming from Nehemiah Church, but there was smoke coming from next door; the Noya family home was on fire. That was the first house to be burnt down during the community unrest in Ambon. I contacted Nevy again and I told him about the situation in Batu Merah. Nehemiah Church had not been burnt down but information that it had been burnt down had reached people living in Amahusu. There, the people also understood that these boundary clashes were a conflict between Salam and Sarane, no longer a case of Batu Merah vs. Mardika.

Zairin phoned again. This time he didn't ask for a camera, instead he asked me to find an unofficial taxi in front of the 'Roda Baru' restaurant. This is because a number of people wearing white head bands[3] had arrived to attack his house. I put down the phone and went out to find a taxi, but there were none to be found. The next day I found out that Zairin and his family had been evacuated by Sandra Lakembe, the daughter of a Golkar politician, Armand Lakembe, to their house in Soya Kecil. This was very risky, because a Salam family had been evacuated to a house in the middle of a Sarane residential area.

Failing to hail a taxi, I returned to the Pemuda Building. The atmosphere the length of Said Perintah Street was very noisy indeed. People in red headbands and carrying machetes were moving towards Silo Church close to the Trikora Monument. Reza Tuasikal, an artist whose studio was directly opposite (now Walang Sibu-Sibu), was standing in the yard of the Pemuda Building. We witnessed all the events unfolding in front of our own eyes, developing from minute to minute. Reza had just left us; his studio had been attacked. His computer and some antiques were destroyed immediately. A wooden sculpture of a person was beheaded and its head rolled into the middle of the street.

People in the mob were carrying machetes and arrows and they were furious. Smoke seemed to be billowing out of Waihaong. The Menara Kasih Church and the old style house belonging to Bert Nikijuluw and his family were burnt down. After that the Alhilal School building was set alight in Anthony Riebok Street and closer at hand, the 'Roda Baru' restaurant. I

---

3   Translator's note: During the conflict In Maluku, people wore white headbands to signify that they were Muslims. People wearing red headbands were Christian.

approached the Trikora monument and watched the mob[4] wearing white head bands gathering in A. M. Sangadji Street. At the same time the mob in red headbands emerged from Said Perintah Street, Diponegoro Street and Dr. Sutomo Street.

The white and red mobs were facing each other, threatening each other and yelling abuse. As the red mob advanced slowly, the white mob withdrew. Then the opposite happened. This action of advancing and then withdrawing was like someone playing a tug of war. This went on for hours until, at last, night fell in Ambon.

I remembered the fast-breaking activity in the offices of the *Suara Maluku* daily newspaper in the Pemuda Building, a week before the end of Ramadan. At that time, Nevy and I talked with Rustam Kastor, the former military commander of 174/Pattimura. It started with us discussing a few articles that had been published in *Suara Maluku*.

The discussion then moved on to the problem of peace and order in society. Kastor said that Ambon should be well-guarded. This was because the Salam-Sarane population was almost equal in numbers. If a conflict erupted in Ambon it would be difficult to control. It was different to the towns of Pasuruan and Situbondo in East Java. There, the majority of the population was Salam. So if conflict broke out, it would be over quickly because the Sarane couldn't put up any resistance. Now, before my eyes, the Ambonese Sarane were running amok. What Kastor has predicted the week before has come true.

Daeng in the Home of an Elder of Silo Church

That night I didn't go home. I stuck it out in the *Tabaos* office until morning together with Roby Lakembe, Adri Latupeirissa and Keety Renwarin. Roby was the staff member who worked on the layout of *Tabaos*. Adri was a member of the Red Cross teenagers, while Keety worked in the GPM chemists. That day Keety and I should have been discussing our plans to get married. However, the topic got buried in the drama. I held Roby, Adri and Keety 'hostage'; we stayed up all night in the office because the situation outside the office was totally unsafe.

In the morning, I escorted Adri and Keety to Airmata Cina, near the fruit market. There, the market buildings had been turned into ashes. The remaining embers emitted smoke that made our eyes smart. We dropped

---

4   Translator's note: The Indonesian term is 'massa', literally 'masses'. Massa usually connotes a crowd out of control.

in on the family home of Julius Luhukay, a retired civil servant from the Ambon City Council offices. I had been part of their family since 1983. Papa Ulen had become like my foster father and his wife, Mama Titi Lawalata, had become my foster mother.

I was shocked when I entered their house on the banks of the Wai Batu Gajah stream, close to Latihan Primary School. There were so many people hiding in the kitchen, under the dining table, near the stove and close to the bathroom door. One of the people hiding was the next door neighbour, Daeng Batako (our nickname for him because he had a business selling bricks or *batako*). His real name was Haji Hama, but we had grown to like his nickname, Daeng Batako. He, with his wife, children, in-laws, and his grandchild who was still a baby, together with several of his workers, were all there. I counted a total of 28 people both adults and children. They sat and slept with a look of fear in their eyes.

'Don't get close to the door or the windows. Somebody might see and then we would have problems,' Mama Titi reminded us over and over again.

I was really impressed by the Luhukay family in this situation. At this time, their home was the subject of a civil law suit. In the case before the Ambon Court of Justice, they were up against a businessman of Chinese descent from Saparua. This businessman was defended by the lawyers Richard Louhenapessy, Abraham Malioy and Adolof Saleky. When Daeng Batako was called to the court as a witness, his testimony implicated the Luhukay family. As a result, they lost the case.

Now, the lives of the extended family of Daeng Batako were threatened. They were descendants of the Bugis people and Muslim. The conflict in Ambon erupted at the same time as the anti 'BBM' (Buton-Bugis-Makassar) sentiments spread, appearing as though there was a war between Salam and Sarane. On the other hand, the Luhukay family were members of the Protestant Church of Maluku (GPM). Mama Titi was an elder in the Silo Church. Some of her children were committee members and other regular members of the Youth Movement of the church (AM)-GPM.

When Muslims and Christians were caught up in a war in the city, the Luhukay family, who were Christians, were willing to give full protection to the family of Daeng Batako. The Luhukay family did not hold a grudge after losing their court case. They compassionately looked after their neighbours, who sought refuge. Mama Titi, Papa Ulen and their children did not display any sign of being put out or objecting to helping these refugees.

Three nights were passed in that house and the atmosphere was increasingly tense. The most influential man in the Airmata Cina area, came onto the verandah of the house. He pushed Daeng Batako's motor on to the road and set it alight. This man started shouting; he was urging others to set fire to Daeng Batako's house. It wasn't long before the flames spread from room to room. The flames climbed from the first floor to the second floor and then on to the third and fourth floors.

Daeng Batako's three grandchildren were sneaking a peek through the shutters of the window. 'Look at the flames, they have reached your bedroom', shouted the little boy. The two little girls watched the flames lick the concrete.

'In a minute the flames will have reached my bedroom,' said one of the little girls without any expression of distress.

Mama Titi came back inside the house. She looked tense. She phoned the police and reported the situation in her home. 'Yes, they've already been here three days in my house,' she reported.

Within less than half an hour, a number of police arrived at the house. They evacuated these 28 people to the Perigi Lima Police Station. They were all safe. Papa Ulen and Mama Titi were very content that not one of Daeng Batako's family members had become a victim.

It turns out that there were many tales originating from many different places of Sarane rescuing Salam or of Salam rescuing Sarane. Some help was given secretly, while in other situations people gave help openly for all to see. A number of teenagers, who escaped from the massacre that took place at the Fisheries Campus in Hila, where they were involved in a Bible Camp, also brought back stories being helped by Salam from Buton.

Salam who lived in the hamlet of Selayar on the west coast of Kei Kecil also have similar stories. When they were under attack by people from several villages, they escaped by getting on to fishing platforms and outriggers. During their journey, because too many people were trying to escape, the weight of these people almost made the fishing platform sink. The Sarane of Ngilngof, picked them up at sea and brought them back to the village hall. In the hall, they were fed and entertained. They were then given food supplies and taken back out to sea on a speedboat owned by a pearl company, to the island of Ohoiwa close to Ngilngof. This story is similar to that of the leader of the Khoiril Ummah Muslim School in Kobisonta North Seram, who gave protection to Sarane people.

A fellow journalist from the *Ambon Ekspres* newspaper, the late Hamid Kasim, also had a similar experience. On the first day of the community unrest, he was trapped in Batu Gantung. His plan to go to Waihaong had to be postponed because the road in front of Rehoboth Church was crammed with mobs of people wielding machetes. Hamid ran quickly to the Pasanea family home. Mrs Pasanea was the leader of the Walang Talenta workshop. Occasionally, when doing work for the *Suara Maluku* newspaper, Hamid had interviewed Mrs Pasanea. Hamid took sanctuary in her home until he could be evacuated.

Gathering at TIRUS

On Tuesday, 26 January 1999, Nus Ukru invited me to come to the Rinamakana office on Pattimura Street, Ambon. Many NGO staff had already gathered there. Cesar Riupassa from the Birdlife Organisation, who until then had only been involved with birdlife, also came in support.

In that meeting, Nus explained that after the conflict, many humanitarian coordination posts had been set up. The coordination posts were good in themselves but they only served their own communities, for example, the Justice Coordination centre, the Alfatah coordination centre, the Maranatha coordination centre. There was, therefore, a need for one emergency team to resolve the Salam-Sarane polarisation. A team of volunteers for humanitarian causes (TIRUS) was thus formed. The volunteers were Salam-Sarane; their aim was to help victims of conflict without heeding their racial or religious background. I immediately volunteered to become part of TIRUS.

As a TIRUS volunteer, I organised communications and information. In the beginning, this job was simply to support the internal work of the team of volunteers. However, during the two weeks of community unrest in Ambon, it was clear that the information being circulated was strongly biased. I blame the media in Jakarta as the main reason for the media plunging into the abyss of war journalism. Using information from secondary sources, Jakarta media quickly broadcast inaccurate news. In addition, there was a stream of information on the internet. News on the internet was in high demand, although the veracity of this news was questionable.

TIRUS also looked after the medical needs of the refugees. It proved very difficult to get doctors and nurses to support the work of the team. I invited Keety and Adri to become involved with TIRUS. Thankfully, Keety was willing, although it meant being absent from her work. From being an associate member of the medical team, Keety was then given the responsibility of being the medical team's coordinator. Not only that, Keety even held a stethoscope to examine patients, as if she was a qualified doctor.

My heart pounded when I saw Keety's determination, as she held a stethoscope and examined patients. Keety was not a doctor but only an assistant chemist. I expressed my concern but I was relieved when I heard her explanation.

'This is an emergency. In situations like this, everyone has to do something to save other people. I am willing to take responsibility,' she explained.

TIRUS had several coordination centres, including the Rinamakana office, Creusa 'Tetha' Hittipeuw's house in Mardika, Ansye Sopacua's house in Passo, a shophouse in Batu Merah and Baileo's office in Wailela. These coordination posts made it easier to help the victims of community unrest, which had spread across Ambon. TIRUS focused on at least 14 refugee camps. TIRUS' workload was intense. Fortunately, dozens of volunteer teams were at work, although there were occasional shortfalls and weaknesses because it was the first time they had experienced a situation as bad as this.

I was also moved when working within TIRUS, because I met up again with the Tujuh Lumut, who were so adept. They even slept with the refugees in the tents so they could make an assessment and obtain accurate data about the refugees' situation. Their assessment became the basis for the distribution of aid.

'We really are like moss, we can survive anywhere, even in the toilet', said Daniel Utra.

Even more amazing, a number of the young nature lovers who been involved in writing the Natsepa Declaration on 17 January 1999, joined TIRUS. They were then placed in the Batu Merah shophouse coordination centre to make it easier to access the camps inhabited by the Muslim refugees.

'So, this is our first task in defending the environment that we love so much,' I remarked to Dino Umahuk.

Working in the midst of an escalating conflict sometimes made the volunteers uneasy. For example, when the Salam and Sarane volunteers were gathered in Mardika, a conflict suddenly erupted and a citizen was killed, resulting in the atmosphere in the city becoming tense. The atmosphere often caused the nerves to fail. Several of the Salam volunteers whispered to Dino.

'Are we safe?' That is how they expressed their anxiety.

Dino guaranteed that they would be safe. But so that they really could be safe, they had to go back to the Batu Merah shophouse coordination centre.

Keety and I decided to spend a night at the Batu Merah shophouse coordination centre, so that we could gain the confidence of our friends. Apparently every day the Muslim volunteers went to the Mardika and Passo coordination centres, while the Christian volunteers almost never went to the Batu Merah centre. Linda Holle, Dewi Tuasikal and other volunteers greeted us on the second floor. Within three hours of being at the Batu Merah centre, a volunteer suddenly came up from the first floor. He brought news that I had a visitor. My chest heaved. Who would come looking for me in Batu Merah, at nine o'clock in the evening, during the conflict?

It turned out that a soldier and Nus Ukru had come looking for me. Nus had come to tell me that there was rumour in the Sarane area that two Sarane were under siege or had been kidnapped in Batu Merah. To put a stop to the rumour, Keety and I were asked to leave the Batu Merah centre. We all regretted this, but the situation demanded it. So Keety and I returned to the Mardika centre.

One time, after helping the refugees in the TNI barracks in Suli, the Salam and Sarane volunteers met at the Passo centre. To wind down, several volunteers formed a circle. They sang lively songs, while Julius Lawalata accompanied them on the guitar. One song led to another. I don't know how it happened, but eventually we were no longer singing pop songs, nor reggae, nor dangdut but a Sarane hymn.

> Jesus takes care of
> The lives of every person
> Those who are broken are put together
> With compassion
> Jesus takes notice of
> Every tear drop
> He knows my heart regrets my sins

Such is the refrain of the hymn 'Current Trials'. At this point, several Salam volunteers stepped out of the circle. They weren't against the Sarane hymn but hearing the words made them suddenly feel on edge. According to a few Salam friends they find the hymn, 'Onwards Christian Soldiers' horrifying to listen to, because during several of the clashes between the two mobs, Sarane mobs sang that hymn. Since that time, every time the young people wanted to sing, they were very careful not to get so carried away with their singing that they spontaneously broke out into singing hymns again.

News of Suffering

Although the war was raging in Ambon and I was actively involved in TIRUS, my friends; Polly Joris, Nus Latekay, Vonny Litamahuputty, Firel Sahetapy, Mon Sahuleka, and I were still able to publish one edition of *Tabaos*. We wrote about the murder of the bride and bridegroom, Marlen Sitanala and Lucky Palijama. However, after that, *Tabaos* was not published again because the journalists had to save their own lives. That was much more important.

Occasionally, indeed, I was afraid that I was going to die. This was mainly because of our experiences in Mardika. A bomb exploded on the boundary between Batu Merah and Mardika, close to the tofu factory. People from Mardika escaped, leaving their house which was smouldering close to the retaining wall. From the Mardika volunteer centre, Keety and I ran to an empty building. Josep Renleuw also joined us carrying his handycam camera. From the roof of the building, on the third floor, we could see four men dressed in green camouflage uniforms across the Batu Merah River. They were directing their rifles at the house that was still smouldering in Mardika.

When Josep emerged with the handycam, Keety straight away pointed to the direction of the four uniformed soldiers. But one of them directed his rifle in our direction. A bullet whistled above our heads and made us lay face downward on the ground. After one minute had passed, Keety lifted her head. Suddenly, a bullet hit the wall where she was standing. If the bullet had been another 30 centimetres higher, Keety's head would certainly have exploded. Since then, I am very suspicious if I see anyone carrying a rifle. Perhaps he is not protecting the peace but he is shooting at the people. So, it is better to be alert and withdraw if you are unsure, rather than dying unnecessarily.

At the beginning of the community unrest I went to check on *Suara Maluku*, the only daily newspaper at that time. The editor in chief, Elly Sutrahitu, admitted that he was confused. First, he didn't know how the journalists could report news that was so racialised. Second, how could journalists in Ambon cover news stories and then get to the office in Halong? They would have to go along dangerous roads. Third, if the newspaper was published, who would distribute the newspaper to the readers and the subscribers?

'Rud, we have agents and people to deliver the newspapers, but almost all of them come from Southeast Sulawesi. With the anti-BBM issue, they are, of course, very frightened. We can guarantee their safety. But where are they all at this moment? We will just have to wait and see,' said Sutrahitu who was well-known for his column under the title, 'Tali Hulaleng'.

Suara Maluku was finally published in February. Before that, however, between 19 January and the beginning of February, thousands of pieces of information about the conflict in Ambon had spread through a variety of channels. Newspapers and TV from Jakarta, foreign media and online media were all full of news about Ambon. While reporters in Ambon were overwhelmed by shock and confusion because they were undergoing such astonishing experiences for the first time, the media outside Maluku was fast and far ahead.

Unfortunately, the news about the suffering in Ambon was inaccurate. The majority of news produced by media in Jakarta came from secondary sources. The news reports constantly repeated the origins of the conflict at the boundary between Batu Merah and Mardika. Some of the media wrote that Yopy Saiya was a Sarane thug, who was angry with a Salam driver called Nursalim. In addition to not being accurate, the information was wrong and back-to-front. In fact, the driver's name was Yopy Leuhery while the person who tried to extort money from Yopy was called Mursalim, not Nursalim.

Facts that were the wrong way round, dominated much of the news. Many of the news broadcasts could even be called fictitious. The fiction contained 'facts' and 'information' that were figments of the writer's imagination. Truth in the field was like that.

For example, there were news items describing that Republic of South Maluku (RMS) flags were flying on Mount Nona, when community unrest broke out on 19 January 1999. These flags were held afloat by gas balloons. It was said that the flags were red in colour with a white trim on the edge and a white cross in the centre.

I asked some young Ambonese people, what colour is the RMS flag? They replied: red, blue, white, and yellow. Armed with this information, I made corrections to the information through AJI Indonesia. Later on, it was discovered that there was no yellow colour on the RMS flag, it should have been green. Too late. AJI had disseminated this correction everywhere, it was even quoted in a book. But this mistake demonstrated that the youth of Ambon really didn't know anything at all about RMS.

I also felt uneasy when a few community leaders in Ambon claimed that a pregnant woman from their community had been killed and the foetus had been extracted from the mother's womb. This lack of clarity continued without any verification. Sidney Jones, then Asia Director of Human Rights

Watch, who has always emphasised the method of fact-finding also came to the conclusion that it was only a baseless rumour.

Later, I visited the Salam-Sarane refugee camp at Rindam Suli. There I came across a little girl who caught my attention. She was 4 or 5 years old. Wherever her grandmother went, she was always present. She didn't want to be separated from her grandmother, even for a second. When I was standing with them for a moment, the grandmother always held the girl's hand tightly. Even when she went to the toilet, her granddaughter had to go with her.

'Oh dear, can't you be separated from granny at all?' I said while taking hold of the little girl's hand. The little girl withdrew her hand and hid behind her grandmother.

'She is still afraid because she saw her mother cut to pieces in front of her very eyes. She herself almost died. Luckily I quickly hid her under my *kain* [batik wraparound],' explained the grandmother.

According to the grandmother, an attacker waving a machete wanted to slaughter her granddaughter. The grandmother grabbed her granddaughter and hid her between her legs. As a result, the machete hit the grandmother's behind.

The hottest piece of news concerned the former Mayor of Ambon, Decky Wattimena who was accused of being a provocateur. Or so the Jakarta media wrote. Decky, it stated, was being interrogated in Jakarta. Other news stated, that after inciting the mobs to conflict, Decky had fled to the Netherlands.

I went to Airlouw, to Decky's home, precisely at the time the Jakarta news media stated that Decky was being interrogated and that Decky had fled to the Netherlands. In the peace of his home, Decky was mowing the grass in his front yard. He was surprised because I had brought a journalist from *Tempo* magazine with me, Veriyanto Madjoa, who had come from Manado. I also sent the interview with Decky to the Jakarta tabloid, *Tokoh*. They had asked for my help after I had sent a complaint about the news through AJI Indonesia.

Decky made an interesting statement about the problem of the people from Buton. According to Decky, some Butonese had lived for more than a hundred years in Airlouw. You could see the proof in the existence of a Butonese grave there. In addition, Decky countered the reports that he was anti-Butonese.

'When I was still the mayor, no Ambonese wanted to be a pedicab driver. All the pedicab drivers came from South Sulawesi and Southeast Sulawesi. If I was opposed to the Butonese, of course I would have got rid of all the pedicabs in Ambon,' he remarked.

Then Decky told a story about a meeting of all Indonesian mayors in Bali. At that time, the mayors had agreed to get rid of pedicabs throughout Indonesia. But Decky stood up. He then asked for an exception to the rule in Ambon.

'Pedicabs in Ambon can be organised,' he explained.

Decky explained about his policy concerning the colour of the pedicabs. Red pedicabs could operate on Mondays and Thursdays, yellow pedicabs could operate on Tuesdays and Fridays and white pedicabs could operate on Wednesdays and Saturdays. On Sundays all pedicabs were free to operate.

Retreat

Being in the middle of a war situation, I felt I was caught between two choices. Should I be on the front line, so I could obtain accurate news or should I protect my safety, and as a result not be able to guarantee the accuracy of the news? I chose to survive and not be reckless. Keety and I had promised to get married soon. In addition, I felt that Salam and Sarane journalists could work together. Although coordination was difficult then, because mobile phones were not as widespread as they are now, at least there was a way to help each other.

For example, at the beginning of the community unrest, Thamrin Ely and Dino Umahuk at the MUI centre told me that some people in the Salam community were disappointed with the Otto Kuyk Hospital in Hatiwe Kecil. They felt that the hospital was only helping Sarane patients and had refused to accept Salam patients. The people, who had complained, wanted to set fire to the hospital.

Thamrin and Dino contacted me and told me about these complaints. At TIRUS I was in a team with Sister Fransisco Muns PBHK, a nun, who went to Otto Kuyk Hospital and asked for a list of patients undergoing treatment. A number of patients with Salam names were on that list. I sent this list to Thamrin and Dino, as evidence that Otto Kuyk Hospital did not reject Muslim patients. Imagine what would have happened if Thamrin and Dino had not tried to obtain confirmation or had not worked with me and my colleagues at TIRUS. This incident encouraged me that, even in the middle of a war situation, there is always a way, even if the road has many twists and turns.

There was still a lot of biased information needing correction during the conflict. I was challenged to do something about it but my commitment to Keety made me withdraw. We got married in the chapel of the Daughters of the Sacred Heart Nunnery in Ambon, 14 July 1999. The next day, we were married according to the Kei traditional custom in Batu Gantung. Before that, we had both resigned from TIRUS. Not just because of the wedding arrangements but Keety and I began to feel there was something unsavoury about the team. There were volunteers and NGO activists who came with different motives from the volunteers who had been working there for months. Their motivation was to find work and to find money within the team of volunteers.

The Kei Way of Doing Things

After resigning from TIRUS and getting married, I went to Kei on an assignment from Roem Topatimpasang from Jogjakarta to interview a prominent community leader, J. P. Rahail, the traditional chief of Watlaar, whom I admired. In 1973, when I was still young, the chief built a house in Watdek, only about 100 metres from our house on the banks of the Rosenberg Strait. Now, 25 years later, I was going to meet the chief.

In Watdek, I met with chief Rahail. He was old, but his face looked fresh. He spoke calmly, clearly and firmly. I was able to meet with the chief every day but I needed between one and two hours uninterrupted for a structured interview. At this time, the chief was leading the other chiefs and local leaders around Kei to bring about reconciliation.

I could only meet with him a few minutes before he left his house at 7am or a few minutes after he arrived home at 9pm, so realistically I couldn't do the interview. I was forced to leave a list of questions, which the chief then answered.

In a short meeting with the chief, he said that he was in Jakarta attending the Alliance of Traditional Societies in the Archipelago Congress (Aman) when the conflict broke in Kei. Many people in the *Ratskap Maur Ohoiwut* (local traditional council) in Kei Besar wanted to go to war and reduce the village of Bandaeli to rubble. This is because people from Bandaeli who lived in Ambon took a leading role in the war.

'Wait until I return and I will lead all of you. Nobody should do anything until I arrive in Watlaar' said the chief by telephone to his people.

The people obeyed their chief's command. When the congress was over and the chief returned home, he gathered together the prominent traditional figures of the *Maur Ohoiwut* and their people. 'There will be no war', he said firmly, in front of all his people. His command was again respected. The chief then returned to Kei Kecil. He asked the Regent Husein Rahayaan to lead the traditional leaders and go from village to village. The regent agreed but because he was busy as head of the region, his agenda of visits was never carried out.

The chief took the initiative to lead traditional leaders of Greater Kei and travel from village to village, both to Salam and Sarane villages. As well as calling for reconciliation, they also heard the complaints of the people in each of the visits. The *tasdov* ceremony, where everyone sits down together to discuss their problems, was carried out every day. This is not a formal mechanism like a modern court. A person can talk for a long time narrating the genealogy, the history of their origins, tales of war, *tea-bel* (*pela*), *koi-maduan* (two villages that help each other), *yanur mangohoi* (two traditional communities that are bound together because of marriage), and so on. A speaker can be angry, curse, even sob without interruption. This is the mechanism in Kei. As a result, the chief's party got larger every day, as all the villages they visited agreed to support reconciliation. This was the reconciliation process according to the Kei custom, which I had the opportunity to join.

War Contributions

In Tual, I heard about an unpleasant incident in Ambon. The story was told that the Sarane had made their way up to Mount Nona and were waiting to be slaughtered. I phoned Keety, and she said she was fine in Batu Gantung. Eventually I returned to Ambon. I arrived at the house at 10pm bringing with me three boxes of nutty *embal*.[5] Keety and I only had three hours of happiness because at 1am there was an explosion on the roof of the house. After that, there was non-stop shooting in Batu Gantung close to the Modal Shop with troops in front of the Telkom office.

Keety and I were living in a house belonging to the family of Go Kim Peng alias Petrus Sayogo, next to the Modal shop. Throughout the night, hundreds of bullets whizzed over our roof. It was as though the corrugated iron sheets were going to explode. I urged Keety to leave the house, to find somewhere safe. She refused.

'No. In the process of looking for a safe place we might be shot. Let us stay here so that if we die, at least our bodies are already in the house,' she answered.

At 7am the sun rose. The last bullet stopped exploding after the six hour shoot out. There was a knock on the kitchen door. A tall bearded man was standing at the door. He spoke very politely. 'If you have any hot water, can I ask for a glass?' he spoke in a quiet voice.

---

5   Translator's note: *Embal* is made from cassava.

Luckily, Keety had just heated some water in a large pan. The water had just boiled and there was enough coffee to go round. Apparently behind the kitchen, there were around 30 people sporting red headbands. They all had a morning drink behind the kitchen.

'Can you eat *embal*?' asked Keety.

'We Ambonese and the people from Kei eat the same food. There is no difference between sago and *embal*', replied the bearded man.

Three boxes of nutty *embal* were demolished in seconds. That was our contribution for the red troops in Ambon.

Two days after that, there was a ship going to Tual. Keety and I went to the docks via the police headquarters. We were carrying clothes and books in six cases. I asked the help of several students from Darussalam University to carry our luggage on to the ship. The ship had divided the passengers according to their religion. Because our luggage had been carried by students from Darussalam, we were given places in the hold of the ship where all the passengers were Salam. During the journey from Banda to Tual, two men passed round a bag.

'Collection for jihad, collection for jihad!' shouted one of them.

Keety opened her purse and gave a contribution of Rp. 50,000. Two days before, we had contributed *embal* to the red troops, now we contributed money to the white troops.

Peace Journalism

My first child, Alfa Luci Velisia, was born in the Sacred Heart Hospital in Langgur, November 1999. I was working, helping two NGOs in Tual and almost didn't plan to return to Ambon. One year after the conflict in Ambon, Dino Umahuk phoned me. AJI Indonesia and the Press and Development Study Foundation (LSPP) had given him the responsibility of organising training in peace journalism.

In January 2000, Adolop Unawekly, Hasan Pataha and I arrived from Tual. After much difficulty, we finally reached the Hotel Wijaya II and checked in. There were, in fact, no Sarane journalists staying there, except the two of us. When Sien Luhukay found out that I was staying there, he also checked into the hotel on the following day. On the third day, almost all the Sarane participants had plucked up enough courage to stay at the hotel.

Even so, every evening we became anxious. This is because there were five well-built dark-skinned men wandering up-and-down and going in-and-out of the hotel. They didn't go anywhere but were always in the lobby or the courtyard of the hotel. There were rumours amongst the Sarane journalists that these men were from Hitu. What are they doing here?

On the last evening, Rev. John Ruhulessin and Thamrin Ely were panellists. When Ruhulessin arrived in the courtyard of the hotel, the men from Hitu, bowing, rushed to shake hands with the minister.

'How are you? What are you doing here?' asked Ruhulessin.

One of the well-built men explained that Salam and Sarane journalists were staying in this hotel. To guarantee the safety of the participants, they had been assigned the task to keep watch so that nothing happened to the Sarane journalists because Hotel Wijaya II was in the Salam area. We laughed uproariously when we heard this explanation, because we had been afraid for a week. Apparently the apparitions we were afraid of were, in fact, people assigned by the management of the hotel to provide our protection.

The training made a big impression on the fifty or so participants. We began to understand war journalism and peace journalism. Maluku needed the intervention of peace journalism. We practised planning, reporting and writing news from the perspective of peace journalism. In our group task, we wrote using the material gathered by field reporters. One of our group's articles was entitled, *'Bang Becak Bung Becak'*.

This is the real story about the emergence of pedicab (*becak*) drivers in Christian residential areas who are not called *abang* but *bung*. This is a new element in the history of Maluku because Sarane Ambonese are now willing to become pedicab drivers. Our feature told of the *Bang Becak* who were Salam and were able to drive their pedicabs into the Sarane areas. Conversely the *Bung Becak*, who were Sarane, were also brave enough to drive their pedicabs into the Salam areas. According to our group feature, *Bang Becak* and *Bung Becak* were pioneers for peace at the deepest grassroots level.

A number of speakers, such as Rusdi Marpaung, Albert Kuhon and Ignatius Haryanto, came to Ambon for this training and changed the direction of the news trends of many journalists in Ambon, although it was a long process. Establishing the Media Centre (MMC) in 2002 further reinforced the campaign for peace journalism in Maluku.

My Loved Ones

When the training was over, Dino asked me to postpone my departure because Megawati, the deputy president, was coming to Ambon. I had no business with the deputy president, so I decided to return to Kei. I had been there just one week, when some unpleasant news arrived from North Maluku.

I received information that a group of jihadists had attacked the village of Wayamega, on the island of Bacan. This news made my head explode. My father, Paulus Fofid, and my two older sisters, Maria Fatima and Petronela, were in that village. Wayamega had become our second home. Since 1976, my father had built up that village, had become the village leader and had built a mosque and a church there.

I graduated from a Catholic primary and a state junior high school in Labuha, the main town in the district of Bacan. We, the peoples of Kei, Tanimbar, Ambon-Lease, Seram and Timor, had become one community – the people of Bacan were outsiders. Besides that, there were also Chinese, Arab, Butonese, Sangir-Talaud, Minahasa, Tobelo, Galela, Makian, Tidore, Kayoa communities. All these communities were greeted as Bacang *mayawa* (people of Bacan). Of course, there were also original Bacang communities in Amasing town, Amasing Goro and Mandaong.

The news that a group of jihadists had attacked my village in Bacan made my blood freeze. I couldn't cry and I couldn't laugh. I could only remember the good days when we walked around the town of Popo, crossed in front of the Sultan of Bacan's Palace, through Benteng Bernavel Street, and turned at the Yellow House that became the *Paparisa* Olesio. From there we walked by foot to the church with the weathercock, then stopped for a while at Lorong Kereta Mati.

Sometimes I would also stop off at the home of Aba Feisal Alkatiri, a poet who sent his poems to the media using the pseudonym Evasakti. I was friends with his twin sons, Farid and Faruk. Although I only asked for a glass of water, quite often I was offered sago, fish and spicy pickles.

Walking from Labuha, we would go home together through the village of Tomori, arriving at Mandaong. The beautiful journey would take us through sago forests, picking fruit; and we would see thousands of yellow butterflies on the rough paths. We also passed *langsat*, *duku*, *durian* and *rambutan* trees, laden with fruit. Or the lush fields of tall grass, where we suspected the Tobaru head hunters were hiding.

I still remember February 1995, when my mother passed away. I flew from Ambon to Ternate and then took a boat to Labuha. When I arrived at the house, I felt put out, watching three old ladies sobbing in front of my mother's corpse. They were weeping more emotionally than I was. They flung themselves on the ground and their voices were hoarse. Who were they?

'Those women come from Makian. Your mother used to buy brown sugar from them,' explained a relative.

There was a distance of 10 kilometres between our village and Makian. When those women came to sell three baskets of brown sugar, my mother would buy all three baskets to send to Ambon. My mother would offer them food before they returned home. This friendship had been going on for years, just because of brown sugar.

Every time I thought about the harmonious life in Bacan, I also imagined what had happened to my father and my two sisters. Clear news finally arrived from refugees who escaped the attack on our village. They told me that my father and my two sisters were shot dead, together with a lady from Minahasa, Ida Makalo. When the jihadists shouted 'God is great' at the edge of the village, a tug-of-war took place between some men and my sisters. These men tried to force my father to escape, but my father didn't want to go. My two sisters also obstinately refused to leave the house.

'I don't have any problems with Salam or Jihadists. So go away,' he said. When the situation became impossible, eventually all the people escaped to the jungle. The next day, the bodies of my family and the Minahasa lady were discovered charred and cut into pieces. They were buried by Salam from Wayamega.

Chasing Headlines

In 2001, I moved to Tomohon. Elnino Clemens Justin, my second daughter was born there in Mount Maria Hospital. I worked as executive editor for the daily *Patroli Manado*. But a year later I and the majority of the other journalists resigned in protest over the newspaper's management only giving reporters a wage of Rp. 200,000. The main reason for resigning, however, was that I had discovered that the newspaper was funded by an investor in illegal logging.

I returned to Kei in 2002 and I collected stones, sand, and cement to build the foundations of a house. In July 2003, however, my older sister, Victoria, who then held the position of temporary head of the finance section in the regional transportation office of Maluku, had passed away in Waitatiri. I had again lost someone I loved. If my father and my other sisters died during the time of community unrest, Victoria died when Ambon was peaceful. She suffered from cancer.

Since then, I have not gone back to Kei. Keety followed with Alfa and Elnino to Ambon. In the same year, Novi Pinontoan and Elly Sutrahitu, who led the daily *Suara Maluku*, decided to separate from the management of the *Jawa Pos* Group. A day after that decision was made, I returned to work at the daily *Suara Maluku*. I felt I had returned to the family home and also the journalistic campus that had nurtured me and so many journalists in Maluku.

In 2003, I also became editor of the website, www.malukumediacentre.net. This website was constructed by AJI Indonesia to practise peace journalism, and to be an alternative source of news in the midst of confusing information about the conflict in Maluku. In 2005, in the land of eucalyptus trees on the island of Buru, Moluccan journalists chose Hanafi Holle and me to become the secretary and coordinator respectively of the Media Centre (MMC) until 2007. We were given the job to campaign for peace journalism. There are many journalists who have now learnt about peace journalism through MMC.

I wrote these scattered notes in January 2009, ten years after the conflict broke out on the Mardika–Batu Merah boundary. When the conflict broke out, I was still single. Ten years on, I have three daughters. The youngest was born in 2006 in Hatiwe–Otto Kuyk Memorial Hospital, in Passo. Because she was born in Ambon, I named her after the fortress and also after my sister: Helena Victoria.

In these ten years, I have heard, seen, thought and felt that there are so many great stories that have not been recorded. Not just in these small jottings but also in records in the mainstream media. I feel that the conflict that took place from Morotai to Wetar has destroyed many fascinating things. Issues, gossip, intrigue, provocation, and manipulation of information has buried many amazing stories about the wisdom of the Moluccan people before, during and after the ugly war.

Just as fire can destroy a house and a village, spears and bullets can pierce a heart, thus biased information and neglecting to record the facts have also buried many great truths. I believe that there are thousands of stories in Maluku that could be headline news all over the world. To present them, however, each Moluccan needs to write down their own life stories as they really are, without pretence. Let the writing flow without the pressure of deadlines. As long as they are honest, then these great truths about the sadness and joy, anxiety and hope of the people of Maluku will shine brightly for the future. If not, a thousand tales will emerge in the future about a generation that was caught out in 1999. If that happens, I would feel that I have not even written one letter in the historical interest of the nation.

Chapter 2

STICKING TO PRINCIPLES

Zairin Salampessy

The Story of Lorong Mayang

One morning in 1972, in the Lorong Mayang area of Ambon, an athletically-built young man was playing an old guitar. The melodious strains of his songs, praising the beauty of the sea and the beaches, could be heard. Sometimes he also sang songs that praised the mother figure or women in general and sometimes he sang spiritual songs. Every so often he would stop strumming his guitar so he could rock the hammock made from a sarong, which hung directly to his right. A two year old boy was sleeping in the simple hammock. The young man's voice melodious as he hummed a song, lulling the little boy to sleep. At his side there was also a four year old playing with his toys on the floor.

Those two young boys who were being watched by the young man, were none other than me and my younger brother Zulkifli. The young man strumming the guitar was our neighbour, Edy Papuling. At the time, my mother and father, who were religious education teachers teaching Islam, were not at home, because they had gone to work. Mum was a teacher at Primary State School (SDN) 10 Ambon, while my dad taught at the Commercial Senior High School (SMEA), Ambon. The young man we usually called Edy looked after us, from lulling us to sleep, to feeding us, and to bathing us. Edy was a soldier in the Indonesian Army. His musical hobby was channelled through playing in a band at his work. It wasn't just Edy, who looked after us. There were also Granny Auw with her daughter, Mother De Nussy, and her sons, Nyong and Angky.

The house where we lived in Lorong Mayang was in an area where the majority were Christians. If I am not mistaken, there were no more than ten Muslim families living there. But as long as we lived there, the residents never identified themselves by the religion that they adhered to strictly. In that narrow alleyway, we all lived in a warm family atmosphere, based on the philosophy of *hidop orang basudara* (living as brothers and sisters) without regard for a person's origins, race or religion. My father and mother therefore had no hesitation in leaving us in our rented house, next to Mother De and her family, as my little brother Zul and I were safe with them until my parents came home from work.

Our relationship with Mother De, who was a nurse in the Military Hospital (RST) Ambon, and Papa Wem Nussy, who was also a medical aide at the same hospital, were like family. After we finally moved to the Mardika area, our close relationship has continued to the present day. Zul and I see them like our parents. In the same way, we see their sons as our older brothers.

I still remember how every time Zul and I visited their house, we would be given pocket money when we went home. The amount was more than enough to buy sweets. This custom was not stopped even when we were teenagers. But then it was for a different reason, the pocket money was to cover the fares of minibuses or pedicabs.

Another routine custom was taking food parcels to each other's houses. Taking food parcels to each other's houses is a tradition amongst the Salam (Muslims) and Sarane (Christians) in Ambon, with most people being involved in this tradition then. The tradition of exchanging cakes or food and drink took place the day before a major religious festival, such as Eid Al Fitr, Eid Al Adha or Christmas. Usually when it was time to go home, the person who had come bearing food parcels would go home with special edible treats as a thank you.

One time we took two bottles of orange juice or pineapple juice and a tin of biscuits to Mother De's house on Christmas Eve. When we went home we would be given special cakes (*kue bruder*) or a container full of stew (*serantang stof kentang*). Then, the night before Eid Al Fitr, when one of Mother De's children, Usi Uce, came to our house she brought with her a cake (*bruder*) or biscuits and canned drinks, and she would go home carrying some of the food prepared by our family that night. She would take home a chicken dish cooked in a coconut milk spicy sauce (*opor ayam*), rice cakes cooked in a leaf casing (*ketupat*), or various savoury snacks (*gogos, namu-namu*), and cakes (*kue cara*), which we would usually eat while drinking tea after we had returned from the *Ied* prayers.

Anger at Mardika – Batu Merah

On the morning of Eid Al Fitr, 1 Syawal 1419 H., Tuesday 19 January 1999 at 05.15 am, the echoes of the call to prayer at the main An-Nur Mosque in Batu Merah could be heard in the Mardika area. The fresh morning air greeted us as the sun came up, in this area where the majority were Christian.

I still felt a bit sleepy as I took steps towards the bathroom. Other members of the family were already up. Several of them had even got ready to go to Merdeka Square, the only football field in the centre of the city, which had become the place where Ied prayers were held if the weather was good. There, the majority of the people of Ambon would carry out the Ied prayers together.

On the road in front of our house, we could see many people on their way to the Ied prayers in Merdeka square, either on foot or by some form of transport. My parents' house was in the Mardika area only fifty metres from the boundary with Batu Merah where the majority of residents were Muslim.

Besides my parents, my two younger sisters lived in the house. One of them was married and had a three year old son. My nephew's name was Dhidit. He was three years younger than my daughter, Inda. After getting married, I and my family lived with my in-laws in their house in the Tantui area. Two days before the end of Ramadan we came to Mardika so that we could celebrate Eid Al Fitr with Inda's grandparents.

The messy house in Mardika in which we lived, belonged to the Department of Religious Affairs of the Province of Maluku. Inda's grandparents were listed as civil servants in this department and were thus given the opportunity to live there. If my memory serves me correctly, we had lived there since early 1973. There was a feeling of security living in a building whose architecture was a remnant from the Dutch period. The doors and windows were large and a wooden tiled roof made the circulation of air in the house cool and comfortable. This large building had been partitioned into four parts, according to the four civil servant families from the Department of Religious Affairs who lived there.

* * *

The digital clock in the right hand corner of the monitor of the computer showed it was 3pm. I had not yet succeeded in completing a game of Spider Solitaire that I had been playing for half an hour. Inda was sitting faithfully by my side as I was filling in time playing a game while waiting for my colleagues from the Baileo Maluku Network and the daily *Suara Maluku* to arrive. They had not yet arrived, although for the past two hours they had bragged on the telephone that they would arrive soon to scoff the meal cooked in a spicy coconut milk sauce and rice cakes cooked in leaf casings made by Inda's grandmother.

Still in front of the computer, I lazily moved the mouse around. When my head started to nod, once in a while, in the direction of the monitor because I was sleepy, Inda immediately pinched my arm. Really, she couldn't wait to take my place.

Inda's wait was successful. Fifteen minutes later drowsiness overcame me. My two eyelids began to close, forming a line as thin as a pencil line. I staggered and threw my body on to the sofa. It was understandable because I had gone to bed rather late the night before. I had helped my wife clean up the house, reorganise the tables and chairs and change the curtains. After that I had the chance to chat with Frans Pattirajawane. He was a neighbour, whose house was in front of our house and coincidently was a Christian. He had brought round two bottles of orange squash and a tin of Khong Guan biscuits. After Frans went home carrying a container of chicken cooked in a spicy coconut milk sauce and rice cakes cooked in a leaf casing, I went to bed.

'Yes ... yes ... yes!' shouted Inda. She was really excited, punching her fists into the air, over and over again. Earlier, she had been itching to play her favourite pinball game. She was happy because her patience had been rewarded. I gave in to sleepiness and she took over the position in front of the computer.

I slept quite well even though it was for a short time. At approximately 3.30pm a noisy disturbance was heard not far from the house. Our house was on the main road, not far from the local minibus terminal for the Hatukau (Batu Merah) route. Our house was also nearby the Victoria cinema, then one of the most popular cinemas in Ambon. The terminal and the cinema were precisely at the junction between three areas: Mardika – Batu Merah (village) – Batu Merah Dalam, or as it was usually called Asrama Militer (Asmil, Military barracks) Batu Merah, because there was a military barracks there.

There were actually frequent, noisy disturbances at this junction. We had become accustomed to the noise. Adolescent crime was the main cause for disturbances. When adolescents taunted each other and bumped against each other, someone would be offended and it would end up in a scrap. Noisy disturbances were part and parcel of the area.

Sometimes the disturbances were triggered by minor things. For example, people placed bets on how many segments were inside a mangosteen fruit. Usually there was always someone who didn't play fair, who didn't want to admit that they had lost, so it would end in a fist fight. The fight would start between two young men who were involved in guessing about the mangosteen segments. If they were not satisfied with this tussle, it would spread, involving brothers and other family members, until it became a disturbance between the two residential areas. So a clash would occur between Mardika and Batu Merah.

But clashes between Mardika and Batu Merah usually didn't last more than two days. It was as though there was an unwritten agreement that on the second day everything would go back to normal. Everyday life would return to normal. The residents of Mardika would return to shopping leisurely at the Batu Merah traditional market, the school children or the office workers would pass Mardika, laughing or joking on their way.

Unfortunately, the disturbances that took place on 19 January 1999 were different. In the beginning those involved in the clash were the residents of Batu Merah, who were bunched together on the bridge, with their opponents being the residents of Asmil Batu Merah, who lived near the Hatukau minibus route base.

But suddenly a group of youths wielding machetes came from the side of the Victoria Cinema. They had tied white ribbons on the handles of their machetes. There were no more than ten people; far less than the number of Batu Merah residents who were standing on the bridge. They had athletic bodies and were running with short, steady steps.

I was shocked, because this group that emerged out of nowhere were running in our direction, towards the residents of Mardika. At that point bystanders had been watching the clashes between the people of Batu Merah village with the residents who lived near Asmil Batu Merah. Frans, Josias (a prominent figure amongst the young people in Mardika), Mr Cas Noya (the head of the neighbourhood watch in our area) and I were standing in front of the others and were suddenly caught by surprise and then we ran helter skelter.

I didn't get a chance to notice what happened to the other Mardika residents, who had also been standing in the front with us, because I was busy avoiding the strikes of the machetes that were aimed at me. Other residents who saw us being chased spontaneously pried ornamental paving blocks (shaped like bricks), to throw at these youths. Their intention was to cut the youths off, so that they would withdraw.

Probably because people were getting very emotional, some of the paving blocks were thrown quite hard and landed close to the group of Batu Merah residents, who were involved in throwing things at the residents, who lived near the Asmil Batu Merah. Something that was thrown strayed far off target and provoked the attention of the residents of Batu Merah. Scores of Batu Merah residents headed towards Mardika. Would a clash occur as was usual in the tradition of Batu Merah versus Mardika? No, that was not the case.

This time the clash of Mardika versus Batu Merah was different to the previous clashes of the past. Shouts of 'God is Great' and the hymn 'Onward Christian Soldiers' became part of this particular clash. I don't know who started this. But it was the first time since I had lived in Mardika that I had heard the shouts of 'God is Great' and the hymn 'Onward Christian Soldiers' reverberating as a clash occurred between Mardika and Batu Merah.

A number of unknown youths of athletic build had now advanced and attacked the Mardika area. They were exactly in front of our house which was fifth in line from the boundary. Wielding machetes, they shouted 'God is great' with enthusiasm. There was not one among them whose faces I recognised.

Stones landed in various places: the wall of the house, on the road, or on the slates on the roof. There were some that landed in our living room, after that some wooden slates that made up our roof broke because they had been pounded by stones. I tried to peep through the shutters of the windows of the house, the stone throwing continued violently. The size of the mobs increased. Smoke rose up from Mr Cas Noya's house. His house was exactly on the boundary. It was the first house that was burnt down in the outbreak of the Ambon conflict.

After that I took good note of what was going on. Among the youths carrying machetes tied with white ribbons, others were also carrying jerry cans. This was clear when they targeted a building functioning as a shophouse with a small garage beside it. This building was not only ransacked, but also sprinkled with kerosene from a jerry can they carried. One of them found old oily rags close to the garage and set them on fire. These rags were then thrown in the direction of the shophouse, using the end of the machetes. The fire flared, adding to the heated atmosphere.

Their actions didn't stop there. The Corputty family home next to the shophouse was their next target. The window's glass louvres were shattered. The curtains were set on fire. The painting of rice fields that I had painted on the inside wall of the house could be clearly seen from our house across the road. Frans Pattiradjawane's family home next to the Corputty's house was then ransacked and was about to be burnt down.

Fearing that our family home was likely to become a target, I spontaneously put on a Muslim cap, wrapped a prayer mat around my neck and clutched an Al-Quran, and then I went outside the house. Coincidentally, several youths from Batu Merah, friends from junior high school, were standing on the steps in front of the house. I glimpsed several youths from Batu Merah pulling at the curtains in the Corputty home and Frans' home. They were trying to prevent the flames from getting bigger and burning down those houses. In the meantime, the shouts of 'God is Great' were getting noisier.

'Be calm. We will help to keep watch out here, so that nobody will cause chaos in your house. We don't know these people, we don't know where they have come from,' remarked one of the youths from Batu Merah. He was in the year below me at junior high school but I have forgotten his name. He also said that he did not know a number of the athletic young men, who acted very smoothly, compared to the other mob, the Batu Merah residents.

Feeling somewhat calm; I went back into the house. With the assistance of a telephone book I tried to contact City Police Station, but the phone was engaged. It was the same with the office of the District Military Headquarters.

I was somewhat relieved when I was finally connected to the Military Police Office. I notified them about the clashes that were going on in front of my house. But I wasn't totally relieved. This is because I learned from the officer of the Military Police on duty, that they had already heard about this incident. They had also contacted the police as the party that was most competent. 'We ourselves can't do anything, because many of our members have taken leave for the Ramadan holidays. But we have coordinated with the police,' replied the officer-on-duty by phone.

Thankfully, less than an hour after the mobs began facing each other, several members of the intelligence service, wearing batik shirts, emerged. I don't know which unit they were from but because they were carrying pistols and walkie talkies, I was certain that they were intelligence agents. A few of them shot their pistols into the air.

The mobs who came from the directions of Mardika and Batu Merah retreated to their original positions. But not long afterwards, both sides slowly advanced again. With every sound of shots, they retreated. Then when the warning shots could no longer be heard, both sides would start to advance again. This continued over and over again, in the end the intelligence agents were at a loss to know what to do.

Fortunately, after almost two hours of continuously hurling stones at each other, a truck full of police arrived. Fully armed, they immediately moved to partition the area into two halves by stretching out pieces of wood on two chairs that belonged to residents who lived close by. They created a simple barricade. One side was directly in front of the Victoria Cinema, bordering the bridge and the Batu Merah area. The other side was about 75 meters in the direction heading away from the bridge inside the Mardika area.

With positioning like that, houses that were in the area between the two barriers, including our house, were automatically in the neutral zone. The steps in the front of our house then became the place for policemen to sit.

The angry shouts of the two mobs vanished. The throwing of rocks or Molotov cocktails that had occasionally fallen on the roof, was no longer heard. Although Molotov cocktails had landed on our house, the house was not burnt down. When they landed, the flames went out by themselves.

Although we were a little relieved, those of us in the house were not yet calm. We didn't know what was going to happen next. Besides myself, there was my wife and daughter, my younger sister with her husband and son, and my youngest sister and my parents, all together in one room 3 x 6 metres in size. We were ready with bags filled with valuables that we would take to safety, if we were forced to leave the house.

Places of Worship Burnt Down?

While the disturbances and the hurling of objects between the two mobs had been going on, I took the opportunity to contact relatives and some friends to ask them to find a car to pick us up from the house. But my cousin, Saleh – who worked as a driver of a rental car – couldn't leave his house. He said there was a commotion amongst the people who lived near his parents' house in the Benteng Atas (Bentas).

The residents of Bentas, who lived close to the mosque, were mainly Muslim and had gathered to look at Mardika and Batu Merah. Geographically, they were higher up and they discussed and watched the flames, but weren't clear where they were coming from. They were guessing whether the fire was in

Mardika or Batu Merah, when an unknown person drove past on a speeding motorbike shouting that the main An-Nur Mosque in Batu Merah had been burnt down by Christians. I tried to explain to Saleh what had happened in front of our house. But the people who lived near my cousin's house were in a panic. They were consumed by the rumour spread by that unknown person.

It was a different story with my office colleague from *Suara Maluku*, Nevy Hetharia. Earlier he had planned to come to my house with his son Alfi and another friend from *Suara Maluku*, Rudi Fofid. However, the plan was cancelled because someone in Amahusu, where he lived, had said that there was chaos in Batu Merah. Then he was told that the church in Batu Merah had been burnt down. I clarified the issue straight away to Nevy and Rudi. It was not the church that had been burnt down, but a house and a shophouse. But it was too late. The residents of Amahusu were consumed by the rumour that the church had been burnt down. Rudi and Nevi finally cancelled their visit to our house.

I phoned Novi Pinonton, a friend from *Suara Maluku* who had promised to visit with his wife and child, asking him to cancel the visit because the situation make it impossible. Earlier, Novi had insisted that he would still come because he thought the situation was similar to the usual conflict between the kids of Mardika and Batu Merah. Novi finally cancelled his plans after I told him what the situation was like this time.

What made me incredulous then was that in a number of areas where the majority were either Muslim or Christian, rumours were spread simultaneously by unknown people. The rumours spread that a church had been burnt down by Muslim mobs and that a mosque was burnt down by Christian mobs. The issue was concocted on purpose to provoke the anger of Muslim or Christian citizens. In a similar way, the Mardika versus Batu Merah conflict was purposely used to trigger conflict in other areas in the city of Ambon. This is because in less than a day, the Mardika versus Batu Merah clashes had spread to other areas in Ambon. The flames in Mardika, right in front of my house, had spread to other spots in Ambon. The atmosphere at night in this small city was tense.

Salam in a Sarane Area

A solution to our uncertain waiting in the frightened atmosphere of the 3 x 6 metre room was finally reached when I telephoned Sandra Lakembe, a colleague who was also an activist in the Baileo Maluku Network. Sandra, who was observing the situation, told me that she would pick us up in a vehicle that would be guarded by security forces. To begin with, family members were a little uneasy. This is because my mother and two sisters wore jilbabs (Muslim women's headcoverings), and at that time an impression was developing that a religious conflict was taking place. Why weren't we being evacuated to an area with a Muslim majority, but instead going to Sandra's home in Soya Kecil, an area with a Christian majority?

Around 10pm, Sandra came to pick up my family. She arrived in a minibus, guarded by security forces carrying rifles. Without waiting too long, we got in the vehicle. The roads were quiet when we drove in the direction of Sandra's home in Soya Kecil.

We were deeply touched when we arrived and were greeted by Sandra's family. Her father, Armand Lakembe was chairman of one of the factions in the Ambon Legislative Assembly at that time. His polite and friendly manner made him highly respected by others. Uncle Man, as he was called, was very active as an elder in the church. Staying in the Lakembe home made us feel safe and at peace.

After drinking tea, we took a shower and then had our evening meal. We then shared stories about about what had happened in the last few hours. That night we all slept well without any burden. The anxiety and worry, which we had felt since late afternoon, just melted away, leaving no trace.

For almost a week we camped in the Lakembe home, my family stayed indoors, or just went into the yard. The neighbours knew that a Salam family had been evacuated to a Sarane area. However, they respected our presence among them. Several young people I knew well, came and chatted on the verandah, just passing the time with me and Sandra.

My wife and my sisters would also sometimes join us in chatting on the verandah or just sitting beneath the leafy trees that were in their front yard. The yard at the Lakembe home was quite extensive with various types of trees planted there.

A few times, however, my sister and mother, who were wearing jilbabs, were asked to go inside the house. Especially when we heard the sound of the electricity poles being struck, as this was the warning sign that an attack was imminent. If the electricity pole was struck repeatedly, it was certain that within seconds there would be a spontaneous movement of mobs in the direction of the boundary with Mardika. Soya Kecil Road was one of the roads that was used to go to Mardika. One of the spots where a concentration of mobs in Mardika assembled was not far from Sandra's home, a distance of no more than 200 metres.

Our time seeking refuge in the Lakembe home eventually ended. A week after the conflict took place, there was no sign of groups facing each other on the boundary. It was as though people were experiencing a 'ceasefire'. Everyone was busy with their own activities. Although the area close to the dividing line seemed tense, my sister-in-law, Inggrid, and some friends came to the house from my in-laws' house in the Tantui area, to pick us up. The vehicle naturally had to be escorted by security personnel for protection. Didith's father also arrived at the same time, with another vehicle also protected by a security forces' escort. Awin, Didith's father, did not come with us, when we were evacuated. He chose to hide in the house in Mardika, in case there was any looting at night.

After saying goodbye to the Lakembe family and to our extended family, we went our different ways. Inda, her mother and I left with Inggrid to go towards the Tantui area. While my father, mother, sister, brother-in-law and nephew went to Kebun Cengkih. They would stay at Madrasah Tsanawiyah Negeri (Muslim State Junior High School) Kebun Cengkih. My father was the headmaster at this school.

Journalists and Religious Segregation

One day, I forget the exact date, but it was definitely at the end of January 1999 – the phone in the house rang several times. Inda's granfather told me that someone called Aji had rung me. It turned out that I wasn't phoned by someone whose name was Aji, but rather someone from the head office of the Alliance of Independent Journalists (AJI) in Jakarta. We had access to one of the organisers of AJI before the conflict broke out, or more precisely after Reformasi. An activist friend, Saleh Abdullah, who had once been the general secretary for Sri Bintang Pamungkas in the organisation they formed, organised for me to be put in contact with the general secretary of AJI, Lukas Luwarso. We had sounded out the possibility of forming an AJI Bureau in Ambon. We had been going through the process of forming an AJI Bureau in Ambon when conflict had broken out in the provincial capital.

The phone call from AJI central office was to confirm my presence (I was then the chair-elect of the AJI Bureau, Ambon) and also the presence of Rudi Fofid (Secretary-elect of AJI Bureau, Ambon), to take part in training in peace journalism and multicultural journalism organised by the AJI Central Office in Manado. I assured AJI that we would make an effort to attend, particularly because our friends really hoped that Rudi and I could bring a supply of stories about what had happened in Ambon to enrich the training.

But fate decided otherwise. Just before we were due to depart, the conflict intensified in Ambon. In various spots on the island of Ambon there were clashes between mobs, which lasted for several days. People were afraid to drive cars. This was even more so if anyone wanted to go to Pattimura Airport because vehicles had to pass through a number of areas. In some of these areas the majority of residents were Sarane, while in other areas, the majority of residents were Salam. We cancelled our trip because there was no transport to Manado.

On 10 February 1999, a few weeks after we cancelled our trip to Manado, I (a Salam) and Rudi (a Sarane) as the AJI Bureau, Ambon – although we had not been officially inaugurated at that time – sent an email to the AJI Central Office. We explained several things about the community unrest in Ambon. We hoped that what we conveyed would be a useful comparison to the mainstream news in the mass media, or that it could provide material to reflect on the ethics and freedom of the press post-Reformasi.

Rudi and I told them that the Humanitarian Volunteers Team (TRK) Centre Ambon was in Mardika and had participants from different religious backgrounds to keep track of reporting of the mass media about the community unrest in Ambon. On occasions Salam and Sarane volunteers from TRK went together to various refugee camps in Muslim or Christian areas. We didn't, of course, do anything during times when there were clashes between the mobs.

From our activities and seeing the situation at that time, Rudi and I came to the conclusion that journalists in Ambon had great difficulty covering the news. This was because, in order to obtain the most up-to-date data on the incidents of 19 to 25 January 1999, journalists' movements had been limited by religious segregation. The Christian journalists were frightened to approach the mobs and groups of Muslims. In reverse, Muslim journalists were not free to approach the mobs and groups of Christians. This was because the psychological state of the mobs during the community violence made the situation very sensitive.

At that time, we also noted that in order to obtain news, journalists stayed close to the entourage of the Governor, the Commander of VIII/Trikora Command or other officials who were closely guarded.

There were also journalists who stationed themselves at military installations, especially in the Regional Police Information Department or the 174/Pattimura Regional Command Information Department. There was very limited reporting directly from the field. Our colleagues who were Muslim journalists could mingle amongst the Muslim mobs, while Christian journalists could mingle amongst the Christian mobs. The Muslim journalists could easily collect data at the Al-Fatah Mosque and Batu Merah and the Christian journalists could also easily collect data at the Maranatha Church or at the Silo Church. But this data was biased to the interests of each side.

A few of the journalists chose to station themselves at home and receive information from various groups by phone. Each method, of course, had its own limits, so journalists were unable to work as effectively as possible. When the situation improved they had missed a number of incidents and journalists could not get facts from primary sources.

Although they could not work freely, journalists in Ambon also then became the source of news for various media, both national and international. This bewildered some high-ranking officials in Ambon, because incidents that occurred the previous evening in Ambon would be broadcast in America, Australia and the Netherlands the next morning.

Several news items from Jakarta-based media showed that there was a tendency for some journalists to allow their emotions to become involved when reporting the news. It definitely seemed that the journalists had lost their independence and were writing unbalanced news. In addition, some journalists reported inaccurately; even information claiming to be factual was actually the reverse of the truth (perhaps on purpose).

The notes that Rudi and I sent to AJI Central Office included a description of the conditions of the disaster, as experienced by a number of journalists. This information was posted everywhere and we became the reference points for a number of national, and even international, media. Rudi and I were also interviewed several times by a number of national and international media. However, our report was to be the first and also the last in the name of AJI Bureau, Ambon. This was because we became busy after that, with humanitarian activities with the Humanitarian Volunteers Team (TIRUS). Our intention to establish the AJI Bureau, Ambon was therefore forgotten. Our intention was ultimately buried in the commotion of the community unrest in Ambon.

From the commotion of biased news media at that time, Rudi, Dino Umahuk and I were entrusted as volunteers in the information section, agreeing to find impartial news to distribute to the community. We accessed a number of national media sites to obtain news that did not demonstrate partiality towards Muslims or Christians.

Generally, the news was about the conditions for the refugees, activities carried out to help the refugees or calls for peace from national leaders. After we printed and made photocopies, a group of volunteers, both Muslim and Christian, helped us to sell the news sheets at locations near where newspapers and magazines were sold. At that time, it was difficult to send national newspapers to Ambon so our photocopied version became the information that circulated. So people weren't suspicious of us, we sold photocopies of news that we had downloaded from the internet.

Driven Out from the Land of My Birth

My activities as a volunteer with TRK Ambon and the Baileo Maluku Network aroused suspicion. It made sense. As one of the senior Muslim activists involved the Baileo Maluku Network, I would sometimes enter or cross between Muslim and Christian areas. Several times when there were unexpected clashes between the mobs I was in a Christian area. This was strange for some people, who had been strongly influenced by the conflict. They felt certain that the conflict taking place was a conflict between religions. This meant that a Muslim should only be in a Muslim area. Conversely a Christian should only be in a Christian area. But it was not only in Muslim circles that people became suspicious, because similar thoughts emerged in Christian areas. Some became suspicious that perhaps I was a spy.

The suspicions about my activities and my presence, heightened when Nus Ukru, a few friends and I, representing the Baileo Maluku Network and TIRUS, were waiting for a commissioner from the Human Rights Commission at that time, the late Asmara Nababan, in the grounds of Maranatha Church. The Human Rights Commission was taking part in a dialogue with some prominent Christian leaders inside Maranatha Church, after carrying out the same thing with prominent Muslim leaders. We, as TIRUS, had made an appointment to meet Nababan after his meeting with community leaders in the church. Our plan was to express our concern about the conflict situation.

My presence with several colleagues from TIRUS in the Maranatha Church grounds was noticed by a few acquaintances. The rumour about me spread in various circles, particularly among people who knew me quite well. The liveliest rumour that spread claimed that I was an apostate. 'Imagine it, there is a conflict like this but he was in a church,' was among some of their utterances when they questioned my presence there.

One of the consequences, was when I was in the grounds of the main Al-Fatah Mosque and I almost had a bad experience. At that time TIRUS was just formed. In order to publicise TIRUS among a number of people we thought could be approached to join with us, I went to the largest mosque. My intention was to meet with Mr MW, who I had known since I was still a student and when I was still editor of the bulletin, *Marinyo*, published by the NGO, Hualopu Foundation. Mr MW was a researcher in an educational institution and as far as I knew he was like an activist, because he often contributed articles for that bulletin.

The day I was to meet with him he was busy in the Al-Fatah Coordination Centre. I was pleased to be able to meet with someone who would probably have the same vision as us in working for humanitarian causes. I conveyed our intention from TIRUS to invite him to be involved as an older person in this umbrella organisation. I was, however, taken by surprise. He rebuked me and said he saw me as a traitor, because I worked together with Christians.

His rebukes and his shouts caught the attention of a number of young people who were sitting on the terrace of the mosque. Several came in our direction with questions on their faces. But when they saw Mr MW point in my direction and say that I was a traitor, their faces changed and they became very angry. Fortunately, a few young people who knew me then put their arms around me and led me out of the mosque saying that I was an older brother to them. I was almost beaten up or, even worse, possibly killed in the grounds of the Al-Fatah Mosque because of the rebukes and shouts of Mr MW, who seemed to have changed and was not the person we had imagined.

This was not the only time that my colleagues and I found ourselves in a dangerous situation. We always believed, however, that the Lord would protect our activities, which we carried out sincerely for humanitarian reasons. We were sometimes frightened that we would lose our lives, or die in a meaningless way, so we always monitored the situation before we went to one of the locations of the refugees. If ultimately we were 'trapped' when there was a concentration of mobs, we had to force ourselves to be calm and not to panic. Panic would attract attention and suspicion, which would end in death. Fortunately, we were always saved from dangers that threatened us.

Once, the vehicle used by the team of volunteers was caught in Hatiwe Besar, a village where the majority of residents were Christian. This village was not far from Wayame where the residents were still of mixed religious backgrounds, Salam and Sarane. However, at that time, there was a rumour of an attack on Hatiwe Besar, the source of this rumour being unclear. The residents were grouping on the side of the road wielding sharp weapons. Our vehicle, which was going in the direction of Wayame, was suddenly stopped by a young man. If I am not mistaken, the youth, who wielded a machete, was drunk. The vehicle came to a halt and we wound down all the windows to avoid any unwanted incidents; particularly given that several other young people were also coming towards the vehicle.

The drunken youth approached the window. I was sitting precisely next to the fully open window. Looking at us fiercely, he asked what our religion was. Without saying much, Lina Oktoseija, a colleague from the Baileo Maluku Network, who was sitting next to me, pulled out the chain that was under her shirt. The cross that was hanging on the chain said enough. I almost lost my nerve, though, when I saw that the youth was pointing his machete at my neck. But I tried to be calm and didn't panic. Finally, he let us go with an apology and a comment to drive carefully.

Eventually I couldn't cope with living in Ambon and being involved in activities with friends from TRK Ambon, helping refugees. My colleague Nus phoned me and asked me and my family to get ready to be evacuated from Ambon because there was a group who were suspicious of my presence in the Mardika area, the location of our coordination centre. One side accused me of spying for the other side. While another group suspected that I was an apostate. To them it was the same as being a traitor. It was rumoured that both these groups had made me a target. Therefore, Nus asked me and my family to leave Ambon as quickly as possible.

While I was living outside Ambon, I still helped friends via advocacy to stop violence and gathering humanitarian aid for refugees in Maluku. I was involved in activities with the Baileo Emergency Team (E-Team) in Jogjakarta and Surabaya. There were also activities with the Advocacy Team for Case Solving in (Tapak) Ambon, in Jakarta.

After nearly eight years working outside Ambon, I eventually returned to Ambon at the end of 2007. The situation there had really changed by then. I was no longer a target and the rumours about me had been clarified with the passing of time. Hopefully the bitter experience of the human tragedy in 1999 has been a valuable lesson for all. Isn't living together in difference something beautiful? Like a beautiful rainbow that decorates the heavens because of the fusion of its different colours.

The fusion of the rainbow is shown in the social and culture institutions of the Moluccans of *Pela* (brother- and sisterhood relationship between two or more villages with different religious backgrounds or even the same religious background)[1] and *Gandong* (womb, kinship and friendship

---

1   *Pela* is a pact of brother- and sisterhood between two traditional villages, it usually occurrs as a result of helping each other in a disaster or having experienced conflict between the two villages. This brother- and sisterhood relationship is secured with a traditional oath and is set in a framework of a number of traditional regulations that

relationship because people originate from the same ancestor). These institutions inherited from the ancestors, still have strong roots within the society.

My wife and I often told Inda, from when she was little, about this harmonious and kinship relationship. I come from Pelauw-Ory on the island of Haruku which has a Gandong relationship with the people of Titawaai on the island of Nusalaut. This kinship relationship between the two villages has been very strong for generations. By telling these things to Inda, we hope one day (without orchestrating it) that she would have a friend from the village that has a Gandong relationship with the village that her father comes from, and they would have an authentic kinship and friendship relationship. Like her father, who has a close friendship even now with Jimmy Ayal from the *Antara* News Office in Ambon, whom I have known since we worked together at *Suara Maluku* in 1994.

The culture that has been handed down by our ancestors for thousands of years is also evident in the feelings of solidarity and assumption of responsibility. For example, when a mosque is built in a traditional Salam village, brothers from a Sarane village will come and help until the mosque is finished. Likewise, the opposite happens when building a church.

The kinship and friendship culture between people was, at least, acknowledged widely with the staging of the National MTQ[2] in Ambon in July 2012. The success of the staging of this great religious event had a double effect on promoting the recovery and raising Ambon's image nationally and internationally. Genuine kinship and friendship was also widely discussed, after it had sunk to its lowest point because of the human tragedy in 1999.

Thousands of people now hope for a peaceful life, caring for and loving each other, especially in 'Beautiful Ambon' (*Kota Ambon Manise*).[3] Beautiful in friendship, social relations, companionship and beautiful in the various development programs for the welfare for all citizens who live there in the future. I hope so.

---

have to be kept within this brother- and sisterhood relationship. The two villages involved in this brother- and sisterhood relationship can be of different religious backgrounds or from the same religious background.

2   Musabaqah Tilawatil Quran, contest of Koranic Recitation
3   Translator's note: Most cities in Indonesia have a standard slogan or motto. (See www.kaskus.co.id/thread/563b7a059e7404e0788b4569/slogan-kota-kota-di-indonesia/9 for some examples.) Ambon Manise means 'Sweet Ambon', but 'manise' is also an acronym for *maju, aman, nyaman, indah, sehat dan sejahtera* (advanced, peaceful, safe, beautiful, healthy and prosperous).

Chapter 3

I COVERED A STORY, I TOLD THE STORY, I WEPT

Novi Pinontoan

After New Year 1999

On 4 January 1999, I went to Jakarta because I was invited, as a journalist from *Suara Maluku* newspaper, to cover the inauguration of Prof. Dr. Mus Huliselan, as the Head of Pattimura University. The inauguration was to take place in the offices of the Ministry of Education and Culture of the Republic of Indonesia. I travelled by plane with some of the staff from Pattimura University and stayed in a guest house not far from Senen, in central Jakarta.

After the inauguration was over, I was given money to pay for my return ticket and also for my services in covering the inauguration so that I could return to Ambon on 6 January 1999. Because I wanted to spend some time with family and friends who had moved to Jakarta to work, I chose not to return home by plane but by a Pelni ship that was due to leave for Ambon on 7 January.

While waiting for the ship to leave, I met with family and old schoolfriends from Ambon. While going around Jakarta, my journalistic instincts came to the fore. My instincts made me want to observe the situation in Jakarta after the incidents of community unrest by the mobs in 1998 and the community unrest that took place in Ketapang, an area of Jakarta, between thugs of Ambonese background and the local people. These latter incidents of community unrest occurred after the end of the New Order, when President Soeharto stepped down.

The remnants of tension and vigilance could be seen in various strategic areas around Jakarta, like the National Monument, the area close to the presidential palace, Menteng, especially along the roads leading to the personal residence of the former President Soeharto in Cendana Road, the Hotel Indonesia roundabout and other places. At these locations, rolled barbed wire fences closed off half the road and tanks, with members of the Indonesian army and police armed with rifles, kept an eye on the vehicles and people who passed by.

The situation and conditions in Jakarta provided the material for me to write an article, which was published in *Suara Maluku*. I deliberately wrote that the demands of Reformasi and the large demonstrations, which toppled President Soeharto in Jakarta, also had implications in Ambon where a demonstration ended in a clash between students and soldiers. This incident is known as 'The Grey November Incident'.

When the time came from me to return to Ambon on 7 January 1999, I sailed on the ship 'KM Rinjani'. At about 1.00pm, I took a taxi to Tanjung Priok docks. I didn't have much luggage and I had bought a first class ticket, so I was not in a hurry to board the ship. When it was announced that the ship would be leaving in a few minutes, I boarded the ship and found my first class cabin.

The atmosphere aboard the ship heading towards Ambon, however, was different to normal. Usually it would be full of sounds of the laughing and joking normally displayed between Ambonese who know each other. People would be exchanging greetings, telling stories, roaring with laughter and generally being cheerful. This time it seemed there was tension and silence; people huddled together in groups, especially groups of sinister looking youths. As a journalist, I asked the question, 'What is going on?' Out of curiosity, I went from deck to deck, hoping I would come across some Ambonese youths that I knew and whom I could ask.

My curiosity was answered when I met an old school friend, Samsudin Rumakat, who was at school with me at Junior High School No. 6 in Ambon. We shook hands, gave each other a hug and discussed many things. From Samsudin and other acquaintances I met on board, I discovered why the passengers, especially the groups of Ambonese youths on board ship, weren't mixing freely, but were tense and sat in distinctive groups. I became even more curious when I noticed that the Ambonese groups were sitting together according to their religion. The Salam (Muslims) were gathered on one deck while the Sarane (Christians) were positioned on a different deck.

According to my sources, the clear lack of unity among the Ambonese on board ship was because the majority of the young people returning home to Ambon had been thugs and debt collectors in Jakarta. Most had experienced bad luck as a result of being involved in the community unrest in Ketapang; this had made the Ambonese young people suspicious and seeking revenge. They were returning home in such large groups to celebrate Eid Al Fitr, while the Christians said it was because they hadn't had the opportunity to return home for Christmas and New Year.

The atmosphere was tense throughout the whole journey from Tanjung Priok docks, through Tanjung Perak Surabaya, Makassar, Bau-Bau to Ambon. I felt ill at ease whenever I took a walk on deck or went to the restaurant. What surprised me was that the first class corridors, which were usually deserted and quiet, were full of Ambonese youths who either slept or sat in groups playing cards.

On 11 January 1999, Rinjani docked at the Yos Sudarso docks in Ambon. Not only were there large numbers of Ambonese thugs on board ship ready to disembark, but the quays were crowded, as youths gathered to meet their colleagues. There were clashes between the groups on the quays. Fortunately, the police immediately drove them out of the docks.

These Ambonese youths who had returned home from Jakarta could be seen in various areas in the city, such as the mini-bus terminal, the Mardika market, the Pelita shopping complex (now the location of the World Peace Gong Monument) and Ambon Plaza. The level of criminality also rose, especially cases of violence and extortion.

One evening, after returning to Ambon, I stayed up late with some friends and ate saffron rice together on A.M. Sangadji Road near the Simpang area. Suddenly two youths came running from the direction of the docks and approached us. One of them asked us if anyone had a motorbike. We told him we didn't. When we asked him why he was in such a rush, he told us that he and his friends had been beaten up and almost stabbed by BBM in the Mardika market. When we asked him what the meaning of BBM was, he replied that it was an acronym for the people from Buton, Bugis, and Makassar.

'If someone has a motorbike please give us a lift to Kudamati, call the guys there to come here so that these BBM people don't act as though they own the place. The BBM people want to take over the market and the mini bus terminal in Ambon,' stated the youth. After speaking with us they left us at the saffron rice stall and hurried towards the Trikora Monument in order to catch a minibus going to Kudamati.

My friends and I were somewhat shocked and we laughed at the use of the term. Usually that term was used as an acronym for petrol.[1] But soon after hearing these youths, who looked like thugs, using the term, it soon came into regular use.

After the conflict broke out in Ambon on 19 January 1999, my feelings and intuition about the Ambonese youths on board the Rinjani became clearer. The electronic and printed media, observers and community leaders began analysing and giving opinions about the trigger for the conflict. Some said that it was the impact from the community unrest in Ketapang, Jakarta involving thugs from Ambon and that the native Ambonese population were jealous of the BBM people.

Irrespective of the quarrel over the information concerning the preconditions of the conflict, 19 January 1999 became a personal story for me, my wife and my child. My life and the lives of my family were 'saved' by my good friend Zairin 'Embong' Salampessy. Embong and I worked together at *Suara Maluku*. I started working at *Suara Maluku* before him. At that time, Embong was occupied with his hobby as a pavement artist. He got the nickname Embong (Javanese for street) as he earned his living on the streets. He was thought to be a little strange by some people, even more so when he chose to use the pavement in the A.Y. Patty area as his studio and showroom. But his career began on the pavement of A.Y. Patty Road Ambon. In 2004, *Suara Maluku* asked him to produce caricatures while becoming a journalist. Embong was well equipped to do this, because he had been an activist involved in the campus press and had taught himself photography and artistic design. At *Suara Maluku*, he was immediately placed on the same level as those of us who had been working there before him because he had access and a style outside the mainstream. Embong focused his coverage on what was happening on the streets, beside the sea, on the outskirts of the city, among village people, and he rarely entered government establishments. His reports were published as features and were always given prominence in *Suara Maluku*. Embong and I grew close, especially when I specialised in covering sports events. At that time, I was the sports editor and went with him to cover National Sports' Week (*Pekan Olahraga Nasional*, PON) 1996. Since then we have been like brothers.

The story of how Embong indirectly saved my life took place at the beginning of the conflict in 1999. In cancelling my visit to his home, he saved my life. At that time, I, my wife and my eldest child were planning to visit Embong and his family, who lived on the border between Mardika-Batu

---

1 Translator's note: *Bahan Bakar Minyak* or refined fuel oil.

Merah. We were going to go there by motorbike, when the phone rang. My wife answered the phone because I was already in position on the motorbike. She told me that Embong asked us to postpone our visit because of an incident between Mardika-Batu Merah. Clashes between these two areas were actually a type of 'tradition'.

Clashes occurred almost every year but they were always over within a short time. While I was concerned by the information that there was a clash between these two areas, I was still ready to go with my family to Embong's place. But not long afterwards, Embong phoned again and asked us to cancel our plans because the situation was developing into something different to the usual clashes. By then, houses had been burnt down and he had heard religious slogans being shouted.

According to Embong, what was strange was that although he and his family were strict Muslims and his father was the head teacher of a Muslim school, among the mob from Batu Merah were a number of athletically-built youths with short back and sides haircuts, who wanted to attack and burn down his home as well. Embong also asked us to help him by finding a taxi to evacuate his family.

Having received the news of the arson, I cancelled my plans to go visiting. I am thankful to the Lord that Embong asked me to cancel my visit to his home, although I had been determined to visit him. My plan had been that after visiting Embong I would continue my journey to Batu Merah village, to visit Mama Yam, a local midwife who helped look after my wife when she gave birth to our first born at the General Hospital. After that I had planned to visit two other friends from *Suara Maluku*, M. Kiat and Ahmad Ibrahim, who also lived in the Batu Merah area. I don't know what would have happened to me and my family if Embong had not informed us about the situation at that time.

After the onset of community unrest, Embong and I met a few times at the Governor's Offices. Then he decided to join other activists in the Humanitarian Volunteers Team (TRK). Embong's involvement with TRK in humanitarian activities meant that he had to take risks, going in and out of the segregated Salam - Sarane enclaves. In turn, this meant that his life and the lives of his family were under threat. Embong was then the only Muslim at TRK. They later recruited a number of Salam volunteers. Because Embong was the most senior of the Salam volunteers, however, he was the most active person to work alongside the Christian volunteers, to bring humanitarian aid to the needy.

Embong and his family were eventually evacuated out of Ambon by the Baileo Maluku Network. He then led the volunteers in Jogjakarta in humanitarian work through the Baileo Emergency Team in Jogjakarta, and then he joined the Ambon Advocacy Team for the Resolution of Cases (Tim Advokasi untuk Penyelesaian Kasus, Tapak) in Jakarta as coordinator, taking over from his colleague, Nus Ukru, who returned to Ambon to continue involvement in the activities of the Baileo Maluku Network.

While in Ambon, Embong and his colleagues carried out advocacy work, both at the national and international levels. It has been noted several times that he was a member of Indonesian NGO delegation who participated in the Assembly of the UN Human Rights Commission in Geneva, Switzerland. Tapak Ambon also published a book about the human tragedy in Ambon. Now Embong and I are together again in Ambon. After he returned, he wanted to help to improve the quality of photography through the Maluku Photo Club (MPC), and his expertise helped to enrich the editions of *Suara Maluku*.

Moved to Tears at Malino

12 February 2002. I am reminded of the small town located in the cool hills of South Sulawesi, called Malino. Although it is only a small tourist town, during the Dutch colonial times, Malino became famous as the place where the agreement was reached between the Dutch authorities and the leaders of the struggle for Indonesian independence.

Malino has played an historic role in solving communal conflict in various regions of Indonesia at the beginning of Reformasi, including the conflicts in Poso, Central Sulawesi (Malino I) and Ambon (Malino II). For Ambon, the peace process involved the two disputing parties and it was called the 'Malino Meeting for Maluku'.

This meeting was overseen by two national leaders at that time, Susilo Bambang Yudhoyono (SBY) in his capacity as Coordinating Minister for Political, Legal and Security Affairs and Jusuf Kalla (JK) as the Coordinating Minister for Health and Welfare, supported by the then Governor and Deputy Governor, Saleh Latuconsina and the late Dra. Mrs. Paula Renyaan. The Mayor of M.J. Papilaja, the Pattimura Military Commander Brigadier-General Muhtadi, the Regional Police Chief Brigadier-General Soenarko and prominent religious leaders, members of the community and people who represented the two sides in the dispute were all present. In addition, there were members of the press, both national and those from Ambon. After being screened or selected, participants were then issued with an ID card from the Ministry of Political, Legal and Security Affairs. No one could enter the Malino area without an ID Card. This rule applied not just to the journalists from Ambon but also to all journalists from the national media and journalists from South Sulawesi.

As far as I can remember, journalists from Ambon at that time consisted of Ahmad Ibrahim (*Ambon Ekspres*/now *Radar Ambon*), Martin Langoday (*Siwalima*), Ongen Sekewael (Radio Republic Indonesia, Ambon), Lucky Sopacua and Hamzah (Television of the Republic of Indonesia, Ambon) and myself from *Suara Maluku*.

We departed for Makassar in the second group; among our group were the former deputy governor, the late Paula Renyaan, and several officials from the provincial government, and also prominent grassroots leaders from both sides.

We had an interesting experience when we were about to leave. The plane was full because the general public was also travelling on the plane. There were, however, four leaders from community organisations who had only announced at the last minute that they were prepared to attend the talks. What happened? The plane's departure was delayed because they needed to work out how these four community leaders could leave for Malino.

Deputy Governor Paula Renyaan, with an attitude that was both motherly and as firm as a police brigadier-general, was sitting in the front of the plane. She began inspecting[2] the passengers. To begin with she approached the group of journalists to ask them to delay their departure and fly the next day. We refused to leave the plane because our news coverage would be late, given the meetings were due to commence the next morning.

Mrs Paula Renyaan gave up and checked the other passengers. She came across several of the staff and officials from the provincial government who did not have any direct connection to the meeting, therefore they were asked to leave the plane. The atmosphere changed from tense to relaxed, despite the unhappy faces of the passengers who were forced to get off the plane.

Once we arrived in Makassar, the two delegations, Muslim and Christian, stayed in separate hotels. We journalists stayed in a hotel in the Losari Beach area. The next day under tight escort, the coaches of the two delegations including the journalists and support staff from the provincial government made their way to Malino. On arrival, there was a thorough security check carried out by fully armed members of the mobile brigade using metal detectors. They checked every delegate, journalist and support staff from the provincial government at the entrance gate of the conference centre. Those who

---

2   Translator's note: The term used is the English word 'sweeping'. This word, used in Indonesian, means a 'raid'.

did not have an ID card issued by Ministry of Political, Legal and Security Affairs were not allowed to enter the complex.

The journalists followed all the proceedings and experienced the tensions in the atmosphere, the debates, and the emotional exchange of opinions between the delegates themselves and between the delegates and the officials from central government. When it came to making a decision there would be a deadlock. The mediators would lobby and even the meetings led by central government figures needed coordination. There was tension between the Pattimura military commander and the regional chief of police, particularly in relation to security and order.

We were careful about the contents of our coverage and the information we sent to our editors. Data and information that we received was in a written form or in the form of an official statement. We were only free to write about the atmosphere within the meetings or our observations of what was going on. The journalists and the Muslim and Christian delegations were not free to go where they liked during the proceedings. They were only free to move about after the meetings were over for the day and before they continued the next day.

The journalists from Ambon, Makassar and Jakarta had to fight for places in the pressroom in order to write up the reports and send them to the various media. We stayed in a guest house not far from the conference centre and it was there we also wrote our reports. The cold evening air in Malino was not able to cool down the tension of the 'hot' news reports because of the heated debates and the emotional outbursts of the members of the two delegations in the conference room.

SBY and JK acted on behalf of the central government aided by officials from the national army and police headquarters. The meetings in Malino were so difficult and serious, that both SBY and JK had to stay in the conference centre. Twice I came across SBY in the toilet. I also came across JK once, in the same place. Their faces looked serious and tired, one time they were seen contacting Jakarta by telephone.

One evening when the meetings were in recess we were taken by surprise when the Chief of the Moluccan Police Force, Brigadier-General Soenarko, unexpectedly invited the journalists to take a breath of fresh air with him outside the conference centre. Together we crossed over to the other side of the road and we sat down in a cafe and drank coffee. At that time, he looked exhausted and acknowledged that his head was reeling from the arguments put forward by the two delegations and also from the officials representing the central government.

We also witnessed the sudden departure of the Pattimura Military Commander Brigadier-General Muhtadi from the conference centre while a debate was going on about the responsibility for security and the involvement in the conflict. The reason given was that he had to go to Jakarta immediately, because he had been summoned to coordinate with the military headquarters concerning the developments of the conference.

When he left the conference centre he looked very tense as he went towards the vehicle that would take him to Makassar. There are many stories to tell about the atmosphere of the meetings. However, there was a strong determination to bring an end to the conflict. Although there were heated arguments and the parties threw accusations at each other, eventually the Malino meetings produced an agreement known as 'The Malino Declaration' with several clauses agreed to, and signed by, both parties.

The signing of the agreement was very emotional. The Chairman of the Muslim Delegation Thamrin Elly, the Chairman of the Christian Delegation Toni Pariela, the chairman of GPM Synod Rev. Hendriks, the chairman of MUI, Rusdi Hasanusi, the Muslim figure Ustad Polpoke, the bishop of Amboina Mgr. Mandagi, the Governor Saleh Latuconsina, the mayor of Ambon Jopi Papilaja, the territorial military commander, the regional chief of police, SBY and JK and the other members of the delegation, all shook hands, embraced and some even wept. I also wept, shedding tears because I was moved to witness the atmosphere surrounding the peace agreement.

Being thankful for the outcome of the peace agreement, Jusuf Kalla who comes from South Sulawesi, invited the two delegations and the press from Ambon, plus the support staff from the provincial government to an evening meal at his house in the Haji Bau Road district of Makassar. All members of the delegations mixed together. There was no segregation or separate groupings anymore. All became united, caught up in the enthusiasm for peace.

There was an historic moment that will not be forgotten by the two delegations. When the delegates left for the meetings in Malino, two different commercial flights were used. For the return journey to Ambon, SBY and JK suggested that all of the group should take the same plane. Due to the large number of the delegates, press and provincial government support staff, it was decided that the whole group should be transported by an Indonesian air force Hercules aircraft from the Hasanudin air force base. The tense atmosphere turned into laughing and joking. This is because in the belly of the aircraft we couldn't sit separately. Whether we liked it or not we had to mix and sit close together. Besides that, not everyone got a place to sit on the seats provided by the air force, some had to sit on the floor of the plane, others sat on top of the crates of cargo, and even some had to lie on the giant tyres that were carried in the Hercules.

I will never forget the shared enthusiasm. The atmosphere in the belly of the aircraft was as though that there had never been a conflict in Ambon. The characteristic Ambonese humour surfaced. Once in a while, raucous laughter erupted because people cracked jokes and were teasing each other, while trying to rest in a sitting or crouching position or lying on top of the cargo. We really suffered the same fate. Nobody was arguing, there was no sense of conflict. It was an unforgettable experience.

'Brain-washed' in Bogor

Precisely a year before the Malino meetings took place, in February 2001, the town of Bogor played its own particular part in the Maluku peace process. There, at the Salak Hotel Bogor, journalists from Maluku and the North Maluku, both Muslim and Christian, gathered to form a united vision on how to cover the conflict and contribute to the peace efforts.

Our gathering was facilitated by BBC London and the Alliance of Independent Journalists (AJI). The chief editors of the print media and the electronic media and the field reporters were all included so that together we could find a solution and develop a perspective on peace journalism. This was so that the pattern of news coverage could be changed from attacking, accusing and blaming each other's media or group in the community. These meetings also aimed to avoid provocative news reporting, which worsened conflict in the field. Our mindsets were well and truly changed from the attitude and style of the news coverage that had been prevalent from the beginning of the conflict.

The journalists from Ternate, Ambon and Tual, all stayed together at Hotel Salak. Being outside Ambon, there was a warm atmosphere of harmony and togetherness between the journalists. There was no demarcation line in the activities. There was no suspicion or accusation. The atmosphere was free from such attitudes and full of comradeship. Discussions were carried out to breakdown the situations of the conflict in the field, analyse erroneous news coverage, study data and facts on the ground. The participants agreed that provocateurs were involved on both sides, including acknowledging the fact of the involvement of army and police personnel in the efforts to achieve security.

We analysed everything fully and held an interactive discussion together with several resource people from the BBC, AJI, the head of the army information centre, Major-General Husodo, the police, chairman of the press council, Atmakusumah, and the chairman of the Jawa Pos Group, Dahlan Iskan. There were also several experts and historians such as Prof. Dr. Teterisa from the University of Indonesia, senior journalists from Jakarta, the Governor of Maluku, Saleh Latuconsina and others. The head of the public relations office for the province of Maluku, at that time Drs. Cak Saimima, and his staff, Mrs. Els Pattiasina, also participated and helped us coordinate the activities.

Sitting together and holding discussions between Muslim and Christian journalists from Maluku and North Maluku eventually helped to make things clear. We realised that the pattern and style of our news coverage until then had been provocative, although unconsciously so, in most cases. We expressed our disappointment with our colleagues from the national media in Jakarta, both print and electronic, the majority of whom had disseminated biased news. They pushed aside one community and used data, facts and unclear sources, which were not independent. This had dire consequences for Ambon. The national media didn't know what had really happened; they also did not understand the Ambonese character. Ambonese could be very emotional when defending their homes, their belongings and their lives.

We agreed to prioritise peace journalism, with the aim of touching the feelings of the disputing parties and avoiding long term provocation. Peace journalism was the appropriate way out to contain the emotions of the general population in the two communities.

We reached an agreement, set out in a number of points and given the name 'The Bogor Declaration'. One of the points was to establish a centre for both Muslim and Christian journalists in Ambon, which would be facilitated by the BBC and AJI. This centre came into being and was given the name Maluku Media Centre (MMC).

We rented a small building in the yard of the Amans Hotel, Mardika and this became the MMC office, the first home for journalists. This location was chosen because it was on the border between the two disputing communities, so journalists from both communities could reach this office quickly and also seek shelter if riots erupted suddenly.

The first chairman of MMC was a member of staff from AJI Jakarta, called Wahyuana Wardoyo. As time went on, a member of local staff, Dino Umahuk, was appointed as coordinator. Lucky Sopacua, Udin Kelilauw, myself and others were appointed as directors in the early stages of MMC.

At the MMC office, Muslim and Christian journalists could mix, work together and cross-check data and information related to the conflict. We were not influenced by the conflict in the field, even when the conflict occurred in several locations. On the contrary, we gathered together at the MMC office. We would monitor the situation and contact sources on the ground to verify data and information.

Thus MMC became known nationally, as well as overseas. Many foreign reporters contacted MMC to verify data and information about the conflict. We endeavoured to protect the independent nature of MMC. Everyday Dino Umahuk, two friends from *Suara Maluku*; Febby Kaihatu and Rudi Fofid, Saswati Matakena and Cak Tulalesy (*Siwalima*); Lili Ohorela (*Surya*); Sukirno (*Republika*); Sahlan Heluth (*SCTV*); Ahmad Ibrahim, Ongky Anakoda and the late Hamis Kasim (*Ambon Ekspres*); Mochtar Touwe (*Tempo*); Hanafi Holle (*Detik.com*); Ongen Sekewael (*RRI*); myself and others met at the MMC office, together with members of the faithful staff such as Yayat Hidayat and others.

Besides producing the declaration which initiated the 'base camp' at the meetings in Bogor, we, the journalists from Maluku and North Maluku, were taken to see the work models and policies of the leading media in Jakarta such as the *Kompas*, *Republika* daily newspapers and Detik.com. For me, the experience and history in Bogor provided a contribution to the regional journalists in aiding the peace process during the conflict. The proof being that one of the photographs from the meetings at Bogor is hanging on the wall of the World Peace Gong Monument Museum on the site of former Pelita shopping centre in Ambon.

Sorrow at *Suara Maluku*

Suara Maluku, the place where I worked as a journalist, was the only daily newspaper in existence at the beginning of the conflict in 1999. It also became a victim of the conflict. The oldest newspaper, which was still part of the *Jawa Pos* Group, became the focus of attention, positive and negative, local and national. Not to speak of the internal pressure and the struggle to maintain the unity of the staff and Muslim and Christian journalists. At one point we stopped publishing. Sorrow, weeping, the shedding of blood and tears, stress, exhaustion, threats, feeling trapped, enduring cold, crossing mountains and seas, and terror, didn't curb our enthusiasm to starting publishing again in February.

We were determined to return to the routine of publishing *Suara Maluku*, although we faced challenges and obstacles during the heightened escalation of conflict. Our 'HQ' in the Halong Atas area was very quiet, not like normal. In order to reach the office, we had to travel along roads that were dangerous, or travel by speedboat which was also a hair-raising experience. Another option was to take the winding mountain route which was steep, slippery and prone to landslides.

In telling this story, I am overwhelmed by a feeling of sadness. What my friends and I went through at that time was aimed at just circulating information and providing a service to our readers and our subscribers. Many of us at *Suara Maluku*, including newspaper sellers, agents, staff and journalists had lost our homes. Some had even become refugees. Newspaper sellers and agents no longer worked with *Suara Maluku*, those who placed advertisements and subscribers did not pay for their newspapers or for their advertisements for months on end. We sustained unspeakable material and non-material losses.

'We were not able to collect the cash from the newspaper sellers, agents, and about a thousand subscribers. We didn't know where we should go to collect it, if we wanted to collect the money. We no longer knew their addresses, because no doubt some had evacuated as refugees, moved house, returned to their home towns, or become victims of the violence. We had to accept the situation because everything was chaotic. *Suara Maluku* felt the effect of the conflict, it is a pity that we didn't receive any support from the government', the former Chief Editor of *Suara Maluku*, the late Elly Sutrahitu, complained, before he passed away in October 2005.

While we were struggling to publish the newspaper and maintain the unity of the staff, a decision by the directors of the *Jawa Pos Group* in the middle of 1999, took us by surprise. The directors had decided to introduce a new newspaper, *Ambon Ekspres* (Ameks), designed for and managed by the Muslim staff and journalists who no longer worked at *Suara Maluku*, because our main office was in the Halong Atas area where the majority of the residents were Christian.

The directors' decision made us feel sad and upset but we couldn't do anything about it. The decision of the *Jawa Pos* Group to create two newspapers in Ambon, an area experiencing conflict, and managed by two different communities, also gained the attention of the national government. The Coordinating Minister for Political, Legal and Security Affairs expressed his regret at the decision. Important community figures in the national press also conveyed the same opinion. Dahlan Iskan, the then general director of *Jawa Pos* Group, however, rejected the accusations. He stated that he was just concerned about the Muslim journalists and staff, who were not working but still receiving their wages.

'There is no other way. If we sack the Muslim staff, this would be a great mistake because they are hard up. How long will the business continue to exist if you allow them to continue to receive their wages without working? The best way ahead is to create a new newspaper for them, and then they will work and run the newspaper in order to still receive their wages. That's what I think,' such was the opinion of Dahlan Iskan. He was the Minister for State-owned enterprises in the period 2011-2014, and has used every opportunity to defend himself.

The birth of *Ambon Ekspres* resulted in *Suara Maluku* having to let the majority of our Muslim crew leave us. Not only were our houses in separate areas, but our places of work were different, so the feelings of togetherness slowly began to fade. The conflict also resulted in some of the *Suara Maluku* journalists leaving their jobs to find work outside Ambon.

Nevi Hetharia moved to *Jawa Pos* Jakarta edition; in 2014 he was appointed deputy editor of the newspaper *Seputar Indonesia* (Sindo) Jakarta. Muhamad Sirham was the general manager of *Gorontalo Pos*, Sien Luhukay became the coordinator for new coverage at *Tribun Kaltim* (East Kalimantan), Joko Sriyono joined the daily *Suara Karya* Jakarta, Muhamad Tan Reha moved to *Jawa Pos* Surabaya, the late Yongker Rumthe worked as a correspondent for *The Jakarta Post* in Manado, Hidayat moved to Malang and a few other friends also left Ambon.

Besides those already mentioned, other close friends moved to *Ambon Ekspres*, including Ahmad Ibrahim, the late Hamid Kasim, Mahfud Waliulu, also Ade Ipa Assagaf, Nurlela, Trisno, Jamal Samal, Ade Samanery. The only Muslim member of the crew who has stayed with *Suara Maluku* until now is Rohim Markalim. He has chosen to stay with the newspaper that has produced so many good journalists.

It was sad to separate after working together for so many years. However, separation is not death, it is not the end of our work. Together with the general editor, the late Elly Sutrahitu, and the founder of *Suara Maluku*, Etty Manduapessy, we were determined that whatever happened, *Suara Maluku* had to continue to exist. In the middle of dangerous and risky conditions, we were still determined to maintain this historic newspaper.

The presence of two newspapers belonging to the *Jawa Pos* Group, run by the two different communities, came to the attention of the writer Eriyanto from Jakarta. He came and researched the roles of *Suara Maluku* and *Ambon Ekspres* in the conflict, resulting in his book, entitled 'Media and the conflict in Ambon' (The cases of the *Suara Maluku* and *Ambon Ekspres* newspapers).

While the crew and I were trying to maintain the existence of *Suara Maluku*, the management of *Jawa Pos* Group created a new policy – a new storm to strike us. Around 2003 we were asked to change the name of the newspaper to *Maluku Pos*.

This command came from the eastern regional management of the *Jawa Pos* Group based in Makassar. We experienced turmoil because we had an emotional tie to the historic name of the newspaper. We cried tears of sadness and felt angry at the same time. There was no other choice but to challenge the decision and reject the name change. We suggested that both *Suara Maluku* and *Ambon Ekspres* be closed and one newspaper created, by joining the two crews together.

While negotiations were still going on, another option was suggested by former members of the *Suara Maluku* crew who had left the newspaper and journalists from other media. The latter had been recruited by the management of the daily *Fajar Makassar*, which was the coordinator of the eastern region of the *Jawa Pos* Group. They said they would join together and create a new newspaper called *Maluku Pos* to replace *Suara Maluku*. The staff and journalists of *Suara Maluku* were given time to join with them or put an end to the working relationship. We were opposed to what had been proposed.

I was commissioned to meet the boss of the *Jawa Pos* Group, Dahlan Iskan, in Surabaya. The outcome of the meeting was that Dahlan Iskan allowed *Suara Maluku* to continue to exist but the layout had to be changed and would be under the direction of head office. Another decision made was that *Suara Maluku* and *Ambon Ekspres* would each have their own offices but the newspapers would be printed at the same printers. This was carried out for a while but did not last long, because the situation was not yet back to normal.

Makassar then took over the negotiations again. We still refused to change the name of the newspaper. Eventually our firmness bore fruit, as the rival newspaper *Maluku Pos* was stopped after its third edition. Negotiations between Elly Sutrahitu and me and the head of the daily *Fajar*, Alwi Hammu and his staff in Makassar, didn't go fairly. Sutrahitu refused to sign the agreement to change the paper's name and rejected the option of stopping cooperation with the Group. We stuck with the option of staying in the Group, but not to change the name of the newspaper.

Sometime after that, my signature and Sutrahitu's signature were forged by someone (if indeed there were any signatures), it seems that a decision was made that the two of us agreed to leave the Group. They also cited that we weren't cooperative and we didn't submit a regular quarterly report on circulation and financial developments for almost two years.

While every day there were sounds of gunfire and bombs exploding all over Ambon, how could we possibly sit down and complete regular financial and circulation reports? Even getting to our office in Halong Atas was difficult. If we managed to save ourselves and our families, we were thankful and that was our main duty. Every day and sometimes every few hours we had to move to a safer location, evacuating ourselves and our families.

Citing the reason that we were not cooperative in providing the regular quarterly report was not a wise action. The directors showed lack of concern for the staff who were fighting for their lives in the middle of the upheaval of the conflict. This could be said to be a barbaric policy decision!

Negotiations and various attempts at 'wooing' failed to melt the hearts of Sutrahitu, myself and our friends into changing the name of *Suara Maluku*. As a result, a letter arrived, breaking off the working relationship with the *Jawa Pos* Group, also forbidding us to use *PT Suara Maluku Intim Press* as the name of the publishers. It is strange that this letter was not signed by Dahlan Iskan, but by the acting director of the Eastern region in Makassar.

We could have questioned the legal status of the letter because the decision was one-sided; it was not made by the top-level leadership of the *Jawa Pos* Group that was in the list of patrons of *Suara Maluku*, of which Dahlan Iskan was the general director. In addition, there was no explanation about our rights as staff and journalists, nor was there any mention concerning the assets of the business or who was responsible for the bank account. It was only stated that we could continue publishing *Suara Maluku*, but under the flag of a different publisher. We were not allowed to use the name of the *Jawa Pos* Group, and they were not to be held responsible for any debts incurred. The management had forgotten or perhaps pretended to forget, that they had stopped or blocked the distribution of production materials, such as paper and ink. Meanwhile, the money in the bank account was in the hands of the directors.

We felt abandoned. We did not, however, lose our enthusiasm. We had worked for several months without wages. In October 2003, our cooperation with the *Jawa Pos* Group came to an end. *Suara Maluku* was one of the eight founding papers of the *Jawa Pos* Group, which we had nourished into becoming a giant media conglomerate.

Etty Manduapessy, the founder of *Suara Maluku*, had a working relationship with Dahlan Iskan and had processed the permits of the weekly newspaper so that it could become a daily. Etty had even been a member of the development board of the *Jawa Pos* Group at the beginning of that cooperation. Etty Manduapessy supported us in our efforts to persevere with the name of *Suara Maluku*, whatever the risks were! We took the risks and got on with it. Thus from the end of October 2003, we decided that we wouldn't print our newspaper at the same printers as *Ambon Ekspres*.

Eventually *Suara Maluku* was printed at the State Printing Firm. The size of the newspaper had to be reduced in accordance with the paper that was available. The newspaper continued to be black and white, and the name of the publisher, *PT Suara Maluku Intim Press*, was removed. The layout was changed slightly to fit in with the size of the printed newspaper. We became totally independent. Our crew used the term 'newspaper of unity'. Given that the situation had not yet returned to normal and was not yet conducive, we left our offices in Halong Atas. We moved our simple office equipment to the home of journalist Febby Kaihatu in the Skip area.

A year later, *Suara Maluku* moved to a rented office in the Paradise area, close to the Sumber Hidup hospital. We were there for four years, then in 2008 we moved our office again to Paradise Tengah, not far from the previous location. In March 2011, the *Suara Maluku* rented office moved again to Rijali Road in the Belakang Soya area.

The official *Suara Maluku* office in Halong Atas is dilapidated and neglected, with refugees living in it. We have left it as it is, because the directors of the *Jawa Pos* Group should not be one sided in their claim to ownership, without taking into account our time of service and our rights as journalists and staff, without remembering the sweat and tears we had shed in helping the newspaper develop. The important thing was our efforts to protect the office from the angry mobs when the conflict broke and during the escalation of the conflict until 2002. If we had not done that, the building would probably just be a shell.

Going through the dynamics of conflict and peace in Maluku was a bittersweet experience. By relating the details of the dynamics of conflict and peace over this time I have learned that no matter how horrifyingly the conflict ripped to pieces the social relationships within society, it could not quell the overwhelming desire for peace in the hearts of each member of the community. It just remains for us to discover, take care of it and nurture it in order to achieve peace in the wider sense.

Chapter 4

A LESSON FOR PEACE IN MALUKU

Dian Pesiwarissa

19 January 1999

That morning, like any school child who was enjoying her holidays, I spent my time reading storybooks and magazines. My hobby is indeed reading, and the quiet atmosphere of the village supported this. I spent most of my holidays in my village of Naku, in the Leitimur Selatan district, Ambon.

Before Eid Al Fitr, my family from my mother's side had planned to visit various families who lived in the village of Hitu Lama, in the Leihitu district of Central Maluku. This had become an annual trip because my mother's parents had some 'foster children' (workers, who had lived in their house) of Butonese descent who had settled in Hitu Lama. Although it was in a different regency, it was still on the island of Ambon, so we didn't need elaborate preparations to visit the village.

There was a very close relationship between the people in Hitu Lama and my mother's family. They frequently stayed in Kilang (mother's home) and helped grandad in the forests, especially when it was time to harvest the cloves and nutmeg. They didn't just work in the plantation or go into the forest; they also exchanged ideas and learnt about Christianity from my grandad, who was a Sunday school teacher and a prominent religious leader in Kilang. He was also very nationalistic. When I was small I used to think that grandad was strange; he had workers who were Muslim, from the Buton area, not from an area in Ambon or Maluku. But as time went on, I began to understand that close relationships and love went beyond the distinctions of race or religion. They even called my grandparents Mum and Dad.

La Ata and La Duka were the two workers whose names I remember most. They were strict Muslims. If I am not mistaken, La Ata was an *imam* (leader of prayer) in the mosque where he lived. As a result of their discussions exchanging understanding of each other's religion, La Ata could recite the Lord's Prayer fluently.

I don't know why, a few days before, our plan of going to visit was cancelled because La Ata and La Duka wanted to spend Eid Al Fitr in their ancestors' village, in Buton, South East Sulawesi. In retrospect, I am thankful that we did not take the Eid Al Fitr trip to Hitu Lama that year.

Towards late afternoon, the quietness of my village was shattered. Community unrest broke out in Ambon, on the border between Mardika and Batu Merah, between Christians and Muslims. Although Naku was about 8 km from the city of Ambon, the news travelled fast. A few days later waves of refugees started moving to the mountainous regions, including my village. Members of my family who lived in the city also evacuated with their belongings.

Over the next few days, I heard news every day about which areas had suffered from community unrest, how many houses had been burnt that day, which churches or mosques had been burnt down, how many people had died or were wounded. The young people and the men in the village didn't want to be left out; they went to the boundaries between the two communities to defend the district. Machetes and arrow heads were sharpened as weapons of self-defence, in order to defend religious beliefs. They wore red head bands. What went through my mind at that time was, if the situation continues like this, when will my holiday be over?

Food became scarce. We couldn't go to the Mardika market anymore. The majority of shops were closed. An impromptu market emerged in Batu Meja, but this was only for vegetables and fish. My mum experienced difficulties in obtaining sugar, rice and kerosene. If she did find some being sold she would have to queue to buy sugar or kerosene. On 23 January 1999, my dad's aunt passed away after an illness. The most difficult thing to find was the black cloth used in the making of the coffin.

We didn't go to school for almost two months. At that time, I was in the first year of senior high school at Vocational Senior High School No. 1, Ambon. At about the beginning of March 1999, we went back to school. Unfortunately, only half of the students in my class returned to school. This meant that the two first year classes in commerce were put together to make one class and this lasted until we graduated from high school. There were no longer any Muslim students or teachers in the school because it was situated in a Christian area.

The school activities did not run smoothly that year. Sometimes we were sent home early or given a day off because of the conflict. If the noise of bombs exploding and shots being fired went on all night, we would always be given the next day off.

If conflict occurred during school hours usually we would have to gather in the schoolyard and be given instructions as to which were the safest ways home for us. From school we couldn't take the main road in Karang Panjang because there was a danger of being hit by stray bullets. The alternative route went past Pondok Patty, Gang Singa and Belakang Soya. While our friends who lived on the other side of the Trikora monument were forced to take an alternative route through Batu Gajah climb up through Pandang-pandang which would finally come out at Mangga Dua. This alternative route needed much more time because of the distance involved. Everyone was forced to take a route that had many twists and turns compared to the normal way of getting to and from school.

A thought once crossed my mind: what would be expected from us if attending school was so difficult. What sort of Senior High School graduates would we be? News about the stabbings, murders, shootings or abductions made people afraid to go far from their houses especially as evening came.

These conditions prevailed for the whole time I was at Senior High School until I graduated and went to university. I spent three years at Senior High School without Muslim friends. I then started to experience campus life. But the Pattimura University campus in Poka was burnt down and we were forced to go to lectures at the alternative campus at the Teacher Training College for Primary School Teachers. It was only when I was at university that I started meeting with Muslim friends again.

The campus was indeed a neutral place for the two conflicting sides and it was guarded tightly by security forces. But this position was quite precarious if conflict occurred because it was located on the border between the two communities. Several times when we were at lectures we were forced to run out of the lecture room to save ourselves.

Once we ran helter-skelter out of the lecture room, in an effort to save ourselves. We climbed the high wall at the back of the campus. We heard a lot of shots being fired in front of the campus. Many of the female students fainted because they were really frightened. Some of them fainted because they were crushed and trampled on by other students as they all ran, trying to save themselves. One of my friends, Jaklin, was one of those who fainted.

Even now, when we get together and reminisce, Jaklin becomes the butt of our jokes because she fainted then.

There was no place to hang out with friends after coming home from the campus, especially because Ambon Plaza was located in a Muslim area. There was no franchise like KFC, cafe or public place that was comfortable like there is now. The place where we often used to hang out was the length of the main Pattimura Street, which at that time was full of kiosks and makeshift food stalls. There was no place of entertainment. The Christians' room for movement was limited to the Christian area. It was the same for our Muslim friends; they could only move around in the Muslim areas. We could only meet with our Muslim friends when we had lectures together at the campus.

Close to Christmas or Eid Al Fitr we were sometimes frightened to go to the campus. We were frightened that the conflict would break out again. Our interactions with our Muslim friends were very limited, including communication with our workers who lived in Hitu Lama.

As the years went by, the situation in Ambon started to improve. The construction of Unpatti was underway in Poka. One semester close to the time of our internship, lectures started again on the campus in Poka. The interaction between Muslims and Christians improved. Although our generation was the one to experience the conflict directly, there were no barriers between the Muslim and Christian students on the campus. We worked on our tasks together, we even joked and laughed as usual. But at that time we were still afraid to visit the homes of our Muslim friends.

There were only a small number of Muslim students in our department and in my year. Many of my friends had lost their houses and also people close to them during the conflict. But when we were at the campus we mingled in the usual manner.

Our communication with La Ata and his relatives in Hitu Lama started to go smoothly. For two clove harvests they returned to help grandad in the usual manner. I often talked with my Muslim friends, or sometimes with La Ata. They really regretted that this conflict had taken place and didn't want it to happen again. La Ata once said, 'We don't want a repeat of the community unrest again. We suffered. Although the village wasn't burnt down and we didn't have to evacuate, life was still difficult. It was especially difficult when the youngsters wanted to go to school.' Such were the hopes of La Ata, whose children were still small at that time.

* * *

After the conflict, I didn't have too many Muslim friends. Around 2007, I met with some journalists who shared a concern about the developing rumours of conflict in Maluku. Mass media played a significant part concerning the issue of conflict. News about the conflict often became headline news in the newspapers or the main news item in the electronic media.

For example, a headline in the news such as 'Ambon Heats Up' influenced the viewpoints of people who lived outside of Ambon. Who would want to come to Ambon if conflict was the only news they heard about Ambon. Just hearing the name Ambon made people frightened. You would certainly die if you visited Ambon.

Very few journalists wrote about other aspects of life in Ambon after the conflict. For example, the matter of the Pela and Gandong relationships,[1] families who had met up again after being separated because of the conflict, interesting tourist attractions or traditional customs worth seeing and other human interest issues.

Embong Salampessy, Rudi Fofid, Saleh Tianotak, Merlin Nussy, Daniel Nirahua, Azis Tunny were among some journalists from the two communities who had the idea to establish *Radio Vox Populi*, a radio and online news website, which made me become interested in being involved in the world of journalism. I was recruited to become one of the reporters together with Iin Makatita, Halid Sabban, Richard de Fretes, and Julaila Papilaya.

At that time, my interaction with Muslims increased. From Embong I learnt how to write news reports from a peace perspective. Embong also taught me how to write news items about conflict, but to emphasise the human side. He also showed me the technique of reporting about the Ambon that wants to live in peace; the Ambon that still has white sands

---

1   *Gandong* is a kinship relationship based on a blood relationship between two or more traditional villages. The villages that have this gandong relationship believe that their ancestors were related by blood before they dispersed and settled in different places within Maluku and set up new village communities. The gandong relationship is also strengthened by an oath and set in a framework of binding social regulations that have to be obeyed by all those who are included in this relationship.

and gentle waves so that you can enjoy swimming; the Ambon that still has many traditional dances, the rhythm of the *tifa* and the *totobuang*; and about Ambonese children who still like to play in the shallow waves when the tide goes out, who like to catch fish, sea worms and squid and who have a hope and a future.

As time went on the online news website changed its name to become *Radio Baku Bae*[2] and much more has been written about Ambon at the website www.radiobakubae.com. Although the radio never went on air to become a radio station as we had hoped, I am glad that I was involved in the process. I am thankful that I could report to the world outside Ambon that Ambon was not as frightening as many people reported.

At the end of 2009, I became an employee of one of the groups belonging to the Astra International Group that is Federal International Finance, Ambon branch. Many of my workmates come from outside Ambon and felt anxious when they heard that they had been transferred to this small town with a beautiful bay, admired by the former colonisers.

Although the civil unrest in Ambon took place some time ago, in their minds Ambon was still an unsafe, 'turbulent' city. They arrived in Ambon full of dread. But once they settled in, they admitted that it is not as scary as they had imagined. On the contrary, they feel that Ambon is safer and friendlier than other Indonesian cities. They do not need to be afraid that they will be held up at knife point if they go out at night. They are also amazed that this city was once in total chaos because of conflict. Some of my friends even cry when they are transferred to offices outside of Ambon.

I hope that the conflict that once smashed the very foundations of Ambonese life will be a valuable lesson for all of us. It can become a story that will make our descendants learn to respect differences, be tolerant and forgive. There isn't a religion that teaches us to abuse and kill each other; on the contrary, religion teaches us to love and forgive each other.

When I was writing this, I asked Christian, a friend of mine whose house, in the Mardika area, was burnt down twice during the conflict, in 1999 and again in September 2011, if he had any feelings of resentment towards

---

2   *Baku Bae* means too make amends, to do good to each other.

Muslims. He answered firmly that he did not. For him, being resentful would become a burden. Being able to forgive makes him calmer.

I was reminded of the inter-faith tolerance that I had witnessed in the lives of my grandad and his labourers when I was little. They cared for each other and accepted each other's differences without being offended by other peoples' beliefs.

'An, the Christian faith does not teach us to condemn other religions. Opening our lives to others and other religions will help us to learn more about life. Jesus taught us to love our neighbours, not just those who are fellow believers,' said my granddad one day in the forest while we were standing between cloves trees that were once harvested by La Ata and La Duka.

Chapter 5

HOLDING ONTO BELIEFS

Dino Umahuk

That afternoon, 19 January 1999, at about 1pm, after taking part in the Eid Al Fitr prayers in the Darussalam University Campus and having visited lecturers and relatives, I decided to go to my cousin's house in Benteng Atas.

I was still wearing an Arab style cap and traditional Muslim clothes; I took a Waai-Ambon city minibus. The minibus journey to the Mardika terminal went smoothly. From Mardika I took a smaller minibus to the house. When I arrived at the house, my cousin and a number of neighbours, who were sitting on the verandah, immediately bombarded me with questions.

'What is the situation like in the town? They say that Batu Merah and Mardika have been involved in a brawl'. I replied, 'Nothing was going on. Though when I got off the Waai minibus, they told me to leave the terminal immediately.'

I entered the house and paid homage to the family. However, within a few minutes, the neighbours sitting outside starting shouting – clouds of thick smoke could be seen from the direction of the city centre. It seems that the reported conflict had spread. I stuck it out in my cousin's house for the next seven days.

On the seventh day, at around 10 o'clock, I borrowed my uncle's motorbike and went to Tulehu to get some clothes, because on Eid Al Fitr I came only with the clothes on my back.

A lot of damage had been caused by the conflict, which had by then been going on for six days. From OSM to Batu Gantung, a number of burnt-out cars and motorbikes could be seen strewn all over the road. Many buildings and houses had been destroyed – burnt down and left in ruins. The same could thing could be seen in other areas such as Silale and Mardika.

Before I continued my journey, I stopped off at the home of Go Kim Peng alias Petrus Sayogo, next to the Modal shop. This was because I had been living there for the last year together with my 'adopted' older brothers, Rudi Fofid and Frans Watratan.

Seeing me turn up unexpectedly, Frans was startled and looked as though he was about to panic. His attitude was highly unusual. I greeted him and went into the back to find Rudi. But it turned out that Rudi wasn't at home. Hearing a noise in the back, I went straight to the source of the noise. It turned out that at the back of the house there were a number of youths, who were blind drunk. I understood why Frans seemed to panic.

Calmly I greeted these youths. Up to now they had known me as Frans' younger brother. To avoid any unpleasantness, however, I only stayed a short time and then I excused myself and went on my way to Tulehu.

When I wanted to return to Ambon, after getting my clothes in Tulehu, my mobile phone suddenly rang. It was Zairin Salampessy, who asked me to meet him at Sandra Lakembe's house in Belakang Soya. He said that there was something important we needed to discuss. I then collected Dewi Tuasikal and we went there.

Zairin and a few colleagues were there and they invited me to join them as a member of the volunteer team for humanitarian causes. I was also asked to invite other Muslim friends, because at that point in time Zairin was the only Muslim volunteer. Dewi and I then joined the team. After the meeting, we returned to Benteng Atas. Zairin promised that he would contact me about the next meeting with our friends from the NGO.

Tuesday, 26 January 1999, I asked Dewi to come with me to the Rinamakana Foundation in Pattimura Street, Ambon. Apparently a number of activists from different NGOs had gathered together there. Chalid Muhammad, at that time the director of WALHI (Environmental Concerns Indonesia), who was on his way to an activity in Tual, Southeast Maluku, was also present. At that meeting, the team of Volunteers for Humanitarian Causes (TIRUS) was formed. The team of volunteers that we formed would serve victims of the conflict without regard for race or religion.

Chalid's presence at that meeting was a story in itself. At that time people were frequently asked to produce their identity cards by the mobs. Chalid, who is a Muslim, was staying in a hotel in a location behind the Governor's office. The majority of residents in that district were Christian. Friends who feared for his safety asked me to find him a hotel in a Muslim district.

After the meeting had finished, Chalid, Dewi and I tried to find an alternative hotel. It turned out that all of the hotels in the Muslim districts were full. In the end with the help of a friend we registered Chalid as a patient of the Army Hospital, Ambon. So Chalid stayed in one of the VIP rooms for four days while waiting for a ship to leave for Tual.

As a TIRUS volunteer, I helped Rudi and Zairin to organise communication and information. Besides this, my main job was to recruit other Muslim friends to become volunteers.

On the Point of Death

One day, I forget the exact day and month, my colleague, Oni Tasik, and I went by car to Rinamakana. Oni sat in the front seat next to the driver, while I sat behind him. From the TIRUS coordination centre the situation seemed calm and there was no sign that community unrest was likely to explode. When we arrived in the area of Belakang Soya, however, for some unknown reason a mob suddenly filled the road. Barricades were put in place and they started sweeping each vehicle that went past. My reflex was to take out my wallet from my trouser pocket and throw it underneath the car seat.

I can't describe my feelings of panic and fear adequately. Our car crawled forward slowly. The mob asked us to wind down the car windows. When the car windows were wound down a machete appeared in the left hand window while an arrow was placed right at my neck through the right hand window. In the front of the car, Oni and the driver were barraged with a number of questions. The mob also asked to see their identity cards.

Instantly, I shouted, 'We want to go to Rinamakana. We've got a meeting with the bishop there,' immediately the machete and the arrow were withdrawn from my neck, when they heard the words Rinamakana and bishop. Then they asked us to divert our car via Karang Panjang, because they had blocked the road in front.

Eventually we were able to travel peacefully to Karang Panjang, where we took a breather until the situation began to calm down. This incident was one of the most traumatic incidents that has stuck in my mind.

Back to my job of recruiting Muslim friends: to be honest, I wasn't courageous enough to do anything at the beginning. So for a while after the meeting at Sandra's home, only I, and sometimes Dewi, went back and forth to the TIRUS coordination centre, which was situated at the home of Creusa 'Tetha' Hittipeuw in Mardika. We routinely went back and forth but when the situation got worse, it was impossible for us to go there anymore. Our TIRUS friends also agreed that Dewi and I should avoid going to the coordination centre until the situation improved.

Coincidentally, there was an invitation to participate in training for peace journalism in Jogjakarta that was organised by the British Council and Institute for the Study of Press and Development (LSPP) Jakarta. I took part in this activity. Besides that, I also had the opportunity to take part in a Workshop on Reconciliation Empowerment that was organised by the Centre for Study on Reconciliation, Duta Wacana Christian University (UKDW) Jogjakarta.

Returning after training activities in Jogjakarta, the situation in Ambon had deteriorated. It meant that it wasn't possible for me to be involved at the TIRUS coordination centre. I eventually decided to help Thamrin Ely at the Indonesian Council of Muslim Scholars (MUI) coordination centre. My job at that time was to prepare the press releases and coordinate the secretariat. Then one day Sandra Lakembe phoned me and told me that TIRUS, specifically the Baileo Maluku Network, would send volunteers to take part in Sanitation and Fresh Water training in Jogjakarta. I invited my colleague Hanafi Holle to go with me as a volunteer.

While we were in Jogjakarta, besides participating in the training, Hanafi and I also helped Zairin and friends of the Emergency Team (E-Team) who at that time were promoting endeavours to put a stop to the violence in Ambon, as well as gathering humanitarian aid to Maluku. Before that, because of safety considerations, Zairin and his family had been evacuated to Jogjakarta. There, the E-Team was formed, facilitated by the Institute for Social Transformation (INSIST), with Zairin as its coordinator.

Returning from Jogjakarta, Hanafi, Dewi and I started to recruit Muslim friends and opened a TIRUS coordination centre in a Muslim district, in a shophouse in Batu Merah. Muslim volunteers joined us there, such as Linda Holle, Iksan Mahu, Ruslan Latuconsina and Biduran Kaplale. The Batu Merah shophouse coordination centre was purposely opened to give easier access to the camps where the Muslim refugees were living. This is because the main TIRUS coordination centre had been moved from Tetha's home in the Mardika district to Ansye Sopacua's home in the Passo area.

Sometimes the volunteers felt anxious working in an atmosphere of escalating conflict. For example, once when the volunteers had gathered in Passo, the conflict suddenly erupted and the atmosphere in the city was frightening. Muslim volunteers whispered to me, 'Brother, is it safe?' Such was their anxiety about the situation. I always guaranteed their safety. However, even when the security was guaranteed a hundred per cent, we were forced to return to the Batu Merah shophouse coordination centre.

So as to relieve the tension, sometimes I came up with some strange ideas, which made our friends to laugh. For instance, one time we had to attend a meeting of all the volunteers in Passo, at a point when the situation was quite tense. I asked Mahu, one of the volunteers at the Batu Merah coordination centre, to paint two broom handles black.

When we were on the way to Passo, I then asked our friends to wind down the car windows a little and let the broom handles jut out as though they were rifle barrels. Fortunately, the car windows had tinted glass, so no one could see inside the car. The atmosphere in the car, which had been tense, changed and felt more relaxed. Some laughed, some smiled a little.

One day on our way back from Passo, there were clashes between people living in the Batu Merah Bawah area. A mob attacked a minibus. When we arrived on the scene, the first thing I saw was four people surrounded by a crowd and a youth who was bruised black and blue. I asked Fadli Wasahua, who was driving, to stop. I then made my way through the crowd and shouted 'stop-stop'. The volunteers followed me. We were then involved in arguments with the mob. I dragged the youth, who had been beaten badly, into the car followed by other friends, who also brought a mother and two female senior high school students.

We drove them to the Army Hospital. Apparently the youth we helped was the son of a lecturer in the Economics Faculty of Pattimura University (Unpatti).

Another time, I was having my evening meal in front of the main Al-Fatah Mosque when the telephone rang. Handoko phoned and asked me to go immediately to the coordination centre, because soldiers had arrived. The Batu Merah shophouse coordination centre had not long moved from Block F to Block A.

I returned to the coordination centre immediately. An army truck was parked in front of the centre with at least a dozen soldiers standing on guard. I parked my car behind the army truck. Inside, my colleagues were being questioned by some soldiers. Of the three soldiers, one was an officer and the other two were ordinary soldiers.

I introduced myself and asked them the reason for their visit. It seems that they had come to ask for the head of the coordination centre to go to the district military command base (KODIM) on the excuse that we were holding illegal meetings in our coordination centre.

I found out later that it was Lieutenant Colonel Suharto, of 111 Bukit Barisan Battalion. He said that he had been ordered to arrest me as the coordinator of the centre, because I was accused of organising an illegal meeting to reject the presence of TNI security forces in Maluku.

'Who said that we have had an illegal meeting here [literally, 'a meeting in the dark']? The proof is that the eight 40 watt neon lights are all working at this moment. How can you say that we are having a "meeting in the dark"?' I challenged Lieut. Col. Suharto. Because the situation was becoming more agitated. In the end, I, Mahmud Rengifurwarin (who at that time was the chairman of the Ambon branch of HMI) and Hanafi Holle who was also at the coordination centre at that time, agreed to go with the soldiers to the Military Command HQ.

When we left the coordination centre, the soldiers who had been on guard immediately took hold of our arms and forced us to get into the army truck. I stopped in my tracks and told Lieut. Col. Suharto that we did not wish to get into the army truck. 'If we have to get into the truck, we won't go to Military Command HQ. If he wants to, Mr Suharto can come with us in our vehicle.'

Eventually Lieut. Col. Suharto gave in and went with us in our vehicle. Escorted by the army truck, we went to the Military Command HQ in the Batu Meja district. During the journey, Lieut. Col. Suharto apologised for frightening the volunteers. He admitted that the new troops had just arrived that morning, and that evening he was ordered to take us into custody.

When we arrived at the Military Command HQ, the three of us (Mahmud, Hanafi and myself) were taken to a hall and left there until the middle of the night. At 2am a middle ranking officer opened the door and allowed us to go home. We returned to the coordination centre.

A number of volunteers joined us at the Batu Merah shophouse Block A coordination centre, making our numbers swell. They included members of an outdoor pursuits group called PPSWPA Kanal and a number of young people from the villages of Liang and Tulehu, such as Handoko, Hadi, Mukhlis, Memet, Yayat, Ani Wakano and others.

Peace Journalism

My personal relationships with NGO activists and journalists in Ambon and Jakarta meant that LSPP Jakarta made me the coordinator of peace journalism training in Ambon in January 2000. It was the first time since the conflict in Ambon had begun that the journalists met together. Besides introducing the concept of peace journalism, this forum started to think about the need for a media centre for journalists.

This training made a great impression on all the participants. Our journalist friends started to realise that they needed the intervention of peace journalism. The experience of this training helped to turn the trend of news reporting by journalists in Ambon. After the Media Centre (MMC) came into being in 2002, it further strengthened the campaign for peace journalism in Maluku.

Accused of Being a Provocateur

A number of NGOs from outside Maluku who were concerned about the conflict in this region began to trust in the developing TIRUS coordination centre in the Batu Merah shophouse. Organisations – such as KontraS, the Volunteer Team for Humanitarian Causes (TRK) Jakarta, even Palace Volunteers (Relawan Istana) that had been formed by Mrs Sinta Nuriyah Wahid – developed a good relationship with us in Ambon. Our colleagues at the main coordination centre allowed us to work with whoever we wanted, as long as it was according to humanitarian principles.

Besides being active as a TIRUS volunteer, I also became a volunteer for KontraS and the Palace volunteers, along with working as a journalist for the daily *Ambon Ekspres*. Together with Thamrin Ely and Yusran Laitupa, I also founded an NGO called Maluku Watch.

One day, I forget the exact date, Mufti Makarim Al-Akhlak of the Palace volunteers, phoned me and told me that they were in the middle of sending aid to Ambon. This aid would be sent via a ship, Lambelu. He and Abu Said Pelu from KontraS would travel on the ship along with the aid.

At 5am the next day, I went with a number of volunteers to the Yos Soedarso docks, Ambon, to meet Mufti and Abu Said, in order to collect the goods which included medicines, instant food, milk and clothes.

The joint forces of the army and the police had placed the docks under tight security. This was understandable, because there had been rumours that Laskar Jihad[1] had started entering Maluku. We went onto the docks because the ship, Lambelu, had already docked. Around 6am, Mufti and Abu Said left the ship. We discussed how to organise the transport of the aid to the TIRUS Coordination centre. We already had some trucks ready for this.

---

1   Translator's note: Laskar Jihad is an Islamist vigilante group founded in 2000, literally 'Soldiers of the Holy War'.

Something strange then happened. The army and police joint forces, which we thought were carrying out raids against Laskar Jihad, confiscated our goods, which had been placed on the quay. They individually checked each box we had piled up on the docks with a metal detector. A number of members of the joint forces ruined some of the cardboard boxes, filled with aid, with their bayonets.

Abu Said and I took the initiative and asked them what was going on. Their reply made us speechless. The joint force operation was aimed at capturing provocateurs, and also to seize communication equipment that had been sent by the Republic of South Maluku (RMS).

We protested that we were doing nothing wrong. A number of soldiers, however, started putting some of the boxes, which they had separated from the others, into an army truck. It turned out that the goods taken were communication devices including 70 walkie-talkies and two CB radio receivers, with their relevant equipment and transmitter, which had been sent to help the volunteers who worked for the refugee coordination centres.

I was still dumbfounded and full of disbelief, when a patrol car arrived suddenly. A police officer got out of the car and came over to us. Without introducing himself he asked us 'Who is responsible for these goods?' Abu Said and I answered together, 'The Volunteer Team for Humanitarian Causes'. The officer asked again, 'Who is its leader – Abu Said?' and I replied, 'The two of us, Sir.' The officer, whose name and rank I don't remember, said, 'Come with me to HQ.'

As we had noticed signs that things were not good, Abu Said and I asked our colleagues to take the goods, which had not been confiscated to the TIRUS coordination centre and asked them to take Mufti with them. At the time of this incident, a number of journalists, who were my friends, could be seen busily taking photographs and interviewing several of the army and police officers.

Our colleagues then transported the aid to the Batu Merah shophouse coordination centre. Because the coordination centre was full, I asked my colleagues to leave some of the goods at the Watch offices in Perigi Lima and, at the same time, take Mufti to check in at the Abdulalie Hotel that was in the area. In the meantime, Abu Said and I were taken to the Sectoral HQ (HQ of the security forces in the former Village Cooperative Central Building (Puskud) on A. Y. Patty Street

When we arrived at the Sectoral HQ, we were put into a small room and told to wait. After about an hour, I was summoned by a soldier and told to appear before the commander.

The commander asked me, 'Name?' I gave him my name. 'Occupation?' I replied, 'Journalist and humanitarian activist, Sir.' 'Do you know why you are being held?' I replied that I didn't know. The commander then went on to explain many things about why I had been detained, none of which made sense. In essence the army and police had received intelligence reports that a provocateur was at work, who had brought aid in the form of sophisticated communication equipment intended for RMS activists in Maluku. I then explained the contents of the aid, including the communication equipment that they had confiscated.

Apparently the commander of this sector who held the rank of Lieutenant Colonel didn't know who the First Lady was. He even asked us, 'Do you mean that the aid was sent by Mrs Megawati?' At that time Megawati was the Vice President of Indonesia. I replied straight away with a smile. 'Sir … Sir, Megawati is the Vice-President of Indonesia. The First Lady is Mrs Sinta Nuriyah, wife of Gus Dur, the President of Indonesia.' Out of the blue the two soldiers, who were standing to my right and left, suddenly hit my temples with the butt of their rifles.

They hadn't finished yet. The commander asked me again, 'Do you know the name Munir? I answered, 'I know him, Sir. He is the Coordinator of KontraS, my boss. I am a KontraS volunteer, Sir.' I hadn't finished speaking, when the commander rattled on, 'That means that you are a Jewish spy? How come you know Munir?' I replied again, 'No, Sir. I am a journalist and a volunteer for humanitarian causes. I know brother Munir from the office. He's my boss.' Because they thought I had shown contempt to their commander, the two soldiers shouted at me and hit me again with the butt of their rifles.

I don't know why, after that the commander suddenly changed his attitude and became friendly. He then asked me to explain in detail about myself, and my connections with KontraS, the Palace Volunteers, and about my work with TIRUS. After I had explained in great detail, the commander gave the impression of befriending me, asking, 'Your friend standing outside, tell me about him.' A naughty thought came to me. I replied, 'The one standing outside is Mr Abu Said Pellu, SH. Munir's lawyer. He has been sent here, besides bringing the humanitarian aid, also to observe the situation and conditions. The results will be reported to the president.'

When I replied, I stoked up courage to stare straight in the face of the commander. He looked surprised when he heard my answer. With a smile on his face, the commander then asked me to leave the room and asked me to summon Abu Said to appear in front of him.

Outside I told Abu Said that if he was questioned, he should be angry and if needed he should slam the table. I told Abu Said about what had occurred when I was interrogated. It is true, Abu Said's loud voice could be heard venting his anger in the commander's office.

After 15 minutes Abu Said came out with a big smile on his face. We were asked to sit in the waiting room. Not long after, we were given two packages of Padang rice and two bottles of mineral water. After eating, we were taken to the Regional Police HQ for Ambon Island in Perigi Lima.

When we reached the Regional Police HQ, we were taken to the Regional Police Chief's office. It's a pity I have forgotten his name. Fortunately, the Regional Chief of Police had been a student of Munir's at the Police Academy (PTIK). We chatted in a relaxed manner in his office.

After a while, we were asked to go the interview room so that the official report could be typed up. However, the policemen were confused about how to write the report and the two of us didn't want to sign it, so the Regional Police Chief let us go home with himself as our guarantor.

From the Regional Police HQ, I took Abu Said to Abdulalie Hotel and then I returned home to Kebun Cengkih to take a shower and have a rest. Because I was exhausted, I decided to take the day off and stay at home, and then in the evening I would meet with Mufti and Abu Said, to discuss their plans.

But what can be said. That evening, at 8pm, the Ambon Station of TVRI broadcast the news of the capture, by joint forces of the army and police, of provocateurs together with the evidence. My face and that of Abu Said were shown on the television screen as convicts. I immediately telephoned Abu Said and Mufti. Apparently they had also watched the news. We agreed to stay calm and keep an eye on developments. I also asked the volunteers at the Batu Merah shophouse coordination centre to be on guard.

At about 11pm, I phoned Abu Said and Mufti again. However, I couldn't contact either of them on their mobile phones. I decided to check on Abdulalie Hotel. Apparently they had checked out. Confused and in a panic, I tried to contact several colleagues. It seems that no one knew where the two of them were. Because there was no news, I decided to return home. I finally heard from Mufti. The night before they were evacuated to the Mobile Brigade HQ in Tantui and from there early in the morning they were taken to the airport and flown to Sorong in a Hercules. From Sorong, the two of them were then flown back to Jakarta.

Mufti told me that a number of people had come to look for them at the hotel. Fortunately, the hotel worked in coordination with the police in order to evacuate the two of them.

Three days after the news broadcast by TVRI Ambon, the situation in the city of Ambon heated up. Conflict broke out again. This time the Mobile Brigade HQ in Tantui, the campus of the Indonesian Christian University in Maluku (UKIM) and the Unpatti campus were burnt to the ground.

Personally, my family and I did not feel safe. Especially as our first born, Vinapora Lailiani Setyananda, the result of my marriage to Dewi Tuasikal, was just over a week old.

A number of soldiers I didn't know suddenly started visiting us routinely, so did some of the members of Laskar Jihad. An even more dangerous incident occurred when one day when I was in the Watch office. When I opened a window, shots were heard including the sound of bullets whizzing past me. Apparently the two bullets hit the wall to the left of the window only a few inches from where I was standing.

I closed the window and phoned Sandra Lakembe straight away. Sandra then told me to go home immediately and wait for news from her. When I arrived at the house, I told Dewi to be prepared for all possibilities. Not long after that, Sandra phoned me and told me to be ready to be evacuated to Jogjakarta.

That evening, with the help of Alissa Wahid (Gus Dur's eldest daughter) our family left Ambon. We left on a boat. Lambelu, Dewi, Nanda and I headed towards Surabaya. From Surabaya we caught a bus to Jogjakarta.

For three months, our family stayed in the home of Arifah Rahmawati in the city of Gudeg. Arifah is an activist at the Centre for Security and Peace Studies at Gajah Mada University, whom I had known since I had been involved in dealing with the conflict.

I was then summoned to Jakarta to help KontraS. In this organisation I was assigned to the investigation division and I also organised the KontraS bulletin. For the first three months, we were put up in a safehouse that was also the residence of Mrs Ade Sitompul (humanitarian activist and one of the founders of KontraS).

When I was at KontraS we had the opportunity to make a documentary film about the conflict, the result of cooperation between KontraS and the Set Foundation led by Garin Nugroho. This film was shown at the Jakarta International Film Festival (JiFFest 2001) and was an entry as one of the best film in the human rights category. Besides that, I was also involved in the organisation of the meeting between the traditional chiefs, part of the Baku Bae movement.[2]

We moved to Otto Iskandardinata Road and moved again to the Warung Buncit district. When I was living in Warung Buncit, I had been moved from KontraS to the *Voice of Human Rights* radio. There I was neighbours with Zairin, who had been moved from Jogjakarta. Zairin was moved to Jakarta because Baileo had closed the E-Team in Jogja. Together with several organisations in Jakarta we came up with the idea that brought the Advocacy Team for solving the conflict in Ambon (Tapak Ambon) into being. First, Nus Ukru was asked to be the coordinator of Tapak Ambon. Then, when Nus was transferred to Ambon, Zairin took over the position.

After almost two years in Jakarta, the Alliance of Independent Journalists (AJI) Indonesia set up the Maluku Media Centre (MMC). MMC was formed after AJI - Indonesia facilitated a meeting of Muslim and Christian journalists from Maluku and North Maluku in Bogor in 2002. I was asked to return to Ambon to head up MMC taking over from Wahyuana as the coordinator. My family and I returned to Ambon.

My first job was to reorganise the MMC, which was in a mess. At that time MMC was located in a small building in the corner of Ambon Manise Hotel (Amans) grounds. I then invited Yayat, one of the TIRUS volunteers, to help me there.

I realised that the hardest job would be to develop trust, both between journalists and MMC, and amongst journalists themselves. To achieve this, one of the things that I did often, was to go by motorcycle at night across the demarcation line in the border areas, to pay a visit to the *Suara Maluku* office in the Skip district. At that time *Suara Maluku* was using the home of one of its reporters, Febby Kaihatu, as an emergency office.

At *Suara Maluku*, we would often meet, drink coffee and chat. This continued when *Suara Maluku* moved its office to Anthony Rebook Road. We also visited other media such as *Dewa* newspaper and Radio DMS.

I often invited Azis Tunny to come with me. Maybe because he was brave or stubborn, Azis came with me every time I invited him. He had been my junior at university and in the outdoor pursuits' organisation PPSWPA-KANAL, which I founded with some friends when I was still a student

---

2 *BakuBae* means to be on goods terms. The opposite of being angry with each other, the term *BakuBae* used in the movement has been adopted from children's games in Maluku. In this game the children touched each others little fingers as a sign that they are angry with each other, conversely they touched each others' thumbs as a sign that they wanted to make up and be friends again.

at Darussalam University Ambon. I also invited Azis to come and live in my house in Kebun Cengkih which was one of the former volunteer team's coordination centres.

Gaining Trust

MMC had the job of campaigning for peace journalism. MMC is recorded as giving the most opportunities to journalists to participate in training activities in professional journalism. A number of journalists even had the chance to have an internship with one of the national media in Jakarta such as *Kompas*, *Tempo* and *Republika*.

Carrying this heavy burden made me realise that this endeavour must involve as many people as possible, not just journalists. In September 2002, Azis and I therefore came up with the idea of gathering around 50 outdoor pursuits' enthusiasts in Ambon, both Muslim and Christian, for an Outdoor Activity Training.

MMC was used as the secretariat, and Azis acted as the chairman of the committee. Rindam Suli became the camping ground. During the day we learnt navigation, hiking, rafting, caving, survival, photography and environmental journalism.

At night time, we sat around the bonfire and played the guitar. Although the Outdoor Training became the means for learning and activities of the outdoor enthusiasts, the main enthusiasm came from true reconciliation. During these activities I got to know Lieutenant Colonel Yudi Zanibar, the commander of the Infantry Regiment Regional Military Command (Rindam), who recently helped my friends and I in bringing about reconciliation.

Azis and I were of the opinion that too many activities were being held in the name of reconciliation and that these had been proposed by the regional elite, and tended to be mere formalities, ceremonial in nature. We wanted to create activities where reconciliation really took place, carried out in the open air, without being set artificially and involving lengthy discussions, without binding regulations in the meetings, and without boring agendas.

In a short space of time, MMC gained the sympathy and the support of the journalists, students and outdoor pursuit's enthusiasts. The journalists made MMC their base camp. Those who were reluctant to begin with now stopped by frequently. At MMC, we carried out frequent public discussions, both offline and on air, inviting prominent persons, journalists, students and outdoor enthusiasts. We even watched the European Cup together in 2002.

This continued until I left MMC on 26 April 2004. By then, MMC had moved to a five-storey building in A.Y. Patty Street.

Besides being the MMC coordinator, I was also a reporter for detik.com and the Liaison Officer for the National Independent Team of Investigators (TPIN), which unfortunately has now been disbanded, without any results being revealed to the general public or even to me, who was an actual member of that team.

I also wrote a column in the *Info* newspaper. I mention this because I once wrote a series of articles with the themes of 'Governing by the Gun' and 'Strike the Ordinary People Force (PPRC)'. At that time, The Indonesian army was carrying out a Quick Response Strike Force (PPRC) exercise in Ambon. It seems that Ryamicard Riacudu, the Army Chief of Staff, at that time, was offended.

This is how the story went. That morning the high ranking army officers arrived in Ambon for the opening of the PPRC exercises. The journalists headed to the Pattimura Airport to cover the arrival of the general. In front of all the journalists, the Army Chief of Staff was very angry with the head of information for the military command, about my two articles. I received this news directly from Saswaty Matakena who phoned me from Pattimura Airport.

To begin with I thought Saswaty was joking. It didn't make sense that a general would be angry with the likes of Dino Umahuk. However two hours later, Lieut. Col. Yudi Zanibar who at that time was Commander of the District Military Command of Ambon Island, arrived at MMC and invited me to meet the Territorial Military Commander XVI Pattimura, Major General Joko Santoso. The two of us went in his official car to the Territorial Military Command HQ in Batu Meja.

When we arrived there, we went straight to the office of the Territorial Military Commander, Major General Joko Santoso who greeted us in a friendly way. After shaking hands, we were asked to sit down. He then told us a lot about the Indonesian army and how it did its duty in defending the country, protecting the sovereignty of the country. In essence he asked me not to write any more articles, which would discredit the army.

When we were about to go home, the Major General challenged me about a certain program. His brother worked in the Social Services Ministry in Jakarta and had a reconciliation program for young people, but as yet it had not been carried out. Joko Santoso asked me to organise this outbound program, involving 50 Muslim youths and 50 Christian youths. I agreed to do it and asked for three days to organise it.

When I arrived home from the military HQ, I asked Agil and Handoko to gather our university student, Senior High School student and outdoor pursuit's enthusiast friends. That afternoon we held a meeting to discuss the agenda for the outbound event. Friends from both communities were present; we asked them to coordinate their friends so that we would get the required 100 participants.

Three days later, at precisely 8 o'clock in the morning, one hundred young people consisting of university students, high school students and outdoor pursuit's enthusiasts, male and female, gathered in Merdeka Square ready to be taken to Rindam.

For a full week we took part in the outbound reconciliation program, we really enjoyed ourselves and were very happy. We learnt to build togetherness, trust and working together in groups. Everyone mixed well together and there was no segregation among us.

After the Outbound, Azis and I organised a Band Festival for reconciliation, which took place in Merdeka Square, Ambon. As far as I know, this was the first such activity to be held after the conflict in Merdeka Square. We didn't think we would get permission to hold the event at that location because of security issues.

Fortunately, this event had the full support of the district military commander for Ambon Island, Lieut. Col. Yudi Zanibar, who acted as our guarantor. He was also prepared to be a sponsor of the event. Although only local bands were involved, the musical performances by Ambonese youths entertained the audience. The enthusiasm of the band members and the audience demonstrated that the young people needed entertaining. MMC also sponsored this event.

Not only that, with the help of Lieut. Col. Yudi Zanibar, I built an artificial climbing wall in Merdeka Square and held an exhibition of wall-climbing amongst outdoor pursuit enthusiasts. The climbing wall became a spot where young people of the city of Ambon met and practised wall climbing. Sadly, the climbing wall has since been dismantled by the Ambon City Government.

Crossing the Demarcation Lines

The conflict in Ambon caused demarcation lines to appear between Muslims and Christians. Beginning with residences, markets, transport routes, hospitals and even educational institutions. In short, everything was divided into two sections, Muslim and Christian.

At that time when life was full of segregation, I still held the belief that the conflict that occurred was not a religious conflict. I have made this conclusion based on my experiences as a volunteer with the Volunteer Team for Humanitarian Causes (TRK) Ambon, also based on personal experience where I interacted with and built up relationships with Christian friends.

Sometimes I would travel from the MMC office in A.Y. Patty to Kebun Cengkeh, on to Air Besar, Ahuru, Karang Panjang, Kopertis, Kayu Putih, descend to Batu Meja and return to MMC. Often, I was in a Christian area when the conflict was raging and I was perfectly safe.

One time, Iin Purwanti, a friend from Jakarta, asked me to accompany her and a friend to meet the *Agas* kids (young teenagers who were involved in the violence during the conflict). She and a Japanese friend were making a documentary film about the involvement of these kids in armed conflict. So Iin, her Japanese friend and I often went back and forth to the Kopertis district to interview and photograph the *Agas* kids.

I witnessed the skills of these kids in their early teens. They showed their abilities in dismantling and reassembling weapons, both automatic and homemade. Several times they taught me how to shoot. The conflict and violence had taken away their childhood, which should have been full of laughter and happiness.

On other occasions, the three of us went to the cross on the hill in the Mangga Dua district to enjoy the view of the city of Ambon at night. They stayed in Mutiara Hotel, so I would go back and forth from Kebun Cengkeh to pick them up and take them where they wanted to go. Sometimes they returned to the hotel in the middle of the night and I had to manually open and close the barricades that were placed close to Maranatha church.

On another occasion, two friends, Irine from the Social Politic Research Centre, LIPI, and a friend from the Friedrich Ebert Stiftung (FES) organisation asked me to accompany them after the evening meal. We went to Latuhalat beach and enjoyed the full moon until late at night.

It was quite tense the time when I accompanied Stevani, a reporter from NOS, a Dutch television station. That evening we interviewed Berti Coker in his home. I knew Berti from when I had lived in Bantu Gantung. When we were in the middle of the interview with Berti, a volley of shots was heard from the direction of Batu Gantung.

I panicked a little, making the camera I was holding shake. Particularly when Berti's wife brought us a drink and suddenly remarked, 'Those Muslims, they are always up to something. What do they want?' The camera which was running almost fell out of my hand. Fortunately, I was using a tripod. I tried to stay calm until the interview was over. We then chatted with Berti and a few of his men. Around 2am we went home because the next day we had to film in Waai, Tulehu and a number of refugee coordination centres in the city of Ambon.

In the middle of uncertain situations, sometimes I would need to joke and journalist friends became my victims. One night, Agil, Yayat and I were having a meal at food stalls in front of the main Al-Fatah Mosque. We were enjoying our meal, when the late Hamid Kasim a journalist from *Ambon Ekspres*, approached us. Without beating about the bush he asked in his characteristic Ternate accent, which he never lost despite living in Ambon for years, 'Dino, you have a car don't you? Let's go for a ride'. I replied, 'Yeah that's right, but hang on a minute, let us finish our meal'.

After eating, we went towards the car; coincidently Ongki Anakonda also wanted to come with us. I drove the car along A.Y. Patty Street. Then we headed in the direction of Maranatha Church, to Pattimura Street. We stopped in Batu Meja in front of Wisma Game. The whole length of the journey, Hamid was the butt of our jokes. But when the car entered the Christian district, he went quiet and didn't utter a word.

After I parked the car at the side of the road, I got out and met a few friends who were sitting on the pavement enjoying the local liquor (*sopi*). They were student friends and outdoor pursuit enthusiasts.

I had deliberately opened the car windows. While shaking hands and hugging these friends, I shouted, 'Wow! There's a Muslim in the car', Ongki and Hamid became more and more afraid. Agil and Yayat, who understood what was going on, split their sides laughing. The two of them got out of the car and joined us. After we finished talking to our friends, we went home. The whole of the journey, Ongki and Hamid didn't stop cursing at us as they laughed.

One evening, when I was visiting the *Suara Maluku* offices in Anthony Reebok Street, clashes occurred at the traffic lights close to the City Police Station. The mobs from the two communities had gathered and Sultan Khairun Street had been blockaded. Rudi and I went outside and mixed with the mobs that assembled in front of the public prosecutor's office. About half an hour later the mobs from the two sides disbanded. Rudi and I returned to the office. An hour later I returned home.

Leaving Ambon Again

It never crossed my mind that my family and I would have to be evacuated from Ambon again. The cause this time was also as a result of a news report.

As I have already explained above, MMC often held public discussions inviting people from different circles.

The plan for the April 2004 edition was the discussion of the topic 'RMS – between Myth and the Dreams of the Indigenous Population', with speakers including the regional chief of police, Thamrin Ely and Rev. Jhon Ruhulessin. I don't know why, but on 21 April, *Ambon Ekspres* led with the main story that MMC would facilitate a dialogue between the government and RMS. This news item also stated that the regional police were the main supporters of this discussion, which was due to take place in the Amans Hotel. MMC provided clarification but unfortunately there was no response from *Ambon Ekspres*.

The next day, 22 April 2004, the head of IAIN (*Institut Agama Islam Negeri*, National Institute for Islamic Studies) Ambon, M. Attamimi, immediately issued a statement strongly objecting to the planned dialogue. Attamimi even threatened to mobilise mobs to burn down the Amans Hotel if the dialogue were to take place. The situation continued to become more heated. MMC again sent a clarification and the right of reply, that this activity was just the usual public discussion not an event to facilitate a dialogue between the government and RMS. Again, *Ambon Ekspres* didn't provide a response or make any clarification or respect the right to reply.

The following day, 23 April 2004, I was giving a session on journalistic training to students from State Senior High School No. 5 in Galunggung, when my mobile phone rang. It was Isaac Saimima the Regional Secretary for the Province. When I responded to his greetings, Mr Cak told me that the Governor, Karel Albert Ralahalu wanted to speak to me. I agreed to speak to him. It seems that the Governor was really angry with me about the news report in the *Ambon Ekspres* two days before.

I explained what really happened. However, the Governor's wrath did not abate. He snapped at me, 'I don't want to know. If anything happens, you will be held responsible.' I felt that I hadn't done anything wrong, so I replied 'Why should I be held responsible? You're the Governor, not me.' He replied 'I don't want to know.' I then replied, 'I also don't want to know. Am I the Governor?' He hung up on me.

On 25 April 2004, the Ambon conflict erupted again. The conflict was triggered by the flying of the Republic of South Maluku (RMS) flag and a procession of supporters of RMS from the residence of Alex Manuputty (FKM Executive Chair) in Benteng district to the regional police headquarters in the Batu Meja area. During the procession, close to the Trikora Monument, another crowd of people emerged from the direction of the Al-Fatah Mosque.

The two groups faced each other. The clashes started with hurling insults at each other, followed by stone throwing, accelerating into attacking each other with sharp weapons and Molotov cocktails. Not long afterwards, rifle shots and homemade explosions completed the community unrest of the mobs.

In a short time, Muslim and Christian communities faced each other again on the borders of the residential areas of the two communities in almost all areas of Ambon. Clashes also occurred between the mobs in Anthony Reebok Street. The UNDP office that was in this street was burnt down. The community unrest even spread close to MMC. At that time, my family and I had moved from Kebun Cengkeh and were living on the fifth floor of the MMC building.

In the evening, I received a telephone call from Tessa Pipper (MDF), one of the organisations that supported MMC and Santoso (Director KBR68H), who happened to be in Ambon at that time. They had been staying at the Mutiara Hotel, but they had been evacuated, together with a group of foreign NGO workers and other UN personnel, to the operational HQ of the mobile brigade in Tantui.

They asked us about the condition of our families and the situation in Ambon. I gave them a description of what the situation was like, including the condition of my family. They asked us to be ready to be evacuated to Jakarta the next day. I talked with my wife about the situation and for safety reasons, friends suggested that we should be evacuated for a while.

On 26 April 2004, we left Ambon again. At 5am we went by car to the coast at Mardika market. From there we took a speed boat to Laha, then we continued by car to Pattimura airport. At the airport, we met with Tessa and Santoso, who gave us two plane tickets in their names for us to use, because other tickets had been reserved for them. So we were evacuated to Jakarta. I have never returned to Ambon.

Although I have never returned to Ambon, the story above has left its mark on my life, especially because my four children now live in Ambon with their mother.

It hurts to hold on to a belief that what happened was really not a religious conflict. I have paid a high price for my ideals, including the loss of my family and my aspirations. But never mind. It has happened and we can learn from these experiences to make us wiser. In this way, life can perhaps have meaning.

Such is part of my journey that I tell you from among many stories that I can't possibly tell for various reasons. Sometimes I can smile while I tell these stories and sometimes I cry. How rumours, gossip, intrigue, provocation, manipulation of information have destroyed things that were charming and beautiful and buried people's talents before, during and after a war that was not beautiful.

As a conclusion, allow me to quote a poem that I wrote in 1999 when I was still in Ambon. I hope it is of benefit to us all.

THE RELIGION OF SUICIDE

If later on this morning you go to Friday Prayers
Perhaps at the Al-Fatah mosque
Or on Sunday
You go to a service or take Mass
Perhaps at Maranatha Church
Perhaps at the Cathedral
Please ask Muhammad
And Jesus the Great
Do they teach in God's religions
That we should kill each other?

If that is so
Why does religion forbid me to commit suicide?

Dino Umahuk
Ternate, 7 August 2012

Chapter 6

TRACES OF ENCOUNTERS

M. Azis Tunny

That afternoon, 23 February 2002, when I returned home from lectures at Darussalam University (Unidar) Ambon, I received a letter from Hanafi Holle, my senior at the university. The note asked me to come to Ambon as quickly as possible. Hanafi invited me to work at *Info*, a new newspaper that had recently come into being, three weeks after the Agreement in Malino had been declared.

When I started working at the *Info* newspaper, Hanafi and I were the newcomers in the 'world without commas'. Beforehand, the two of us were just campus journalists, and had founded the student bulletin 'Tafakur' during the time we were involved in the Student Press Association (LPM) in Unidar.

Becoming a journalist at *Info* was my first experience of the workplace and the start of living an independent life. At that, I was still a student in my sixth semester at Unidar, and I was very dependent on my monthly allowance sent by my parents who lived in Masohi, Central Maluku.

It is not an exaggeration to say that *Info*'s presence gave new hope and new enthusiasm, not just for me, but for Maluku. Yusnita Tiakoly, as the chief editor of this newspaper, succeeded in overriding the pessimism of members of the Ambonese media, who were uneasy about working together in one newsroom. She initiated something new by employing journalists from the two religious communities to work together in one office.

Yusnita realised that building media in a post-conflict region that still had the potential to erupt into a new conflict, needs to accommodate various perspectives from all parties. From her earlier experiences during the conflict she knew that news media added fuel to the flames of hatred and enmity. Even though the profession demanded that both sides should be covered in order to give a balanced report journalists and media tended to be biased towards their own religious communities. Journalists in Ambon ignored the universal journalistic norms when the region was beset by conflict.

The concept of covering both sides objectively is an ethical norm in journalism that cannot be forgotten, however, the reality of the situation was different. Discussing journalism in a region experiencing the violence of conflict is often paradoxical and controversial, especially for local journalists who live in the area of conflict.

When the conflict smouldered, journalists covered pages and pages of newsprint with incidents of bloody war. Vulgar news reports were violations of the norms and ethics of journalism, which protects the use of every word. Journalists dramatically broadcast every incident by radio, their broadcasts spiced by the sound of guns going off and bombs exploding, giving the impression of a horrifying conflict. Television broadcasters didn't want to lose out and provided news of the war with moving narratives which made the viewers angry. The public could guess immediately which side the media was on, merely by watching the news.

This situation arose because the journalists and the media were compartmentalised through the segregation of districts. This community unrest with a religious nuance split the journalists into two camps emotionally, making them fight over the truth of information. The conflict led to journalists' ideology and politics fusing with the news reports of the conflict. As a result of domestic factors and the journalists being too close to the waves of communal conflict, news was published using the terminology of 'friend and foe'.

The hard and brutal conflict also resulted in many local journalists becoming victims of the conflict. The house belonging to Max Apono, a journalist from *Suara Maluku*, was burnt down in the Pohon Puleh district. Poly Yoris, also a journalist for *Suara Maluku*, was once left adrift for hours in a speedboat where the rest of the passengers had been killed by a sniper shooting at them, and only he was saved. The house of Dien Kellilauw, journalist for *Antara*, was burnt down; as was the house of *Ambon Ekspres* journalist, Ahmad Ibrahim, in Nania; and *Siwalima* journalist, Saswati Matakena, in Wailete. More than fifty journalists became victims of the conflict, their houses were burnt down, or their relatives were wounded or died.

As in Samuel Huntington's thesis in 'The Clash of Civilizations', conflict terminology used in a news report emphasises the identity of one group and ignores the other group. This phenomenon describes the journalists' working environment. In the end, it was difficult for journalists to free themselves from the 'traps' set by their working environment and the places where they lived. The situation got increasingly out of control because the roots of the conflict were very personal for everyone, because they were based in religion. In the end it was difficult for journalists to act ethically.

When ethics became an expensive commodity in the struggles faced by the media, *Info* tried to be different and to avoid becoming trapped in the prevailing situation. Although *Info* only lasted nine months and eventually collapsed because of management problems, its presence marked a new beginning in the development of post-conflict mass media in Ambon. Vincent Fangohoi, Harry Radjabaycolle, Lisa Woriwun, Gery Ubro, Mozes Fabeat and Sintya Latumahina were Christian journalists, who didn't hesitate to cross the demarcation line that separated the two domains.

Info was located in a Muslim enclave, which didn't daunt our Christian colleagues. Mochtar Touwe, Tahir Lating, Insany Syahbarwaty, Tahir Karepesina and Hamdi Jempot, senior journalists at *Info*, succeeded in convincing them and gave our five colleagues assurances of safety.

'*Info* was a concrete example of reconciliation demonstrated through the media. We employed journalists from both communities at a time when other media in Ambon who did not have enough courage to do so', said Insany Syahbarwaty.

Gambling with Death

Before reconciliation was achieved the conflict in Ambon hardened into anti-Muslim and anti-Christian dimensions. Religion had become the legitimating reason for certain groups who had political or economic interests in the conflict. Even now, I still ask why it is so easy to use religion in this way. Is it too difficult to compromise the difference between faith and beliefs, when we can negotiate the conflicts between economic and political interests? Don't all religions on the face of this earth teach their followers not to hurt other people, let alone kill each other?

The conflict carried out in the name of religion in Ambon abandoned the traditional promises and the local wisdom of '*ale rasa beta rasa*' (what you feel, I feel). The city whose inhabitants had lived together harmoniously smouldered with an anger, which burnt the moral code of orang basudara to ashes. The pela–gandong cultural relationship, which was the social capital for long periods of time, lost its meaning and rituals in a moment. Ambon was ablaze, houses were burnt down, lives were lost and vandals scrawled blasphemous graffiti on the walls of burnt-out houses and buildings already destroyed in the conflict. Social conflict spread to other islands in the archipelago: Seram, Halmahera, Kei, Lease and Buru were also torched. I therefore began wonder if there was a future when today is so frightening?

The conflict made many things difficult. The journey from the Unidar campus in the village of Tulehu where I attended lectures, is 24 kilometres from Ambon. It was really difficult to get to the city. Although the distance was relatively short, it was very expensive for me as a student and also for the general public. This was due to the barricade that blocked the borders between Muslim and Christian areas, not unlike the walls that separated the residential areas of the Protestants and Catholics in Northern Ireland.

The cost of a single journey from Tulehu to Ambon could be up to Rp50,000 because we had to take a long detour along the Leihitu peninsula on the northern coast of Ambon. If we took a direct route from Tulehu to Ambon, the journey would be less than 30 minutes. The cost of public transport between Ambon and Tulehu before the conflict broke out was only Rp3,000.

When the conflict erupted, the journey between Tulehu-Ambon required two public transport rides from Tulehu to Liang and from Hitu to Poka, plus two speedboat trips from Liang to Hitu and from Poka to Batu Merah. This journey would take more than two hours. The rise in transport costs, multiplied many times, made all the cost of living skyrocket, because the price of other basic goods also shot through the roof. The impact of conflict in Ambon not only made life feel unpleasant and uncertain, but all aspects of life also became desperate.

In addition to the alternative route which made the journey longer, during the breaks in the conflict or in the cooling down periods, members of the armed forces offered direct transport: a direct Ambon to Tulehu route had a cheaper tariff of around Rp10,000 to Rp25,000. The cost of the transportation was still expensive because the passengers had to pay the extra cost of protection to the members of the army or police who 'sold' this protection service.

Usually, two to four fully-armed members of the armed forces provided the protection. The vehicles used included cars, trucks used for troop movement (belonging to the army or police) and goods trucks. Sometimes, passengers who boarded the goods trucks had to be prepared for the worst, as though they themselves were goods. Whether they liked it or not, they would sit bunched together and covered with plastic tarpaulin, to give the impression that the truck was carrying goods.

Few people wanted to take this direct form of transport. Most people chose to take the long, convoluted route. Although the journey was much longer and more expensive, this route was safe. A number of vehicles, together with their passengers, had been caught in chaotic incidents and burnt by the mobs. This made people feel scared to take the shorter journey. It could just be bad luck; a person could unwittingly shorten the path of their own life by taking the direct route.

I took the direct route from Tulehu to Ambon on a number of occasions. I spent some minutes of the journey having misgivings, wondering whether I would arrive safely or not, as though I was gambling with death. Muslims regarded the villages of Passo, Lateri and Galala as red zones that were hazardous to pass through. For our Christian brothers and sisters, the hazardous zone was Batu Merah, starting from Galunggung through to Batu Merah village.

When entering a red zone, your adrenalin would start to pump. Whether you liked it or not, you would be prepared to die and relied on the power of prayer alone. If you were unlucky and got caught in a situation, anything could happen, even the worst could happen, an untimely death. Fortunately, on the occasions I crossed the barricades, no bloody incidents took place to block the road.

Rusmin Saimima, a friend who shared lodgings with me in Tulehu, once reprimanded me for my habit of taking the direct route to Ambon to save money. 'If one of the passengers is unlucky that day, all of the passengers will be unlucky. So think about it when you want to take the land route,' Rusmin reminded me.

Baku Bae on Pantai Mardika

Pantai Mardika Street is a stretch of road in the Mardika district, Ambon. When the conflict broke out, this district was like hell. Hundreds of two-storey shophouses were burnt to smithereens by mobs. Most of the goods from the shops were looted and the rest went up in flames. Before the community unrest, Pantai Mardika was a busy area because it was the centre of commerce for the community and in addition, the Mardika Terminal was also in this area. Several renovated shops became the headquarters for the soldiers who guarded the border area.

Although traces of the conflict were still evident, and when night fell, the atmosphere was scary, the seeds of reconciliation also originated in this area. The *Bakubae* market was one form of grass-roots reconciliation which emerged in this area without any engineering. The length of Pantai Mardika Street, directly in front of Amans Hotel, members of the Muslim and Christian communities mixed and became one in their commercial activities.

At the *Bakubae* market, the divide was almost invisible. They were united by the market for the very simple reason; they needed each other. The market was able to unite them, free from racial religious prejudice. At this market, the vendors were Muslim, while the majority of the buyers were Christian. There were no signs of doubt on either side when transactions took place.

The *Info* office was in this area. When I left Tulehu for Ambon, I immediately became homeless. The result being that the *Info* office became my place of work and also the place where I lived in Ambon. But sleeping at night was a rare event given that the pace of a media office almost never slows down. Late in the evening when the city's streets are quiet, the work in the editor's office increases in intensity.

This work rhythm meant that I stayed up late every night. I felt that I would miss something if I went to bed too early. As a new journalist, I tried to make the most of the opportunity to learn what I could. Harry Radjabaycolle and I would sit with the editors until the lay-out process was finished and ready to go to press in the early hours of the morning. Harry, one of my friends, who is a Christian, more often than not slept at the office. Now he has become a journalist at TV One, while I have become a correspondent for *The Jakarta Post* in Ambon.

When the newspaper had been printed I still remained awake, often taking time to go for a walk close to the office in the early hours. At that time of the morning, the pavements and the middle of the road the whole length of Pantai Mardika Street were usually busy with the activities of the vendors arranging their vegetable, fruit, and other basic materials in the *Bakubae* market.

Still in Pantai Mardika Street the seeds of reconciliation also grew and blossomed. The Maluku Media Centre (MMC), 'joint base camp' for journalists in Maluku, was founded at the end of February 2001 to unify the journalists of the two communities and to spread the mission of peace fired by the enthusiasm of 'peace journalism'.

To carry out this mission, Wahyuana was given a mandate by AJI Indonesia. He was flown from Jakarta to Ambon. For almost two years, from November 2001, Wahyu attempted to build trust and balance in journalist circles. The 'man with slanted eyes' [Wahyu] was terrorised and received quite a few threats. Wahyu succeeded in unifying Muslim and Christian journalists under one roof in MMC. Unfortunately, Wahyu was freaked out by the the amount of terrorising and threats. People who didn't want to see reconciliation between Muslim and Christian journalists, tried to drive him out, using dubious methods. They succeeded. Wahyu returned to Jakarta in a very shaken state.

Many people see MMC as one of the community's efforts to find a solution to the conflict. MMC was present long before the Muslim and Christian leaders agreed on peace at Malino. In 2007, I was given the responsibility by journalists in Maluku to lead MMC, together with Saswati Matakena as secretary.

At MMC, I met up with Dino Umahuk, who was above me at Unidar and also in PPSWPA-KANAL, the outdoor pursuits' organisation. At the beginning of the community unrest, Dino joined the Volunteer Team for Humanitarian Causes (TIRUS). The Muslim and Christian volunteers gave aid to the causalities of the conflict without regard for religious or racial background. TIRUS was also the first emergency team that was able to cut through the segregation of the Muslim and Christian communities at that time. Dino decided to move to Jakarta because he felt that Ambon was no longer friendly.

Although Dino was above me at the university and involved in the same outdoor pursuits group, we only met face-to-face for the first time when AJI Indonesia sent him back to Ambon to lead MMC, to take over from Wahyuana. I only knew about him from what friends had told me. It didn't take long for the two of us to get to know each other and become close friends. I was invited to stay in his house in Pandang Street, Kebun Cengkeh, one of the former TIRUS Coordination centres.

One thing that the two of us used to do frequently was to go out on the motorbike at night, crossing the demarcation line in the border areas, just to visit the *Suara Maluku* office in Skip. At that time Febby Kaihatu's house was used as the emergency office for *Suara Maluku*. We often met to drink coffee and chat at the *Suara Maluku* office.

As an outdoor enthusiast, in September 2002, Dino and I came up with the idea of gathering about fifty Muslim and Christian outdoor pursuits enthusiasts together in Ambon, for Outdoor Pursuits Training. I was chairman of the committee and we used Rindam Suli for the camping area. During the morning we learnt skills together such as navigation, hiking, rafting, caving, survival, photography and environmental journalism.

In the evening, we sat around the bonfire and played the guitar for the four nights of this event. If you wanted to sleep, you just chose whichever tent you wanted. The tents were only divided by the sexes, other than that everybody mixed together and became one. Although the Outdoor Pursuits training was organised so that we could learn skills and relax together with other outdoor pursuit enthusiasts, the participants' main enthusiasm was for true reconciliation.

Dino and I were of the opinion that many activities that had been proposed by the elite and held in the name of reconciliation, tended to be formalities, ceremonial in nature. We wanted to create activities where reconciliation really took place, carried out in the open air, without being set artificially and involving lengthy discussions, without binding regulations in the meetings and without boring agendas.

Beside the Outdoor Pursuits Training, Dino and I also organised a concert, which was held in Merdeka Square, Ambon. As far as I know, this was the first such activity to be held in Merdeka Square after the conflict. We didn't think we would get permission to hold the event at that location because of security issues. Fortunately, this event had the full support of the district military commander for Ambon Island, Lieut. Col. Yudi Zanibar, who was our guarantor for the event. Although only local bands were involved, the Ambonese youths were able to entertain the audience with their music. The enthusiasm of the band members and the audience demonstrated that the young people needed entertaining.

Crossing the Demarcation Lines

The conflict in Ambon changed the way of life of the city, not just the physical elements, but also the vision of the city. To return to the image of Ambon of '*kota manise*' [the beautiful city], new history had to be made because the conflict had ripped the city apart and left its reputation in ruins. The city, which had received the Adipura award for a clean environment, was formerly also known for its tolerance between religious communities. It had started a new chapter full of blood and tears.

The historic Peace Agreement reached on 12 February 2002 at Malino, South Sulawesi, was the entry point for the people to build on the remnants of hope and start moving towards the return of normal life. Starting from zero, people's optimism began to grow and made slow progress towards escaping the trap of conflict. The people eventually realised that nobody gained from war. Victory turned into charcoal and loss turned into ashes. Both sides of the conflict had to bear suffering and loss. The provocateur won and even now the winner's identity is unknown.

During the transition to reconciliation, it was not easy to even make slow progress in such a difficult situation. Not only the physical facilities needed to be rebuilt, but there was also a need to rebuild a positive and constructive mentality and a community free from all elements of conflict.

As a young journalist, I always felt challenged when I covered news in the Christian enclaves. To begin with I was full of doubts, but eventually it became normal. I often covered the plenary sessions of the Regional Assembly in Karang Panjang (Karpan), one of the areas of the Christian community in Ambon. This did not mean that people's interactions were normal after Malino II. People thought twice about crossing the barricaded areas because of residual trauma.

Some Muslim assembly members went routinely to their offices using their own vehicles to go to Karpan, some even used armed guards. For me it was different. Every day I would take the Karpan public minibus and mix with Christian members of the public. I got on at the 'Christian Terminal', in front of Citra supermarket Mardika on Tulukabessy Street. Because the situation was not yet conducive, the Mardika Terminal was not open to all public transport. All minibuses serving the Christian residential areas lined up along this road.

One morning, when I was returning from covering a news item in Karpan, I boarded a minibus, as usual. When going past Tanah Tinggi, suddenly my mobile phone in my trouser pocket rang. My mother was calling from Masohi. My mother started her conversation with the Muslim greeting, 'Zis, *Assalamu'alaikum*, it's mum.' Spontaneously I replied, '*Waalaikum'salam* mum'. In a second all the passengers in the minibus stared at me suspiciously. Seeing this unpleasant situation, I suddenly became aware that I was a passenger in a Christian minibus passing through a Christian area.

I mentioned that it was a Christian minibus and a Christian area because Ambon had been segregated since the conflict broke out on 19 January 1999. Public facilities, government offices, mass media, terminals, docks, markets, banks, schools, hospitals and transportation, were all divided into two groups. It was as though everything was divided along religious affiliation lines. But I hold to the belief that as long as you have a clear conscience and have no intention of harming others, then the Lord will protect you wherever you are. I held on to this belief when I was working in the field. It meant, however, that I needed to make calculations and rely on my instinct.

Because I usually covered news stories in Christian enclaves, every day I met fellow journalists who were Christian. We worked closely together and often helped each other when covering news stories. We would interview the sources together and share information with each other, filling out the news for our different media. Unconsciously, our closeness had 'deceived' them into thinking I was a Christian. I didn't intentionally conceal my identity. It took some of them one or two years to realise that I am a Muslim.

'I thought you were Christian, because you were always mixing with us,' exclaimed Imelda Simulate. Imelda is a reporter for a local newspaper printed in Ambon. Similar sentiments were expressed by other friends of mine.

On 25 April 2004, conflict erupted again in Ambon. The conflict was triggered by people flying a South Moluccan Republic flag (RMS) and a procession of RMS supporters starting at the residence of Alex Manuputty (FKM Executive chairman) in the Benteng district towards the regional police headquarters in the Batu Meja area. During the procession, close to the Trikora Monument, another crowd emerged from the direction of the Al-Fatah Mosque. The two groups faced each other. The clashes started with the two groups hurling insults at each other, followed by stone throwing, then it accelerated into attacking each other with sharp weapons and Molotov cocktails. Not long afterwards, the community unrest resulted in rifle shots and homemade explosions. Many became victims of snipers' bullets.

It would be simplistic to describe the conflict that occurred as a clash between supporters of RMS and the supporters of the Unitary State of the Republic of Indonesia (NKRI). The dimension of communal conflict being based on religious belief, was still very strong. In a short time, Muslim and Christian communities faced each other again on the borders of the residential areas of the two communities in almost all the areas in Ambon. Clashes also occurred between mobs in Anthony Reebok St and Talake-Waringin.

A week after the conflict broke out on 25 April, causing the meaningless deaths of 38 people, I observed the development of a situation in the area surrounding the Trikora Monument, which is where this conflict started. I met Charles Mayaut, the veteran photographer from *Suara Maluku*, in front of Silo Church which was just a few steps from the Trikora Monument. While we were deep in conversation, we suddenly heard angry shouts not far from where we were standing. The mobs were on the march from the direction of Baru Street (just behind Silo Church) and were forcing their way towards Pohon Pule, which is where a different community lived. Around 20 soldiers were trying to stop them with great difficulty.

Not wanting to miss the moment, I quickly moved towards the mob. I invited Uncle Kace – Charles Mayaut's nickname – to come with me and take pictures of this incident. A look of reticence could fleetingly be seen on Uncle Kace's face at the thought of approaching the mob, but seeing that I was mixing with the mob, Uncle Kace worked up his courage to immortalise the incident from close-up. Suddenly some of the mob noticed Uncle Kace and immediately went berserk and chased him. I suddenly realised that Uncle Kace is a Christian and wasn't safe close to the Muslim mob. Using sign language, I told Uncle Kace to leave the scene as quickly as possible. Fortunately, nothing happened to Uncle Kace who quickly made his way out of the situation.

In the *Suara Maluku* office, which had not yet been 'evacuated' to Febby Kaihatu's house, Uncle Kace was carrying on about his experience. He had escaped from the wrath of the mob, but he couldn't understand how I could be safe in the middle of a Muslim mob. 'That young man is very brave ... ', exclaimed Uncle Kace.

'Who Uncle?' inquired Novi Pinontoan, the chief editor of *Suara Maluku*, Uncle Kace replied. 'That Agil [my nickname] is usually with us at *Suara Maluku*. How come he could be so brave in the midst of a Muslim mob, they didn't do anything to him,' said Uncle Kace using his dialect from his own village of Mahu in Saparua.

'Do you know what religion he is?' asked Novi. 'He's Christian isn't he ... ?' replied Uncle Kace. 'Uncle ... He's a Muslim. Only he's often here with us at *Suara Maluku*,' explained Novi, laughing a little at Uncle Kace's mistake in guessing my religion. 'I always thought he was a Christian', exclaimed Uncle Kace because he suddenly realised, after two years of knowing me, that actually I am a Muslim.

A few days later, the Protestant Church of Maluku Synod (GPM) held a press conference to give their reaction to the case of soldiers from Arhanud 11 who were photographed on 9 May 2004 with an RMS flag, in the church bell tower of the Gatik congregation, Hative Kecil. A fellow journalist phoned and asked me to cover this press conference in the GPM Synod offices, next to the Maranatha Church.

At that time, the main roads in the border areas were deserted. The barricades were still in place because life had not yet got back to normal after the 25 April conflict. Rocks, blocks of wood and branches of trees were strewn all over the road. The pedicab driver was reluctant to take me to my destination, but in the end he was prepared to take me because I said he could drop me off in front of 1504 Military Command barracks, which wasn't far from the GPM Synod offices. The road seemed deserted close to the Military Command Barracks. Exactly in front of the traffic police post, two barbed wire barricades blocked the road as a sign of the demarcation line. I asked the pedicab driver to stop there.

About 25 metres from where we were in the Maranatha Alley, a group of youths was sitting, watching us suspiciously. After paying the pedicab driver, I slowly walked towards the Synod offices. Several of my fellow journalists, including Alex Sariwating, Febby Kaihatu, Saswati Matakena and Max Urusula were already there.

Without my realising it, some of the youths from Maranatha Alley had been following me. They were suspicious, supposing I had bad intentions. Their suspicions were not, in fact, wrongly placed. I emerged from the Muslim community with a rucksack on my back – suppose I had a bomb with me to blow up the Synod offices? After a person working at the Synod explained that I had been invited to cover the press conference, the youths eventually backed down and went home.

When the press conference started, the GPM team of advocates asked for clarification about the photograph of the soldiers with a symbol of the church and the RMS flag. I was asked to sit behind a cupboard in the corner of the room. This was because this press conference was to be recorded by the state television company (TVRI). 'Gil, you sit here, so that you aren't seen on the TV. If you are spotted you'll have problems in the Muslim community,' said Alex Sariwating.

There was truth behind Alex's concern. All incidents can be interpreted differently to the reality. As a Muslim, it is true that I would be asked why I was in the heart of the biggest church alone. The worst speculation that could arise would be that I was a traitor or a spy for the Christians. If that happened, then I would no longer be safe in my own community, even though the reason I was present at the GPM Synod Offices was no other than to carry out my duties as a journalist.

A few days after the 25 April conflict, Rudi Fofid, a senior journalist at *Suara Maluku* phoned me. 'Gil where are you?' asked Rudi. 'Opa (Rudi's nickname), I'm at Mandiri Bank. I'm putting some money in the bank. Opa, what's the matter?' I asked in turn.

'I just want to check where you are. I'm with Bambang (Bambang Wissuedo, a journalist from *Kompas* newspaper). We want to interview the lady village chief from Passo and the village chief from Tulehu,' said Rudi. 'I'll come with you ... ' I replied spontaneously.

'If you want to come with us, we are in a car in Batu Meja, close to the Police HQ. Gil, we will take the mountain route to Passo,' replied Rudi.

'Opa, wait for me. When I've finished at the bank I'll come straight to you,' I said. 'How are you going to get here?' asked Rudi doubtfully. 'I'll take a pedicab, no problem,' I replied. 'It's no problem?' Rudi asked still feeling uncertain. 'Opa, it's no problem just wait for me', I tried to reassure him. 'In that case we will wait for you outside the cathedral. Hurry!' Rudi put an end to our conversation.

Although he was in a car, Rudi couldn't pick me up because it still wasn't safe to cross from one community to another. We had to take the mountain route via the Leitimor peninsula in the south of Ambon island because the white zone in Batu Merah was not safe for Christian vehicles. The Leitimor route was the alternative route used by Christians when the conflict was heated and when the situation was not yet safe, just as the Leihitu route was utilised by Muslims.

After I had finished my business at the bank, I quickly went in the direction of Amans Hotel, because there I could find a Christian pedicab driver. Crossing the Mardika barricade, the pedicab went in the desired direction. Approaching the Cathedral, I could see Rudi waiting for me. Rudi smiled as he saw me approaching in a pedicab.

After that, we went towards the car that had been waiting for us next to the Police HQ. We took the mountain route. We made a stop in Hutumuri. Our journey was continued to the house of the lady village chief of Passo, Mrs. Maitimu. Our interview concerned the efforts taken to bring about reconciliation after the conflict including the efforts of Passo to work together with Batu Merah using the pela relationship between the villages as an approach to open up the 'lower route'.

Once the interview with the lady village chief had finished and before we continued on our journey to Tulehu, a Muslim village in the Salahutu village to interview the village chief, Jhon Ohorella, we stopped off at a seafood restaurant in front of the state Police Academy (SPN) in Passo to have lunch. 'Nobody knows that there is a Muslim in Passo,' Rudi joked.

I got to know Rudi in 2003, when he was the editor of the news website, www.mediacentre.net, and I became one of his reporters. This website was established by AJI Indonesia as a means for practising peace journalism. It also became an alternative news source about the conflict in Ambon. Although we had just got to know each other, our relationship was more than just that of being colleagues. My wife, Nova Senduk, and I, had come to regard Rudi and his family as our own family.

Rudi is from Kei, while I am from Ambon-Lease, we have no genealogical link whatsoever. Rudi's family is Catholic, while my family is Muslim. At Christmas 2004, Nova and I spent the night in Rudi's home in the BTN Waitatiri district. That night, Nova helped Keety Renwarin (Rudi's wife) to prepare the meal for Christmas the following day, while Rudi and I talked late into the night.

We ate our evening meal and relaxed together until almost sunrise. When we got sleepy, we slept with Rudi's children, Alfa and Elnino. In the morning, Rudi and his family went to church. I also went with them and took photographs of the Christmas mass procession at the church. We left Nova alone in the house, preparing the house and the food and drinks needed for the expected guests. Not long after we returned to the house, guests started to arrive to give Christmas greetings. Nova and Keety served the food and drinks; Rudi and I accompanied the guests.

One day in May 2005 Rudi's cousin, Michael, was to take his First Communion at St Joseph's Catholic Church in Passo. Long before, Rudi had asked me to come to his house, the day before the First Communion took place. He wanted me to take photographs of Michael while he received Holy Communion from the priest. He also asked Nova to come and spend the night with them. The atmosphere was the same as Christmas Eve. Nova helped Keety prepare the food for the guests the next day, while we, the men, sat discussing endless topics the whole night, while we played with Alfa and Elnino.

The next morning, I dressed neatly, as did Nova. We rented a public minibus, together with Rudi and his family, to take us to the church. It turned out that the First Communion procession commenced with a service led by a priest. I was confused about what to do; because there was no way that we could leave the church building. 'Opa, it looks like there's going to be a service. What do Nova and I do?' I asked.

'You and Nova just copy us,' he replied. Keety gave the same reply. Finally, I whispered to Nova, 'It looks like we just have to stay put.' Nova nodded slowly in agreement. The two of us took up our positions by the side of Rudi and his family in the middle of a Catholic congregation. The service went ahead; we followed what the others were doing. After the service was over, Rudi said quietly. 'People don't know that there were two Muslims in the Church in Passo and that they took part in the service too,' Rudi whispered half-joking.

Encounters like those above leave traces, make life more meaningful. These encounters made me realise that we are social creatures and by nature need each other. The thing that differentiates us is tribe, religion, race and so on, but our blood is red and our bones are white. I compared it to a large house that we must live in together; however, we need to be tolerant and respect all of the inhabitants who were destined to be different.

Margaret Mead in the 'Coming of Age in Samoa' says that nomads are wiser after they have left their homes, compared to those who have never crossed over their own thresholds.

Religious values are not just based on faith in God or obedience in carrying out religious worship, but also our morality and behaviour in communication with God's creatures. The people who mix with diversity and live in peace for humanitarian reasons, are also religious. This is my small idea for seeing religiosity from a humanitarian perspective. I hope that the future of Maluku will become brighter and the inhabitants of the large house will respect humanitarian values.

Part II

Ain Ni Ain:
We Come from the Same Egg

Chapter 7

WHEN THE CHURCH SPEAKS OUT

I.W.J. Hendriks

This is not intended to be an article claiming that the conflict could be solved because of the role of the Protestant Church of Maluku (GPM). Our experiences demonstrate that only by all of us working together – both Christian (Protestant, Catholic, Pentecostal, etc) and Muslim – was it possible to bring an end to the conflict, to bring reconciliation and the rebuilding of a new Maluku that is safe, just and prosperous. Focusing on GPM does not mean that the roles and active involvement of all our colleagues are ignored.

From Being Confused to Becoming Wise

The conflict or community unrest was an unexpected, bitter experience. We were not prepared to face and resolve such a conflict. We did not read the signs of the times accurately, as the Lord Jesus had warned us. Although we could read them, our sights were perhaps set on heaven, so that the wisdom we gained was not being applied to daily life on earth. For example, in September 1998, a friend told me about his son's experience, when his path was blocked on his way home as he was leaving Amplaz (Ambon Plaza). The people threatened him, saying, 'Don't you know that there's going to be a religious war in the not too distant future?' If we had been prudent, we should have contacted the government or the police so that they could take preventive steps. No steps, however, were taken. We thought the story was just another form of adolescent behaviour.

When the conflict took place, ministers and congregations reacted differently. Some ministers rejected violence; they gathered together in their congregations to pray in times of crisis and then told their congregations to return to their own homes. Of course, some of the members of the congregation protested, but their minister stuck to his opinion. There were other ministers who felt the need to respond to the violence with violence.

I once listened to a sermon by a minister during a service. It was before the Indonesian Christian University in Maluku campus (UKIM) had been burnt down. The sermon doubted the relevance of the teachings about Christ's love, especially the statement, 'If someone strikes you on the right cheek, also show him the other cheek' (Mt. 5:39b). On another occasion a colleague tried to render a different meaning to what Jesus said, by stating that we were not facing the problem of 'being struck on the cheek' but rather 'losing one's head', and we do not have two heads and can't afford to lose one. This attitude and interpretation illustrated the tendency to use the principle of 'a tooth for a tooth' in reacting to the conflict. Some even introduced 'Amalekite theology' (1 Sam. 15:1-3), because the text states that God summoned Israel to destroy the Amalekites. It is therefore understandable if, in the first few years of the conflict, some members of the congregation thought that any efforts to be involved in reconciliation amounted to treason.

I feel that the variety of reactions demonstrated an instinct for self-defence in the face of death. These reactions can be regarded as a form of confusion. But as more experience was gained during the conflict, many people started to question a number of anomalies that have occurred, that have never been answered completely, including:

- How can a clash between two individuals develop into a conflict that involved almost the whole region, over a long period of time and causing so many casualties?
- How can a conflict develop in such a dramatic manner, where people start attacking each other with sticks and stones, but then go on to machetes, spears, bows and arrows, then eventually to guns and homemade bombs?
- How is it possible that local residents rejected the erection of army guard posts in their areas because they claimed that when these guard posts were erected, it became a sign that their house would be attacked? I experienced this when the people of Telaga Raja refused a guard post in their area. The people felt safer without such a post.
- How is it possible that the large numbers of soldiers and police despatched to Maluku did not have significant influence on reducing the escalation of the conflict?
- How is it possible that appeals made by religious leaders seemed to be ignored while the conflict continued to escalate?

These questions made many people suspect that there were irresponsible hands causing chaos. This awareness continued to develop when Christians and Muslims started to exchange information and warn each other when there was news of attacks. Many people became wiser and could no longer be provoked and no longer wanted to become futile victims. They started to think about endeavours towards reconciliation.

Solving the Conflict as the Church

The basic question that became the concern of the executive body of the GPM Synod of the 2001-2005 period was how to react to the conflict as a church faithful to the path of Jesus. As we know, the path of Jesus is the path of love, the path of willingness to sacrifice one's life for the lives of many people. In the atmosphere of the conflict, the path of Jesus was a great challenge to faith, as described above. But for the church, there was no other choice. We had to walk the path of Jesus or we would cease to be the church. We prayed and thought about how to spell out the basic principles so that they became part of the church's policy in solving the conflict. This meant that we had to view the conflict as a theological matter, analyse the conflict from a theological point of view, and there had to be a theological grounding for the church's policy for solving the conflict.

Pro-Life Theology

During the conflict threats to lives were very real experiences. Everyone felt very close to death. People who were out on the streets faced the risk of being shot at or becoming the victim of a bomb blast; but people who were in their homes were also at risk from stray bullets. The most concerning fact was that people would kill each other simply because they had different religious beliefs. Life had no value. What was really happening? Various social, economic and political analyses were carried out and were of great help to us in trying to understand the conflict which had befallen us. As a church, we had to view the conflict from the point of view of our faith. The theme and sub-themes of the Assembly of the GPM Synod noted the following.

From the point of view of faith, all this is not merely an economic, political or social problem but there is a serious matter of spirituality.

This chaos is a manifestation of spirituality, which has been used throughout the life of the community; or our religion is a spirituality that was inwardly directed in the interests of making ourselves happy.

We placed ourselves higher than others. We have been greatly influenced by a dualistic hierarchical ideology. This has been evident in our religious lives and the way we do theology.

If we pay close attention to theological formulae used by religions including Christianity, it is clear to see how a strong, dualistic ideology colours our theology.

The tendency of religions to claim the truth for themselves is one manifestation of this type of theology. This was also prominent in Christianity. For example, for a long time in Christianity we have spoken about *extra ecclesiam nulla salus* (there is no salvation outside of the church).

This is one church doctrine formula that is very pious but very dualistic, because here we see Christianity as the only true religion. Salvation can only be found in Christianity; become Christian to obtain salvation. There are many other dogmatic formulae that say similar things.

Such dualistic theology produces dualistic hierarchical spirituality. Such theology means that religious communities, including the Christian community, are taught to regard their own religion as the one that is really true. This is not really wrong, because every person undoubtedly believes the truth of their own religion.

A mistake occurs when this belief considers other people and other religions as less worthy and therefore encourages aggressive mission work that does not respect the pluralistic nature of the community.

Religious violence has existed throughout the history of religion and in essence originates from such a dualistic hierarchical point of view. Examples include the Crusade, the massacre of Jews in Germany, and the massacre of Muslims in India by a group of Hindus.

Indeed, we have to acknowledge that other factors such as economic and political factors are the main reasons for these different forms of violence. The fact that religion can be used for such goals, however, is proof that in each religion there is a potential conflict as a result of this dualistic point of view. This way of thinking does not just happen between religions but also in the relationships between denominations.

Each denomination feels superior and regards other denominations as inferior. Thus the relationship between denominations becomes an arena for competition and proselytising.

In connection with the internal life of the church, dualistic theology has produced a type of spirituality that tends towards being inward and individualistic. We often feel quite happy if we talk about spiritual matters in church, whereas the problems of social discrepancy, injustice and the violation of human rights are not thought to be related to church matters.

Dualistic theology directs our eyes heavenwards so that we are blinded to worldly matters. Like the teaching at the time of Amos, our religious teachings tend to make us busy over matters of ritual, creating liturgy and worship that is special on Sundays or places where worship is held, but worship that has no effect on our social activities. People can thus be very sincere when worshipping but their hearts are not moved to do something to reduce the suffering of others caused by oppression.

Dualistic theology also tends to make the institution of the church the centre of their church lives. The institution is a symbol of the whole of our Christianity. The authority of the church is seen as a strong institution and energy is directed at strengthening the institution of the church.

In relation to this, church leaders at various levels also can be seen as the holders of absolute power in the church at these various levels within the church. Their words are regarded as commands from God as the people appointed and anointed by God. This turns ministers and church leaders into types of 'spiritual sultans', whose power is untouchable, but at the same time the congregation is made powerless because they await the decisions of their leaders and are unable to challenge whether or not the leader's decision is appropriate.

The above is a description of the resolutions of the General Assembly of the GPM Synod 2001, held in Saparua-Tiouw, on the development of a pro-life paradigm in a renewal of theology and spirituality. Because the spirituality that had developed was dualistic hierarchical theology, as described above, it does not solve the problems, rather on the contrary, it further entraps us in life-threatening practices.

Non-violence

The General Assembly of the GPM Synod in 2001 also included the clarification of theological understanding. Theology is not understood only as an intellectual discourse, abstract theoretical concepts, which are only enjoyed in lecture rooms. The theology that is meant is 'doing theology', theology that is functional, that responds to the challenges and real hope every day. When the community can only see one way of resolving the conflict, that is, by repaying violence with violence, then the church can give voice to a movement of non-violence. We saw the challenge, however, as the risk that we were called to as the leaders of the church.

Non-violence was not the monopoly of the executive board of the GPM Synod. The Women Who Care Movement was formed by Protestant, Catholic and Muslim women who carried out a number of activities to socialise the non-violence movement. One of the activities was the mentoring of children to stop war games and exchange violent games for non-violent games. Parents were also advised not to buy games that could stimulate violent actions. They also carried out a peace campaign by giving out flowers and cloths with 'non-violence' written on them which could be tied around the wrist.

The executive board of the synod itself, together with the church leaders in Ambon, carried out three days of mourning. The community were encouraged not to go to work. It was hoped that the days of mourning would be filled with prayer and fasting according to the traditions of each denomination. Almost all the churches in Ambon took part. We felt real fellowship and solidarity stretching beyond the boundaries of denomination and church organisations. Then we held devotions in front of the Governor's office on 19 December 2001. This action was an act of solidarity with those who were victims of shootings and bombings in Ambon bay, and also a protest against a government that was not able to protect its citizens. These actions wished to teach the community that opposition could be carried out without violence. For the Christian, this is the path of Jesus.

Along with the invitation to bring a halt to the violence, the executive board of the GPM Synod also invited the whole community to propose law enforcement in resolving each clash. In this way, we reduced the role of irresponsible people to carry out provocations that could cause an escalation in the conflict. At the same time, we helped the government to re-establish its authority, especially in the realm of law enforcement. This is because the people did not trust the government, including the army and police. They could not avoid being partisan especially in terms of religion.

Both the executive board of the GPM Synod and the GPM Crisis Centre, alone and with the inter-faith team facilitated by Ambon City Council, also visited the president and government ministers as part of the non-violent action. Visits overseas were also made. The executive board of the GPM Synod and the GPM Crisis Centre visited the Netherlands to talk to the Dutch government. This visit was facilitated by PKN (the Protestant Church in the Netherlands). Together with the inter-faith team, they also visited the UK and the European Parliament.

Dialogue for Peace

Mutual trust became the key to success in the endeavours to develop long-term peace. The Christian and Muslim communities were very suspicious of each other. Therefore, it was particularly important to give the appearance of being people who could be trusted.

In our experiences, consistency in words and actions became very important capital. We had to convince all parties that our words could be trusted. We could not use double standards. For example, we could not emphasise pluralism when speaking to a mixed forum of the communities, then emphasise fanaticism when we were speaking to our own community. Many of our leaders were called hypocritical, which in turn caused many problems to arise.

We knew Wayame as a peaceful village in the middle of the conflict. One of the keys reasons for this was the communities' trust that the religious leaders in the village were non-partisan. I talked to the minister of Wayame at that time and he said that he would take the same course of action if any resident of Wayame did something that would destroy the peace in that village. Thus, when we reject the RMS generalisation used about Christians, we must also reject the idea that every Muslim is a member of Laskar Jihad.

The program of cooperation between the Women Who Care Movement and the Uniting Church in Australia (UCA) should also be detailed here. They had two programs that had a great influence on the peace process; Closing the Gap and Young Ambassadors for Peace (YAP). They started working among women and then expanded to include men. The programs created transformation through the use of games. This process was able to change the participants who, when they attended these activities, were initially very suspicious, rejecting, hard-headed and exclusive, but by the end of the program had all become close friends who trusted, respected and loved each other.

Various NGOs conducted a large number of meetings involving participants from different religious backgrounds. All of them clearly made an important contribution to the peace process. In relation to this, the Malino Agreement needs to be mentioned. Although the Malino Agreement caused much controversy in Christian and Muslim circles, it cannot be denied that the Malino Agreement was a significant turning point in building peace in Maluku. Malino was conceived by the government, in particular the Coordinating Minister for Health and Welfare. The executive board of the GPM Synod welcomed it because it seemed to be a priceless opportunity to put an end to the conflict.

The previous policy of government, using a military approach, had not succeeded. On the contrary, it had resulted in many casualties. Thus, when the dialogue approach was used to resolve the conflict, it was welcomed but was also criticised.

Many people didn't know about the stages of preparation that had taken place. The atmosphere at that time was still very heated, so it was not wise to carry out the preparation openly. The governor formed a small group consisting of five Christians and five Muslims. I still remember the first time we met.

After the governor gave an introductory talk, each group was given the opportunity to express their opinions. We each spoke one sentence. We were very suspicious and didn't trust each other. Trust began to grow from one meeting to another. We each started to become open and also critical about the tendencies in our own communities.

When the situation became more conducive, the teams were then expanded to create a delegation of members of the general population/youth and also scholars and religious leaders, men and women. The Christian delegation consisted of representatives from GPM, the Catholic Church, the Bethel Indonesia Church and the Pentecostal church in Indonesia. The Malino Agreement became important because it was not only signed by the Christian and Muslim delegations but it was also signed by the government.

It is a pity that this agreement was not totally realised. Perhaps the government felt satisfied with the Malino Agreement because it reduced international pressure, but the conflict could not be resolved as quickly as that.

I remember when Soya was attacked: many people were killed, and many houses were burnt down, including the old church. This incident made people very angry. The young people didn't want to be approached. When I talked to one young man, he said, 'You told us to surrender our weapons, we did what you said, and then we were attacked.' This statement made me very sad because it indicated how weak the government was, unable to protect the people.

The support and the involvement of the church in building peace is a manifestation of a renewed theology. The old theology that stacked up exclusive and triumphalistic attitudes was unable to help us build good relationships with our Muslim brothers and sisters.

The old theology drove us to be competitive and led to violence. We needed a more open theology that respected religious pluralism. It is not enough to receive pluralism as a social reality; we also have to receive pluralism as a theological truth. Perhaps God wills there to be more than one religion because of the limitation of humankind in expressing their faith.

An open attitude such as this is not the same as the concept of relativism that regards all religions to be the same. On the contrary, each religion has its own unique, incontestable character. It is more important and more meaningful if the uniqueness of each religion becomes the source of inspiration for sincere brother- and sisterhood, justice, peace and the wholeness of creation.

In relation to this, two study programs continue to be offered and have played important roles in building peace in Maluku. The first was formed by the Inter-Faith Organisation at the initiative of GPM, MUI and the diocese of Amboina. The second is a widening of the focus of study of the Postgraduate Program in the Master's degree in the Philosophy faculty of UKIM. This program was started in 1997 with a focus on 'the Gospel and Tradition'. Since 2001, the focus of this study has been extended to become 'Religion and Culture', giving the opportunity for Christians and Muslims to study together. The process of studying together has brought a positive influence built on mutual trust which will greatly influence them when they work and become leaders in their own communities.

Another fact that needs to be understood is that when religion causes segregation between the communities, then culture can open the opportunity to restore the *basudara* (brother- and sisterhood) relationship. This is also an important lesson learnt from the conflict. Therefore, once again, the old theology is no longer relevant. It regarded local culture as 'pagan' and, in turn, created a dichotomy between the Gospel and Tradition. Everywhere culture and religion influence each other, meaning that, on one side, culture can enable humankind to understand and express their experiences about God and, on the other side, people's experience of God can transform culture. This cycle can be continued as a spiral for the length of humankind's existence.

Final Words

The reality of pluralism will always have the potential for conflict. Our experiences demonstrate that the management of pluralism by using an authoritarian approach will fall into the trap of uniformity that will ignore the sense of justice of the community. Some people will be marginalised and feel oppressed. If this situation goes unnoticed and is not corrected, then dissatisfaction will pile up and become a tinderbox waiting to ignite.

It is the call of the religions not be tempted to use power or to be used by those in power. A critical distance from power will ensure that religions will become the source of inspiration to demonstrate real brother- and sisterhood, justice and prosperity, peace and the wholeness of creation.

Chapter 8

THE TURNING POINT ON THE ROAD OF BASUDARA RELATIONSHIPS

Jacky Manuputty

'Why did you only tell us about the Christians who were victims in Maluku? One of our staff has just returned from Indonesia and has informed us that many Muslims were also victims.' This question was put to me directly in a meeting in the Presbyterian Church Synod office in New York City in April 1999. At that time the weather was chilly at the beginning of spring but in that moment it was as though a burning coal that seared my whole body. I felt embarrassed, I was flustered and I hung my head in silence. The offer from the Synod staff to introduce me to the Muslim prominent leaders in New York City sounded like thunder that shattered my earlier sense of ease.

The meeting described above was one in a series of turning points for me, to give meaning to the conflict as a conflict of humanity, rather than a religious conflict. From that moment onwards, a confrontation and a tug-of-war continued inside me, to choose between campaigning for the universal humanitarian values that had been destroyed, or simply to support the opinion that the Christian community was the party that had been sacrificed in the conflict.

It turns out that the turning point did not completely alter my bias. It needed many other points to strengthen my determination to speak on behalf of the whole of humanity in Maluku.

When I returned to Ambon in September 1999, the conflict continued to escalate in Maluku. There were not many choices to be made in that crazy escalation. Thousands of people died and their belongings were destroyed; it defied reason to hold a neutral position. 'God does not ask us to kill. He asks us to preserve life so that it is not destroyed arbitrarily. Although if we have to kill to preserve life, we have not committed sin.' This was the theology of war that I had previously stated, when I was asked about the legality of killing by young Christians. That theology was really based on confused decision-making in the middle of conflict amongst the *basudara* (brother- and sisterhood), and was out of control and irrational.

I surfed the internet (which at that time could still be accessed) to find a group war strategy. I discussed this war strategy with a group of Christian young people, including giving them spiritual motivation for groups of Christian youths who went to war. This was something I did part-time. All things were rationalised, whether anger, sadness, hatred, revenge, even death.

* * *

From this turning point, a series of many other events took place through enlightening encounters with many friends and our 'Salam' brethren. This included Salam brethren in Maluku, outside of Maluku, or even other Muslim brethren who were not Moluccans. Each encounter began with suspicion: who would trick who? Time and intensity of encounters were needed to build up trust. We needed to work together first in order to test mutual acceptance. Together we made a start.

The 'Baku Bae' movement became one place where I tested myself. Developing mutual trust and acceptance in the long journey together with friends in this movement needed great perseverance.

This started in Jakarta in 2000, where a small group brought together their perceptions about conflict. To begin with, meeting after meeting took place outside Maluku because of fear of intimidation. At that time, anyone who talked about reconciliation in public was regarded as an enemy. The use of the term reconciliation was taboo. The singing of the song '*Gandong*' made people angry. In several of the traditional villages, 'the *Gandong* cloth,' which is a symbol of the unified relationship across traditional villages, was almost ripped up. In Christian communities, whoever was suspected of building relationships with Salam brethren were called 'Judas.' The risk was that they would be kidnapped and murdered. The same thing happened in the Muslim communities.

The result was that I had to experience being two-faced. On the one hand, the Baku Bae strategy was formed in a constructive manner together with friends who were involved in the steering committee of the Baku Bae movement. On the other hand, when I returned to the Christian community, which was still very angry and didn't believe in the effectiveness of peace efforts, we also discussed defence strategy and war.

I experienced suspicion, slander, terror and even death threats in this dynamic situation full of dilemmas. These usually came from the Christian community, or from certain groups in the Muslim community. The journey of the Baku Bae movement was carried out as an underground movement that was stressful and exhausting; however, from the development of mutual trust amongst individuals, it became the source of capital for the next stage of the journey.

It is a pity that the Baku Bae movement was then trapped under the influence of certain key people and finally fell to pieces, just at the time the movement developed the courage to declare its dynamics publicly.

Although in the end the movement destroyed the consolidation that had been built up, the closeness between many individuals, which had developed over the long process of the movement, was not destroyed. The minimum trust between individual members of the movement, especially those who lived in Maluku, became the initial capital that was fed and nourished through various encounters and working together.

The growth of this trust made it possible for me to sit, pray and eat in the house of the late Haji Jusuf Eli, together with one of the leaders of the Christian community who was initially trembling and frightened when we entered the house in the area of the small port, Ambon, at a time when there was a high level of escalation in the conflict.

This feeling of trust also enabled the late Mr Ucu Eli, the late Mahfud Nukuhehe, Bishop Mandagi, Rev. John Titaley and myself to attend the UN Commission on Human Rights Assembly in Geneva and voice our concern together as Moluccans, not as Muslims or Christians.

This feeling of trust also became my capital when meeting and becoming close to Mr Husni Putuhena (Brother Uni) who for the length of the conflict was known as a hard-line figure in the Muslim community. It turned out that we could enjoy drinking coffee together in the restaurant of the Mutiara Hotel, while tapping our feet to the rhythm of *Hena Masawaya*. This song is usually regarded as particular to the RMS movement, however Brother Uni explained that in the beginning this song belonged to the Salam community.

Because of this trust, when the conflict started to de-escalate I developed the courage to cross the demarcation lines late at night with some Christian friends to visit Ustad Mohammad Atamimi (Brother Mo) at his home. We met together a few times and this developed into a close relationship with Brother Mo, a figure who was known in the Christian community as a hard-line Muslim leader.

Hatred and resentment will not stay with us if trust can be developed; and trust is developed if we increase the intensity of our meetings and our conversations with each other, and are willing to listen to one another. From encounters between individuals, trust spreads into group relationships.

Developing mutual trust between individuals and groups by multiplying the intensity of encounters is part of the local wisdom of eastern communities, and also part of the Moluccan way of life. I grew up and experienced the strong social relationships in the custom of 'dropping in' and 'chatting' as part of the community's way to become one and mix every day.

Growing up, going to school and playing with Salam friends like Lutfi Padang, Afras Pattisahusiwa, Rustam Hieriej, Yati Hole made us become close, like brothers. This is because culturally I would feel guilty if I passed one of their homes and didn't drop in. You don't need to make a prior appointment to drop in, as the way things are done in some western countries or as happens in a cosmopolitan city.

To drop in and chat is a sign of the strength of a relationship, even of brother- and sisterhood. Our parents taught us through their own behaviour towards other people. It is not surprising that older people such as Mr Nur Tawainella or the late Mr Ucu Eli, who are Salam, could explain the blood lines of many of the Sarane families in Maluku.

I remember on one occasion when Mr Ucu and I spoke in a meeting held with Dutch citizens of Moluccan descent at the Maluku Museum, Utrecht, Netherlands. At that time a participant suddenly, in an angry manner, interrupted Mr Ucu's explanation of the situation of the conflict in Maluku. Mr Ucu responded calmly and asked this angry lady about her surname. After the lady told him her surname, Mr Ucu continued with some questions about this lady's family tree in Maluku. She calmed down immediately when Mr Ucu clearly explained the lady's family tree and Mr Ucu's relationship with her family in the past.

This proved that sometimes anger recedes if the outline of the story includes kinship ties. Within the framework of dropping in and chatting, there are actions that bring about a cultural responsibility to protect the relationship. Difference should not be used as a reason to clash and be involved in conflict within the *basudara* (brother- and sisterhood) relationship. To break this would be a disaster for our grandchildren in the future, which is how our parents understood it.

The conflict did indeed grind away at much of the local wisdom in Maluku; however, it didn't totally destroy it. It is a bitter lesson from the shameful bloody conflict that tore apart human values; we have been made conscious that something was not right with the way we had protected the local wisdom.

Besides the conflict, the strong capitalist orientation developed in this age has become a sledgehammer that has pounded at the strong cultural endurance in Maluku. Within such an atmosphere we are tied to reaching a series of targets in our work. All our energy is thrown into accumulating a great amount of profit as the final result of what we have achieved. We are forced to move and work in a straight line at great speed for hours on end.

There is no longer any time to 'drop in'; there are not many opportunities to chat. Time runs out because of a need to work 24 hours a day to achieve development goals. Children are forced to become extra-clever human beings. The result is that their time is divided between tight lesson schedules at school and after-school tuition.

Parents do not have enough time to tell stories or pass on the sacred kinship relationships between *orang basudara* (the brother- and sisterhood). The cultural and tribal rules of communal life are transferred to the regulations and conventional laws that are characteristic of a democratic country but, in reality, we trample upon them and abuse them. Eventually we experience law that is paralysed: both conventional laws, as well as tribal law and cultural morality. The barbaric conflict that occurred between us is understood as the incapacity and lack of authority of conventional law, as well as the lack of internalisation of the traditional morals of the indigenous Moluccan people. The impact of the conflict awoke our consciousness to return to scrape together what was left of our cultural structure, while slowly bringing back a sense of basudara and trust amongst us.

* * *

The Inter-Faith Organisation in Maluku (LAIM) became one place where we tried to develop dynamic encounters within the framework of orang basudara, as a strategy to restore kinship values based on Moluccan local wisdom. It started as an underground movement and the embryo of this movement was prepared in stages from the end of 2001 till the end of 2002.

Closed meetings were carried out involving prominent leaders from the different religious communities including MUI, the Synod of the Protestant Church of Maluku and the Roman Catholic Diocese of Amboina. Although the conflict was beginning to de-escalate after the Malino Agreement II had taken place, it was still not easy to talk about reconciliation in public. One of the meetings that took place after the Malino Agreement II had finished was carried out in secret in a room in the Amans Hotel, Ambon.

The main issue at that time, which was the frame for the conversation between these 13 religious leaders, was the desire that we should not allow the peace process to be controlled by certain people and peace networks from outside Maluku. We were determined to put an end to our shame as Moluccans by demonstrating that the religious communities in Maluku could work together to manage the peace process amongst the communities.

We stirred up chauvinism for peace as one way to motivate ourselves to work together, without denying the reconciliation process that was being managed by hundreds of humanitarian organisations both national and from overseas. We channelled the desire for revenge between ourselves by stages to become a desire to take revenge together against our own stupidity, for allowing ourselves to be shamed in the eyes of the world for killing each other. With this enthusiasm, the underground movement grew and became LAIM.

The journey of LAIM for me was one of the many ventures which opened up a non-linear journey to reconciliation. To pioneer a humanitarian movement needed a militant driving force that was consistent and united. At this point, the building of mutual trust and acceptance is an unavoidable necessity. LAIM as an organisation was involved informally, spreading and extending the process of friendship at the community level, as a model adapted from the process of humanitarian dialogue that takes place between followers of different religions. Encounters between friends in public adopted the culture of dropping in and chatting as an activity that is tiring but invigorating at the same time.

Helena Rijoly, Warni Belu, Kiki Samal, Daniel Wattimanela, Sven Loupaty, Olivia Lasol, Abidin Wakano, Ruth Saija, are a few of the many people who became close friends, then began to move and expand into an inexhaustible network of friendship in the public arena. They all have their own stories, both happy and sad experiences that they went through together in order to develop dialogue between followers of different religions based on community participation.

It is not easy to develop a sense of mutual trust between and amongst communities that are suffering and holding onto anger and resentment. Rather than a direct dialogue about theological differences and similarities, in these many encounters my colleagues mainly used a personal approach, based on joint visits and the idea of a shared responsibility to return to order the humanity that had been destroyed.

The basic assumption tested during this long process of interaction was that developing a relationship like that of a close friend or a family member, made possible the growth of mutual acceptance in the midst of the existing differences, including differences in religious beliefs. This did not mean that theological aspects were taboo in every encounter. Conversations about the similarities and differences in points of theology were discussed later, when trust had been developed, as between close friends, and once the feeling of being members of one family within the Moluccan cultural framework had solidified.

Trust did not only grow through the intensity of encounters between friends and kin-like relationships, but it was tested through the willingness to remove sacred meanings from symbols or rituals, which were regarded as taboo by followers of other religions.

The presence of close friends, such as Hasbollah Toisuta, Abidin Wakano and other Muslim friends at the wedding ceremony of Rev. Rudi Rahabeat and Rev. Ruth Saija held at the church in Hatu, was a sign that the presence of followers of other faiths in a church building, and even at a Christian service, need not be taboo for them as long as they didn't take part in the confession of faith.

The presence of Hasbollah and friends at the wedding was a strong indication of the close ties of friendship within the cultural framework of orang basudara, without having to degrade their Muslim identity. Entering a church or mosque is not a taboo within the basudara relationship in Maluku. Within many of the traditional rituals linked to the Pela and Gandong relationships, praying together in either a church or mosque is sometimes an integral part of the ceremony that takes place. Their presence does not affect their integrity as a Muslim or a Christian. In this basudara relationship, each other's integrity has to be protected.

Besides buildings and rituals, it is often regarded as 'taboo' for followers of other religions to read the religious documents and reports belonging to another religion. The reports of the Council meetings of the Protestant Church Synod contain the development strategy for the ministry of GPM for the next five years. In many Christian circles it is regarded as 'taboo' for this document to be left lying around and for it to be read by people from outside of the church. We were happy for this document to be read by our Muslim friends in LAIM. There is nothing taboo concerning these documents, which contain the church's strategy for humanitarian ministry. In reading these documents, Muslim friends can give input to the church concerning strategy for inter-faith humanitarian ministry.

In the same way my close friend, Abidin Wakano, came to the LAIM office and invited us to discuss the content of his sermon which he would deliver at the Eid Al Fitr prayers. Making no apologies, our Christian colleagues gave him some input concerning the reality of human degradation that was needed to enrich his sermon.

The dynamics of such a relationship require mutual trust, enlightening us to criticise things that are often regarded as taboo in the process of crossing the boundaries of our diversity. Within the atmosphere of mutual trust, we could even criticise our diverse ways of doing things, or make inter-faith jokes without anyone taking offence.

We try to achieve our ideals of a clear conscience and close friendships in the context of kinship (*orang basudara*) in post-conflict relationships in Maluku. It may sound like a cliché but we felt that the kinship relationship was diminishing in Maluku. The cultural pillars of the kinship relation seem to wobble from time to time.

The words of our elders about the beauty of basudara relationships in the past have real implications for the confusion about the massive shift in culture nowadays. Our communal home is not able to accommodate the new cultural dynamics that have been dragged along with the economic strengths and power.

Those of us in basudara relationships need time and space to sit down together and seriously talk about the process of renovating our communal home and revitalising the values within that home. Cultural action needs to be taken if we don't want local wisdom to be crushed to pieces like a pile of fossils, made immortal only by the verses of a song but having no authority in our social, political or religious lives. Although we have to acknowledge that our communal home is no longer compatible with the shifts that have taken place, we need to agree to build another home that will guarantee the close relationships of the brethren who inhabit this communal home.

The confusion I experienced when answering the questions posed by the staff of the NYC Presbyterian Synod, mentioned at the beginning of this account, in turn brought me to reflect on how to be a Christian in this communal home. The encounters with Salam brethren in the process of breaking the ground for peace gave me enthusiasm to continue our struggle to be Christians who are Sarane in nature, while supporting our Muslim brothers to become Muslims who are Salam in nature.

I believe that a Christian cannot ever become Sarane without continuing to mix with Muslim brothers and sisters who are Salam, and vice versa. Let us walk together and tell stories about basudara relationships, about supporting one another!

Chapter 9

A SERMON ON PEACE FROM THE PULPIT OF THE AL-FATAH MOSQUE

Hasbollah Toisuta

The main Al-Fatah Mosque Ambon is generally known as the centre for Muslim teaching in Maluku. All types of activities of the Muslim community or Muslim organisations in Ambon are based in this mosque.

I came into contact with the Al-Fatah Mosque when I was still an active member of Young People's Muslim Teaching Program (PPDI) and then the Muslim Students Association (HMI) Ambon branch, 1986–1990. Al-Fatah Mosque has always provided opportunities for Muslim youths to be engaged in activities and even use the mosque as the centre for the Muslim movement. At that time, heated discussions took place in the mosque, about the study of Islam, politics or nationalism, especially the Pancasila[1] as the only foundation for the state. Just imagine, I walked in the early hours of the morning from Benteng, Air Salobar, to Al-Fatah Mosque just to listen to lectures on Islam by teachers such as Ali Fauzi or Bahweres.

Ir. Soekarno laid the foundation stone of the mosque on 1 May 1963. It was not just the pride of the Muslim community, but for all elements of society – in short, it belonged both to the Salam and the Sarane. According to history, the construction of the mosque involved the Sarane community as a reflection of the tradition of solidarity of the people (*laeng tongka-tongka laeng* – helping

---

1   Translator's note: Pancasila, the 'five principles', is the Indonesian national ideology: 1. belief in an Almighty God; 2. humanitarianism; 3. Indonesian unity; 4. representative democracy; and 5. social justice. In the 1980s, Soeharto pushed for all political parties and mass organisations (including religious groups) to adopt the Pancasila as their *azas tunggal* (sole foundation). Muslim groups saw this as an attempt to subordinate God-given principles to those of the state. This was, nevertheless, adopted as Laws No 3 and No 8 of 1985 on Social Organisations.

each other); the Al-Fatah Mosque should therefore return to its true spirit as a symbol of unification and reconciliation for the community.

Through this account I want to share my experiences in initiating the peace process through the pulpit of the Al-Fatah Mosque. This occurred during the time of the harrowing conflict, when it seemed that people could not hear the call for peace. At that time people were frustrated, they did not know how to extinguish the flames of conflict.

First Experience of the Al-Fatah Pulpit

My connection with the Al-Fatah Mosque began in 1986, but at that time it was only as an activist who used the mosque courtyard as a place to hold discussions with friends. Like other members of the Muslim community in Ambon, activists felt something was lacking when we took part in Friday prayers in a mosque other than Al-Fatah. So young Muslim activists always met together at the Al-Fatah mosque for Friday prayers. Attendance at Friday prayers at the Al-Fatah mosque therefore had a special meaning for the activists.

My early experience of the Al-Fatah mosque pulpit occurred at the time of the conflict in the region, from 1999. From the beginning of the conflict I observed that the Friday sermon at the Al-Fatah mosque had become a place from which to summon people to take part in war (*jihad*), whilst only a few preachers touched on the area of character development. As a member of the congregation I knew that a few of the preachers were 'allergic' to peace and were very provocative in their appeals, giving support to enmity and war. At that time conflict had reduced our ability to think positively. People were conditioned to see conflict as a 'holy war', so that they needed to be mobilised.

At the end of the year 2000, after I had finished my Master's degree in Islamic studies at IAIN Alauddin, Makassar, I could see that conflict was causing more concern. The arrival of the Laskar Jihad made matters worse. Some friends and I, who could still think relatively clearly, tried to take an unofficial role to find a way out of the tangled mess of the conflict. We held discussions and we relayed the conclusions through local newspapers in Ambon. I understood that, in reality, many people wished for peace but found it difficult to express this against the tide of opinion that shouted for *jihad* and the defence of Islam's honour through war.

A golden opportunity was given to me by the elders of Al-Fatah Mosque, when for the first time I was scheduled to give the Friday sermon in the mosque in November 2000. I made use of this opportunity to try to guide the congregation to view the conflict in a positive and rational manner. My mission at that time was simple: there needs to be balanced thinking in order to sow the idea of peace. If this did not happen then Ambonese Muslims, who every Friday were indoctrinated with thoughts about war, would be totally destroyed.

In the refugee camps resources were limited and the electricity supply was restricted, so I wrote my sermons by hand. I was inspired by some of the thoughts of Nurcholish Madjid. The theme for my sermon was about the need to develop awareness about peace and plurality when facing conflict.

Taking such a topic at a time of conflict was very risky. The preacher could become a casualty if he was considered to go against mainstream opinion. I realised that to pick the theme of peace and plurality at that time was quite controversial. But at least the congregation needed to be given an understanding of Islam from a different point of view, so that they could develop the hope that peace was necessary.

When I came down from the pulpit and after Friday prayers were over, several members of the congregation came up to me and gave me a hug. The principal Imam of Al-Fatah Mosque, Teacher Ahmad Bantam, showed his appreciation by saying, 'Your sermon was quite good'. From that time onwards I was registered as a preacher at Al-Fatah Mosque. *Alhamdulillah*, it meant that my sermon was received well. It was obvious, however, that many people didn't agree with the thoughts expressed in my sermon. This was evident the next Friday when the Islamic teacher (*Ustaz*), Ali Fauzi, directly opposed the contents of my sermon. Furthermore, the *Ustaz* was of the opinion that I regarded all religions as the same.

What was interesting was the snowball effect caused by expressing my thoughts. The governor, M. Saleh Latuconsina – as I heard from one of my activist friends from the youth branch of the Muhammadiyah – appreciated my sermon. He stated there should be new ways of thinking, like those I had delivered in my sermon.

Even more interesting, the night after I had given my sermon, three visitors came to my house. Two were high ranking police officers while the third, Malik Selang, was head of the MUI work unit. It seems that the three of them had been sent by the chief of police, Brigadier General Firman Gani. My wife's face turned pale because she thought there had been something wrong with the contents of my sermon.

I asked them to sit down and, without beating around the bush, Malik Selang started the conversation. 'We have come to your home to convey greetings from the chief of police'. He continued, 'The chief of police thanks you for the delivery of your sermon. The chief of police has sent us here to ask for a copy of the text of your sermon'. Malik Selang's statement was confirmed by the two police officers. This was the first time that I received this unexpected appreciation from the chief of police. This was an honour and gave me fresh enthusiasm to urge for a more serious effort to achieve peace.

I thanked Malik Selang and his two friends for the attention paid by the chief of police. I couldn't immediately give him a copy of my sermon because it was hand-written and difficult to read. However, they continued to ask for the text of the sermon which they promised they would return after it had been photocopied. I was forced to comply with their request and gave them the sermon notes. A few days later these notes were returned to me.

It is amazing that one sermon could gain such a positive response from two important public figures in Maluku (the governor and the police chief). This gave me hope that I must continue my struggle to sow seeds of peace. From that time onwards I used all of my energy to call for peace through writing articles in the newspaper, dialogues, sermons or lectures. This was done, of course, with the awareness that I would face many challenges.

Coup d'État when Entering the Pulpit

It seems that after my first experience of preaching at the Al-Fatah mosque, sharing ideas of peace and plurality didn't go smoothly. For those who held strong views, my sermon threatened the existence of hard-line Islamic ideology, especially the ideology held by the Laskar Jihad. For that reason, from that time onwards they kept an eye on my preaching schedule and even blocked my preaching.

I had a bad experience when I was due to preach for the second time at the Friday prayers at the Al-Fatah mosque – I forget the exact date but I remember that it took place in 2001. I had arrived at the Al-Fatah mosque to give the sermon but at the moment I was due to preach, suddenly three people appeared, intending to stop me from delivering the sermon. I knew two of the men: they were Wahab Lumaela and *Ustaz* Lukman Ba'abdu, deputy commander of the Laskar Jihad. They asked me not to preach. According to Wahab, they had contacted the elders of the mosque, so that my turn to preach would be filled by *Ustaz* Lukman Ba'abdu. (At that time, the *imam* of the Al-Fatah Mosque, Teacher Ahmad Bantam, was out of town).

I countered, 'Why didn't you contact me before now? Isn't it my turn to preach?' Considering the immediate need for someone to deliver the Friday sermon, however, and so the situation wouldn't get out of hand, I gave way. I realised that if I stood my ground and refused to give them the opportunity, chaos would have ensued inside the Al-Fatah Mosque. The elders of the Al-Fatah mosque learnt from this experience to be more selective in choosing people to preach in the mosque and to control the roster so that no intervention could take place from other groups who were not due to preach.

I began to be aware that the peace ideas I had put forward had become a controversial topic. The Laskar Jihad people were not able to stay quiet. They used various means to provoke others – starting with the pulpits of the mosques (including principally the pulpit of the Al-Fatah mosque), handing out bulletins, even through a radio station known as the Voice of Maluku Muslim Defence (SPMM). At the Al-Fatah mosque they kept an eye on the roster for the Friday sermon that was usually placed on the notice board. If the one who was due to preach held the same ideology as they did, then they left the preacher alone. But if the one due to preach held opposing views to theirs, then they would do everything they could to prevent that person from preaching.

My second experience of being blocked by the Laskar Jihad group happened when the board of the Al-Fatah mosque placed my name on the roster to preach for the third time. The Laskar Jihad saw me as a stumbling block, so a week before it was my turn to preach, they tried to block me again.

This time, two youths approached me with what they said was a message from Abdul Wahab Lumaela. I knew these two people because they were both my ex-students at STAIN Ambon (now IAIN). They were M. Zen Haji Hamzah and La Syarifuddin. After the Laskar Jihad arrived in Ambon they had tried to consolidate their position by developing relationships with hard-line groups in the area, so they were able to involve people like Abdul Wahab, M. Zen and La Syarifuddin.

I invited them into my house. I asked them the purpose of their visit. 'It's like this', said Zen, '*Ustaz* Wahab Lumaela asked us to bring a message to you'. 'Oh, what is the message?' I was impatient to receive their message. 'It's like this, Mr Hasbollah,' Zen continued, 'By coincidence, this Friday *Ustaz* Djafar Umar Thalib is in Ambon. He wishes to consolidate the Laskar Jihad forces. So *Ustaz* Wahab asks that your turn to preach at Al-Fatah on this coming Friday will be filled by *Ustaz* Djafar'. I was startled, and I thought to myself, 'The situation is beginning to become unhealthy again'. Now my turn in the preaching roster of Al-Fatah is about to be blocked again.

'Oh, I'm sorry, I can't give my turn in the roster to Laskar Jihad again', I replied. 'Just a few Fridays ago wasn't my turn in the roster taken by *Ustaz*

Lukman? Please convey my greetings to *Ustaz* Wahab but I can't comply with his wish'. I added, 'I will also communicate this problem to the Imam of the mosque, Teacher Ahmad'. The two of them left to deliver my message to *Ustaz* Wahab.

My answer didn't make them give up. They used various methods to try to persuade teacher Ahmad to allow *Ustaz* Djafar to switch with me. However, it seems that the Imam of Al-Fatah Mosque was fed up with the behaviour of *Ustaz* Djafar and his group, who he believed were provoking people. So, in a diplomatic way Teacher Ahmad said, 'Please feel free to contact Mr Hasbollah. If he is prepared to answer your request, then *Ustaz* Djafar can preach'.

Hearing the teacher's answer, they felt that they had been given a fresh incentive to quickly meet me in order to give me the message that the Imam of Al-Fatah didn't object if *Ustaz* Djafar took my place. Two of the messengers came to my house on Wednesday at about 5:25pm not long before the Maghreb prayer time. This time Zen Haji Hamzah and La Syarifuddin were not the messengers, rather they were two people who were not from Ambon. They told me that they had met the Imam of the Al-Fatah Mosque and he didn't object in principle, and that it all depended on me. I again apologised using the excuse that my previous opportunity to preach had been given to *Ustaz* Lukman. I replied, 'So if *Ustaz* Djafar wishes to consolidate his forces, he is welcome to use the Amal Shaleh Mosque at the Kebun Cengkeh housing estate. Isn't that close to the Laskar Jihad HQ?' I told them that I would convey this decision to Imam Ahmad Bantam.

It seems that teacher Ahmad wasn't happy with what he had said to the Laskar Jihad group. The Imam was known as *tawadhu'* (humble) and as someone who didn't speak much. It was really difficult to imagine what would happen if I surrendered my turn to preach to *Ustaz* Djafar: the Al-Fatah pulpit would become an arena of provocation that would ignite the fires of war, while the congregation (*umat*) was desperate for peace.

This I found out the following day, when I visited the teacher on Thursday morning. It seems that Teacher Ahmad, who was advanced in age, had, with great difficulty, gone to my house on Wednesday morning before the two messengers from *Ustaz* Djafar arrived in the late afternoon. Unfortunately, the charismatic Imam wasn't able to meet me because I was at the campus. When I returned from the campus, my mother-in-law informed me that earlier in the morning Teacher Ahmad had come to the house; I responded coolly to the information. I thought, 'It's not possible that a great Imam of the mosque would come and look for me in my house. Perhaps my mother-in-law was mistaken: someone she thought looked similar to the Imam of Al-Fatah.'

That Thursday morning, when I knocked on the door of his house and wished to give him my greetings, Teacher Ahmad happily greeted me with enthusiasm. Before I had a chance to sit down, the teacher opened the conversation, 'Hasbollah, yesterday I went to your house'. It was then that I realised that what my mother-in-law had told me was true.

'The reason for my visit,' continued the teacher 'was to warn you, not to let *Ustaz* Djafar preach in the Al-Fatah Mosque. If that should happen then we would be at war for ever. *Ustaz* Djafar's sermons were always provocative'. The Teacher went on to say, 'I went to your house early in the morning to give this information to you before the messengers arrived'.

I told the Teacher, 'They (*Ustaz* Djafar's messengers) contacted me yesterday afternoon, but I maintained my position that I would preach on Friday in order to fulfil my commitments'. *'Alhamdulillah,'* replied Teacher Ahmad with joy 'if not, the Al Fatah pulpit will become a platform for provocation'. I expressed my respect and gratitude towards the Teacher and then took my leave and kissed his hand.

As was my custom at that time, in my Friday sermon I conveyed the importance of developing peace and humanity of the Moluccan people. I received news that *Ustaz* Djafar carried out his Friday prayers at Amal Shaleh Mosque, Kebun Cengkeh, with his followers.

The Pulpit of the Al-Fatah Mosque Post Malino II

I also noted some important incidents concerning the pulpit of the Al-Fatah mosque shortly before and shortly after the Malino agreement. The meetings themselves took place from 10–12 February 2002 and resulted in 11 points of agreement that have become known as the 'Malino Agreement'. The pro- and contra-arguments about the process of Malino conference were very strong, from before the two delegations (Muslim and Christian) departed for Malino until they returned to Ambon. This was reflected in the sermons delivered at the Al-Fatah Mosque.

Indeed, from the onset of the conflict the sermons delivered from the Al-Fatah pulpit were dominated by a group of hard-liners. However, there were also a number of preachers who chose to deliver sermons containing moral teaching. Those in this second group really wanted peace but they were very cautious and didn't want to be called 'traitors' of the faithful. But a third group called for peace more openly.

From my observation, on Friday 9 February 2002, KH. Abdul Wahab Abubakar Polpoke was due to preach at the Al-Fatah Mosque. The elderly *Kyai*, a graduate of the Gontor traditional Muslim School, had indeed been organised by the regional government to deliver *tausiah* (wise words) about peace in his Friday sermon and it was hoped that this would be a precondition leading up to the Malino conference. The characteristic preaching style of KH. Wahab was known to be firm and harsh in the delivery of concepts of reconciliation. He gave the impression of not being too diplomatic in the context of the very sensitive situation at that time. This caused the group of hard-liners to react strongly. They did not want the reconciliation process to take place; therefore, they refused to attend the Malino conference. The result was that the elderly *ustaz* was besieged in the MUI offices. He was also threatened with vile remarks before being rescued by the Al-Fatah Foundation.

After the two delegations (Muslim and Christian) returned from Malino, the situation in the city of Ambon didn't become calm immediately. Hardline groups were involved in strongly provoking and agitating people to reject the results of the Malino Agreement. This is evident from the fact that after the Malino Agreement, there were several incidents in Ambon city centre: a bomb exploded in Yan Paays Street, the Governor's office was burned down, the California boat in Baguala Bay, Ambon was bombed, and other incidents also caused many innocent people to become victims.

In this unstable situation the Muslim faithful were preparing for Eid al-Adha (the feast of sacrifice). While I was in the middle of my routine tasks on campus, two staff members of the Regional Religious Affairs office (now the Ministry of Religion) suddenly appeared. I knew them both, they were Sukri Drachman and Rustam Holle. The two of them delivered a message from the Governor through the head of the Regional Religious Affairs office, asking me if I would be willing to preach on Eid al-Adha. The two friends said, 'Greetings from the Governor and the head of the Regional Religious Affairs office, Mr Hasbollah, it is requested that you be willing to preach on Eid al-Adha this year'. I asked in return, 'Isn't there anyone else who is more worthy?' The question was immediately answered by Sukri, 'The choice has fallen to Mr Hasbollah'.

I accepted the mandate with quite a feeling of tension and anxiety, remembering that various violent incidents were still happening. Peace activists were still receiving threats and being terrorised and intimidated at that time. Yet, apart from the feeling of uneasiness, I also felt inwardly that this was an important opportunity to call for peace. I prepared a sermon with the theme of 'The Eid Sacrifice and the Spirit of Solidarity of Universal Humanity'.

As usual to welcome the two main religious feasts (Eid Al Fitr and Eid al- Adha), the Al-Fatah mosque foundation displayed several banners inviting the faithful to flood into the Al-Fatah mosque to take part in the Eid prayers. The names of the preacher and the Imam of the communal prayers were printed on the banners to draw the interest of the faithful.

When my name was included on the banner, I immediately received several anonymous threatening telephone calls. 'Don't try to talk about peace and reconciliation, if you want to be safe'. Such were the threats. Several friends and family were worried, seeing the restlessness of the community at that time. Indeed, the threats were real and serious, because not long after that, the home of the head of the Muslim delegation at Malino, Thamrin Ely, was burnt down by unknown people while he was away from home on official business and his wife and daughter, who was still a toddler, were inside the house (official housing for members of the Regional Assembly). *Alhamdulillah*, mother and daughter could be saved.

My wife and I discussed this problem. We had also been contacted by friends and family to reconsider the preaching roster for the Eid prayers. But for me it was a trust that had to be fought for. It is not just anyone who received the trust of the Governor and the head of the Regional Religious Affairs office to speak in public like this. I convinced my wife that this was part of my struggle: whatever the risks, this was my *jihad*. With the full support of my wife, we then made a definite decision, while inwardly praying, '*rabbi ij`al haza baladan aminan*' – 'Lord, make Ambon a land that is safe'.

As an initiative for self-protection, I asked for informal protection from the police. The chief of Police, Brigadier General Soenarko, DA., happily gave me protection on the day by sending several plain-clothed police to escort me to the Al-Fatah Mosque.

The experience of preaching at the Eid Sacrifice at the Al-Fatah mosque at the time of conflict was quite memorable, because it was broadcast live by TVRI, RRI, and even local and national media. I tried to explain the nature and struggle of the Prophet Abraham AS and the struggle of Rasulullah SAW in sowing the values of love and maintaining universal humanitarian values. I didn't forget to explain the phenomenal speech of Rasulullah in Arafat (in *hajj al-wada'*), whose contents built solidarity and respect based on humanitarian values.

The sermon was well received by the people, beyond my expectations. This good response was a sign that the people had really been longing for peace for some time. The war only created a long human suffering. Nobody won, but what had clearly occurred was never-ending human suffering, misery and sorrow.

After the sermon, one by one the congregation shook my hand or embraced me and gave thanks for the moral message in the sermon. Some even embraced me and spontaneously wept on my shoulder.

In 2003 the atmosphere in Ambon started to recover, with the security status being reduced from civil emergency to civil order. It needs to be remembered, however, that, although the situation in Maluku was relatively calm, the concepts of peace should be promoted continually. Ideas about peace should be a torch, which can lead people towards better values and egalitarianism.

During 2003-2006, my ideas concerning peace development were no longer delivered from the Al-Fatah Mosque pulpit, because I was no longer living in Ambon. Fortunately, I could still write articles in the *Ambon Ekspres*, so that I continued to sow the seeds of peace, democracy and awareness of plurality. From 2008, I was scheduled again on the roster as a preacher at the Al-Fatah Mosque. *Insya Allah* (God willing) I will continue to consistently encourage the creation of lasting peace and the acceptance of plurality in our nation, as long as I live.

Chapter 10

FOOTSTEPS LEADING TO ENCOUNTERS

Weslly Johannes

Making an Escape while Carrying Inner Trauma

Kayeli Bay, 26 December 1999 – Many tears were shed aboard the passenger boat that was heading I don't know where. This boat had just taken on board hundreds of refugees who no longer had a land of birth. From the bridge of the ship to its hold, people were crying. Hundreds of pairs of confused eyes shed tears. These people were not crying for their belongings which had been destroyed, not even for their homes which had been razed to the ground. They were lamenting their shattered dreams, also their vulnerable souls and lives that in an instant had become meaningless and without purpose. In the face of a raging civil war, they had no rights to determine their own lives.

I, one among hundreds of refugees, sat on the deck of the boat packed with people. I held my rucksack which contained all the important documents belonging to our family. My job was to keep them safe. At the other end, young people were sitting and chatting; they were strumming a guitar and singing a song about the island of Buru.

I don't know how many times they sang that song. The longer it went on, the harder it was to tell the difference between the singing and the crying. I was more and more certain that they were not singing. They were crying, they were softly singing the words of the song. I have forgotten the name of the song and the singer. However, twelve years on, I still remember the lyrics:

> Beautiful, green leaves can be seen
> Oh the eucalyptus waves, decorating the dear land
> It is the land where we spilt our blood, I won't forget
> There I was born and brought up, oh Buru …
> Every time I remember you, without realising it I shed tears.

The lament they were singing brought me back to beautiful, almost buried memories of my childhood. Moreover, being aboard the boat that was sailing along coast of Kayeli Bay made this escape feel like a flashback of my life. There was a story wherever the eye could see.

On top of Tanjung Batu there was a large leafy and strong banyan tree. For years it had been a stopping place for the many people who passed by and also for birds, who built their nests in it. The large banyan tree was a favourite on the way from state junior high school Namlea No. 1 that was about five km from our village. Every day, under the shade of the tree we joked and told stories about unimportant things, which made us laugh. After taking a rest, our strength restored, we continued our journey.

The boat continued onwards. We could see the roofs of the houses, schools and churches. Nametek was where I was born and grew up in the same way as other children on this earth. Here I enjoyed my primary school and playing.

I remembered the friends I played with. We grew up together from childhood to senior high school and we were aboard the boat together. I remembered Andri Yudhi Kristianto, Dedi Lating, Ratna Makian, Husein Dokolamo, Lukman Galela, Jailan Makian, Ahmad Biloro, Asril Buamona, Ibrahim Buamona and other school friends. I remembered their faces one by one. How they smiled or laughed when we cracked jokes, or their expressions when they were sulky or angry, even what they looked like when they cried.

Long beforehand, immediately after the 19 January 1999 incident in Ambon, frightening rumours had spread about the 'religious war' that would reach in Buru. We often played together but we had never harmed each other. This prejudice on both sides could never be solved while prejudice existed, because prejudice cannot by conquered by prejudice, but rather by open encounters.

The days went past; people began to leave the village. They looked for protection in Waenibe, a Christian village, which was larger and had more inhabitants.

By the end of 1999 the situation got worse. They started beating and maltreating young people, including a few of my close friends, who were still at senior high school. All of this took place without any clear motives. Indeed, there was never a clear motive and it became acceptable to persecute someone, even though the persecutor was in the wrong. People who are persecuted are left with a lasting anxiety. Persecution also brought the guarantee that a 'religious war' would soon explode.

Everyone was afraid. For me, as a Christian living on the island of Buru, the rumour of a 'religious war' sounded as though we would be hunted down and slaughtered. No doubt the Muslims felt the same feelings if they were living in an area where the majority were Christians. For us, the minority, whether Christian or Muslim, 'a religious war' meant 'hunting', and we were the prey.

That afternoon, 23 December 1999, was the last afternoon in Nametek. While little children in other places were playing, enjoying their holiday, the little children in our village were not allowed to play. The situation wasn't safe. My friends and I who could wield machetes were in a hurry. Feeling threatened forced us to prepare our weapons in case we had to defend our lives. We had received news that war had taken place between the villages of Waenibe and Waeputih.

Evening fell; we waited in the dark and the silence was frightening. We could hear the sounds of the homemade bombs exploding in the distance. Slowly but surely, the noises got louder and closer. A raging mob was moving quickly. We could hear the rioters' voices clearly shouting 'God is great'. We all gathered in the church waiting to die. I no longer felt afraid. Perhaps we were standing too close to death.

I didn't know why the raging mob didn't attack the church building. They only destroyed the houses belonging to the Christians who lived along the main road. The houses were empty, nobody was there. Content with damaging the houses, the mob dispersed when the predawn call to prayer was heard.

Having escaped the threat of death that night, I took the opportunity to return to our house to gather a few important items. At that time, I didn't know that it would be my last chance to see the place where I built my dreams.

I have never seen that house again. That day, about two in the afternoon, two trucks, escorted by police, took our family and all the other people left in Nametek to the police station in Namlea.

Without any preparation, the Christmas Eve service took place meaningfully in the inspection yard of the Namlea police HQ. Under the open skies, sprinkled with drizzle, we sang 'Silent Night' in whispers. This was the most memorable Christmas Eve in my life. The last Christmas I celebrated on the island of Buru. The next day we were evacuated by a passenger boat.

A woman's shouts brought me back from my daydreaming. I instantly turned my head. There, the church tower was upside down. The young people who had sat in a huddle were still strumming the guitar and singing. They were drunk with *sopi* that they had 'stolen' from the police HQ in Namlea. They didn't have any words for this tragic incident except that song. 'The feeling of pain cannot be expressed,' said Richard Rorty, 'it is something we have in common with dumb animals. Thus the victims of violence are humans with few words'.

Kayeli Bay, 26 December 1999 – on board the passenger boat that was heading I don't know where, I witnessed the last sunset in Kayeli Bay, a sad sunset. Smoke was still billowing from the wrecks of boats that had been burnt on the beaches, also from the houses that we had lived in yesterday.

People were still weeping as though the sadness would never abate. But evening came quickly and covered our eyes, preventing us from seeing the view that generally humankind didn't want to see. I am certain that, just as no man wants to witness his house being burnt down, there is no fisherman or offspring of a fisherman who wants to spend time watching his father's boat burning. At this point, I wept without words. And I sailed the sea with hatred towards Islam burning in my loins. Twelve years ago.

A New Identity: Refugee

It was still dawn. The passenger boat was slowly entering Ambon Bay. On 27 December 1999 we arrived at the Gudang Arang quay. I believe that our neighbours and all the residents of Buru Island wanted us to leave. At the least, they let it all happen, even though they could have prevented it. They were Muslims who plotted together to hunt down the Christians on Buru Island. Those were the thoughts that I carried with me since I was saved from great danger in Buru Island.

When we reached the Nehemiah church building, my attention was more focused on the normal things needed for everyday life: food, clothes and a place to lay my tired body because I had been unable to sleep for five nights straight.

I almost forgot to tell you that when we arrived at the Gudang Arang quay and started to get off the boat, we were shot at by people in a speed boat coming from the direction of the Yos Sudarso Port.

This made me more certain that the Muslims of Buru Island and Ambon Island were the same. Islam, wherever it was, was the same. Both were dangerous and both wanted us dead. See how easy it is for people who have had the same bitter experiences as I have to easily link together one incident with another and believe them to be true. Many people in Maluku still think in generalisations like this.

From Nehemiah church we were taken by truck to Amahusu. The government of the village of Amahusu allowed us to occupy two classrooms in the state primary school No. 1 Amahusu. From then on, we were given a new identity – 'refugee'.

This new identity placed us on a lower level of humanity. In the eyes of many people, refugees are human beings whose self-worth is not the same as human beings who are not refugees. Refugees are newcomers in the ranks of lower castes of society. Life became more difficult!

A New Ambition: To Take Revenge

Negative encounters with the mobs in December 1999, had crystallised as generalised prejudice and hatred towards all Muslims. I changed my ambitions, with the thought patterns of a third-year senior high-school student. I initially wanted to become a minister of the church. The desire to become a minister had a sad background. I can always feel my mother's sadness when she told me about it.

On 15 March 1980, Thomas Johannes married Fransina Uneputty and they lived together as husband and wife. They were not as lucky as other couples who married, had children and lived happily together as a complete family, because their two baby daughters died. They did, however, eventually become my parents. Husbands and wives who have experienced this know how painful it is and can easily identify with my mum and dad.

A year went past and my mum became pregnant. This made them both happy and also frightened at the same time. Happy because they were having a child and frightened that they would lose this one like the last. Thus the time of pregnancy was a time of wrestling with the problem. Every night my mum prayed and made a bargain with the Lord. If the child in her womb lived, then this child would be dedicated to serve the Lord. Of course you would think that you can serve the Lord in any profession, but that was not what was in my mother's mind. For my mother, serving the Lord meant becoming a minister.

Once when I was in fourth grade in primary school, my teacher asked us about our ambitions. Of course, I answered with certainty, 'I want to become a minister!' From that time my ambition was to become a minister. But the experience of being expelled from our home village in Buru Island made me change my mind. Secretly, I decided to join the army.

My ambition to be a minister was buried without my parents' knowledge. My desire to join the army was so strong. As soon as possible! My capital was only a Senior High School Certificate and a healthy and strong body. I wanted to hold a rifle and protect my parents and my siblings.

Only now, I understand why so many young people at that time wanted to enter the army or the police force. This work is indeed suitable for people who live in Maluku because the security situation changed like the weather: sometimes hot, sometimes raining. In the middle of the uncertainty of security like that, for senior high-school students like me and my friends at that time, the choice of becoming a policeman or a soldier felt quite strategic.

More than that, I had just come to understand that many girls were interested in policemen or soldiers then. Girls also clearly need to feel safe. Love also needs to feel safe. Don't take this last point too seriously, but you cannot ignore the fact that at that time many girls gave birth to children without fathers.

Finally, I have to be honest about the reasons why I wanted to be a soldier. I have said previously that I wanted to be a soldier so that I could hold a rifle and protect my family. It's true, but it is not the full truth. To be honest, I wanted to take revenge.

Deciding Failures

Life has many flavours that are wrapped up in surprises. Not only is success a decider; failures have the same share in deciding a man's path in life.

A month before the national exams I had an accident. I broke my collarbone, the bone that connects the shoulder and the top part of my right arm. I had to undergo surgery. As a result, I had to take the national exam in the nursing station because the men's wards were not suitable. Afterwards there was no graduation ceremony or scribbling signatures on each other's school uniform, as is the usual practice for many senior high-school students in Indonesia.

The broken collarbone destroyed my ambition. It is not possible for someone who is physically impaired to be accepted as a soldier in the Indonesian army. I wept when I heard that my collarbone could not be returned to its previous state. This is not because of the pain it caused, but because I knew that my ambition to be a soldier was over. I had no other ambitions.

After one year 'hanging around' after graduating senior high school, I started to become bored with life just as it was. I promised to fulfil my parents' request, so I studied at the Theology Faculty of the Indonesian Christian University in Maluku, but my motivation was unclear. I was involved in aimless socialising and caught up in activities involving alcohol and marijuana, which meant that I neglected my lectures.

As a result, two years later I dropped out of university. I did not regret stopping my studies, but I felt disloyal, because I had wasted my parent's hard efforts. Every night Dad went to sea amid the terror of fishermen being shot by unknown persons and Mum sold fish around the village of Amahusu.

After that, I went with my dad to sea at night or did construction work during the day. This was all that I could do to help pay for the education costs of my two siblings. This was a way to redeem myself.

You can see how failures determined the direction of my life.

July 2004 – to cut a long story short, Mum reminded me about her spiritual struggle when she was pregnant with me and about the binding promise that she made with the Lord. I didn't think about it every day, but Mum's story about her spiritual struggle and her promise to the Lord disturbed my 'peace of mind'. I had to return to study at the theology faculty so that I could be a minister. Such was the end of several personal times of reflection that instilled new enthusiasm in me.

Feeling certain, I stepped into the temporary offices of the Theology Faculty of UKIM in the Rehoboth Christian School complex to register myself and settle the administration requirements so that I could take the entry test as a new student. The previous evening, Rev. Ola Subagyo-Noija came to the refugee barracks and prayed for me. If I passed the selection test, then I would not waste the opportunity.

Three times I went back and forth to read the list of names of new students. I read the list of those who passed the test to enter the Theology Faculty of UKIM one by one, but my name wasn't there. I was disappointed. What now?

Heinard Talarima and Vemmy Wattimury – close friends when I had studied previously – came and asked me about the results of my entrance test. I told them what I saw. My name wasn't on the list and it meant that I didn't pass. Curious with what I told them, they went and read the list for themselves.

I sat almost fifteen metres from the notice board where the list of new students was posted. From there they raised their voices, 'Friend, your name is here'. It was my turn to take a look and I moved quickly moved in the direction of the notice board. Indeed, it was true: my name was number sixteen on the list, Weslly Johannes.

Learning from the failures of the past made me wiser in my socialising. In order to redeem the failures, I became more enthusiastic about studying. In this campus I experienced enlightenment that brought me to a paradigm shift and a new attitude. After studying for more than four years, I graduated in September 2009.

To this point you have read a rough summary of ten years in my life. Many changes have taken place in that time. One of these changes, which are the focus of this writing, is the process of my paradigm shift towards Islam.

I hated Muslims. That was in the past, but it is not the case now. I was driven to meet Muslims and Islam became more and more interesting to me. I will tell what changed my mindset and shaped my new attitude towards Islam and the struggles in the process of change.

The Same Fate and the Same Suffering

Suffering doesn't have a religion. Suffering doesn't have a reason to be on the side of followers of a particular religion. It comes and strikes whoever is pushed in front of it. Life in the refugee camp is shoved in the face of suffering and there is no other choice but to face it.

If you asked me to describe what life was like for years in refugee housing, then I would say one word to you: 'Suffering!'

I have relatives who were also refugees, but they lived in a different refugee camp. We faced the same problems. We both experienced conditions that caused us stress and suffering.

We lost our livelihoods; we didn't have any money; we had no land to grow crops; we didn't have much of what we needed to support our lives. We lived with help from other people or charities, or the government. It meant that we didn't protest if it wasn't what we wanted or if what we were given wasn't sufficient.

We regarded physical and psychological pressure as normal for us refugees. Minor issues often led to beatings and maltreatment. Every day we experienced insults and insinuations that lowered human dignity. This situation went on, not for a day or two, but for years. Feelings of inferiority, anxiety, despair and a bleak future were part of being a refugee.

Once I reflected about the fate of Muslim refugees. Did they also suffer? Of course you can answer that yourself. But for me, when I became a refugee,

I got a new friend who was called suffering. From this point I thought that war should continue so that many more people could suffer.

In the middle of the war, from 1999 until 2005, I rarely came across Christian refugees who felt that they suffered the same fate as Muslim refugees. They often scoffed at each other's suffering. Christian refugees saw how Muslim refugees were suffering and claimed it as a Christian victory and the result of karma because they had made Christians suffer. I once shared these thoughts with refugee friends of my age, but their reactions were not what I hoped.

Their reaction didn't change the feeling of having the 'same fate' that was filling my heart. I still held my stance that supporting the war and attacks on others would drive more people to be at the same point at which we didn't want to be. I did not wish for other people to become refugees. Period!

I didn't want war to continue and cause other people to suffer. It's true! But this didn't automatically release me from the suffering I experienced as a refugee. There is something that bothers me here and it is the question of the value or meaning of the suffering I was experiencing. I had to learn the meaning of this suffering. Viktor E. Frankl wrote that humankind does not stop 'interpreting meaning' even in the darkest hour of our lives.

Searching for the meaning of the experience of suffering is a small path that we can take to survive and, at the very least, develop hope within ourselves. Humans are responsible for life, even when they experience suffering. Instinctively, this is so.

This type of thing can only happen to a person who has certain religious beliefs, whether Muslim or Christian. At the moment when the surrounding conditions are unpromising, humankind needs to reassure itself with something outside the realm of rational explanation; when hundreds of possessed rioters surrounded us in the church building, we still hoped that we would live. This doesn't make sense, does it? Therefore, religious values play their role here.

I am not saying that faith doesn't make sense. I only mean to demonstrate that beliefs and the actions of faith sometimes cannot be explained rationally, as stated by Kierkegaard, 'A person must believe not because he knows, but because he doesn't know'.

I usually hear in sermons and have read in devotional books, for example, that people must be patient when facing suffering, because the Lord is never idle, but suffers with them and is carrying out deliverance. This was quite helpful for our family when we faced difficult times and yet could still be hopeful.

In the middle of such a situation, Mum and Dad still encouraged the three of us to continue our schooling. What they did was give me the belief and enthusiasm that suffering and humiliation are to be accepted and that it is entirely up to us whether we choose to continue to be humiliated or to improve our situation.

In short, humankind will, as much as possible, try to avoid suffering. But there are conditions in which there is no choice other than to suffer, in which what we can do is to learn from suffering.

I believe that all that has been written in this book also reflects this. The Moluccan people had no choice but to 'learn from suffering.' Because suffering does not contain meaning within itself, humankind has to learn to give it meaning. This is important, because, if the Moluccan people do not regard the human tragedy that once befell them as something of value, then they will not ever learn from it. If the Moluccan people do not learn from their suffering, then this dark era has the potential to darken other parts of life of the Moluccan people in the future.

The time to weep for the losses and the destruction is over. Now is the time to learn from it all. Learn from the suffering and become wise in looking to the future.

The Benefits of Studying Theology

Extra ecclesiam nulla salus, 'Outside the church, there is no salvation'. This church dogma from early times has long been left behind. I was so surprised when I discovered that the majority of the students who took the Theology of Religions class that was taught by Rev. I.W.J. Hendriks still held strongly to this dogma. An extended debate coloured the second meeting of this class. We were fortunate to learn from Rev. I.W.J. Hendriks and to become enlightened.

The debating in class showed the theological gap between the theologians and the laity. Therefore, an inter-faith 'dialogue' amongst circles of the elite became very exclusive and did not bring about much change because there was a lack of method and space to share in order to build bridges. Also, in preaching this, clerics experienced anxiety.

The debates were a small example of how church teaching influences in the ways people see other religions. I felt lucky to be studying theology. I felt its benefits. The Moluccan conflict with its religious nuances needed theological enlightenment because various parties had an interest in the conflict in sowing hatred, agitating and mobilising mobs to slaughter each other, using religious values that had been manipulated.

It is not my intention to promote institutes of theological education in Maluku, whether Muslim or Christian, but it would be wise to give these institutions serious attention. Teaching staff and students in these institutions must really give special attention to studies on peace.

Studying in the theology faculty was one of the periods during which my views and attitudes towards Islam and its followers changed. I hope that theologies friendly towards difference can continue to be produced and shared, so that all people will have the opportunity to prove their impact on living together in peace.

Several years ago theology students from the year 2005 made a plaque in the yard of UKIM campus, on which this very worthy statement was written: 'Theology is not only a science, but a lifestyle'. I was not only being taught how to interpret the Bible within its context, or learning about what is love, or what is salvation, or what is peace. I was not only taught to understand but also how to put it into practice.

All followers of a particular religion are not only encouraged to understand but also to put it into practice. You can therefore imagine the impact of not correcting religious concepts that are unfriendly to religious differences or that have been manipulated, so people carry out violence in the name of religion, as we have witnessed and experienced in our past.

Healing Oneself in Homogeneous Communities

I am lucky that I was born and grew up in Nametek, a small pluralistic village, different from many of the homogeneous villages on Buru Island and other islands in Maluku. The social segregation and dichotomy of 'us and them' can be found all over the place in Maluku.

When I was writing this section I remembered the history lessons at primary school about the *divide et impera* (divide and rule) strategy, and how the colonialists broke up this nation and sprinkled distrust amongst the people so that they could prevent any coalition among their opposition, and thus conquer and take over with ease.

Segregation gained strength during and after the conflict. You could find out a person's religion by simply asking where they lived. When I said that I lived in Kudamati, then the people listening would immediately assume that I was a Christian. The same could be said for anyone living in Batu Merah, who would without a doubt be Muslim.

This is something that may seem insignificant, but if you trace it back into the past, it is clear that we have indirectly inherited *divide et impera* from the colonialists.

At the time of the conflict and even afterwards, I discovered that many people were forced to synchronise their prejudices against Islam with the new reality of what had recently occurred.

The effort to unify all thoughts was done subconsciously and could be found everywhere. For example, when something bad happened and the victims happened to be Christians, people would say things such as, 'They [Muslims] are indeed like that, don't ever trust them'.

Such reactions indicate that prejudices were already present. The synchronisation with facts was a new step carried out later. Negative incidents that occurred were interpreted by prejudice that was already present long before the incident occurred.

We have lived with the traumatic burden of colonialism, and, with the Moluccan people's traumatic experience of the post-1999 conflict, of civil war. Thousands were mobilised by manipulated religious values and encouraged to slaughter fellow human beings of a different religious background. What is left from this traumatic experience is a strong prejudice that weakened the Salam-Sarane relationship and sharpened the Islam–Christian dichotomy of us and them.

In this context, Islam was not only regarded as one of the world religions, but also as a metaphor for threats. Islam was not a brother; Islam was the enemy. This conclusion was not surprising; the main targets were the church and the mosque. The church and the mosque are not just buildings but glorious symbols of different religions.

In a society such as that of Maluku, in which such strong collective bonds are polarised according to political interests, individuals are unable to think differently and hold stances that diverge from those of the communities in which they live.

On several occasions I was forced to agree with what people said about Islam because I was afraid because I thought differently or had no proof to counteract them, or my voice was in the minority, even though I didn't agree with them. Refusing to be like-minded, of course, has its consequences. It is thus normal for an individual to choose to conform, even if he doesn't agree with the community's actions. In conditions like this, independence and identity are unclear.

What I did to heal myself in this context was not complex. I chose to listen to myself. I thought over the negative narratives about Islam, which were always popping up in conversations in the homogenous domestic realm and tried as best as I could to prove their veracity or inaccuracy.

Thinking about these negative narratives, I wrote down my personal reflections in relation to my experiences during the conflict. I discovered that writing things down could help in healing trauma. I have found out that an alternative way to heal wounds is to tell stories.

In telling stories we accept the painful incidents that have befallen us and try to find meaning in them, including the acceptance that the pain is over and taking revenge doesn't take us anywhere. Taking revenge is like road signs in one place for one group in a parade festival. We only go round in circles in our dark past without being able to see a bright future.

I am lucky to have parents who are there for me and have time to talk about the pain, and about hope for the future and the spirit to fight for it.

A Space for Encounters

Social segregation and prejudices meant that it was rare during the post-1999 conflict for there to be any space for encounters, in either a physical or an abstract sense. People put up many more barriers in their minds because of their inability to expand spaces for encounters and because of their fears about their own difference from other people. There was also fear of others who were not the same as us. There are many barriers in the Moluccan people's minds and it is a pity that they are frightened to open the doors or build bridges to meet others.

Since I was evacuated from Buru Island in December 1999, I have lost contact with my close Muslim friends. Only in 2009 did I start to have Muslim friends in Ambon. The decision to get out and meet friends from a different religious background was driven by my reflections on my experience during the 1999 conflict, which I have written about in a number of articles, some of which I have published in a blog and some I have kept as private notes. To get out and meet people I had to start with challenging myself.

To be honest, I was uneasy about writing so much about inter-faith encounters, the spirit of living in a *basudara* relationship, and the good feeling of culture in the Salam-Sarane relationship in Maluku, when I did not have one good friend who was a Muslim. Such articles would just be nonsense if I didn't try to cross that barrier in my mind and the geographical segregation of space, to actually meet with people from different religious backgrounds.

Martin Luther King, Jr. said some important things about such a situation. 'Human beings sometimes hate each other because they are scared of each other', King said. 'They are scared of each other because they don't know each other, they don't know each other because they don't communicate, and they don't communicate because they are segregated'.

What he said is true. Post-conflict, people have been fed with narratives of hatred, fear, and collective suspicion. They then built large barriers and didn't leave space in their minds for people who were different. These barriers in their minds separated them from others, although they were living in close proximity. Ambon is too small a city for people to use the excuse that the distance between them made it impossible to create enlightening encounters. Moreover, there are no longer barricades to prevent us from meeting.

Crossing the barricades in our minds to meet and get to know people who are different is a choice made by people who are not afraid of their own uniqueness and are not afraid of others who are different to them. Only the courageous can do this.

During the conflict we were brave enough to face each other and hack off each other's heads. Why have we become cowards who need to hide and feel safe wrapped up in a blanket of prejudice? We need to meet and enter our private realms where we neatly keep our suspicions.

The first time I met and talked for a long time with two Muslim friends about our experiences during the conflict from 1999 until 2005, we talked about our fears, involvement and hatred, which the majority of people were keeping a tight lid on.

One of my friends wept when he shared his experiences, but he didn't hate me anymore because I was a Christian. We also laughed about many things that happened, which we did seriously during the dark period. The remainder of the time, we shared our dreams, also the dreams for the future of Maluku, things that couldn't be achieved through war, when we were burning down each other's houses and slaughtering each other.

By meeting and sharing experiences, we discovered the truth. We confirmed and removed the prejudices and understandings that were inadequate or even wrong. It seems that as more things were exposed, the more it became clear that the differences between us were not the roots of the problem.

For me, people who want to appear as innocent, or say that they were not involved – either directly or indirectly – or who were victims, who hid their feelings of suspicion or hatred and pretended to be fine, are people who have not yet recovered from their traumatic experiences.

Know that, when you are brave enough to come out from beneath the warm blanket of your prejudice and cross the cold river to meet someone from a different religious background, you are going to do something important for yourself and for Maluku. You do not know what you will find. Perhaps you will be given a warm cup of welcome and the bonfire of basudara, for which you have been longing for some time?

Chapter 11

TWO OF ABRAHAM'S CHILDREN

A Snippet from the Fajar Hidup Vicarage

Elifax Tomix Maspaitella

Reflection on an Experience

Sumanto Al-Qurtuby, who we usually called Manto, gave me a book by David W. Shenk as a good reference book for lectures and discussions on religion. It was entitled *Journeys of the Muslim Nation and the Christian Church, Exploring the Mission of Two Communities*. Mentioning Manto's name is now like mentioning Shenk's name, because his thoughts have become a reference for discussions on religion in Indonesia. Manto is a thinker, well-known for his critical ability and for his love of discussing matters that are regarded as sacred and carefully-protected in religion.

I borrowed his name here to refer to the fact that our relationship has developed not just into a close friendship but into a relationship such as that between siblings (which in Ambon we call a gandong relationship, like that of siblings from the same mother and father, eating off the same plate and sharing the same pillow when going to sleep). According to Manto 'it turned out to be easy' for a Muslim to experience the reality of living with a vicar and his family in the vicarage that had been built by members of his congregation.

This experience made a deep impression and became a pattern in the efforts to restore the *basudara* (brother- and sisterhood) relationship between Salam–Sarane which had been ripped apart during the Moluccan conflict in 1999. In Ambon, this basudara relationship is a sociological and theological fact that was born and has grown from a mutual understanding based on a rich cultural foundation. I will discuss this in another part of this writing.

I call Manto a brother because our relationship is different to what it used to be when we studied together at Satya Wacana Christian University (UKSW), Salatiga. Our inspirational experiences at university only lasted a year and we were not very close.

I am certain that I should call him a brother. The year we spent living together was far more meaningful than the year we spent together in Salatiga. I made an effort to become his brother, even though it was only accompanying him when he was carrying out research for his dissertation. My family and I promised to help him as a manifestation of the basudara relationship. For us as Ambonese, the basudara relationship is a concept, a definitive fact, or as expressed by Durkheim, an ideal fact, concerning a relation between individuals that is moved by self-understanding and cannot be replaced by any other relationship. A gandong and pela relationship is a definitive manifestation of this relationship and is not replaceable. This is why people from the traditional villages bound in the pela or gandong are not allowed to marry each other, because to marry would be regarded as incest which is a violation of traditional law (*adat*) and the standards of morality.

Because we (my wife, my daughter and I) had promised to help him, it meant that we had taken an oath that I could not break, and, moreover, I could not ask for payment for the things I did. The entire Maspaitella extended family was part of this relationship. Thus, when Manto asked if he could use Maspaitella as a surname, we were pleased. When family members read Manto's article in the *Siwalima*, one of the newspapers in Ambon, and he used the name Sumanto Al-Qurtuby Maspaitella, the extended family felt very proud because Manto had used our family name, a token from our brother, who is Javanese and a hundred percent Muslim.

For a year I became his adopted father and we shared our lives together in the Rumahtiga vicarage, which according to him was 'far from the noise and hubbub of Ambon'.

We built our basudara relationship on the conviction we were different, I as a Christian and minister of the Protestant Church (GPM) and Manto, a Muslim and the general secretary of *Komunitas Nahdlatul Ulama* (Nahdlatul Ulama Community) USA. Indeed, once he claimed that Anthropology was his religion, but my wife and I saw a sincere Muslim, who was faithful to Islamic values. He was accepted by the congregation of Rumahtiga GPM, as a special member of the Yarden-Yabok sector.

We carried out this journey together for a year and the strange thing is that we never discussed religion but, rather, while we reviewed the 1999 conflict and the peace activities consciously carried out by the community, we talked about the everyday lives of the Ambonese/Moluccans, whether Muslim or Christian. On the day Manto arrived (30 March 2010), without asking any questions, he attended the preparation service for Easter and mixed with members of the Rumahtiga congregation. I even introduced him as my brother who had long been separated from me and with whom I was now reunited. The next day, in the Easter service in the Fajar Hidup Church, Wailela, Manto introduced himself and explained that he would be living with us in the vicarage for a year.

The vicarage was quite far from the noise and hubbub of Ambon and was surrounded by the houses of Salam families, and they had no objection to Manto living at the vicarage or questioned why I should want to live with Manto. Indeed, Ambonese have never seen this as a problem. We shared our lives together with no frills. No prejudice was manifested by the local community, either by Salam or Sarane.

I mentioned that we shared our lives with 'no frills' because more often than not we ate fried fish or fried soybean cake with rice, even fried egg with instant noodles, because I lived with our 2 year old daughter Ellexia, while my wife served in the Uweth congregation, in the Taniwel diocese, Western Seram. If my wife came from there, then we would have a full meal, of course, with fish in a spicy yellow soup on the menu, which became Manto's favourite.

I felt an urge to write down these experiences because there are several aspects which I regard as important. One of these is the formation of religious understanding in the Moluccan community [and in Indonesia], starting with the children. The social conflict that dragged in religion or a religious conflict has succeeded in forming a contra-religious way of thinking in the consciousness of the religious community.

When the conflict erupted on 19 January 1999, children of five years old and above inherited a contra-religious way of thinking [us and them, or us and them below or above, showing the location where the Muslim/Christian communities live]. They have grown and inherited this way of thinking and, if it is not managed, it will preserve a dichotomy in understanding.

A transformed religious way of thinking for the generations born post-conflict must be formed; a way of thinking that is based on the values of basudara and peace.

This urge was strengthened when Manto completed his research and returned to Blora to be with his wife and child, whom he had missed, and our daughter, Ellexia, asked almost every day about Manto, Aunty Asri and Viki. The bedroom Manto had used is still called Uncle Manto's room, and the sandals Manto left behind and the doormat always have to be placed in front of 'his' bedroom door. When Manto returned to Ambon on 13 September 2011 to carry out research into the 11 September 2011 conflict in Ambon, without us realising, Ellexia placed his travel bag in 'his' bedroom, although Manto was staying in a hotel together with staff from the Ministry of Religious Affairs. Even now, every time we watch TV and the *magrib* call to prayer appears on the screen, she will say 'Mum/Dad, it's time for Uncle Manto to pray'.

I realise that this experience of a year with 'Uncle Manto' has resulted in the growth of a spontaneous feeling in Ellexia, and she has kept this togetherness in her memory. Every time we communicate with Manto, through texting, e-mail or Facebook, she always asks all sorts of questions, including many questions about Viki and Aunty Asri whom she has never met.

Perhaps this is what James W. Fowler calls basic faith through pre-verbal processes. The more the levels of belief grow, and a child develops through the different stages to reach adulthood and old age, that child's pre-verbal sense of belief also grows until he or she becomes an individual and can differentiate between various religious phenomena and belief in the vicinity. Then the individual reaches the peak of universalising faith and has made the decision to be involved with the One Almighty, as the foundation and source of everything. However, this can only happen when he frees himself from his ego (*kenosis*) and of thinking that ego is the central reference point and the standard for absolute life.

The second point is that we need a model of different religious communities living together. The basudara relationship is a model that is based on our community's cultural foundation. There are a number of basic values which can become joint values and function in the context of life together. Cultural roots can provide a satisfactory reference for this. In culture there are forms of definitive relations such as kinship, consanguinity and basudara.

Inter-faith relationships in Indonesia need to be built on cultural foundations through respect for the local wisdom of the community. We need to do this so culture doesn't have a primordial meaning but becomes universal in meaning.

One Airport, Two Responses

At precisely 11.30 am on 30 November 2010, after we had lived in the 'cold' town of Salatiga, I met up with Manto again at Pattimura Airport, Ambon. This time we were in Ambon, a tropical town that was quite hot, because the weather was so sunny.

'Which one are you, brother?', asked Manto using, his mobile phone although he was only a few steps away. 'Here, you are in front of me, brother', I answered, laughing and aware that he was a little confused.

He may have been a little confused, but we hugged each other like long-lost friends, although he still had to make sure that it was me, 'Is it really you, brother?' I spontaneously replied, 'Are you afraid that I'm a terrorist who will kidnap the secretary general of KNU USA and one of Gus Dur's favourites?'

Then we laughed together. Several acquaintances standing near us also broke out laughing, and one of them even asked me to make sure: 'You have a friend who is a member of NU?' I nodded to confirm that it was true, and they shook their heads and slapped me on my back because they were happy. I am sure that they were happy or amazed at a friendship like that. I dare to say that this was not strange to an Ambonese/Moluccan who was used to inter-faith basudara.

We then we moved towards the car belonging to a member of the congregation who helped me pick up Manto. I remember when I asked a member of the congregation to help (Christ Seilatu, who was also coordinator unit 1 Yarden Sector of ministry, Rumahtiga congregation GPM), he was happy to do so. At that time, I said that I wanted to pick up a Muslim who was going to carry out research for his dissertation and that he would stay with us in the vicarage. He replied spontaneously, 'Fine. We will pick him up together'.

Christ's response and Manto's desire to live with us in the vicarage, were, in fact, something normal. Some people feel that it is not necessary to blow this up into a narrative, as though there was something amazing in these two things.

I remember a series of theories on semantics, adaptation and integration. I also remember a series of theories on symbolism and narration analysis. However, in the context of recovery in Maluku, the two responses make a strong narrative, of how we affirm someone in the context of social difference. Affirmation is a step forward in penetrating the partitions that have been built for centuries and have unconsciously been strengthened behind religious symbols and other social symbols.

In fact, Manto shared his life with all members of the Rumahtiga congregation, especially in Wailela, as was the way of Muslims and Christians in Wailela. In his research, Christ had an important role if it rained. Tony Lorwens was another person who helped if Manto wanted to avoid traffic jams or needed to visit the narrow alley ways in Batu Merah, Kebun Cengkeh, even Air Salobar.

In my opinion, this happened because of that affirmation. I then remembered several Bible stories, such as the Jews' refusal to affirm the Samaritans and Syro-Phoenicians as brothers, which Jesus broke down by befriending a Samaritan woman and a Syro-Phoenician woman [Mark 7: 24-30]. Jesus disputed the stigmatisation of sin that the Jews imposed on them, and, his conversations with them, Jesus announced forgiveness for their sins.

By removing the stigma of sin, Jesus radically affirmed the Samaritan and Syro-Phoenician women. Thus Jesus opposed religious legalism with new action, rather than with new interpretations of religious law. Jesus' religion was not a 'textbook religion' but praxis in an encounter and new meaning of self.

I don't know whether Christ, Manto and I, at the beginning of the encounter developed this life praxis or we were just not bothered with 'textbook religion'. One thing is certain – that the initial responses were positive in the praxis of inter-faith encounters in Maluku and Indonesia.

Ramadan 1431 Hijriah: Sahur as a New Praxis

Ellexia was just 2 years and 9 months old when the Ramadan fast took place. Close to the beginning of the Ramadan month of fasting, my wife, who was the main minister of the Uweth congregation, Taniwel Diocese, West Seram, came to Wailela, because we needed to serve Manto during his fasting.

We agreed to fast together. On the first day of the fast, Ellexia started to watch the *sahur* activities as practised in the Wailela vicarage, with a menu of chicken cooked in a spicy coconut milk sauce, steamed rice cooked in banana leaves, not to forget Manto's favourite fish cooked in a spicy yellow soup.

We 'ate *sahur*' together, and we explained to Ellexia 'Uncle Manto is fasting, so each morning there will be *sahur*'. On the second day of the fast, Ellexia played her role which made me think, 'How come?' She went to Uncle Manto's bedroom door and knocked on it, shouting: 'Uncle Manto, get up, it's time for *Shaun*[r]' – at that time she couldn't pronounce 'r' properly. 'Thank you', called Manto, when he opened his bedroom door to find Ellexia waiting for him. Then *sahur* began, with a menu ordered especially by Manto during the fast month.

That afternoon, Manto and Ellexia were watching TV together as they waited for the time to break the fast. A few minutes before breaking the fast, Manto teased Ellexia and asked her to move forward the fingers of the clock on the wall above my study door. 'Can you move the fingers of the clock along?' While looking at the clock on the wall, Ellexia replied: 'it's too high, Uncle Manto'. We all laughed together, and Ellexia continued to watch TV. A small child couldn't reach the clock on the wall. *Alhamdulillah*, because if she could, then Manto's fast would be cancelled because of the 'clock fingers'.

It was a small thing. For some people this way of thinking and this experience were normal. For my wife and me, however, it was an indication that at an early age Ellexia had accepted the presence of Manto who was different to her. Every afternoon when the *magrib* call to prayer was played on the TV, Ellexia always said to Manto: 'Uncle Manto, go and pray'.

She understood that we went to church on Sunday and sometimes Manto wouldn't go with us. She didn't complain because she also knew 'Uncle Manto is a Muslim'. This acceptance of Manto as a Muslim made me think that, if from early childhood children can be taught to understand the reality of difference through direct encounters such as this, and see how the difference can be talked about in our life together, won't our children be able to break through the barriers of difference in the future?

At least Ellexia has understood that Manto's wife, 'Aunty Asri' and their child, Viki, are part of the family. She complained when on 23 July 2012, a package containing Manto's dissertation arrived at the vicarage. When I read the 'acknowledgments' in the dissertation, it turned out that Ellexia wasn't mentioned. 'I don't like Uncle Manto', she shouted and then ran crying to her room. I phoned Manto and told him what happened. Manto immediately apologised to Ellexia. And as what usually happens with children, Ellexia immediately stopped crying and asked, 'Will Viki go to America as well? I've not met Viki yet.' She had forgotten that Manto forgot to include her name and she protested about an encounter that was probably more important to her than just meeting Manto. Because Manto had once promised that on his return from America and before he went back there to teach, he and his family would come to Ambon. I had once told Ellexia, 'You will meet Aunty Asri and Viki.' Aunty Asri and Viki have become family and it has been recorded in her memory that she has members of the family who are Javanese. I have no idea when they will meet up.

I understood from that situation that children have good memories. Creating an indirect dialogue with children forms the basis of their memory. This will grow and become part of their consciousness that will become the basis of their way of life and their way of thinking. If a child's memory is formed in a good way, we hope that in the future their way of life and their attitudes will become more open and they will accept the differences in others.

Getting Free from of the 'Tyranny of the Text'

To have a religion and to do theology is about dialogues and encounters. The essence of dialogue and encounters will build up an example that can become a new narrative about life. I am not saying that Manto and I have become an example. On the contrary, I want to emphasise that we have also learnt from others who have shown to us how to live together and share the differences between them without questioning.

Perhaps Manto will reflect on the little incidents that took place in our vicarage in Wailela, but I want to reflect on it by looking at how Jesus in the Gospels carried it out.

I took one dialogue from Luke 19:1-10, the story of Jesus and Zacchaeus, the chief tax collector who was short in stature. When Jesus wanted to stay at his house, many people tried to prevent Him because Zacchaeus was regarded as a sinner. At the beginning of the story, Zacchaeus really wanted to meet Jesus, but because he was short, he had climbed a sycamore tree. I am not saying that the initial motive was the reason Jesus forgave his sins.

Rather I want to look at the claims of the majority and Jesus' attitude that was controversial. In spite of the claims of the majority that Zacchaeus was a sinner, Jesus still stayed at his house. Of course Jesus would also be labelled as a sinner. But in order to expose these labels, Jesus acted against them.

Perhaps we do not need to proceed to discuss the power of Jesus to free Zacchaeus from sin. What needs to be discussed here is that a person cannot escape from being labelled and from the theological claims that tyrannise if we do not have enough courage to fight them. This is why the praxis of doing theology and having a religion is put in 'encounter' terminology.

Opposition to labelling takes place when religions discuss human reality and encounters give new spirit for life together. Thus I am convinced that sharing one year with Manto did not only form the religious and theological character of my wife and me, but also formed the religious and theological character of Ellexia, who is 4 years old at the time of writing. I hope that in the future she can understand why Manto lived with us and became a Maspaitella.

Chapter 12

MEETING POINT ON A DIFFERENT CORNER

Notes on Encounters in Makassar

Zainal Arifin Sandia

Mujahadah

A long time before the bloody conflict occurred, between 1991 and 1995, discussion groups about renewal of Muslim thought had wrestled with ideas, concepts, thinking and discourses on friendship, peace, inter-faith dialogue and even searched for meeting points between religions.

We never missed reading all types of literature, books, magazines and the opinions in the newspapers on these topics, and friends at university always discussed these subjects together. We really enjoyed these debates. As long as ideas made sense and could be logically sustained, they were well received. We particularly appreciated, honoured and respected subjects related to meaning and appreciated and trusted endeavours to find the truth.

We felt free to criticise all concepts, whether they came from an *ulama*; from thinkers and world-class intellectuals, who were well-known and respected by the Muslim community; from the text of a collection of stories about the Prophet (*hadis*); or even verses in the al-Quran, whether they were *dhanni* (open and can be understood by the mind) or *qath'i* (closed and cannot be understood by the mind).

At the same time, our openness towards our reading material led us to read ideas, concepts and writings of non-Muslim public figures. We carried this out without any intention of making comparisons to find the weaknesses and shortfalls in other religions. This did not interest us and we regarded any study that compared one religion with another to be a step backwards in the study of religions, considering that it would put an end to healthy dialogue between religious communities and would be very naive in creating space for acceptance of differing religious communities.

Openness to reading material about the thoughts and literature from different religions enriched our perspectives, ways of thinking and discourses about humanitarian themes, friendship, peace, inter-faith dialogue and the search for a meeting point between religions. We could discover a point of view and obtain a description of key concepts in other religions from insider sources that were authentic, competent and authoritative. Interestingly, we considered the reading of such sources more representative than reading a pile of literature with the same focus but written by outsiders. There are, of course, a few authors who have written quite well about a religion that is different from the beliefs they hold. They have allowed themselves to wander in their thinking and their religious experiences are usually quite rich, and they have overcome the partitions of different religions, but you can count the number of these debates on your fingers.

I came to realise that reading about and receiving a belief does not necessarily come just from the indoctrination of texts that claim to be 'holy'; it is more importantly and more decisively a process of experience and of comprehending these texts fully, applied in everyday life whether within communities or between different communities. In other words, a firm belief usually is tested by the experience of dialogue, discourse, spirituality, the practice of a religion and social interaction in everyday life.

Unfortunately, reading literature of a different religion often feels passive, lifeless and naive because the material tends to be a monologue, lacking the experience of an encounter in an interactive dialogue. There is quite a wide gap between the convictions of people based on the text of their 'holy books' and the practical experiences in everyday life. Questions arise, such as: Why should someone need to have a religion? Does someone not need to believe in a religion but still carry out the teaching of different religions? Can someone have more than one religion? What is the importance of claims of truth and claims of salvation for those who have a religion? Why is someone willing to die or be prepared to kill in the name of religion or God? These questions often bothered me when reading the long history of bloody conflict of religious communities.

A Blessing in Disguise

In 1999, a close friend introduced me to a Protestant minister (hereafter I will use the term 'Christian'); let's say he is called JP. After waiting for a long time we eventually found an opportunity. This became a joy in itself. This introduction provided the first steps towards an explanation of the mystery of the questions that had been bothering me for about five years.

JP was a lecturer at a theological college in Makassar. In students' circles, JP was known as someone who was open-minded, critical and independent. Besides being a lecturer, JP was also known as a female activist. JP was involved in many women's movements, at the local and national level. The combination of being an academic and activist gave JP a way of looking at her religious teaching and an attitude towards the religious communities and leaders or institutions of the Christian church that could, in many ways, be said to be special and against the mainstream. Because of her thinking, JP held a special place in the eyes of her students as an icon of Christian renewal in the university. I regarded JP as a Protestant who 'protested'.

Encounters with JP, from one opportunity to another, passed with colourful discussions in a relaxed but critical atmosphere. Our discussions were very varied, starting with the main religious teachings, the religious way of looking at things through to religious behaviour, both in Islam and Christianity. The whole process of our discussions was productive. It gave us the courage to criticise the ways, attitude and behaviour of conservative, conventional religion, which claimed to be taken for granted. After so many discussions, we came to the conclusion, that is, that religious matters were really very personal.

The institutionalising of religion with its many procedures loses the inclusive and accepting nature of a religion and changes it to become exclusive and resistant to other religions. Herein lies the root of the problem of certain religions that claim truth and salvation as their own property. The most extreme manifestations of these two claims are present in flying the flag in the name of religion and of God in bloody community unrest and war between religious communities.

Besides discourse, the quality and productivity of our encounters demonstrated our appreciation of each other's religious convictions. When we held discussions in her house, JP always reminded us to pray when the call to prayer reverberated. JP even provided prayer mats for us. If our prayer time was too short, JP would scold us, 'Why so quick?' This question prodded us and also criticised the way we worshipped as though it was like a package from the post office: regular, special or express.

It was the same during the fast month; JP prepared food for breaking the fast. I joked with JP about breaking the fast that it was written 'anyone who provides food for breaking the fast for someone who is fasting will obtain a reward the same as those who fast'. We laughed out loud because JP happily said that she received a reward from the two of us who broke our fast in her house. 'Two people fasted, so the reward is double. While the both of you will only get a single reward each for fasting', added JP.

Our closeness and trust are not enough to explain the process of change that occurred between us. It was not enough to feel like individuals who had a basudara relationship although we were not from the same blood line. We felt that our togetherness was not limited to just being friends, but was like that of members of the same family, although we were not related. We could be open and share with each other, talking about things that included personal matters.

Through JP I eventually got to know a number of Christian ministers and theological students. We even tried to translate the ideas and concepts born out of our encounters into practical actions, such as strengthening awareness to accept differences, and to build peace and uphold social justice. More than that, a call to moral responsibility and an intellectual restlessness in developing our practical action mission was channelled through a new community that was then growing and developing – that is, the South Sulawesi Dialogue Forum (Forlog SulSel).

Forlog evolved to become a self-supporting movement that worked to spread encounters between inter-faith communities, both on a small scale (internal amongst members) or large scale (encompassing sympathisers).

The Movement

The energetic activities of Forlog were picked up by SA, a woman who was a graduate of a master's program at a well-known university in Chicago, America. She then recommended it to BC, who had studied with her, and who was working in Indonesia. SA appointed JP to meet with BC in Makassar, his new place of ministry. Through JP I eventually got to meet BC. BC was a priest, an Indonesian, who had lived for a long time overseas (the Philippines and America). Naturally, he found several words in Indonesian quite difficult to pronounce. Eventually we learned to accept the fact that our new friend spoke a mixture of Indonesian and English, as a result of being cross-cultural.

BC was a humble, sensitive, critical and open-minded person. His experiences in strengthening awareness of pluralism and peace in the Philippines and America made it easy for him to adapt to the Forlog dynamics. The presence of BC gave me new opportunities in my struggle for an inter-faith dialogue. The dialogue widened to include Protestants and Catholics. We had rich discussions about religious experiences. Along with this, the productivity and quality of our meetings improved with the emergence of ideas about how to 'spread' experiences of different religions in the joint area together with the students. Thus the idea of the Sharing for Peace activities was introduced.

How would Sharing for Peace be organised? We held several meetings to discuss this in the houses of JP and BC. As far as I can remember, we had about seven meetings to talk about the aims, output, outcome, methods, approach and direction of the activities. The intensity and quality of the meetings consumed our energy, strength and thinking. It was tiring because we dreamed of the best or were too involved in our own personal contests. We questioned what we were doing. Why had we become so serious about what we were doing? There was no intention of any proselytising from any party: Islam, Protestant Christianity or Catholicism. In our minds, we only had good intentions and strong convictions about developing peace and strengthening awareness of accepting differences. The most serious matter that we debated was our lack of knowledge about the religious experiences of the prospective participants, which we were sure would be various and unique. How could we share these experiences honestly and openly with other prospective participants without burdening them?

Eventually we agreed to formulate a series of questions in stages to control the level of tolerance, which could be moderated around very personal and sensitive matters. Questions such as, how did they feel about the phenomena of stigmatising a person from a different religious background, labelling them as 'heathen' and saying they would be bound for hell? Or, what was their opinion about bloody community unrest, war and suicide bombing being carried out in the name of religion and God? Or, can we justify and accept that family members can have different religions but all go to heaven? These questions were very sensitive and very personal in nature. But these questions were very important and necessary to discover the religious experiences and potential for encounters, where all participants could be honest, sincere and trust each other. This had to be tried, because this was the process of internalising experience.

Amazing! The process of encounters in the Sharing for Peace program went really well. Worries about sensitivity, suspicion and religious offence proved baseless, as the activities took place with a happiness that was very moving. The participants seemed very enthusiastic to share and listen carefully to each other's stories. The process of asking questions, so that they could fully comprehend what they were listening to, took place while the stories were being told. This was a new experience and was meaningful because they could listen to the religious experiences of people from different religious backgrounds and evaluate 'misleading claims', while developing an understanding of religious teaching.

Participants were students from different religious backgrounds (Islam, Protestant Christianity and Catholicism) who were courageously honest, open and sincere in recalling their religious experiences, including areas that they had previously regarded as very sensitive and personal. The amazing thing was that this process of sharing experiences continued in their rooms until they were overcome by sleep. The rooms were organised so that encounters would take place between participants of different religious backgrounds.

All of us who were actively involved in the three-day Sharing for Peace activities also felt very enlightened with the process of sharing religious experiences. From each participant, we learned many different lessons, which were very rich, varied and unique. All of this added to our treasury and further confirmed our choice to consistently try to empower and strengthen awareness of accepting differences in religion, culture, tribe and ethnicity as something that is given, a certainty (*sunnatullah*).

Spiritual Feast

Our bonds of friendship grew very close. Quite out of the blue, BC expressed his desire to attend the Friday prayers. Initially, we doubted his intentions, but eventually we decided to go to the mosque together to attend the Friday prayers. After the prayers were over, many of the congregation shook hands with BC. We didn't understand why this happened because the local people knew that BC was a priest and leader of the Catholic CICM community, The Stem, located across the road from the mosque. We also never asked why BC wanted to attend the Friday prayers. BC had only asked if it was allowed.

I experienced something similar. I once asked BC if I could attend the mass (English service) that he led. 'Who forbids someone from entering the Lord's house?' asked BC. I was very pleased and enthusiastically attended mass several times, including a funeral, a Sunday service and Christmas, at the Cathedral in Makassar. I was very proud of this experience. Since then I have felt no difficulty in attending mass. I even got to know several priests, nuns and Catholics in the Cathedral. I never once worried that my faith as a Muslim would be damaged or shaken, or even that I might have to make the choice to change my religion to Catholicism. What crossed my mind was how many Muslims have experienced what I have experienced?

After attending mass a few times, I discovered many things which were also taught in Islam. 'These are universal values', I concluded. I remembered BC's question, 'Who forbids someone from entering the Lord's house?' I wanted to ask the same when entering a Buddhist or Hindu temple at some point. Amen. I have remained a devout Muslim, not only in name but also in practice.

Chapter 13

DEVELOPING PEACE WHEN DIALOGUE BECAME DEAD-LOCKED

Abidin Wakano

Dusk on Eid Al Fitr, 19 January 1999, found me with friends who were members of the coordinating body of HMI Sulawesi, relaxing together in our secretariat while watching TV. Suddenly one of the TV stations broadcast news that community unrest had erupted in Ambon, with scores of houses burnt down. I was taken aback and rushed to find the closest telephone kiosk to telephone Ambon. I could not contact any of the five telephone numbers I tried, including the number of the Provincial Regional Religious Affairs office, where my father worked. I became more and more angry.

Finally, at about 7pm, I was able to contact one of my relatives who lived in Batu Merah. When I asked him about the community unrest, he wept. He told me, 'Ambon has been destroyed. We are at war, Muslims against those Christians. Please pray for us'. I couldn't speak except to say that I would pray for them and ask them to be careful.

The next day, the issue of community unrest in Ambon had changed to the issue of the expulsion and slaughter of the people from Buton, Bugis, Makassar (BBM). This issue also made the situation in Makassar become tense. It was not only the Christians who came from Maluku but also we Muslims from Maluku who became anxious, worried in case the issue became an ethnic conflict. Not long after that, the issue of community unrest became an issue of conflict between Islam and Christianity.

A Division in Acts of Humanitarian Solidarity

Because religious conflict was such a sensitive issue, the community unrest in Ambon quickly spread to other regencies in Maluku. The Province of North Maluku which had just been separated from the province of Maluku also suffered. Waves of refugees from Maluku to Makassar were uncontrolled. It was made worse when tens of thousands of people evacuated to save themselves, and university students and school children escaped to Makassar to continue their education. This prompted people from a number of social groups in Makassar to act in solidarity, creating coordination centres to accommodate the refugees.

These coordination centres were varied. Some were based on humanitarian values with no regard to the religious background of the refugees, but others provided help for refugees of particular religions. The majority of Makassarese are Muslim, thus the majority of refugees who arrived in the city were Muslims. In addition, most were ethnically Buginese or Makassarese. The collective memory about the racial and religious conflict in Poso in 1998, in addition to the provocative rumours about religion, meant that most coordination centres were created for Muslim refugees only.

The division of acts of humanitarian solidarity along religious lines could not be separated from the sociological, political and theological backgrounds. The sociological factor was strong because the majority of refugees were Muslim. There was also a political factor because there was provocation from certain groups, who wanted to make political and economic gains. Finally, a theology, which was divisive and exclusive in nature, regarded the community unrest as a religious war (*jihad*) to oppose the infidels and caused people to neglect humanitarian values.

The tension and polarisation caused by the community unrest in Maluku had an impact nationally. Calls to support the Muslims in Maluku, in the form of material aid and prayer, came from different communities in almost every area in Indonesia. Similar things happened in areas where Christians were in the majority. The polarisation between 'us' and 'them' distorted the meaning of genuine humanitarian values. A strong impression emerged that if a person was not one of 'us', that person was a lesser human being, who could be punished or murdered. In such conditions, Christian and Muslim organisations were often trapped into narrow polarisation and lost their humanitarian vision.

Social organisations were also not free from these polarisations. An anti-Christian sentiment drove a number of youth and student organisations to conduct identity card checks, especially among those people who came from Maluku and Poso. If they came across a person with an identity card which indicated that someone was a Christian, the person was beaten up or held hostage. They regarded this as a manifestation of Muslim solidarity (*ukhuwah Islamiyah*) towards Muslim brothers in Maluku. It was also meant to pressure Christians in Maluku to stop the slaughter. In fact, both Muslims and Christians suffered in the conflict.

These identity checks caused deep fear and trauma, especially in children. The economic and educational activities of Christians in Makassar and the surrounding areas was paralysed. The fate of the Christian community became uncertain.

Breaking the Deadlock in Dialogue in the Name of Genuine Humanitarian Acts

Hardly anyone at that time was prepared to defend the Christian minority against these identity checks. Dialogue and religious encounters were almost at a dead-end. Eventually a number of religious leaders, humanitarian activists and intellectuals expressed concern and questioned this practice. They raised the following questions. First, why should we commit violence against Christians in Makassar? What have they done wrong? Second, aren't the Christian refugees from Maluku, now living in Makassar, also victims and haven't they suffered as much as the Muslim refugees? And third, violent acts perpetrated against the Christian minority in Makassar not only contradict basic Muslim values, but also contradict the principles of human rights and the principles contained in the Pancasila.

Besides making appeals to the community, these prominent community leaders also put pressure on the state, especially the security forces, to carry out their constitutional duty. Their duty was to protect every citizen, whether living in Maluku or in Makassar.

In the midst of this all, I chose to join the inter-faith humanitarian solidarity movement. At that time, I considered that defending the innocent and the oppressed, regardless of their religion, was an obligation. As a Muslim from Maluku, and in the midst of waves of solidarity for Muslims in Maluku, this was a very delicate choice.

My inter-faith friends and I then started conducting dialogues and encounters to reduce the provocation that took place when identity checks were made. First, we built a pro-peace network among activists in social organisations, like HMI, the Indonesian Muslim Student Movement (PMII) and

Muhammadiyah Student Union (IMM); second, we appealed for peace and the stopping of identity checks through mass media, stickers and banners; and third, we tried to direct solidarity for Maluku to send aid, like staple foods and medicines. We also tried to help the process of transferring students and pupils to universities and schools in Makassar and to find scholarships for students and pupils who were victims of the conflict.

The inter-faith humanitarian solidarity movement continued until the South Sulawesi Dialogue Forum (Forlog) in 2000. Through Forlog, dialogue to cultivate peace in the province of South Sulawesi began to be developed. It was also developed through encounters among various inter-faith, racial and national communities. In the middle of the politicising and polarising of religion, as a result of community unrest occurring in Maluku and Poso, I resolved to become an oasis for all people (*Rahmatan lil 'Alamin*). In Forlog, my friends and I brought together Muslim and Christian students from Maluku, something that was very difficult at that time. This took place through activities such as breaking the fast together, discussions, joint inter-religious lectures, joint reflections and informal meetings, like visiting each other's digs.

Efforts to become a bridge and an oasis for all people in the midst of that situation, of course, were not easy. I was often labelled 'infidel' and was accused of many things like 'not being consistent in the struggle for Islam', 'a hypocrite', and 'an apostate, who could be justifiably murdered'. Quite often I was terrorised. But for me, this step was a manifestation of the spirit of my *jihad* to defend humanity. When we faced challenges like this, my friends and I never gave up, even though we were sometimes frightened.

Alhamdulillah, the dialogues and encounters we carried out and publicised had quite a positive impact, although on a small scale. At least they reduced the tension and overwhelming suspicion, which had been caused by the identity checks and other acts of violence. The dialogue and inter-faith encounter experiences in Makassar also opened a new chapter in dialogue and inter-faith encounters at various levels, starting from: (1) dialogues about life, which discussed common concerns; (2) social dialogues, discussing social issues such as poverty and inequality, including thinking about the contributions from different religions; (3) monastic dialogues, like an exchange in religious experiences in the form of meditation or live-in retreats; and (4) theological dialogues, exchanging information about beliefs, including discussing similarities and differences.

Fermenting Friendships to Build Genuine Peace

If the situation in Makassar felt quite critical, imagine what the situation was like in Ambon, as the centre of the community unrest and violence. One serious problem in the middle of the conflict, especially in the 1999-2001 period, was the resistance to peace and reconciliation, because most people were experiencing a high level of emotional tension. Anger and revenge led the Muslim and Christian communities to attack each other, sacrificing thousands of lives and almost destroying civil society.

Instead of thinking about peace, in a situation like this, the two conflicting groups only think about of how to survive and be safe, or to attack and win. These tendencies led most segments of the community to contribute to the war – whether in towns or in villages, men or women, or even children, who were known as the *Agas* and the *Linggis* gangs. Religious organisations, social organisations and youth organisations were not immune from efforts to mobilise mobs to go to war. If someone talked about peace or urged people to work for peace, he or she was considered a traitor or not faithful enough to fight for their religion.

This was the challenge my friends and I faced. Hasbollah Toisuta, my senior and my friend who had at that time returned to Ambon after completing his master's degree in Makassar, experienced even greater challenges. As a preacher who held the values of pluralism high, he often faced psychological and social challenges, even death threats. He was often pressured to not speak about peace, because this would weaken the position of the Muslim community.

Hasbollah felt that if we didn't stop the war, when would we be able to live in peace? He asked, didn't the Al-Quran command us to live in peace and command us not exceed certain limitations, especially regarding the wounding and killing of fellow creatures created by God? He added, aren't people who are different from us also part of what God has determined (*sunnatullah*) that we cannot avoid? When almost everyone, including prominent religious leaders, did not want to talk about or appeal for peace because of their resentment, desire for revenge or pressure, Hasbollah was determined to fight for peace. For him this was part of *jihad*. When he was asked by the Imam of the Al-Fatah Mosque, Ambon, K.H. Ahmad Bantam, and Governor at that time, Dr. M. Saleh Latuconsina, to deliver the sermon on Eid al-Adha at the Al-Fatah Mosque, Ambon, the largest mosque in Maluku, he used the opportunity to deliver a message of peace. Though it was very difficult and full of risks, he courageously carried out this task. Then, when the poster announcing the Eid al-Adha prayers with Hasbollah Toisuta as the preacher was posted in front of the Al-Fatah Mosque several days before the event, he received threats and pressure not to preach about reconciliation and peace. However, because he was committed from the beginning, he called for the importance of reconciliation and peace in his sermon. After that, he and his family were often threatened and put under pressure.

From that time onwards, groups that did not want peace or had different perspectives on peace – such as those who wanted to continue attacks until the enemy surrendered and asked for peace – tried to stop Hasbollah's efforts in different ways, including trying to discredit him. But, as time went on, support for my friend from all levels of society increased. The desire for peace and hope began to emerge. Ideas supporting reconciliation and peace began to flow and become a collective strength. Deadlock, fear and panic began to subside. The way to dialogue and encounters began to open up.

As close friends, Hasbollah and I often discussed and shared information, although it was more often by email and telephone. At that time, I was still studying for my master's degree at IAIN Alauddin Makassar. Our communication continued when I went on to study for my doctorate at UIN Sunan Kalijaga in Jogjakarta.

At the end of 2002, when I was on holiday in Ambon to celebrate Eid Al Fitr, I met with Hasbollah. He introduced me to several colleagues, including the members of the coordinating body of HMI Maluku. Through my good friend, the members of the coordinating body of HMI Maluku asked me to be a speaker at the get-together (*Halal bi Halal*) between HMI and KAHMI Maluku. I was asked to talk about the meaning of friendship (*silaturahmi*) in developing genuine peace in Maluku. My good friend was convinced that I could utilise this momentum as much as possible, to share experience and knowledge and to fight for humanity. He calmed me down so that I wasn't afraid of anyone and said that God would protect me. His words convinced me to carry out my obligations. This was the first time I appeared in public in Ambon to spread the values of pluralism and humanitarianism in Maluku.

In 2003, Hasbollah, together with fellow lecturers from IAIN Ambon and graduates from Pattimura University, went on to do further study in both the masters and doctorate programs in Jogjakarta. At that time, I was already studying for my doctorate at UIN Sunan Kalijaga and working at the Dian Institute / Interfidei Jogjakarta, the first inter-faith NGO in Indonesia. Our meetings in Jogjakarta strengthened our communication. We were no longer alone, because many Muslim, Protestant and Catholic friends from Maluku, who were studying in Jogjakarta, became involved.

We therefore formed a community which we called the Tali Rasa (Emotional Ties) Community. In 2005, in Jogjakarta we held a meeting of all the village chiefs from Maluku to develop peace. Almost 200 village chiefs from most of the traditional villages in Maluku attended this meeting. This activity was run by the Tali Rasa Community together with the Moluccan Young People, Pupils and Students Association (IKAPELAMAKU). We also documented our discussions and struggles in a book with the title *Nasionalisme Kaum Pinggiran: Dari Maluku, tentang Maluku, untuk Indonesia* (The Nationalism of the Marginalised: From Maluku, about Maluku, for Indonesia) published by LKiS Jogjakarta (2004).

Based on my experiences at Forlog Makassar (1999–2002) and Dian Interfidei Jogjakarta (2002–2007), I was then invited to join the Inter-Faith Organisation in Maluku (LAIM), one of the first inter-faith organisations in Maluku established by MUI Maluku, the Synod of GPM and the Amboina diocese. LAIM had quite a significant role in developing inter-faith dialogue and ending the deadlock in the relationships between religions in Maluku, especially between Islam and Christianity. The process of how I got involved with LAIM also made a deep impression on me. I was impressed by people's courage and trust in developing dialogue and cooperation.

When the situation flared up again in 2003, a minister from the GPM Synod (Rev. Jacky Manuputty) contacted me and asked me to join LAIM. At that time Jacky and I were not as close as we are now. He asked me to manage of the LAIM program. He said that this had been agreed by the GPM Synod, MUI and the Amboina diocese. He also added that, although I was still studying in Jogjakarta, I could help by contributing ideas.

One day Jacky informed me that he wanted to visit Jogjakarta and visit me at Dian Interfidei. This visit made a deep impression on me. He came without seeming to carry a burden, with sincerity and a clear conscience to develop genuine friendship. Without beating about the bush he immediately said, 'Abid, finish your studies, don't take too long. If you have any difficulties let me and our friends know. Who knows, we might be able to help'.

The fact that the Muslim and Christian communities in Maluku lived separate lives and still attacked each other didn't shake Jacky's intent in extending a hand in friendship. He came as a brother with a clear conscience to share the hope of peace, although his heart was torn to pieces by grief caused by the human tragedy in our land. He always emphasised that there was a need for dialogue between the religions because it was that realm that often experienced 'bleeding' when there was tension. As we witnessed, Muslims and Christians murdered each other, because of the struggle for power and livelihood. The situation got worse because dialogue in the social realms of religion was deadlocked and religious leaders were caught up in this situation.

Jacky's statement was true; the roots of the Muslim and Christian conflict in Maluku lay in injustice, power struggles, the destruction of social capital, and symbolic-formalistic religious patterns. All of these problems had been going on for a long time. It was these latent problems that caused conflict to erupt into community unrest, delete triggered by a fight between a Christian minibus driver and a Muslim thug in the market. Until now, these problems had been settled using the security stability approach of the New Order. This resulted in surface harmony, while the roots of the problem were allowed to rot.

In the middle of these problems, LAIM's endeavours to develop peace and begin dialogue and encounters weren't easy. The mission of pluralism and humanitarianism that this organisation supported, to develop peace and genuine friendship in Maluku, faced very big challenges. Pluralism has been labelled as a western product that is Christian and colonial – it was thus a huge challenge to sow its seeds in Muslim circles. MUI issued a *fatwa* (binding rule) that forbade pluralism because pluralism was regarded as syncretistic and relative in nature. In the end, the pluralism movement that we supported was regarded very suspiciously.

Even so, our resolve to fight for the values of pluralism, humanitarianism and peace never subsided. LAIM carried out several breakthrough dialogues and encounters, through activities such as peace sermons and live-ins, where Muslim participants stayed in the homes of Christian families, and conversely, Christian participants stayed in the homes of Muslim families. We did this in the spirit of reintegrating society that at that time was segregated. Various other breakthroughs included dialogue sessions that we carried out in houses of worship. For example, we would invite a minister or priest to speak at a mosque and, in reverse, a Muslim would speak in a church. I was often invited either as a participant or a speaker. LAIM even cooperated with Dian Interfidei, Jogjakarta and ICRP (Indonesia Conference on Religion and Peace), Jakarta, to organise an Asia-Pacific inter-faith youth conference. We held the closing meeting at the Jami' Mosque, one of the oldest mosques in Ambon. The process towards the closing ceremony was full of colourful dialogues that were interesting because they included the pros and cons of various matters, whether theological or political. My colleagues and I were accused of being apostate, liberal and syncretistic, and so on.

Although it was difficult and full of challenges, we kept going and the dialogue relationship between religions was slowly beginning to form. LAIM started a new chapter in dialogue and religious encounters in Maluku. There is no record of dialogues and religious encounters, until those, which occurred after the 1999 conflict. Previous encounters and dialogues had only taken place in the cultural realm, such as the cultural relationships of Pela, Gandong, *Larvul Ngabal*, etc. The religious realm had become polarised by political interests and strong divisive religious ideologies.

We hoped that through the inter-faith activities we carried out in mosques and churches, which until then had been command centres for war and targets for destruction, these places could return to being the centres of civilisation for the peace movement, functioning as they should, as places for intensive training in faith and morals for followers. Besides this, the mosques and the churches could develop partnerships in facing many types of social problems. The results have been quite significant. Many endeavours to create dialogue and intense encounters between religious leaders and organisations have now emerged.

It must be acknowledged that there are still many difficult problems, like the problem of social segregation, the loss of mutual trust and the stigmatisation of Muslims as 'terrorists' and Christians as 'RMS separatists'. This stereotyping was imbedded so deeply, that it became a kind of 'imaginary enemy', an obstacle in the Muslim-Christian relationship in Maluku. Any struggle to build peace between the two communities must, therefore, overcome these stigmas and stereotypes to build mutual trust. There is a high amount of resistance in both the Muslim and the Christian communities.

Politicised religion became a challenge in the efforts to disseminate pluralism, especially because the social segregation between Muslims and Christians made it easier to polarise and exploit people in the name of religion. The notion of pluralism in the context of social reintegration for peace in Maluku was regarded as without political benefit. The struggle to disseminate pluralism was often obstructed in the name of religious interests, by members of religious communities. In addition, a polarised situation was sometimes cultivated to maintain the solidarity of the group.

People often ask me, 'Why do you fight for pluralism in Maluku? What do you get out of it? Isn't committing *jihad* in the battlefield more glorious?' I believe that pluralism is not created by humans; but rather it is God's will, God's design. Therefore, rejecting or violently destroying the reality of plural living is a clear act of faithlessness. Putting an end to violence in a violent manner only causes greater violence. Religious teaching instructs that the most beneficial solution to prevent destruction is acting in a wise, sound and peaceful manner. If we are forced to act violently, it should never be in a manner that is over the limit (*la ta'tadu*). The fiqih norm states that destruction cannot remove other forms of destruction (*al-dhororu la yuzalu bi al-dhorori*). Syariat Islam in its doctrine and practice strongly reveres humanitarian values, such as those taught in the concept of *al-kulliyahal-khamsah*, whose five universal principles are: (1) guarding the freedom of religion (*hifdz al-din*); (2) protecting the continuity of life *(hifdz al-nafs)*; (3) guaranteeing the continuity of descendants (*hifdz al-nasl*); (4) protecting possessions (*hifdz al-mal*); and (5) guaranteeing creative thinking, freedom of expression, and expressing an opinion *(hifdz al-'aql)*.

Peace and pluralism as part of the mission of religions should be delivered to the general public, not just to groups that are in favour of pluralism and peace, but especially to other groups that are different, including groups that reject it. Here the mosque and the church have important roles as centres for the movement of disseminating pluralism and peace. The fight for peace and pluralism has to be understood not only to overcome and get rid of conflict, but also as a relationship of diversity in the bonds of genuine civilisation. Here the basudara idea of living side-by-side in basudara relationships becomes important. In the wisdom of the Moluccan people, '*potong di kuku rasa di daging*', '*ale rasa beta rasa*,' '*sagu salempeng dipatah dua*'.

Part III

Hena Masa Waya: Village above the Water

Chapter 14

A POLICY OF RESTORING PEACE OF MIND

M.J. Papilaja

A violent conflict always leads to a rise in the level of emotion, sadism, hatred, revenge, as well as other forms of anger. All of these are expressions of feelings of people who have been involved in, heard about, experienced or were present during violent conflict. The people of Ambon experienced this when the violent conflict reached its peak from 1999–2001, and it was still felt until 2003 when the civil emergency status that had been in place throughout Maluku was lifted. With the people of Ambon in such an emotional state, Syarif Hadler and I were appointed as Mayor and Deputy Mayor on 4 August 2001. From 1999–2001, the two of us were mandated, as members of the Ambon Regional Legislative Assembly (DPRD). I became the Chair of the Assembly and Syarif Hadler was the Chair of the United Development Party Fraction of that Assembly.

To lead a city that was in physical and, more particularly, psychological chaos required wisdom when choosing an appropriate strategy. There was a high risk of failure when trying to restore peace of mind and mend the bleeding hearts of the people of Ambon. Our strategic choices were taken because the system and dynamics of the city could not be rebuilt if the people were still yearning for blood and were full of emotion. This choice of strategy, however, also ran a high risk of failing in the mayor's five-year term of office, which might not be long enough for any physical improvements in the city of Ambon to be made at all. But if we didn't start with restoring peace to the hearts of people of Ambon, the rebuilding of the physical city and the system of running the city would easily be damaged by simple provocation.

Therefore, the two of us agreed and were determined to start with restoring peace of mind.

The process of restoring peace of mind wasn't easy because we had to make many choices: what should be a priority? Where should we start, or which segment of the community should we start with? Which locations and which groups should be our target? Early failure would have a negative impact on future success – how should we tackle it? Who should be the people to restore peace of mind to the people of the city? Which social instruments should be applied? What should the government and the politicians do (city, provincial, or central government)? These questions were our first tasks as Mayor and Deputy Mayor. There was a whole string of episodes that preceded various social dynamics, that the two of us went through together, and some I experienced alone before I took office in Ambon Town Hall.

I

Starting in 1999, processes and efforts towards stopping the conflict involved a group of public leaders from different religious backgrounds in an initiative called Team 19, which consisted of high- and middle-ranking army and police officers, both from Maluku and from outside Maluku. Two groups of youth leaders from the Christian and Muslim communities who lived in Ambon were also formed, each consisting of twelve people. The Christian group of twelve often met in my rented home in the Benteng area or in the Diocesan complex. Every time we met, the Christian (Protestant and Catholic) leaders, or those who were regarded as leaders, always discussed what could be done so no other location was burnt down and nobody else died. To this end, we each communicated with our different networks, whether it was friends in our communities or in the Muslim communities, armed forces/police, or other networks. Several of the networks became connected.

This complicated process took time. It can't be denied that some of these connections broke down and some people had 'strange thoughts', some political and some economic. This made sense. It was part of human nature: everyone needed to make a living. But because differences began to surface, the group meetings became less frequent, even coming to a halt. If a meeting took place it was face-to-face, or with just a few people and the full group was not summoned together as had previously happened. This was due to differences of opinion about how to solve the conflict. Some of them urged that a radical movement was needed. As the conflict had been going for a long time, there were many victims and much loss of possession which had affected almost half the people of Ambon and its surroundings. To avoid being offensive, patience and soft methods were needed.

From the dynamics of the Group of 12 meetings, I made some notes: (1) conflict that is long lasting will systematically destroy social-emotional defence; (2) in every conflict there are always parties who try to use the opportunity for economic, social, or political interests; and (3) suspicion within the group and the tendency to use each other also occurs. This shows that whatever efforts to restore peace of mind for the people of the city, various interests also need to be taken into account. If that is so, as the government, what should we do? All people want to feel safe and secure in their environment, as their main desire, so that they are free to choose what they want to do to obtain economic, social or political benefit. In this context, when I started my term as mayor the first thing I had to do to reduce the emotional tension was to invite all elements of the society to return to their true identity as Ambonese, who were all brothers and sisters. I did this so that people would begin to think rationally and were not easily provoked. The methods employed when I was mayor are explained below.

II

The inauguration of the Mayor and Deputy Mayor (4 August 2001) was coloured by demonstrations in front of the Al-Fatah mosque by people who were unsatisfied with the result of the mayoral election (they also demonstrated against the results of the election in front of the Home Office). While the demonstration was taking place, a number of groups attacked the demonstrators, so the demonstration was dispersed. This incident sent a message that the pro-contra in society was not just between communities, but also within the communities themselves.

In the context of restoring peace of mind to the people of the city, this incident was a signal that there was a possibility of moving towards peace. In one religious-based community, there were those who were for and those who were against the new leadership in Ambon, even though they came from a different religious background to that of the group. This meant that, in spite of emotional political bonds, there was a group who were courageous enough to defend the new leadership in Ambon, the mayor (a Christian) and the deputy mayor (a Muslim). Politically, the message in a community experiencing social division was that the just division of political power was important and strategic in the framework of social reconstruction, leading to a dynamic and socially healthy society.

The first days in office in the town hall, as is usual for new government officials, were spent visiting the different departments within the city hall complex and also the offices that were situated in other parts of the city. The atmosphere in these different settings was not the same. The civil servants who worked in the offices in the city hall, which was located between the residential areas of the two religious communities, consisted of civil servants who were both Christian and Muslim. In the offices of the city government located elsewhere, generally within a residential area of one of the religious communities, we found that the civil servants tended to be from the same religious background as the community where the office was located.

The working atmosphere of the civil servants in the two locations, that is, those located in the city hall and those located away from the city hall, seemed very different. This was evident in the body language of the civil servants in each case. Those civil servants who worked in the city hall seemed tense and did not seem to trust each other. The way they stood (because there were no chairs in the office) or sat was always in a group with people from the same religious background. The interaction between civil servants of different religious backgrounds while they were doing their work seemed to be very stilted. The very opposite could be said of those civil servants who worked in offices outside of the city hall, where the work atmosphere was more dynamic, because all the civil servants were from the same religious background.

The working atmosphere manifested by the civil servants of the Ambon city government reflected the social situation experienced by the citizens of Ambon. A guarded attitude, tending towards feelings of suspicion, revenge, even possibly hatred, still coloured the relationships between groups of citizens from different religious backgrounds. Nevertheless, there were a small number of staff and members of the general public who were relatively more open in the way they communicated with those from a different religious background. For me, social conditions such as these represented a challenge and also an opportunity. Therefore, I had to manage the challenge so that it would turn into an opportunity to reduce the social emotional tension, so that the road to peace in the city of Ambon would be laid out before us. I had to commence with the environment closest to me, that is, the civil servants. They had to become agents of peace in their own environments. But how should we start and which issue was most appropriate to start with?

The first thing that went through my mind was: what are the needs of these civil servants? There were many different answers, starting with feeling safe at work, an appropriate salary, promotion, and answers that were linked to the needs of each family, whether it be a house (for those who were still refugees) or schools for the children. I focused my attention on the needs directly connected to the workplace, that is, feeling safe at work, improvement in the salaries of the employees, and the pattern set for promotion.

Improvement in the work environment had to start with the leader of each department, because they were the ones who were closest to the employees. If there were still psychological constraints influencing the head of a department, then all the measures in the workplace would be viewed subjectively. Measures that were regarded as subjective, especially by those of a different religious persuasion, would make the employees distance themselves from one another, especially if they were from a different religious background.

The first step was to eradicate psychological barriers between heads of departments of different religions. The method I used was to invite all heads of departments to the mayor's residence every Friday night to relax and sing songs. Each head of department was required to attend and also to sing a song. Besides singing, we also played billiards and dominoes. This went on for about two months and the stilted atmosphere that was originally felt between the heads of departments began to thaw and even disappear. As a result, the communication between heads of departments, which had tended to be stilted because of psychological barriers, started to become fluent. The *esprit de corps* of the departmental units started to develop. Together with the development of this *esprit de corps*, twice a month on Friday mornings volleyball and football competitions between the different departments were held. As a result, the earlier patterns of sitting together in groups according to religious backgrounds started to change. Eventually there was hardly any awkwardness between the employees.

In addition to the efforts to create a conducive working atmosphere, we tried to find a way to increase the employees' salaries. We adopted the policy of putting an end to the project honoraria, which until then had only been received by the heads of the projects, heads of departments, chief executive officer, deputy mayor and the mayor. The total budget for the honoraria for all the projects was divided equally among all the employees and called the Public Service Allowance. In addition, a transport allowance was given to people who didn't use official transport.

The policy of providing a transport allowance was to stop employees from having to use their relatively small salaries to pay for their travel to and from the office. The employees' salaries could thus be used to provide for their family's needs. Other decisions linked to the improvement of the employees' welfare included the provision of official uniforms – previously they had to buy their own uniforms.

These policies to improve the employees' welfare helped relieve the financial burden on the employees and their families. By alleviating the economic burden and providing an increasingly conducive work situation, the psychological constraints experienced as a result of the conflict was alleviated, not just for the individual employees only, but also in the employees' family and social environment.

After providing a more conducive work situation and improving the employees' salaries, we turned our attention to the matter of promotion. This was a very critical area in managing government in Ambon because one of the issues that stood out in the social conflict was the domination of a certain religious group in the bureaucracy in Maluku, whether at the Governor's office, Pattimura University, or the Mayor's office. So that this sensitive area could be managed well, Mr Syarif Hadler and I held discussions to determine our guiding principles.

We agreed that all positions in the bureaucracy, apart from the position of mayor and deputy mayor, are career appointments, so that any political or subjective considerations would be down the list and not the main considerations. Because these appointments were related to the career structure, there needed to be recruitment system for officials based on competency. A Mayor's Decree was issued relating to the standards of competence related to positions. The standard of competence for these positions, from the Chief Executive Officer to the lowest echelon positions, was to be determined by conditions of rank and skills, according to the main functions and duty of each position.

Once a standard of competence was established, recruitment would take place according to the standards set for each position. In the stages of this recruitment, we worked in cooperation with the School of Further Education in State Administration (STPDN) to recruit heads of departments and heads of sections. One consideration for choosing STPDN, and not Pattimura University or the University of Indonesia, was to avoid suspicion about the results of the recruitment. The recruitment process continued and was open to the general public and reported by the printed media and TVRI Ambon. This transparent recruitment process produced competent heads of departments from the available civil servants, and, most importantly, parties didn't feel they were overlooked or that others were given special treatment. This process reduced the impression of subjectivity and suspicion concerning the placement of certain people in certain positions and led, in turn, to healing the wounds to social psychology caused by the organisation's problems.

After the heads of departments were installed, the next stage in recruiting officials was to fill the next level below the heads of department. The process of filling the lower positions was handed to the heads of departments who proposed two people who met the conditions for all the positions in his or her department. These proposals became a test of whether the heads of departments were really objective or not. What happened when these people were nominated was very pleasing and added new energy to the process of restoring peace of mind to the people of the city.

During this process, one head of department among the 23 departments proposed people for positions within his department who were from a religious background different to his. Amongst those positions there were 4 echelon III positions and about 14 echelon IV positions. At that time, the head of department who proposed these people had asked permission to go for family reasons to his village, where there was no mobile phone reception so we were unable to communicate with him, which created difficulties. Mr Syarif Hadler, the Chief Executive Officer and I were forced to wait until he returned for an explanation about the proposals he had made.

After about a week, the head of department came back to the office. We asked him to explain why all the names he had proposed were from the same religious background, which, differed from his own background, when there was one employee from his religious background who, in terms of rank, would have met the conditions. The head of department answered that he simply wanted to succeed in his job, so he only wanted to select staff that were capable and wanted to work, without heed to ethnic or religious background. His reply startled and moved me. Deep down I immediately shouted … we have succeeded in restoring peace of mind to the staff …!

III

Alongside the process of restoring peace of mind among the staff in the city government, we also held a special meeting with members of the Ambon Consultative Assembly and members of the Provincial Consultative Assembly who represented Ambon, so that our politician friends were also on the right track in the mission to put an end to the conflict.

Linking with politicians in the process of restoring peace to the people of the city was also a strategy, because political support for public policies was greatly needed. With their political and social networks, the members of the consultative assembly could also function as agents for peace. Meeting after meeting took place in the mayor's office, to unite our perceptions about the political steps we needed to take together.

We were not all of the same opinion in our discussions about facts and issues. We differed on a number of issues and facts but we agreed that different and sensitive issues would be ignored for a while, to prioritise a united spirit in stopping violence. Eventually we agreed to meet high-ranking national officials to talk about solving the conflict in Ambon, in particular, and in Maluku, in general. So Mr Syarif Hadler and I, together with 35 members of the Ambon consultative assembly and five members of the Provincial consultative assembly representing Ambon, went to Jakarta on a 'peace safari', meeting the Chairman of the House of Representatives, Akbar Tanjung, the Coordinating Minister for Political, Legal and Security Affairs, Susilo Bambang Yudhoyono, and President Megawati Soekarnoputri.

The main topic of discussion in the meetings with the national leaders was the disclosure of what was really happening in the field in Ambon. A number of policies for ending the conflict by central government were not implemented in the field, because of the inaccurate disclosure of information or inappropriate analysis. The mission of the 'peace safari' was to convey the facts as they stood and ask the central government to take concrete steps to put an end to the conflict.

The first meeting took place in the office of Akbar Tanjung, the Chairman of the House of Representatives. In this meeting, several members of the Ambon consultative assembly wept as they movingly described the situation as it was in Ambon. Mr Akbar also shed tears. This was 'tear diplomacy' at Senayan! Mr Akbar promised that the House of Representatives would urge the central government to take appropriate steps to put an end to the violence in Ambon.

The second meeting was in the office of the Coordinating Minister for Political, Legal and Security Affairs. A small incident occurred in front of this office. Before our party arrived, another party from the Moluccan Provincial Consultative Assembly also arrived at his office. This party was denied access by an official at the office of the Ministry, so they left. In this meeting with the minister, several members of the party engaged in tear diplomacy. Mr SBY also shed tears. Mr SBY promised to use the field reports that we had delivered in coordination meetings between his ministry, the Chief of Police and the Commander in chief of the Army, and other chiefs of the armed forces. After the meeting, Mr SBY invited our party to attend a meeting with President Megawati in Merdeka Palace.

Our 'peace safari' had two significant outcomes. First, we explained that what had occurred in Ambon, and in Maluku generally, really had nothing to do with the local political elite, as several parties in Jakarta had described in their analysis. Our party had consisted of the local political elite who came from the political parties that were dominant in Ambon and Maluku, and came from different religious backgrounds. Second, we placed political pressure on Jakarta to find an appropriate way to discover the political motives of the players in Jakarta who had caused Ambon and Maluku to become political hostages.

IV

On Eid Al Fitr 2001, not long after I became mayor, I went to visit the deputy mayor, Syarif Hadler, in his home in Galunggung, together with a middle-ranking Christian army officer, a staff member of the Civil Emergency Authority. The situation was not at all conducive, as Christians did not dare to drive through Batu Merah, the largest Muslim district in Ambon. We had to go quite some distance into the densely-populated Muslim area, which was about two kilometres from the main road, to reach Mr Syarif's house at the end of one of the streets in the Galunggung area. We drove to Mr Syarif's house without any escort, except an adjutant who was a member of the mobile brigade.

When I got out of the car, I saw a few older people milling around Mr Syarif's house. I approached them, shook hands with them, exchanged Eid Al Fitr greetings and introduced myself. The situation became tense; they were taken aback, but it was also very moving.

The people cried when they kissed my hand. I asked, 'Why are you crying?' They replied, 'Christians and officials have never come to see us'. Mr Syarif was also taken aback and definitely became tense because I had arrived without letting him know in advance, while close to his house were many outsiders hanging around in three-quarter length trousers.

From this visit to Mr Syarif's house and meeting with the local people, including their expressions and their moving utterances, I grasped one message. Until now the government had let the provocateurs infiltrate every area of the people's social life in the city! Spreading of provocative rumours had triggered tension and the rumours were sometimes exploited, leading to communal violence.

The next day, I contacted RRI Ambon. I asked them to be on the air 24/7, so I, the police chief or the military commander could clarify an incident that might have occurred somewhere or dispel untrue rumours being spread among the people.

To obtain information about incidents or rumours circulating, I used the available intelligence network. I also formed my own network by giving mobile phones to people in all the different residential areas. Their job was only to give me information about an incident or a rumour that was circulating in their areas. They had to send me a text message and weren't allowed to phone me. The information from this network was used by me, the police chief or the military commander to deliver a message via an RRI Ambon broadcast.

V

In 2003, I gathered representatives from senior high schools. Each school was represented by six pupils and we met on the 4th floor of the city hall, to eat and sing together. The room was prepared with a number of round tables with six chairs set at each table. Each pupil was free to choose where they would sit. Representatives from each school tended to enter the room together and sit together at each tables.

I noticed they displayed awkwardness, stiffness, tension, suspicion, even hatred, when they saw pupils from other schools of a different religious background. While they had been at junior high school and senior high school, they may only have had contact with pupils from the same religious background. After the conflict broke out in 1999, they were all still at primary school, with the majority of pupils being of the same religious background as themselves.

This meant that outside their homes they had never mixed with others from a different religious background. From the age of 10-16 years, they only had friends who were of the same religion as themselves, and had developed feelings of hatred or enmity towards people of a different religious background.

I was the host at that event and began with singing a few teenage pop songs. I was helped by a local singer, who had been invited to the event. I then invited all the pupils to sing with me. To begin with, the pupils sang very softly and were almost inaudible. I continued to sing these teenage songs to elicit a reaction from the pupils. Sometimes I pretended to forget the lyrics, with the hope that they would correct me. Indeed, some did spontaneously correct me. I would walk towards the pupil and hand him or her the microphone so that he or she could finish the song, and I encouraged all the pupils to sing along with this pupil.

Spontaneously the majority of pupils started singing, and as time went on more and more joined in. The expressions on their faces which had initially displayed awkwardness, uneasiness, tension, suspicion, even hatred, started to change, and the situation became quite relaxed. I stopped the singing session and continued with introductions. Each pupil had to introduce themselves, starting with their name, current and previous schools. This was so we could find out if some had previously been at the same school together. After the introductions we had lunch together.

The food was a buffet set on one long table, so all the pupils had to take food from the same place. This was organised on purpose so that they would have to queue for food and when they queued close to each other, they would perhaps greet each other. In this process, I observed what was going on while I also queued for food and also engaged in small talk. While waiting in the queue, some were quiet and didn't greet other pupils who were not from the same school or of the same religious background. However, there were others who invited each other to eat. Some came across friends from primary school and they greeted each other.

After taking the food and finding somewhere to sit, they started to mix and sat at a table together. In planning this event, I had selected a number of pupils who were known to have good communication and social skills. They were asked to greet other pupils at meal time who were not from the same school as them and who were from a different religious background. At meal time, they were encouraged not to sit next to friends from the same school but rather with pupils from different schools and different religious background.

The results were pleasing; a number of the pupils who had been prepared beforehand and others who had been at primary school together or had once been neighbours mixed with others when they sat down to eat. They started to talk to each other. To begin with, it was still very flat, and this could be seen from their facial expressions. Eventually they started to become friendly, smiling, and exchanging mobile phone numbers. I observed their behaviour seriously, so that I could measure the effectiveness of this event, whether the goal was reached or not.

The aim was to encourage these children, who were at a critical age and were so easily provoked and used to carry out violence or other dangerous acts that could trigger conflict, to communicate with children of their own age but from a different religious background. For more than four years (since 1999) they had lived and gone to school in their own communities and never interacted with others. After seeing the intimacy between these senior high school students at the end of the gathering I decided that I would organise a similar event with pupils every week from different schools, so that we could cover as many pupils as possible.

The greater goal of these gatherings was to erode asocial perceptions which were the result of the conflict. Since the conflict broke, these children were restrained in a narrow social reality. They played, interacted and went to school only in their own religious communities. Perhaps they believed that they could only interact with people from the same religious background, that they didn't need to interact with those from a different religious background, and they had already become enemies. It was hoped that through these events that this asocial perception could slowly disappear. Negative perceptions such as suspecting each other or harbouring vengeance would dwindle or gradually even totally disappear.

VI

The fragments described above, are just a small segment of my experiences as a decision maker when the conflict was smouldering. There are many other things I could disclose, but because of time limitations and editorial policies, this is all I can offer. Hopefully this offering can become a reference for policies that can be carried out by governments dealing with conflict or potential conflict so that peace of mind can be returned to the people, without having to become a project in the national and civil service budgets. Another message from this offering is that whatever small things a government does for its people should be done sincerely. I hope that is so!

Chapter 15

WHEN THE CONSCIENCE SPEAKS

M. Noor Tawainela

When I was small, Dad told me about his genealogical relationship with the family in Waai which went back hundreds of years, before the West Christianised Waai. I almost don't remember anything of the story because I was too small at the time.

I only remembered that if the roof over my ancestors' grave was to be replaced then a great number of families from Waai would attend. The atmosphere was lively, serene, and full of kinship and friendship nuances. There were songs – *cakalele, tifa* and *totobuang, pantun* and *lania* – that were sung in a language I found difficult to understand and sung in rhyming choruses calling back and forth. There were *pasaware* that told of the history of the relationship of their descendants, the history of the traditional villages and how they came into being, before the West set foot on the land of their birth, whether it is Honimoa, or Lataela, or Harua or Lataenu.

At this point there was no Islam or Christianity. All that was present was family (*basudara*) from the same pool of genes. In their happiness, they danced, they wept, linked arms, greeted each other in the beautiful intimate traditional languages: *sau, wate, uwa* and *bonso*, because they were all from one spring of life and they were 'gandong'.

Such was my experience when I was small in the village of Tulehu, the place I was born and grew up, where I was spoilt with the fertile land on the slopes of Mt. Salahutu. Almost 40 years later, when I read *Colenbrander*'s report, quoted by Karel Steenbrink's book *Dutch Colonialism and Indonesian Islam: Contacts and Conflicts, 1596-1950*, in which he writes about Waai being Muslim twice and Christian twice, I realised how long and complicated it was. But the history of the journey of my ancestors was also very enjoyable.

It's not surprising that they guarded this kinship relationship like a mirror which should not be dropped or scratched.

They realised that, although they had become Christian or Muslim, their kinship relationship should not be broken or become vulnerable. The roots should still go into the earth and the dense foliage on the branches will always protect their descendants at all points of the compass, for all seasons and for all time.

Suddenly I remembered the utterance of two wise Moluccans, Watloly and Ajawaila. Their utterances rang in my brain. I meditated on their sayings as a reflection on the richness of their social convictions, which were full of humility. For them *basudara* (kin) is a cultural reality that is not limited to a genealogical relationship, as I had understood, rather covered an extensive cultural geographical area, which is not confined to an administrative region, but is the 'historical' Maluku. The historical Maluku, as in the *jazirah al-Mulk* of Ibnu Batutah, covers the coastal area for the length of the Pacific Ocean. Their cultural characters are happy-go-lucky, loud, and they tease one another by the bonfire when the full moon sails across the blue horizon and gently shines on the white spray of the waves. It isn't just *Maloku Kie Raha* (North Maluku consisting of four kingdoms), because *Maloku Kie Raha* is an emotional and rigid point of view which is not historical, and contains many legends.

I remember, in the 1980s, many women from Tulehu, my mother's sisters among them, would go to the islands of Saparua and Nusalaut to sell their goods. There, in Saparua, Haria, Porto, Paperu, Mahu and Titawae, they were not treated as though they were just ordinary Muslim peddlers, but they were treated as *'tuang hati jantong'* (my dearest) a beautiful expression carrying deep meaning, but difficult to explain. Once when these acquaintances had wanted to return to Saparua from Ambon but missed the motor boat, they went instead to the homes of their kin (*basudara tuang hati jantong*); they stayed the night and were received well in the same manner by the women of Tulehu as these women had been treated in Saparua, Haria, Paperu and Titawae.

This beautiful cultural phenomenon did not arise from a worldly idea, but grew from a spiritual esoteric reflection that was not orchestrated. It grew naturally. Humanity that shines a beautiful light from transformative religions – Islam and Christianity, both of which have their roots in Abraham's religion – reflects pluralism in the human character in history. As is known in the journey of Ishmael (which means 'God hears'), he was the descendant of Abraham, Abraham-Hagar's child. His descendants lived on in the Baca valley, on the slopes of Mt. Paran. Hira cave can be found on the slopes of Paran. It was there a great-grandchild of Ishmael, called Muhammad, continued the mission of the prophecy concerning Abraham and Ishmael. Abraham and Sarah produced Isaac whose seed ran through Jacob (Israel) to Jesus who, according to Muslim belief, furthered the prophecy of Abraham.

Thus there is a kinship relationship (*basudara*) – Muslim Ambon – that is represented by Muslim Tulehu and Christian Saparua, which is one of hundreds of manifestations of Moluccan local wisdom. Therefore, whoever denies this reality has transgressed against history and culture. This is not forgivable according to the historical kinship relationship between Muslims and Christians. This record of local cultural practice will continue to be the heritage of our descendants forever. Those who have tried to erase this by creating conflict will have the same fate as Cagliostro in the Middle Ages in Europe.

The experience above is only a drop in the ocean of the local cultural practice that is pleasant to remember and reflect on as an internal statement, experienced by all Moluccans: Salam-Sarane.

I

In 1955, I lived in Mardika in order to continue my education and I lived with *Uwa* Etty Bakarbessy. I had to call her '*Uwa* Etty'. *Uwa* in the local language used in Ambon and Lease means the sister of my father. According to old people in Tulehu, my father, my grandfather and the village chief of Waai were almost identical. It was almost impossible to distinguish which was the Muslim grandfather and which was the Christian grandfather. Again, this is linked to the gandong gene relationship.

So gandong is not just a concept in a cultural structure that was developed by our ancestors. The cultural structure has strong supports that can protect our descendants for hundreds of years against the heat of the sun and the threat of storms of change in each era. It is so strong because it has been built with a sincere and sacred intention, without the need to question the religion held.

In Mardika, I lived with *Uwa* Etty and her husband Uncle Obi, who were polite and showered their love and attention on their Muslim nephew. There was another *Uwa* who married *Wate* Beng Sohilait, from Allang, who also lived in Mardika. According to my father, this *Uwa* was the spitting image of my elder sister. At the *Golden Spoon*, there was a fussy, but good-hearted, granny and an *Uwa* who married a Tanamal. They were all my father's relatives even though they had different religious backgrounds. Once my father explained that there was another *Uwa* who became a Muslim and married an Arab.

II

I remember on the banks of the Mardika River, there was a leafy banyan tree, where we used to play. It is still fresh in my memory that I would carry little Meyti on my back when I came home from school. Ida and Truitje Latuheru, Elsje Maruanaya and Nus Ophier were also there.

When memories flood the consciousness and form an artistic frame then the colours will decorate a sort of cosmic mosaic. The kinship way of life is a pluralistic, cultural reality that is part of the richness of the Moluccan people. The conflict almost broke all the strings of the kinship fellowship. Thus we confidently declare to all nations that the Moluccan people have a rich mind, that is, local wisdom.

Humility and a humble approach, to borrow Sir John Templeton's words, will lose their strength in humankind's spiritual ocean if the desires of cleptocracy and hypocrisy are given high value like arrogance in the kingdoms of the heart. Then the heart and the spirit will become miserable, poor and destitute; and devilish behaviour as the dominant role will destroy angelic behaviour. As Francis Fukuyama said, we can only repeat our historical experiences to prove that the local cultural practice of our ancestors, which they established, should be kept and become the mindset of the sons and daughters of the beautiful land of Maluku, wherever they are.

How wise our ancestors were. They built the institutions of *gandong, pela, badati, masohi, tuang hati jantong, ale rasa beta rasa, sagu salempeng di pata dua, maano, lania-lania, dorabo-lolo* to decorate the heavens of this green and fertile land, from the furthest north to the furthest south. This concept is like Ajawaila or Watloly's explanation. For years I lived in Mardika, looked after by my Christian relatives, but I didn't become a Christian. On Saturdays I was told to go to Tulehu to study the Quran but I had to return to Mardika to go to Sunday school. I am, however, still a Muslim. Group 11 even accused me of being a 'radical Muslim' when I rejected several points in the Malino II Agreement.

Thinking about it again, I really enjoyed my past. To reminisce is not a sin. On the contrary, humans are motivated to enjoy again the essence of the intrinsic. Humans will reflect the essence of the philosophical kinship values, whether it is genetics or ideology. We cannot deny variety, because variety, according to Claude Levi Strauss, 'is behind us, in front of us, even surrounding us'.

Stories about our past experiences show how wonderful and beautiful pluralism is in social relationships. Pluralism is a reality in the historical journey, not just a guess or an idea. Variety and plurality are a mosaic – a beautiful, spectacular garden. Whoever pops in will never feel bored. The local cultural practice of the Moluccans has been collected from identities that stand independently, but are harmonious in the differences between these identities.

III

When the conflict in Ambon occurred, the world around us changed continually. These changes have denied the boundaries, choices and ethics of our beliefs. The ferocity of the conflict has caught the attention of researchers, who then produced speculative explanations that the traditions, customs and inherited norms of the ancestors have been buried and will never rise again.

This explanation about the kinship relationship that used to be sacred, polite and intimate, as shown above, has been ripped apart and it will be difficult to stitch it back together as it was in the past. Can people in their right minds, however, accept such explanations, analysis or assumptions? Are people prepared to just erase the traces of genetical history that are summoned up in the term '*basudaragandong*', or '*basudara*' expressed in the emotional expression '*tuang hati jantong*'?

The natural realm of the Moluccan people, the tempestuous nature, thundering like waves crashing against granite rocks, perhaps forms their physical posture, starting from their hair and their sharp, eagle-like stares. But their hearts are so gentle and full of love for humankind – that '*basudara tuang hati jantong*'. Because of this love you will never hear of anyone dying of hunger in Maluku.

Indeed, during the totally unexpected conflict, all people in this land experienced a great upheaval, both in the social order and the cultural order.

We witnessed the city of Ambon and the traditional villages become necropolises; conscience and sane reasoning stopped functioning; people didn't know why the conflict occurred or at whom it was directed.

The conflict spontaneously created a group of emotional solidarity internationally. Common sense became paralysed. *Basudara, tuang hati jantong,* gandong, pela and various value systems of local cultural practice, inherited from the ancestors, were forgotten by the conflicting groups. They were possessed by the devil. The devil is an evil spirit, a deceiver, who is always whispering ethological desires – borrowing Stuart Mill's expression – so that humankind is far from the whispers of the gentle streams of light that shine from the glorious descendants of Abraham.

Today the conflict is a thing in the past for the Moluccan people. It has become a valuable lesson for people to reflect on. It is a part of the history of the Moluccans that needs to become a wise foundation and step in making decisions – in all aspects of development – to bring about a just and prosperous future in the historical pluralism of Maluku.

There has been a renaissance, *Aufklarung*, enlightenment, or whatever word you want to use, to describe the new situation of the Moluccans. Everything changed, and in that change here was differentiation and deviation. There were innovations, lively discourses, a spirit to build justice, prosperity and victory within the Republic of Indonesia, that hopefully is far from the chaos of separatism, political thuggery, inflation of democracy, the evils of corruption and discrimination, using new terms that were worse such as 'indigenous'. This evil was encouraged by a state that was in chaos and powerless, and entrapped by the moral evils of collusion and nepotism. Strangely, the Lord's name was invoked in this evil.

In speeches, briefings, workshops, meetings, taking oath for new positions and transfer of power – I don't know what else – people automatically lift up their hands, close their eyes, but in reality they didn't worship the Lord. The Lord became the black sheep of helplessness and hypocrisy.

Believe it or not, we are a nation under the sun that too easily uses the Lord's name, but most of us do not understand what we are saying. We only love 'the name', not His laws. It seems that our utterances about the holiness of friendship, about nationalism, about justice, about self-worth, about unity in diversity, don't arise from the depths of conscience, but from mathematical logic that tends more to calculate strategy for the gain or loss of interest.

Our character is a character of pretence and conventionality. We even pretend to the Lord and utter polite phrases, so that Sindhunata alluded to a nation that is dazed, a confused nation, perhaps the nation that makes the least sense in the world. Are the Moluccan people also a nation that likes the culture of pretence and conventionality? I am certain that the brother- and sisterhood, that we understand, besides the genetic relationship, that we call *basudaragandong*, and the explanations of socio-anthropology about brothers in cultural concepts, is very close to the character of the Moluccan people. How the non-Moluccan brothers, both Muslim and Christian, for scores of years – perhaps even hundreds of years – have settled here and become Moluccans. They have become part of the fermentation of Moluccan culture. They speak the Ambonese Malay dialect, marry and have children here, in the fertile land of spices, a beautiful, but tempestuous, mosaic on the edge of Oceania.

I know several students who have a Moluccan surname, but these students do not originate from Maluku. When I asked, 'Why do you use a Moluccan surname?' They answered that the surname was given to their ancestors almost five generations ago, because of the close relationship of their ancestors with the people who bestowed on them this surname. It is amazing. Only because of this close relationship, they have been given the right to use this surname. They feel proud of their surname and even feel that they are true Moluccans. Interestingly, they were given land belonging to the clan and acknowledged by all the family members of the clan. This is an interesting cultural, ideological phenomenon from the spirit of local cultural practice that can only be found in Maluku.

There are many interesting stories that appeared during the conflict that some who evacuated and chose to leave Ambon were not received as brethren in the land of their ancestors, who had the same genealogy, but were treated as Ambonese refugees. They were foreigners, newcomers, in their ancestral homeland. Because of their Moluccan sense they felt offended. They felt tortured and didn't feel at home. Eventually they returned to Maluku, the place where they belonged.

In the month of Ramadan in 2005, together with Prof. John Lokollo and Semy Toisuta, I was invited by the East Seram regional government to be a member of the jury for a competition to design a symbol for the East Seram Regency. When we arrived in Bula the problem of food and drink for Prof. John and Semy weighed heavily on my mind, because the vast majority of the people of Bula are Muslim and are still very traditional. The same thoughts were worrying the wife of Mr Rahman Rumalutur (Chief executive officer of the East Seram regional government). When I was told about the concern by Ahmad Sopamena (an official of the East Seram regent's office), I explained that Islam is a blessing for all (*rahmatan lil alamin*), as practised by the prophet in Medina. One of the beautiful aspects of its teaching is respecting and always treating guests in the community well whether they are non-Muslim or Muslim. This is one of the conditions of Islamic law. Islam is not a religion that is very rigid in its regulations. Therefore, sincerely demonstrating the beautiful face of Islam is a form of worship. Looking after Prof. John and Semy with a sincere heart, as guests of a Muslim in the month of Ramadan, is a social form of worship. From that moment onwards until we returned to Ambon, the wife of the chief executive officer, as a strict Muslim, continued to look after the needs of Prof. John and Semy, both in the morning and in the middle of the day.

The above experiences are the reality of a life of friendship among the Moluccan people, with its cultural and religious plurality. Respecting plurality and diversity is the essence of Islamic teaching. I am convinced that it is the same in Christianity. Respecting and honouring variety within culture and religion is the holy mission of all the religions. Humankind is of the same blood line for the length of history. Humankind is descended from humans. Humankind is not descended from a chimpanzee or African gibbon. They were born from one source in history. A difference in religious belief doesn't mean we have to be enemies each other. My *Tauhid* is not the same as Prof. Dr. A. Watloly's Trinity. In understanding each other, the beauty of friendship is full of peace and enjoyment.

I was taught that the prophet Mohammed SAW was not sent to curse or be an enemy of difference but rather to unite the differences in a religious community system called the Madaniah community, where humane pluralism was developed. Whoever betrays, wounds or disparages the essence of humane pluralism has betrayed himself. The essence of universal humanitarian values of religion brings to earth the majesty of the love of God in the theological privilege that causes us to tremble. This is wisdom that has to be sought by all of humankind who are categorised as believers, wherever they are.

IV

Man or woman is really a cosmic body that is also a creature that possesses a mind and intelligence, which, according to Aristotle, is always linked to his or her experience. These experiences are spiritual privileges. We like to read and listen to them when they are expressed. For wise people, they are a mirror that can be used for introspection. Thus what I have written is the smallest part of the wanderings of the Moluccan people, who are usually equated as Ambonese. The Ambonese have spread civilisation and knowledge the length of the Halmahera coast line and its surrounding areas, in Papua and the Balim valley, who then after they had learnt to play the flute and learnt to read the Latin alphabet, became clever and created an 'Anti-Ambon Movement'.

I, like you, truly love the land of our ancestors, a beautiful land full of natural resources. Deep in the earth various metals can be found and there is a rich sea, green and fertile jungles, but the people are poor because they have been impoverished by a very corrupt system full of mafia.

Finally, in concluding this article, gathered from a treasure of experiences, I need to emphasise that pluralism is the richness and beauty of creation. To make a pilgrimage to pluralism is to make a pilgrimage to human existence, which is fascinating and thrilling. Syncretism, on the other hand, is a shallow, confusing ideology in the understanding of religion itself. Islam teaches that pluralism is the character of the treatise but firmly rejects syncretism as in traditional religious beliefs. Humankind was created from the elements of man and woman, then tribes and finally nations were created, with different cultures and beliefs. In these differences, humankind is inter-dependent, needing each other to know each other in universal humanism. Whether spirituality is holy or not depends on genuine worship of the Lord. Hurting others is the same as hurting oneself. Whoever is wise about himself will also be wise in his relationship to the Lord. This is not syncretism but *Tauhid*.

What I have written is only a flashback, like an imaginary illustration by the Brazilian writer Erico Verissimo, after meeting Abidin and Rudy of the Inter-Faith organisation, in a car heading towards Darussalam University Ambon.

Chapter 16

MALUKU ASHAMED

Steve Gaspersz

I want to start my story with my own experiences. I was born in Surabaya and then grew up in the town of Malang, East Java. I went through the educational system there. When I graduated from senior high school I was confused: where do I go from here? I once had a desire to be a minister – a strange ambition when compared to the great expectations of those who were graduating from senior high school at that time. This ambition was almost forgotten. Then Dad reminded me that he had once made a promise to God that one of his children would become a minister. Dad asked me and I didn't object.

Dad gave me a choice of theological colleges after my senior high school graduation and I spontaneously replied, 'I want to study in Ambon.' Amazed at my choice, Dad said, 'Strange. Many kids from Ambon want to study in Java, but you, who are living in Java, want to study in Ambon'. The decision was made for me to study theology in Ambon. My reason was very simple: I didn't like being called *ambonkaart* or 'Ambonese on his identity card', that is, someone with an Ambonese surname but doesn't know anything about Ambon and has never lived there. I wanted to experience life in Ambon. The atmosphere, kinship relationships, food, teasing one another – I wanted to experience all of these as part of my identity on becoming Ambonese.

Sadly, Dad didn't have the opportunity to see me ordained. He passed away too quickly, taking his last heavy and bitter breath after being hit by a bus in the Pasar Rebo area in Jakarta in 1994. My last meeting with Dad was when he accompanied me to the Tanjung Perak docks in Surabaya, where I boarded the ship that would take me to Ambon in 1990. But Dad's instructions are still clear in my mind: 'If you want to become a minister, you have to become a smart minister'.

* * *

Going through the early stages of living in Ambon as a theological student was not as easy as I thought it would be. I didn't have any difficulty making friends, but I did have difficulty adjusting myself to the Ambonese way of thinking and their way of life. When I lived in Malang, I was usually indifferent to people around me. This type of attitude was not acceptable in Ambon. Several times I almost got into a fight because I didn't greet people when I entered the area where they were living. Fortunately, university friends taught me many things about how to become Ambonese, including the tradition of greeting people in the street which in Ambon was seen as a sign of respect. It's like when we enter someone's house, we have to ask permission to enter.

The experience that made the most impression on me and most influenced the way I looked at Ambon was my involvement the city-cleaning project set up by the mayor of Ambon, Dicky Wattimena. Students were given the opportunity to become members of the cleaning service. My friends and I volunteered. We were accepted into the program. Our group was given the job of cleaning an area that consisted of Mardika Terminal and the length of the Mardika beach. We were supervised every night, because we worked at night, and our supervisor gave us our wages once a week.

It was not much money, but it was enough for us to buy a banana snack, which we ate sitting on the retaining wall on Mardika beach, while teasing a few transvestites from the Gambus market. Our small wages also made us happy because we were able to buy a few books that we needed for our courses. What was more valuable for me, though, was that I was really enjoying becoming truly Ambonese. I could be involved and see the struggles of the 'people of the night' in the untouched corners of Ambon city.

* * *

My desire to get to know Ambon and Maluku pushed me to explore village by village. We (my college friends and I) did this by agreeing every holiday to go to their villages: Porto, Haria, Haruku, Oma, Hulaliu, Kairatu, Piru and many more, including, of course, Naku. Our exploration helped me understand the wealth of local wisdom still alive in Moluccan communities.

I was fascinated by the beautiful scenery in the villages, intoxicated with the different fruits that were seducing us with their flavours for the length of the fruit season, and engrossed in the rhythm of the different unique dialects in the villages. From my exposure to these Moluccan communities, I got to know that Ambon wasn't just Christian but rather an area where the Christian community and the Muslim community lived together in the atmosphere of the local community, that gave the spirit to the expression of a tradition rich in kinship values.

I had almost no knowledge of this precise, sociological description when I lived in Java. When I lived in Java the stories I heard about Ambon and the books that I had read were about Christian Ambonese. The vast majority of the Ambonese I met in Java were Christian. That is what made me think that Ambon was a Christian area. Now, after going from village to village, I could see that Ambon was a cultural world that brought together so many expressions of religions – including world religions – always in creative tension, even dominating each other, in a long, socio-historical narrative.

Exploring the villages also opened my eyes to the local traditional beliefs (*alifuru*) that have been woven together with Christian and Muslim ideas and practices, forming a distinctive Moluccan religiosity. Christianity and Islam have been creatively earthed in the cultural use of the terms, 'Salam' and 'Sarane'. The use of Salam and Sarane as friendly terms tended to mock the dogmatic repression of formal religious institutions, which used up their religious energy in doctrinal debates to defend the truth. Salam and Sarane offer a way of looking at things and a down-to-earth religious life, and therefore refuse to argue over who should to go to heaven and who should end up in hell. The main issue is how to live together, with a religious energy which invigorates cultural ties. I think this is a brilliant religious way of life, because there is awareness that we must develop religious responsibility together on earth, together in the one place, and not up in the heavenly clouds with the beautiful angels.

* * *

In the middle of that day, 19 January 1999, the roads in Ambon were deserted. It was the Eid Al Fitr holiday. A few friends had invited me to go and visit them in Waihaong and Batu Merah, but I couldn't go with them because I had to do some writing. On that holiday I was busy with my fingers dancing on the computer keyboard in the GPM Mentoring office (LPJ-GPM).

The telephone rang, stopping my fingers in the middle of their dance. Nancy told me to come home quickly because the people of Mardika were involved in a clash with the people of Batu Merah. I sneaked a peek through the windows of the LPJ-GPM office on the second floor of Baileo Oikoumene and saw clouds of black smoke rising up. I was reluctant to go home because I still had to finish the writing, but I caught the anxiety in Nancy's voice and I felt that the situation was becoming problematic. A relative phoned me and told me not to go in the direction of Batugantung because a car had been set on fire and mobs had spilled into the road. Minibuses were no longer operating.

Coming out of the LPJ-GPM office, I saw many people running, holding machetes, wood or metal pipes in their hands. All of them were wearing the same coloured clothes: red shirts with black head bands. I asked one of the young people but he only answered by shouting, 'Everything is out of control!' I didn't understand what he was talking about. In the middle of the confusion, a youth suddenly asked where I wanted to go. I replied 'to Kudamati'. He immediately responded by saying, 'You can't go in that direction. They have burnt down a mosque and a church.'

Confused about the situation, I decided to go to Karang Panjang (Karpan), to Nancy's parents' home. No public transport was operating. In just a few hours, the city of Ambon had become totally paralysed and was frightening. I walked to Karpan along roads that were deserted. People gathered in their own residential areas, with whatever weapons they could find. Everyone seemed hypnotised by the horror. Nobody knew – or perhaps just a few knew – that this was the beginning of a human horror that would tear apart Salam and Sarane in Maluku. This was the beginning of a long and tragic story.

I became involved with the UKIM Crisis Centre for a while and was one of the witnesses of several vicitims' moving and heartbreaking stories about the 'community unrest' that hit Maluku. In the scribbled chronological reports of the incidents, which I had to write to document these incidents, I found it hard to describe the heartbreak upon heartbreak. But working with colleagues, one of them being the Rev. Jacky Manuputty, gave me the chance to learn a lot about conflict management and how to map the developing issues, including conflict analysis which could be directed towards the reconciliation process by empowering the cultural strengths of Salam-Sarane.

Here, I have to relate the heartbreaking stories that disrupted the Moluccans' self-esteem and culture. Religions reacted arrogantly, with fierce faces ready to indiscriminately wipe out their kin. Physical bodies were torn apart in rage, social bodies were splintered into artificial, arrogant factions shouting slogans from the Al-Quran and the Bible and singing spiritual songs, to draw God into the cruelty dealt out to Salam and the Sarane kin.

However, Salam and Sarane cannot deny the necessity of history, which etched the bitter sketches that future generations will remember. Should it be forgiven when bodies were torn apart by revenge? Do we have to live side-by-side while memories are still crammed with poison of hatred that gnaws at the heart of the community? A long line of questions and anxieties are still visible. We do not need to stir up the bitter dregs of the past, but they are a sign of the cultural frailty that is scraping away at the Moluccan identity.

I started with a story about my own experiences that were caught up in seeking my identity and 'becoming Ambonese'. I went in all directions to find traces of what being Moluccan means, even returning to the ancestral lands in the hope of discovering the roots of the myths that brought about the ontological unity of '*Nunusaku*'.[1] This is, indeed, a personal narrative. But I felt drowned in the collective memory that reflects the socio-cultural narratives of others, who experienced similar anxieties.

This story is not over yet; it is still in process. This story does not need a conclusion, because it is being pieced together with local fragments that are rising, opposing the narrowness of homogeneity and the appeal of globalisation. Perhaps, this narrative is only a small part of resisting the label of *ambonkaart*; perhaps this narrative also reflects my discontent at being anonymous. Anyway, this narrative is a link in the cultural chain, which releases a cultural turn with a thousand and one meanings.

We are increasingly crushed by suffocating fashion and technology. We no longer have cultural backyards where we can tell stories about ourselves, about our sea, about the ancient tales of the pela-gandong relationship, whose verses we have almost forgotten; tales about lands made barren through uncontrolled greed; tales about the cooking utensils used to roast food over coals, which have been exchanged for modern crystal dishes with asparagus soup, and about tastes that are more familiar with *brinebon* (foreign food) rather than the traditional vegetable dishes of *ganemo* or *arwansirsir*, with

---

1 Translator's note: A place in the mountains on the Island of Seram.

chicken from McDonald's or KFC, feeling that it is softer than the local fish dishes of *cakalang, kawalinya, momar* and *komu*.

Can we create a new backyard? Or will the children's games of *apiong, mutel, asen* and *benteng* just be myths, about which future generations will only have a vague knowledge? Then *Hainuwele* (a princess in the mythology of Seram Island) would only be a set of scribbles on a faded piece of paper that the MTV generation in Maluku can't read, eroded by the heroism of *Naruto* or *Ben-10* and the lures of Barbie. Lips would be more familiar with the lyrics of Michael Jackson or George Michael rather than *Hena Masa Waya* or *Hio-Hio* that have already almost disappeared; even the agility of the moves for *saureka-reka* and *cakalele* seem awkward compared to the moves in hip-hop and moon-walk or are just dished up to satisfy tourists' desires for the exotic. The little hands playing the wooden clapper are becoming stiff because their fingers are more used to running up and down a Blackberry keypad.

I have tried to reflect on the essence of becoming a Moluccan. Maluku now – after being struck by a great tumult – wishes to resurrect its vital signs that have collapsed. I have never being embarrassed to be a Moluccan. I am, however, ashamed when my generation and the generation after me do not spur themselves on to learn to put in order the future of Maluku, with its bitter history that perhaps still scars us and with as yet undetected infections. I am ashamed because we allow ourselves to be caught in the strong current of change, as if we want to give full rein to a greed repressed by the hypocrisy of 'praying in the midst of community unrest', while not learning from history, which sooner or later may become a 'suicide bomb' that will explode in a future generation. Ashamed, because if that is the case, what is the difference between this situation and 'the stupidity of tripping over the same stone twice'?

In the words of the song: *Sayang dilale ... apa tempo tuang bale?* (Don't forget ... when are you coming back?)

Chapter 17

WHEN THE NATION IS SILENT

Theofransus Litaay

The morning of 19 January 1999 started just the same as any other day in our lives. It was special because it was the Eid Al Fitr holiday. Many cities were flooded with people going home to celebrate Eid Al Fitr with their families, or just going home for the holidays. In the middle of the day, we received news that violence had broken out between the people of Mardika and Batu Merah in Ambon. The situation changed very quickly because crowds were being mobilised everywhere. On hearing the news, we Moluccans living in Java felt little urgency.

It was only on 20 January 1999, when the chaos had not subsided, that we began to realise that this was not an ordinary incident. Furthermore, the media reports added to the confusion, because their sources and the angles of their reports were unclear. In the meantime, many people had become casualties in Ambon. News that was circulated by e-mail was quicker and clearer and helped us to comprehend that violent incidents were taking place that were controlled by unidentified groups in the community.

Early analysis, based on information from Ambon and Jakarta concerning the incidents of violence in Maluku, suggested that these incidents had not just occurred by accident. The larger scenario, too strong to be dismissed, seemed to be linked to the agenda of and conflict between the political elite. This reality raised concerns that this violence would continue for some time depending on the 'author of the scenario'.

If the situation continued like this, then an advocacy process with a strong analytical basis was needed. It was difficult to hope that this would come from Ambon, because safety had deteriorated to the extent that people didn't have time to think about anything else except saving their families. Advocacy for the victims of violence was, therefore, needed from outside

Maluku. Based on this understanding, the Moluccan Intellectual Network for Java and Bali was formed, led by Rev. Dr. John Titaley.

From the beginning, Moluccan intellectuals living outside Maluku hoped that there was still enough social capital strength left in the community to reject the provocation of violence. However, from time to time, despite civil society's resolve to maintain its unity, the community seemed to be forced, through armed combat, to separate into religious factions. This resulted in the community being segregated. As a result, the different religious communities became suspicious of each other. Indeed, several parties used this situation for their own interests. This is also the reason that, from the beginning, advocacy by groups of Moluccan intellectuals outside Maluku was also separated along religious lines.

People felt isolated, marginalised and threatened by the constant violence, destruction, the ineffectiveness of the law and the dysfunctional state. On one hand, it seemed as though the state was not taking action to end the violence. On the other hand, the state continued to convey the message that this violence was a 'horizontal conflict'. The Moluccan Intellectual Network, in its communications on both the national and the international level, always rejected the official state view.

As it developed, the Moluccan Intellectual Network saw that the violence had triggered conflict at various levels. The conflict could be called a multilayer conflict. The various discussion forums organised by the Moluccan Intellectual Network at that time always recommended, therefore, that the problems should be resolved cautiously, layer by layer. For example, there was conflict between the national political elite (thereby involving elements of the government in the violence), but there was also conflict between the regional political elite and between villages, as well as between members of the security forces.

Given that there seemed to be perpetual violence in Maluku, many people felt that it was useless to rely on the government to solve the problem. This was because the government itself was not united (there was, at that time, tension between President Wahid and other key political figures) and it seemed that a number of political figures were using the chaos in Maluku for their own interests. The only way to get out of this chaos seemed to be by asking for international help. That is the reason that the process of international advocacy was developed.

By advocating at an international level, the problems that had struck the people would be known in other parts of the world. The world community could then urge the Indonesian government to be more serious about resolving the problems in Maluku.

During the process of international advocacy, we were involved in preparing and disseminating information, as well as coordinating the various parts of the Moluccan Intellectual Network in Java, Bali and Ambon. International advocacy was useful to neutralise the distortion of information.

Over time, through discussion and analysis within the network, we started to develop communication with grass-roots organisations in Muslim communities in Maluku. We gradually became aware that we could only develop communication and peace if we talked about culture and tradition. We disseminated the ideas to the various people in this network on an interfaith basis. From within the Moluccan Intellectual Network, leaders like Jacky Manuputty, Piet Manoppo, Tony Pariela, Dicky Mailoa and Jopie Papilaya took on the role of strongly pushing for more intense inter-faith communication.

One thing that helped was the emergence of internet network communication through the Masariku mailing list, developed by Peter Theodorus and Eska Pesireron. This Masariku mailing list became the discussion forum for various groups in the Moluccan Intellectual Network, where they could exchange ideas, provide affirmations and raise awareness.

In Jogjakarta and Salatiga, there were intensive discussions and the members ended up publishing a book together with the title, *Nasionalisme Kaum Pinggiran*, or 'the Nationalism of the Marginalised', a collection of articles written by young intellectuals calling themselves the 'Komunitas Tali Rasa' (Emotional Ties Community) that was led by Rudy Rahabeat, Has Toisuta, Abidin Wakano, Angky Rumahuru, Welly Tiweri, Rio Pellu, Fahmi Salatalohy, etc. This was the first book that was the result of inter-faith collaboration of young Moluccan intellectuals. Rio Pellu and Fahmi Salatalohy were the editors of the book. The other amazing thing about the process of making the book was that writers in different cities were connected by the internet.

History also proved that although people are now talking about virtual collaboration, the Moluccan young people were practising this a number of years ago. Several of the contributors have still never actually met each other in the flesh, but trust developed between them because of their love for Maluku.

The turning point for all the processes in the Moluccan Intellectual Network was becoming aware of our unity and developing trust with our Muslim brothers. Our suspicions shifted because when we looked into and studied the ongoing national political conflict, inter-faith intellectuals increasingly comprehended that the violence in Maluku was being exploited. Such violence can only be fought with a peace movement or reconciliation.

One good thing about the reconciliation process in Maluku is that it started at the grass roots level. Before the Baku Bae movement began, the peace process had been pioneered by several groups who wanted peace. I think this was strengthened by the Malino II agreement. There has been much discussion about the significance of the Malino II agreement, but I, personally, see it as providing very important momentum. It was a springboard from which we could demand that the state take responsibility for solving the problem in Maluku. I also see it as the result of a long process of advocacy about the Moluccan tragedy.

The reconciliation process, which is still taking place, has brought many benefits. It was very important for us at the Satya Wacana Christian University (UKSW) Salatiga. Why was this? It was because, through the idealism of reconciliation, we, at a Christian University, were given the opportunity to closely and intensively interact with our Muslim brothers from Maluku. Through the presence on campus of Muslim students from Maluku who were studying at UKSW, as a result of cooperation with the Indonesian Christian University in Ambon, commitment towards peace was not just a matter of words, but had been put into practice.

This was felt to be very important for an educational institution like UKSW, because the university campus is a place to sow seeds of peace. This would have an impact on the community on a larger scale. Many Christians living in Java at the time of the violent tragedy in Maluku were frightened. At that time, a group of people calling themselves the Laskar Jihad started to collect money at intersections with traffic lights in the main cities in Java. Their presence caused Christians, especially those from Maluku, to feel apprehensive and anxious about their personal safety. The reconciliation process taking place in Maluku, however, assured us that the Laskar Jihad's actions were not representative of the attitude of our Muslim brothers in Maluku.

In order to strengthen the capacity of the institution (under the leadership of Prof. Dr. John Titaley), UKSW then developed cooperation with a number of IAIN campuses nationally (especially in Semarang, Lampung, and Mataram) in a program of conflict resolution, working together with Arizona State University in the United States. This program succeeded in developing cooperation between intellectuals from these universities, both directly with those in Indonesia and also with those in the United States. Case studies have been one of the focuses in this cooperative study.

From the peace movement's point of view, the situation in Maluku has progressed very well. People are very critical about the wrong use of power and incitement based on religious beliefs. Members of all communities do not want to be easily provoked again. I was very happy when I celebrated Christmas in Ambon in 2004 and saw Muslims visiting their Christian acquaintances to wish them a happy Christmas. The tradition of togetherness has started to grow again.

There are still, however, many unresolved problems for the victims of the conflict. This incomplete work includes housing for the refugees; finalising of the civil rights of citizens in relation to ownership of houses and land; and the right to obtain social assistance. All this is the responsibility of the state.

Another problem is the lack of transparency about the results of the independent team of investigators into the violent tragedy in Maluku. The results of the team's report were not published openly for the public to read. As a result, there have been many questions. The perpetrators or the intellectual actors behind the tragedy have never been clarified. This question will continue to be asked until one day someone finds the answer. I hope it will happen!

Chapter 18

TRAGEDY AT THE CROSSROADS OF TRANSITION

Almudatsir Z. Sangadji

Conflict is a limited but universal experience in our culture. Throughout history, human beings from various cultures have grown, developed and created their own stories. Some of them have competed to defeat each other. The losing group is forced to follow the victor's culture, if it does not wish to be destroyed.

Bloody conflict leaves feelings of anger, sympathy and curses in its trail. Israel and Palestine, the experiences in Northern Ireland and Hitler's fascism in Germany tugged at the conscience of the world's citizens. Africa, with its more characteristic and limited experiences, is also legendary for the subduing of certain ethnic groups by others. Finally, in Maluku, the area where there had been relationships between villages (Pela – Gandong), the fires of conflict burned the orang basudara's morals to ashes. It was a tragedy that occurred at the crossroads of transition, when Indonesia was celebrating victory at the start of democracy and was leaving behind authoritarianism.

The conflict involved not only feelings of nationalism, but also ethnic and religious narcissism, the most intimate feelings in the experience of humankind. Historically, conflict occurred in a struggle over food and for genetic preservation, but the methods are now more modern, sophisticated and conscious through the use of technology and fabricated ideologies.

In ethnic conflict, for example, the enemy is another human being, a friend from a different ethnic background, or a neighbour from a different tribe, group or religion. In situations like this, conflict changes and even temporarily breaks social relationships, which had been connecting links for the exchange of values, experiences and culture.

A common saying, therefore, is that the first victim in conflict is truth. Using more reconciliatory language, the saying could be 'the first victim in conflict is peace'.

Global Context: A Critical Study

War, conflict and disasters have determined the course of civilisation. In various situations in the world, war, conflict and disaster have left many victims and much damage. Experiencing war, conflict and disaster has also led to the exchange of values, experience and culture.

In Europe's and America's experiences, the long periods of conflict and suffering disaster led the two continents to consolidate democracy and modernisation. Europe, for example, passed from tyranny, monarchy, oligarchy and social revolution to democracy. America has gone from being the land of cowboys, Al Capone, civil war, social movements, towards democracy.

The most brutal conflicts of the 20th century were those between countries, but after the 1990s most of the largest conflicts in the world have occurred within countries. Between 1989 and 1996, for example, 95 of the 101 conflicts occurred between ethnic groups within or against a country, either for self-determination or just to assert acknowledgement of communal identity.

In the Serbia–Bosnia conflict (1991), 200,000 were massacreed and 2.5 million became refugees. In 1994, the ethnic war in Rwanda between the Hutu and the Tutsi tribes led to the deaths of half a million people. Research by the Baku Bae movement indicates that the latest episode 'in our own home' – the three-year Moluccan conflict – resulted in three times as many victims as in 23 years of military operations in Aceh. A combination of identity issues with wider perceptions about economic and social injustice often rekindled 'a rooted conflict', to borrow a phrase from David Bloomfield and Ben Reilly.

Two strong aspects are often brought together in a conflict like this: the strengthening of the solidarity of communal identity (ethnicity) based on race, culture, religion and language, as well as the distribution of social and economic justice. The unjust distribution of natural resources coincided with a difference in identity. For example, if one religious group experiences a lack of resources that are owned by other groups, this can trigger (even cause) potential conflict.

The conflict in Maluku can be understood as the result of the transition to democracy due to a difficult compromise between fast social change in the midst of democratisation and increased identity awareness. Oshu, a Japanese author, metaphorically describes the change as a transfer from being the 'rose' region to becoming the 'sword' region.

Looking for a Needle in a Haystack

Democracy can be established if people's social and cultural prerequisites are strong enough to support it. If we are only involved with regulations and procedures, democracy cannot build dialectically to access life's energy.

Substantively, democracy is always dynamic, living alongside the existing cultural and social reality. Without it, democracy is just plastic packaging that is, in reality, authoritarian and tyrannical in nature.

When democracy starts to leave authoritarianism behind, social and cultural tensions may arise, which can turn to violence. The transition to democracy is usually risky. If wrongly managed, then it will often reverse and return to authoritarianism.

Democracy on the local stage can produce a very worrying situation, even appearing as a deviant euphoria. For example, in a number of situations, where new regions have been established it sharpens the perception of being 'against outsiders'. This can be seen when local culture (democracy) is not ready to accept change, so it is susceptible to conflict because the 'egotistical' attitude is very strong and closed off.

Europe was able to join democracy and monarchy, as, for example, in the United Kingdom, the Netherlands and Spain. In Indonesia, however, particularly in the multi-ethnic sphere, local cultures still encounter difficulties in conducting dialogue and living alongside each other, without the tension caused by democracy and modernisation.

Indonesia, especially during the time of the New Order, ignored pluralism as the basis of the nation's identity. The motto *Bhineka Tunggal Ika* in the centralistic political practice was fragmented into the application of the phrase '*Tunggal Ika*' (unity), while '*Bhineka*' (diversity), the reality of the variety, was allowed to be restless, oppressed and slowly die. The implementation of Law No 5 of 1979 on Village Government severed the cultural practice of traditional villages in Maluku for 20 years.[1]

Therefore, looking for and explaining the authenticity of local culture (not just in the meaning of the symbols, but also the behaviour) is like

---

1   Translator's note: Law No 5 of 1979 placed *desa* (villages) and *kelurahan* (urban neighbourhoods) as the lowest administrative units of government. *Desa* had originally been self-governing. The Law required that, in principle, heads of *desa* were elected and assisted by an elected council of representatives.

looking for a needle in a haystack. It has been gone about incorrectly – an arm could be wounded, blood shed and conflict inflamed. The local culture is increasingly suppressed, resulting in cultural or social bleeding.

Japan is an example to learn from, as it arose from bankruptcy and conflict. Hopefully, after the three years of conflict (1999–2002) in our country of a thousand islands, there will be a renaissance and the people of Maluku (and Indonesia generally) will show themselves to be more advanced and civilised. Conflict and war have brought unique experiences in how a civilisation eclipses the previous generation. Japan is one country that has been able to balance its national culture with democracy and modernisation.

Conflict, Exodus and Returning Home

I passed from adolescence to adulthood in the middle of the transition to democracy in Indonesia. A month before I graduated from senior high school, on 21 May 1998, the authoritarian New Order regime under Soeharto collapsed. At that time, as a teenager on the verge of adulthood, I was looking forward to experiencing my first love.

Before I experienced that first love, however, on 19 January 1999, six months after I graduated from senior high school and seven months after Reformasi, conflict broke out in the land of peace, which had been bound by the cords of Pela Gandong (brother- and sisterhood). I had not started to admire the student movement, which had created history by destroying the New Order. I failed to become a university student because I didn't pass the state university entrance examination in 1998. While waiting to take the exam the following year, hoping to go to Unpatti in June 1999, the second chapter of conflict wreaked wrath, revenge and blood.

On Eid Al Fitr, 19 January 1999, when doors were wide open and people were asking each other's forgiveness,[2] I went to Rumah Tiga – the Unpatti lecturers' housing complex – to visit Uncle Idrus Tatuhey (Drs. Jusuf Indrus Tatuhey, MS, lecturer in social and political sciences at Unpatti, who at the time of writing is chair of the Moluccan Electoral Commission). Around 3pm, I asked permission to return home. Together with my cousin (Amang, the son of Uncle Idrus) we chose the route along the bay. We didn't go straight to Ambon; rather we stopped off at Dayan Tawainella's house, a close friend of Amang from the Economics Faculty at Unpatti, who lived in

---

2   Translator's note: The custom at Eid Al Fitr is to visit people and ask forgiveness for wrongs committeed, in thought and deed, over the past year.

the provincial government housing complex, Poka. I knew Dayan because he was chairman of the outdoor pursuits group, Kadal Adventure Club, of which I was a member.

After exchanging greetings, we talked, had a drink, and then excused ourselves. However, before we could turn on the engine of the Vespa we were riding, Dayan gave us news that he had received a telephone call. He told us that there was conflict in Batu Merah. The information wasn't surprising. During the time we lived in Batu Merah, while at Junior State High School No. 2 Ambon (before Uncle Idrus moved to Rumah Tiga in 1996), clashes between youths in Batu Merah Dalam were quite normal.

Dayan went on to say, 'The conflict has spread a long way. Mobs of people are gathering along the roads leading to Ambon'. Confirmation was made by telephoning a few friends who lived in different places. Mobs of rioters, especially at several points in the city of Ambon, were gathering as the result of a quickly circulating rumour. Most people, myself included, immediately thought of a religious war.

We decided not to continue our journey to Ambon. We returned to the lecturers' housing complex in Rumah Tiga. There, for about a week, we experienced a range of emotions, from uneasiness, to a degree of calm, to extreme anxiety. In the first two days, rumours circulated quickly. There was a rumour that the main Al-Fatah Mosque had been burnt down by Christian mobs. This rumour incited the mobs. Mobs of people from the Leihitu peninsula, with lightning speed, combed the roads leading to the city of Ambon. There were many casualties.

The situation was no longer safe. Every night, we took it in turns to keep watch, together with others from the housing complex. Uncle Idrus' house was located at the back of the Denzipur V barracks. Every day, however, new rumours would bother us. Our adrenalin went up and down. We didn't sleep well; we didn't enjoy our food. The arrival of refugees from Benteng Karang, whose houses and land had been destroyed by mobs from the Leihitu peninsula, made the situation even more tense.

We held out in the house for three days. Because the situation was becoming increasingly tense, on 23 January we evacuated to the Denzipur V barracks, together with the refugees from Benteng Karang and the surrounding areas. In the barracks, we were safe. Others had been evacuated because of violence, while we were there because we were afraid. After four days in the barracks, we decided to return home to Tial. On 27 January 1999, escorted by security forces, we went to Tial. We brought all of Uncle Idrus' belongings from his house with us.

I don't remember much after that. However, because of the ferocity of the conflict, whether I liked it or not, I had to make a decision. After failing the state university entrance examination for Unpatti in 1998, I had asked permission to study at a university in Makassar. But my mother wouldn't give me permission because of the cost involved. In 1999, after the first chapter of the conflict was over and the general election, with 48 political parties involved, went well in Maluku, I took the state university entrance examination for the second time. While I waited for the results, the conflict erupted again.

My mother decided that I should join the 'exodus' to study in Makassar. Coincidently, my two cousins (Ipul and Ona) also decided to transfer from Pattimura University to Hasanuddin University, Makassar. On 16 August 1999, the three of us, accompanied by Uncle Salim Tatuhey (my mother's older brother), went to Makassar. A month before, another cousin of mine (Fat) had gone to Makassar, also to study.

We boarded a Pelni ship, Dorolonda, heading for Makassar, via the Halong naval base. We arrived at the Murhum port of Bau-Bau, Southeast Sulawesi on 17 August 1999, on the 54th anniversary of Indonesia's Independence Day. I noticed the red and white flag flying in the port. I felt that the flag seemed to be in tatters, because our kinship relationships in Maluku were in tatters.

The next day, on 18 August, we arrived in Makassar, after an 18-hour sea voyage. We had decided that if we couldn't find anywhere to stay, we would sleep at the mosque. At that time, we felt no better than homeless people. The first time I set foot on Makassan soil, was exactly 21 years after my mother gave birth to me in the village of Tial (18 August 1979).

I wanted to study in Makassar because I hadn't passed the state university entrance examination. I was mentally prepared to study and gain experience. I was not, however, mentally prepared to be part of the exodus to Makassar.

My thoughts were always far away in Maluku, in the village of Tial, 22 kilometres from the centre of Ambon, where my parents, siblings and grandparents lived. I was beset by negative thoughts, afraid that death would take them away one-by-one; I was often haunted by such thoughts. I would often cry when I was having a meal. Physically I had joined the exodus but my mind and my anxious thoughts never left Ambon.

After I had registered for a first degree in Journalism at STIKOM FAJAR Makassar, I suddenly received news from Ambon that I had passed the state university entrance examination for the Social and Political Science Faculty at Unpatti. I wanted to return but sadly the information arrived too late. My mother wouldn't agree to me returning to Ambon to study.

When I suggested that I returned Unpatti, my mother replied, 'If you came home, you would get involved in the war. You have two younger siblings (now four younger siblings); if you and your father became casualties who would look after them?' My mother's words halved my negative feelings. I had to focus on my studies and then I would return to Ambon to look after my siblings, as my mother hoped.

One year was enough for me at STIKOM FAJAR. Apart from the language problems, the only Moluccans studying there were myself and Syeihan Rumra (a journalist at the daily *Fajar*, who now works at the daily *Radar Ambon*). Lonely, I moved to the Indonesian Muslim University (UMI) Makassar because there were hundreds of students from Maluku studying there, and studied law. With more people about, my homesickness for my brethren in Maluku reduced. I was considered an introvert then, a little closed and critical in comparison to Syeihan, who was quite open and a little moderate.

At UMI, when I understood how brilliantly the students had brought down the New Order in 1998, I became obsessed with the emerging student world. UMI, in particular, had the reputation of being the most popular campus in Makassar for holding demonstrations. On 24 April 1996, a tragedy had struck this campus, when students clashed with soldiers and some people died and others were wounded.

This incident is known as 'AMARAH' or Bloody April in Makassar. From the documentation that I have seen, tanks attacked the campus. At that time the military commander was Agum Gumelar, and the chief of police was Da'i Bachtiar. In May 2004, a similar incident took place in UMI. This time the clash was with police, and is known as 'MEMAR' (Bloody May in Makassar). No one died but two people were shot and around 300 students were wounded, although some say that 500 were wounded, mainly in the head.

While I was living in Makassar, I and the others living there were often emotionally caught up in the conflict in Maluku. Our analysis of the conflict was narrow and tended to be emotional and, in our expressions of sympathy for our fellow Moluccans, we seemed to be inviting others to see things from our perspective.

On one occasion at Friday prayers at the main Al-Markas Al-Islami Mosque, Makassar, we had heard news of the massacre of about one thousand people in Tobelo, North Maluku. The situation became quite heated. While taking part in Friday prayers, for the first time I saw a preacher being interrupted by one of the worshippers who was trying to stir the fires of jihad through war. That Friday there was an attempt to provide clarity so Muslims would not be provoked by the incident in Tobelo.

It didn't, however, calm the worshippers. The sermon made many tense, including me. My emotions were stirred up, not because of the call for a jihad war, but because there had been so many casualties, yet the police and soldiers hadn't immediately tried to stop it.

After Friday prayers, a crowd gathered spontaneously. Some of the crowd were still wild and wanting a jihad war. A few friends and I took the initiative to demonstrate at the local police station in Makassar. With only a small number of people, we completed a long march of around one kilometre from the Al-Markas Al-Islami Mosque to the local police station in Makassar. Slowly the crowd gathered in large numbers.

The mob delivered an ultimatum. It demanded that in two days the police and army had to catch the provocateurs and other parties that were behind the incident in Tobelo. If this didn't happen, the mob shouted that Makassar would be hit by the same conflict.

The people of Makassar were not influenced. It seems that the demands were only from a small amount of people. 'Makassar is not Maluku, if you want to be involved in a jihad war, please go to Maluku. Don't do it here. It is enough for us to commit to jihad with prayer and aid', said some of the people responding to the demands.

On the campus there were frequent arguments and moving discussions among both radicals and moderates about the conflict. Discussion material was available, some of it humanitarian and some of it put out by 'cannibals'. We often met with anger and concern in these conditions. We were told to weigh things up, to change our perspective. Our emotions and thinking depleted, and I changed my way of thinking.

The issues of our demonstrations at the end of 2001 and the beginning of 2002, close to signing of the Reconciliation of Malino II, had moved far away from the issue of religious conflict to solving the conflict. Our demonstrations had changed and we now asked for the government to be resolute, especially for the police and army to be firm and fair in stopping the conflict.

More than that, we were involved in finding humanitarian aid in the form of medicine, food and second-hand clothes to be distributed in Maluku. We also helped the casualties of the conflict who were sent to Dr. Wahidin Sudirohusodo General Hospital in Makassar. The last people we helped were two burns victims (I forget their names) of the 25 April 2004 conflict. Unfortunately, one of them passed away.

As I started to read other motives behind the Moluccan conflict I became more and more annoyed. When the conflict struck again on 25 April 2004, on the historical RMS anniversary, I was very surprised. The mass media was full of allegations of fraud in the legislative election, which was being contested by 24 political parties. Every day the media reports spotlighted the issue of electoral fraud.

After the 25 April conflict, the headlines in the media changed, from election fraud to the issue of the Moluccan conflict. As someone close to the world of journalism, I was quite sensitive to the change in issues in the mass media. The power of the explosion of the sporadic and wide conflict increased its interest as the main item of news, following the dictum followed that bad news was good news. The media preferred headlines on the Moluccan conflict, because the issue of electoral fraud was not as bad as the Moluccan conflict with its many casualties.

When there was no conflict to report, Maluku was not newsworthy. If there was any news, it would, at most, be reported concisely on one of the middle pages in the mass media. Any incident that occurred in East Java, Greater Jakarta or West Java, for example, in the elections for regional leaders, or political behaviour, including the results of surveys complete with analysis, would be discussed in greater depth, filling one page. Main issues would appear on the front page of the newspaper.

After much thought, I put my reflections into an article entitled, '*Tiga Motif Conflict Agama*' (Three motives behind religious conflict), and sent it to the daily, *Ambon Ekspres*. The message was clear; conflict can be managed. Two motives that were present earlier, that is, the issues of religion and RMS, were not the most significant facts for the instigator. The intellectual actor was looking for a spark to inflame the anger of the mobs, like oil that was ready to be burnt in the stove of religious emotion, with the issue of separatism acting like dry leaves.

I believe these two factors were only used to bring out sensitive emotions. The provocative situation then developed to become an arena that would easily draw blood, because the intellectual actors, with the appropriate stimulants, were able to make the situation worse and increase the frequency of clashes. The work of the provocateur was only to cause friction in the midst of anger, after he had previously studied and mapped the situation accurately.

A letter arrived from my mother, telling me that our Christian relatives in Tial had to leave the village. In Tial there were around 20 Christian homes. They all came from Tial and were all descended from the Tatuhey family, with the same surname as my mother. Some of them had other surnames but had married wives who were from the Christian Tatuhey family.

A mob from another area had entered Tial. Two residents of Tial became victims (Ashar Tuarita, 23 years old, and Sedek, 18 years old). The conflict that occurred on the border between Tial and Suli made the Christian residents of Tial a target. My mother wrote in her letter that she took some old people in. Later I found out that other families also 'saved' Christian relatives from the threating mob outside the village. They were eventually evacuated safely by security forces from Rindam Suli.

What made me sad, however, was that my class teacher from first to sixth year at State Primary School No. 2 Tial, Mrs Tapilouw, couldn't be saved. She was regarded as a 'spy', so she was targeted by the mob, who came from outside. She had lived in Tial for almost 30 years, and didn't want to leave Tial at the time of the conflict. 'People had already tried to suggest that she should leave the village, but she said, what's the point of leaving. If I'm going to die, let me die here,' a primary school friend, Ayat, said, repeating Mrs Tapilouw's words, when we talked about our teacher. I hope that her soul has been received by the Lord.

Here is a story of how Christians with the Tatuhey surname came to live in Tial. It is said that at the beginning of the 18th century the third generation of Tatuhey, a man called Korbow, had two sons. The older child was called Tiar and the younger Thaib. The two often hunted for tuna fish in their junk. Because they frequently stopped at Hutumuri to rest and eat, Thaib fell in love with a girl in that village.

Then Thaib, when he got the opportunity, asked his father's permission to marry. His father was confused, as he had never seen Thaib with a girl, so he asked, 'Who do you want to marry?' Thaib replied, 'A girl from Hutumuri'. However, there was a condition, said Thaib, he had to change his religion to that of the girl. His father gave permission and Thaib got married to the girl. After getting married, his father told Thaib to settle in a location that was close to the beach in the western part of Tial. His descendants lived there for 300 years, until they were 'evicted' on 19 September 1999.

It is interesting that the people of Tial have never called that location 'Christian Tial', but rather 'Amang Kakoin', or small village. The houses of Amang Kakoin are only a stone's throw away from the other houses in Tial. There was no segregation so everyone mixed socially, like an extended family. Amang Kakoin was like a room in a large house, or like a chamber in the heart that enabled the dynamics of family life in Tial to continue to throb.

There had been thirteen generations of Christian Tatuheys in Tial since Thaib became a Christian. They were given a hamlet, land and garden to provide them with a livelihood. From this story it is clear that the kinship feelings have always been there. By leaving his parent's religion, a child did not destroy the kinship relationship.

The Christian relatives from Tial lived as refugees in Rindam Suli, and others mixed with the people of Suli. However, after the conflict calmed down and the situation became more conducive, some started to live near the river Waiyari and others near Waitatiri. Often, when travelling from Ambon to Tial, I would see the GPM Tial church sign in front of the Suli Indah Inn, as a sign that they used it as a church for worship. Their church in Tial was badly damaged and left in ruins. It was destroyed along with their homes, which were also razed to the ground.

They have woodlands and other extensive lands in Tial. They should, in the interests of history, return to Tial. There have been attempts made to encourage them to return but these overtures have, to date, been unsuccessful. As far as I know, one of people involved in these attempts was Uncle Idrus Tatuhey as someone from the same bloodline working together with the government. It seems that, having been refugees for a long time, they have now bought land and built permanent houses. They are, however, still acknowledged, as they should be, as traditional descendants of Tial.

I had never thought, until my mother's letter made me aware of it, that I have an intimate experience of a kinship relationship with Christian families from Tial. Especially at the beginning of the conflict, my emotions were always caught up with thinking about Muslims versus Christians. My thoughts were filled with the segregation of religious war. The arrival of my mother's letter made me feel sad, because I realised that I knew some of them as relatives.

As someone whose genes are from Hatuhaha, because my father is from Rohomoni, I also tried to find the story of how the village of Hulaliu became Christian. In the book *Potret Retak Nusantara* [Portrait of a Splintered Archipelago], a collection of articles and case studies from various conflict regions in Indonesia, Rev. Jacky Manuputty and Daniel Wattimanela wrote about conflict in Maluku, including the history of Hulaliu becoming Christian to reduce the spread of the Alaka war (1625–1637) and protect their four sister villages, Pelauw, Kailolo, Kabau and Rohomoni.

In deliberations with the VOC (Netherlands), in which Hatuhaha was represented by Hulaliu, the VOC asked that one of the five villages become Christian. If they refused, the Dutch would wage a war against the strength of Islam in Hatuhaha. Out of love for her four sisters, Hulaliu was prepared to become Christian and the four other villages wept. Because of this, in Dra. Maryam Lestaluhu stated in her book, *Sejarah Perlawanan Islam terhadap Imperialisme di Daerah Maluku* [The History of the Resistance of Islam towards Imperialism in the Moluccan Region], the Alaka War was a war without defeat.

In another version, Hulaliu becoming Christian had nothing to do with deliberations with the VOC, in which Hulaliu represented Hatuhaha Amarima. A part of oral history mentions that Pikay Laisina (the ancestor of Hulaliu) left Amahatua (in the hills) for Amalaina (on the coast) after an agreement with the leaders of the four villages, led by Patty Kasim (or Patty Hatuhaha). Laisina objected, but Patty Kasim persuaded him and Laisina eventually prepared to leave Amahatua. Weeping, the four leaders let Laisina go. Laisina sobbed as he left them.

When he went down to the coast, Laisina built a mosque in Hualaliu that is Nambuasa Mosque. After they became Christian, Nambuasa Mosque was moved to Rohomoni. The mosque was not moved in its entirety, but the preaching cane and the left-over stones that were usually used to burn dry resin on the 25th day of the fast month were moved.

These stones, in the Hatuhaha dialect of Hulaliu, are called 'Haturessy', which means 'remaining stones'. In order to reflect on the history of Islam in Hatuhaha, Nambuasa Mosque was deliberately built in Rohomoni, next to the Hatuhaha Mosque. The two-storey mosque is, however, much smaller than the Hatuhaha Mosque, which has three floors.

The Alaka war took place in three stages over 12 years. Hulaliu became Christian in the last stage of the war, around 1630. They were baptised by the Dutch and were bathed in a small stream, now called *Wae Uru Mau*. The story goes that after they were baptised, the Laisina headbands (*lahatale*) worn by Hatuhaha male adults were removed and exchanged for *capeu* (hats). Laisina felt that his head had shrunk, so the stream was named *Wae Uru Mau*, which means 'shrunken head'. After that, the Dutch built a church in Hulaliu, giving it the name Santatheo.

Whatever the version, the five villages, Pelauw, Kabauw, Rohomoni, Kailolo and Hulaliu, are still called *Amarima Lounusa*. *Amarima* means 'five villages', while *Lounusa* means, 'return to land of origin'. Thus *Amarima Lounusa* is the expression of the desire of the kin when the five villages were still Amahatua, especially when they were together in the Uli Hatuhaha kingdom.

History, experience and critical reflections like this have formed my philosophy of life in understanding the conflict, separation (exodus) and kinship. I went to Makassar as a rigid Muslim, trying to be at peace with feelings of anger and revenge because of the conflict, so that I could return to the village of Tial as kin.

After being introduced to Karl Popper's *Open Society*, I can forgive everything, because conflict reflects all human experiences from a variety of cultures to the best civilisation. According to Popper, the best civilisation is an 'open society', tolerant and always willing to learn. Reading Nietzsche's ten utterances, however, made me erase all the truth that I felt I knew; the most telling utterance for me was 'the truths of mankind are the mistakes of mankind that cannot be contradicted'.

In December 2005, I graduated in law from UMI Makassar and returned home to Ambon in April 2006. I married my 'first love', Nurmarwati Wadjo, on 11 June 2006 and at the time of writing we have two children, Eka (2 years) and Mahatir (2 months). I feel that we have all had enough of the bitterness of conflict.

I don't want my children to experience conflict in the future – if possible, not for seven generations. That is why I often write essays and give my opinions. That led to Rudi Rahabeat asking me to contribute to this book. I only have one goal – that we abandon violent conflict, by developing a healthy dialogue about peace for humankind and for God. Amen!

Chapter 19

WHEN POLITICS SPEAKS

Thamrin Ely

A good world needs knowledge, kindliness and courage; it does not need a regretful hankering after the past or a fettering of the free intelligence by the words uttered long ago by ignorant men. It needs a fearless outlook and a free intelligence. It needs hope for the future, not looking back all the time toward a past that is dead, which we trust will be far surpassed by the future that our intelligence can create.

(Bertrand Russell: *Why I am not a Christian*, 1957)

Observing the violent political conflict in Maluku since 1999, people could draw the conclusion that this archipelagic province has a thousand potential conflict flashpoints ready to be ignited at any time, borrowing a conclusion from *Newsweek*, 9 July 2001.

Whether this was the case or not, two types of conflict occurred almost simultaneously: horizontal and vertical conflict. Horizontal conflict is conflict between two groups within society, often known as 'social conflict' or 'communal conflict'. Vertical conflict occurs between the state and civil society. If Talcott Parsons states that conflict takes place because of clashes of interests, then in the eyes of Dahrendorf, conflict is greatly influenced by the role of the actors in the organisation, who are supported by ideologies and particular interests.

Louis Kriesberg offers four factors in recognising conflict: first, the issue that brought about the conflict; second, the characteristics of the groups involved in the conflict; third, the relationship between the conflicting groups; and fourth, the methods implemented by each of the conflicting groups.

The violent conflict that took place on Eid Al Fitr, 19 January 1999, was triggered by a dispute between individuals within the general community but the conflict was immediately formulated as a religious conflict. Yopi and Salim, who are seen to be the triggering factor, were, however, not religious leaders or leaders in the general population, who had the capacity to call for war. The same pattern of violent political conflict occurred on Christmas day, 25 December 1998, in Poso. This was triggered by Roy and Akhmad (who were also not religious leaders) but it became a religious issue immediately, because it involved religious symbols.

The people who held the reins of the political conflict consciously used the characteristics of the people of Maluku. Moluccans are hard and emotional but known for their tolerance, so that they want to fight continuously and can also be transformed any time, with the intention of taking care of the conflict so that it continued, whether the stakeholders, their target, realised it or not.

After the conflict on Eid Al Fitr 1999 in Ambon, the conflict changed many times, becoming a vertical conflict, raising the issue of separatism. But, strangely, the groups in the conflict were not the state versus civil society, rather the supporters of NKRI against those who were supporters of the FKM/RMS separatist movement (2000). In the conflict between the supporters of NKRI and RMS, the victims of the anonymous snipers were the supporters of NKRI. Then questions arose, were the snipers members of the RMS armed forces, or was it an attempt by the national intelligence to put a stop to the conflict? Until now, not one case of the violation of human rights has been brought to justice.

This was followed by horizontal conflict between religious groups to gain hold of the sources of politics and economy. Then there was the conflict between military units and the police, as a result of the reform of the security sector, which to date has only dealt with a very limited number of legal and structural reforms but has not yet dealt with the behaviour of the security forces.

Conflict also occurred between neighbouring traditional villages of the same religious background or between traditional villages with different religious backgrounds, whether caused by disputes over village boundaries, or just the dynamics of actions by young people. Mysterious shootings and bomb explosions added to the list of violent conflict. These conflicts always smelt of the security forces' involvement, particularly given that the firearms, which caused many casualties, were rarely detected by intelligence agencies. We don't know whether this was caused by weaknesses in the organisations which decipher state codes or whether other institutions became directly or indirectly involved in the conflict, or were co-opted into supporting the political conflict. Maluku even became the object of global intelligence operations.

Political conflict 'to the last drop of blood' is very militaristic; so military circles worldwide do not really like peace politics. In Indonesia's modern history, we can see how the attempt to maintain Indonesian independence led to differences between General Sudirman, who fought in the jungles of Java, and Soekarno-Hatta-Syahrir, who chose the diplomatic route. Similarly, resolving the issue of Aceh's Independence Movement (GAM) involved the military with a huge budget, but that was brought to a halt by Jusuf Kalla through more economical peace diplomacy in Helsinki. What Jusuf Kalla had done in Poso and Maluku, he continued in Aceh.

Wiranto rejected the accusations that TNI was the controller of the political conflict in a number of regions. TNI said these were not in line with the concept of 'ideological compromise', new steps which redefined, repositioned and implemented the role of the TNI. Wiranto claimed that many intelligence operations were carried out without the knowledge of the TNI HQ. We often witnessed this during the violent conflict in Maluku.

The style of the violent conflict in Maluku indicates that there was an intellectual actor, key figures, a central issue and a group of leaders, who instigated the violent conflict. The central issue and the group of instigators were clearly visible. The intellectual actor and key figures, often said to be the provocateurs, are still camouflaged. While the Malino Agreement on 12 February 2002 decided to form an Independent Investigation Team (Presidential Decree No. 38 of 2002 on the Formation of a National Independent Investigation Team on the Conflict in Maluku), the results of this investigation have never been made public.

The Relationship between Islam and Christianity in Maluku

With the map of the conflict like this, we need to consider the relationship between Islam and Christianity as the object of violent conflict, through the role of leading organisations in each group. Their relationship had, in fact, experienced ups and downs – with several variants – since the colonial period. But the groups were carried away and trapped by the strategy of political conflict (often with violence), without being aware that they were only objects. Others profitted from the violent conflict.

This started with the colonists who came to Maluku in the guise of continuing the mission of the Crusades. It turned out, however, that they were only interested in trading and depleting the natural resources of Maluku. The Dutch East Indies Company (VOC) introduced the conflict theory of divide and conquer.

The Indische Kerk (the embryo of the Protestant Church of Maluku – GPM) knew this theory well. In *Chabar Ambon* (a monthly newsletter of the association of credited clergy which was legalised by the Decision of the Governor General No 32 of 19 January 1924) we find news (in volume 32, no 1 of 4 October 1924) of the Lombok War. This report mentions that an 'army chaplain was honourably discharged because of sickness, and has been replaced by another army chaplain' (National Library, Jakarta – Port III No 11).

This quote from *Chabar Ambon* shows that the church, as a religious organisation, was ready and adept at anticipating emergency situations, regardless of how bad it was, as seen in the appointment of an 'army chaplain'.

Unsurprisingly, after the conflict of 19 January 1999, GPM quickly formed the Communication Forum (Bankom), Crisis Centre, and Church Lawyer Team (TPG). This last organisation was then disbanded by GPM. Several activists then joined FKM and continued the same mission as they had in TPG. Possessing modern organisational experience and with congregational loyalty, GPM was perhaps able to exceed the limitations of their authority. Officials, businesspeople and politicians, who were symbiotically involved in the activities of GPM organisations, often placed GPM in a non-independent position, both politically and economically.

MUI Maluku is an organisation that is not on the same level as GPM, which has a structure that reaches to the branch level. MUI only goes as far as regency level. Sunni Islam in Indonesia does not have the concept of *imamah* (leadership), as do the Shiites. The organisation and the congregations tend to be against structure and are therefore difficult to organise.

During the violent conflict, which took place from 1999, MUI was only able to form a Unit for the Dealing of Casualties of the Bloody Eid Al Fitr Incident (Satgas IFB) on 25 January 1999; this was later disbanded. The Joint Muslim Secretariat (Sekber UI) was formed in 2000 but its offices were turned upside down and its radio transmitter destroyed in an unclear incident. A number of organisations emerged in the form of pressure groups and (Sekber UI) established a new radio transmitter, until the Grand Muslim Conference created the Board for the Welfare of Muslims in Maluku (BIMM). It was hoped that these organisations would perform the same role as GPM, but for a variety of reasons, these organisations didn't function.

In general, it must be acknowledged that religious organisations, from the leadership at the top to taskforces or pressure groups, tended to be exclusive and were formed to strengthen the conflict. People proclaimed 'love' and '*ukhuwah*' (solidarity) only for the in-groups; everyone outside those was a competitor who was in diametrical opposition. There was no effort to create initiatives where both sides worked together, except in forums formed by a third party or the government.

Experience in Maluku shows that, in reality, the syncretic tradition played a greater role in social integration than that played by religious organisations. This has occurred through the pela-gandong institution or other local traditions, although in a limited capacity.

Final Words

Looking ahead, there is much to be gained from reading again the words of Bertram Russell quoted at the beginning of this chapter.

We need to have the courage to reflect and be aware of our own weaknesses. If we don't know each other, we won't be able to respect each other. On the contrary, group egotism and claims to truth will dominate.

A strategy is therefore needed to strengthen society based on faith and culture, to improve social relations, including the development of a better self-image. If the Christian church, especially the Protestant church, could be more like the Calvinists with their Protestant ethics as its foundation, then the work ethos of the congregation would be encouraged, and the congregation would not depend on government bureaucracy, a confusing paradox. The conflict in Maluku which was triggered by the general population, because the economic imbalance needs a joint thought-out plan to stimulate prosperity in a more systematic program. The GPM structure which reaches down to the lowest level in society could introduce economic activities that are more based on natural resources.

A prosperous, peace-loving nation will feel disturbed if there is conflict; on the contrary, a poor nation will use conflict to become prosperous but in doing so will sacrifice humankind.

The rest, only God knows.

Part IV

Hiti Hiti Hala Hala: Enjoying the Good Things Together and Facing Difficulties Together

Chapter 20

WE ARE ALL BROTHERS AND SISTERS

Hilary Syaranamual

The first time I arrived in Maluku was in October 1993. I had just got married to Reza Syaranamual, who is Ambonese. We travelled to Ambon, taking the Pelni ship, MV Rinjani. The sea in Ambon Bay looked beautiful and was not yet polluted by rubbish.

It turned out that in Ambon the weather was really bright and sunny during the month of October. The water in the bay was still and shimmering like a mirror and dolphins danced alongside the ship as it made its way to its mooring at the Yos Sudarso Port. What a wonderful gift for a bride who for the first time witnessed the natural beauty of Maluku.

Although I had lived in Indonesia – in Malang, East Java – for ten years, I didn't know anything about the culture or the language used in Ambon. Beforehand Reza had told me that the language used in Ambon was the same as the Indonesian language that I had used in Malang. We spent the first few weeks getting to know the family, including starting to understand the language being used around me. Granny (my mother-in-law's mother) lived in Wayang. We often visited her and got to know her neighbours. I remember the first time I tasted *papeda* together with the extended family. This happened when the family gathered when grandpa died (my father-in-law's father) in Amahai on the island of Seram.

The majority of our time was spent in full-time ministry in the church, thus our social circle was often limited to the people in our church and their needs. However, we also met with my husband's friends. They were friends from primary school, junior high school and senior high school. There were also the friends with whom he used to play football. Besides these, Reza also had friends who lived in the vicinity of the military hospital (RST) Ambon. Reza's family, including his grandparents and both his parents, had worked at the hospital, so from his early childhood he was familiar with the people who lived and worked near to the hospital.

We also had the opportunity to visit the village of Nolloth on the island of Saparua which is where Reza's family originated. In going to Nolloth we were able to get to know the extended family of my father-in-law. We also went and watched the 'Pukul Sapu' ceremony, which takes place in Mamala and Morela,[1] an example of the culture on Ambon Island.

After a reasonable amount of time of living in Ambon, I began to understand that for the Moluccan people the important thing was to identify a person's place in the social order. Who are their parents? Where have they lived? From which traditional village does the family originate? Where did they go to school? Once a link had been established with a person, then that person would feel free to spend time talking to us, because he/she understood that the person he/she was speaking to was a fellow Moluccan. The first time two people met, they always tried to understand the exact relationship between the two people holding the conversation to establish what they had in common or who they both knew. Once this link was established, then those involved in the conversation felt at ease. After living and being assimilated into the daily way of life in Maluku, I discovered that the bonds of kinship between the Moluccan people are very strong.

A Feeling of Restlessness in Malang

In May 1998 we moved to Malang so that Reza could complete his Bachelor's degree. When we arrived in Malang, a city where I had lived for several years previously, I felt like a stranger. I wanted to return as quickly as possible to Maluku. I didn't remember a single word of Javanese, although I had been familiar with the language previously. Perhaps this was because I had become used to speaking the Ambonese dialect over the years that I had lived in Maluku. This made it difficult for me to communicate with others

---

1 Translator's note: *Pukul Sapu*, or 'hitting with brooms' is a traditional ceremony held in the neighbouring villages of Mamala and Morela at the same time. Two groups of youths in short trousers (one group in red and the other in green or white) beat each other on their backs and chests with brooms made from the spines of palm leaves until their skin bleeds. The ceremony marks the defeat of Kapiten Tulukabessy forces to Portuguese and Dutch VOC forces in the 16th century. This resulted in the Kapapaha Fort falling to the invading forces. The troops were said to have whipped each other with palm leaf spines in the wake of this defeat.

during the first weeks after we arrived in Malang. Eventually we started to readjust to the situation in East Java, the place where Reza had returned to complete his studies at the Southeast Asia Bible Seminary, Malang.

On 19 January 1999, Reza made a phone call to Ambon to wish a member of our former congregation a happy birthday. This friend of ours happened to live directly opposite the main Al-Fatah Mosque. We were shocked when we heard from this friend that clouds of smoke could be seen coming from the Silale area and that the home of the Nikijuluw family had been burnt down. That house was not far from granny's house in Waihaong. Reza often went to that house because Heidy, Reza's school friend from kindergarten through to senior high school, lived there. Reza's mother was also a school friend of Heidy's father. We phoned our home in OSM to check on Reza's parents. It turned out that Reza's mother was in the Soabali area visiting her friends who were celebrating the end of Ramadan. We felt helpless, living far away in Malang, because we couldn't do anything about the situation. Late in the evening we received news that Reza's mother had arrived home safely.

It was almost impossible for Reza to concentrate on his studies. We continued to receive news from Ambon which made us feel very anxious but we couldn't do anything about the situation. The people who rented granny's house in Waihaong had to run away to save their lives. The members of our family who lived in Hunuth were forced to seek refuge, and we received news that one of our relatives had been killed when he drove a truck to pick up the children who had taken part in a retreat. The retreat had taken place at research facilities belonging to the Fisheries Department of Pattimura University (Unpatti) close to the village of Hila.

After living a year in Malang, we moved to a house which was close to the Merdeka University (Unmer). The main reason for this move was that the local church had asked us to minister to students. At the same time, I was also asked to be the advisor to Christian students at the same university. When we started to get to know the students at Unmer, it turned out that many of these students came from eastern Indonesia, including Maluku. There were also students from Maluku, whose families had moved to live in Papua or other areas in Indonesia. We decided to make our house an open house, especially for those students from Maluku whom we ministered to. Not only that, the house was open to anyone who passed by and wanted to come in.

We tried to create a home-away-from-home atmosphere, so that those students who were far from their parents could experience the warmth of those who came from the same region. As time went on the language used in our home was the Ambonese dialect. Thus anyone who came through our doors, whether they liked it or not, had to learn the Ambonese dialect, including students with Javanese, Dayak or Batak backgrounds, who also used to come to our home. We did this so that those who were living a long distance from their parents could express how they really felt about things in a language that was close to their hearts. Thus students from Sumba, Timor, Papua, Toraja, Manado and Maluku could communicate far more freely.

Our main aim was to give spiritual guidance. Our hope was that these students would become more mature and would be able to complete their studies, which had been disrupted because of the effects of the community unrest. The students were very worried about their parents, also the flow of funds needed for their studies and everyday needs were no longer running smoothly. With help from friends in Malang, cartons of instant noodles were dropped off at our house. Funds were also made available that we channelled according to the needs that arose. Besides activities of a spiritual nature, we also helped mentor a vocal group. This group was already in existence before we met them. During our time in Malang this group was able to perform all over East Java; they even had opportunities to perform in Denpasar, Palangka Raya. They were able to record two albums, although only for limited circulation. For those who preferred sport, we mentored a group of footballers who took part in an Army Strategic Command football competition that took place in Malang. The aim of all these activities was to channel all their energy channelled into positive activities. Although there were quite a few Moluccan students in Malang, it was free from problems related to religion. Everybody was free to come and go and mix in our house. The problems that we dealt with were usually related to boy- and girlfriend issues and the usual problems related to student life. If the problems turned out to be quite difficult to solve, my husband, who is a pastor, would sort the problems out and, if necessary, he would involve Ambonese soldiers who were stationed in Malang.

There was only one incident that occurred at Unmer that we felt had been engineered from outside the university. One day Ambonese students ran to the house to tell us that an Ambonese Christian student had been attacked in the Economics Faculty building by an Ambonese Muslim student. Eventually we were able to calm down the students so that they did not become involved. It seemed this incident was in response to a previous incident when an Ambonese Muslim student had been attacked by another Ambonese Christian student. After it was investigated, it turned out that this person had not attended lectures for some time, so we were confused why he could have been involved in such an incident. Exaggerated reports from mass organisations from outside the university meant that this matter was brought up in the Student Executive Body. We were not directly involved in the process of solving the matter on the campus, but we gave input to the students under our guidance in the Christian fellowship that the root of the problem needed to be clarified and the matter should be resolved in a wise manner. Eventually the problem subsided, because it was acknowledged that both sides had lost out and, to protect the harmonious atmosphere on the campus, the problem should not be magnified.

Although we were living outside Ambon, we felt the impact of the community unrest. We therefore tried to help students, not just to continue their studies but also care for others. We were involved in providing guidance for 44 police cadets from Ambon who had been assigned to complete their training at the Mojokerto Police Academy. They also felt far from their families and every weekend some of them would come and stay with us. Before their training was over, we were given permission to organise a retreat for them in Pacet and students from Unmer were involved in giving guidance to these police cadets.

While we were in Malang, our student friends became skilled in selecting and sending second-hand clothes that we received from acquaintances, who wanted to help people in Ambon. Although we lived in Malang, our attention was focused on the situation in Ambon and we endeavoured to return home to Ambon when we could.

Sadness in Ambon

The first time we returned home to Ambon was the end of semester holiday in June 1999. We boarded one of the Pelni ships and we arrived at the Yos Sudarso port. This experience was very different from the first time I arrived in Ambon. We felt happy because we had an opportunity to go home and bring aid in the form of medicines, underwear and sanitary items for the people in Ambon. But we were anxious when we stood on the steps of the ship. There was a trembling and a feeling of fear when we started down the steps of the ship. These feelings emerged because we didn't know how to get to the house. Nobody had come to meet us. We were frightened that we would get on the wrong public transport. I felt sad because my husband was returning to the place where he grew up but we didn't feel calm.

While we were in Ambon we tried to understand what had really happened there. Because I am 'fair skinned', we felt it was unwise for me to immediately visit certain places. It might be lead to misunderstanding if people didn't know me. At that time there was still open access to Waihaong and we wanted to go and visit our neighbours who still lived there. Reza went down the alley way first to see what the situation was like. Once he felt it was safe, then the two of us went in the direction of granny's old house.

The families who lived in the vicinity were very pleased to see us. They hugged us and wept with joy when they knew we had come to find them. Some of the newcomers in the area asked what we were doing there. Our old neighbours told them, however, that we were members of their family. We entered their house and we chatted with them. They explained what had gone on in the area close to our old house. Although we were of different religious backgrounds, it didn't stop us enjoying the warmth of family relationships in Maluku.

That time we joined together with a few friends from the medical profession to organise free medical treatment at the Army officer's training School at Suli (Secata). We had brought medical supplies with us donated by friends in Malang to be distributed among the refugees. We treated all the refugees living there, irrespective of their religious or ethnic background. Our aim was to help fellow Moluccans; we were not concerned about their beliefs or racial background.

The next time we went to Ambon, we boarded a Hercules plane that was flown from the Abdul Rachman Saleh Air force base in Malang. We had completed all the paperwork several days before we were due to leave; an official had come to the house and checked our identity cards. We had also paid for the flight before we were due to leave. When we arrived at the air force base and were waiting for our bags to be weighed, a member of the intelligence service approached us and informed us that we were not allowed to fly because I represented a threat to security in Ambon. The reason I was deemed to be a threat was because I was 'fair skinned'. I was taken aback because my papers including our family registration card, identity card and driving licence were issued in Ambon. The interesting thing was that a few seconds later, a different official came and told us to get ready to board the plane. When he gave the signal we had to run quickly to the plane. We had paid for our tickets so if we didn't take the plane then they would have to refund the money.

We finally took off and flew via Jogjakarta and Makassar and eventually arrived at the air force base in Laha, Ambon. The day we arrived it was the time for a change in the tour of duty for the air force special forces. When we glanced up we could see several security forces lined up on the nearby hills with their weapons aimed at the airport and the air force base next to it. The friends who were due to pick us up were late. We were frightened because we didn't know how to make our way out of the air force base if nobody picked us up. After waiting for some time, we were picked up. Then we had to learn how to take a speed boat to Gudang Arang and then take public transport to our house.

Every time we returned home to Ambon, we tried to visit the families of our students in Malang. We did this so that their families would know that there were some adults who were keeping an eye on their children. In 2003, when the situation started to recover in Ambon, we returned, bringing with us the vocal group we had mentored, so that they could entertain and encourage the refugees. We took one of the students who came from the village of Waai to meet with his grandparents, who were living in a refugee camp in the Barito complex in Passo, Ambon. Another time we also visited this family once the people of Waai had returned en masse to their village. At that time people were frightened to go Tulehu. People were amazed when they had heard that we had visited Waai. We then explained that there was no reason to be afraid when passing through Tulehu on the way to Waai. People were frightened because the majority of the people of Tulehu are Muslim.

Once we saw that Ambon was more and more conducive and almost all of the students we had mentored had graduated, we decided to return to Ambon. We also decided that we would be freelance in order to help build up Maluku, so that we would not be tied to just one congregation.

Friendship Ties

Many stories could be told, but I want to focus on the restoration of bonds of friendship in Maluku. What I noticed, after we returned to live in Ambon, was that there were efforts made by many parties to try and build up these ties of friendship, which had almost been severed. Reza had gone to State Junior High School No. 3 and State Senior High School No. 1. He and his friends renewed contact, after such a time of separation. They had lost contact with one friend and nobody knew where he was or where he had moved to during the community unrest in Maluku. Eventually, after a long search, we got news that he was living in the Bekasi area of Jakarta. Everyone was happy that they had eventually found him. Friends from Junior High School No. 3 held a reunion as a manifestation of the friendship ties in Maluku. The atmosphere of the reunion was very friendly and all enjoyed getting together again. Since then, there have been many occasions when old school friends have got together in Jakarta or Ambon and they still continue to keep in contact.

We have also been involved with musicians and journalists. We were given the responsibility to organise the *Kacupeng* children's magazine. Although we have faced problems getting the magazine published regularly, the aim of the magazine is for children to understand their culture and to learn to accept and respect each other. The same thing has been manifested in the photographic community, with the establishment of Performa and what has become the Maluku Photo Club (MPC).

The incident on 11 September 2011 shocked everyone, and trust between different members of society almost disappeared. However, I found some of the developments interesting. That day we were returning from Aston Hotel in Natsepa and we passed through Batu Gantung. Everything looked very quiet. A few minutes after we arrived at the house, we received a text message from one of our former students who was living in Masohi. He asked if the news was correct that there had been clashes between people living in Waringin and those living in Batu Gantung. We immediately contacted friends and we found out what had happened. Reza went back in the direction of the city to find out exactly what was going on. All through the night into the early hours we were in contact with our Muslim friends keeping an eye on the situation and sending clear information to them. For me, the grass-roots movement worked hard by sending correct and accurate information to counter incorrect information that was circulating. I don't think this sort of thing happened in the past, but now the friendship ties are much stronger and can be used to reduce feelings of fear and suspicion that emerge when unwanted incidents occur.

For me, the friendship and kinship relationships of people in Maluku are far deeper than it was a few years ago, and the important thing is trusting one another so that suspicion and fear can be reduced when unexpected incidents occur. Some people are beginning to understand the values that were sown by their ancestors. I hope that, with people understanding more about traditional and cultural values, the everyday lives of the people of Maluku will be enriched.

Chapter 21

PEACE IS JUST ONE BREATH AWAY

Sandra Lakembe

dust and earth
form has been created
breath has been given
transform one
truly does not have the right
to change the design
in forming one's own nirvana
given a glorious position
given a command
strength in the banquet
every drop of blood
gives life to every substance
dissolves thick darkness
in the sky
only elements
a dot in the silk illusion
transforming times
but just a dot
not having a second life
not having a thousand hands
only hoping

ONLY DUST

Beginning with a flashback of what happened in the 1999–2004 era is like uncovering a struggle between sanity and insanity. Everyone living in Maluku has stories, opinions, and assessments about the causes of the social disaster that happened in Maluku. I also have my own assessment.

However, above all, great appreciation should be given to the genuine heroes in life. They were the agents of social economics who risked their lives above all. They remained consistent to their vision of life, fulfilling the needs of their families and serving humankind in the worst of conditions, without looking for a reward.

The highest appreciation goes to the sellers in the Mardika market Ambon, the labourers in the Yos Sudarso dock Ambon, the minibus drivers, truck drivers and humanitarian volunteers. They stayed sane in the midst of the insanity of the situation and conditions of that time and still hold their line consistently today. Thank you for being a breath of fresh air in between the weeping, screams of anger, the red of the raging flames and the spilt blood on Maluku's earth.

I don't remember that much from the five-year period of darkness in Ambon. I can only remember only one true value of diversity that strengthened my movements, my thoughts of staying in Ambon and not leaving the beloved place of my birth.

Many friends living outside Ambon often asked me then, 'How can you handle being in Ambon and not be provoked by the situation? Why don't you get out of Ambon?' At that time, I only had one answer, 'Try to keep sane'. When the social disaster happened (forgive my words) 'those who were sane became insane' and 'those who were insane became sane'. Only those who in that situation were generally called 'insane' didn't get involved in aggravating the situation and taking part in the social tragedy. They only sat laughing as they watched 'sane people blaspheme and kill each other'.

Child: Dad, what's this picture?

Father: This is the path to eternal life ... the place where there is no famine, no one is angry, no one fights, there is no envy, no one denigrates other's beliefs, there are no poor or rich, all are the same. There, everyone who draws breath gives thanks ... There are blessings ... There is love ...

Child:	You mean it's heaven? [She quickly countered.] But why are there many roads that branch off? There are also all different types of people there!
Father:	Child, there is only one road to heaven. There is only one Lord. The branches in the road are when we visit a new place, and we would really like to go there, however we can't go alone. We need to be given guidance so that we don't take the wrong road. The one who guides us and directs us is not just anyone or a human being.
Child:	Oh, like a guide, Dad?
Father:	[Smiling] Yes, something like that. Our guide leading us to the one Lord can be different. Our guide is Jesus; if it's Mama Tja, Tji Loen or Uncle Musa, their guide is the prophet Mohammed. If the people are Buddhists, their guide is Sidharta Gautama, etc. We go along different paths, and then we will meet at the crossroads before in the end we will travel together to the ideal place.
Child:	So we will all go there, won't we?
Father:	Yes. All people from all tribes, nations and religions, if they have done good deeds all their lives on earth, carrying out the Lord's commands and believing in Him, this will bring you to a place in heaven. The Lord never taught about differences, but the Lord teaches us to accept diversity. People don't have the right to judge. Only the Lord has the right to judge.

That is part of a conversation I still remember from when I was just four and a half years old. This simple teaching that I received from my late father has become the strong foundation in my life's journey till this day. It is simple … not difficult to describe diversity in belief.

When formal religious teaching is received, the term that we learnt was 'difference'. It didn't matter, this term didn't influence the way I regarded family, relatives and friends, who have chosen diversity in another religion.

My father provided me with a lesson on life, based on what he told me and taught me when I was small, by his clear attitude wherever he was. Thankfully, I was raised in a diverse family so I could experience the beauty of respect, the beauty of acknowledging others' choices, the beauty of visiting on the diverse religious celebrations. Easter, Eid Al Fitr, the Pilgrimage feast and Christmas are the four great phenomena of family life that are inseparable from my life's journey for the last 30 years, before it was forcibly taken away by insane people. But only the physical can be taken away, not our basic convictions of belief.

I didn't really understand the last sentence uttered by my father. I only really began to understand the truth when I lost my dear uncle who passed away in Dobo, and when my elder brother was maimed for life, all because of the judgement of dust and earth that acts in the name of 'defender of truth, defender of religion, defender of the Lord'. Who knows which Lord was being defended … who knows which religion was being defended?

The last message of my uncle to the family before he died was, 'Don't retaliate'. When my father and mother received the news of my uncle's death, I saw my parents crying for the first time in my life.

My father's message to the family when my brother hung between life and death was, 'Don't retaliate, because we don't have the right to judge'. In a piercing voice my father also declared to others (who at that time wanted to act as heroes and retaliate), 'Is it your right to retaliate, we don't need to be defended … Our family sees this as fate, the trials of life given by the Lord … So why are you angry … ? Why do you have to use our family's name in order to retaliate?'

The greatest loss in the richness of my life and, indeed, in my family's life happened during the social catastrophe from 1999 to 2004. Our extended family had to leave Ambon for Banda, Southeast Maluku and for Southeast Sulawesi (Buton). We felt it even more when we began the fasting month. There were no more get-togethers in Air Puteri, Belakang Kota, Poka and Tulehu on Eid Al Fitr and there was no cheerfulness at Christmas. There were no more trips in the early evening close to the breaking of the fast along the street in front of the Al-Fatah Mosque. The days went on as usual. Everything was just routine.

My sadness was cured a little because I could still go freely wherever I liked. I could still meet up with my uncle, the late Yusuf Elly, and Aunty Fat. I could still stay over at their house, chat with them, and discuss many things about how this could happen and why we all had to be forced apart. Fortunately for me, I don't look very Ambonese, and my dialect isn't too Ambonese, which made it easier for me to cross the imaginary border. I still remember (and perhaps all Ambonese still remember) Uncle Utju's utterance describing the social disaster in Maluku: 'other people strike the *toto buang* (traditional instruments), we dance, and the other people got up and left but we continue to dance without the *toto buang*'.

People regarded him as a controversial figure, but for me he was still my Uncle Utju, my uncle didn't change. He helped many people but not many people knew. There is one story that I need to tell about that time, because it would have been impossible to say anything at the time. When the incident happened in 2002 the people of Waai had to leave their village. Food stocks were very difficult to obtain, especially milk for babies and toddlers. I wasn't at home because I was staying at the home of Uncle Utju. Early in the morning I received a phone call from my brother who asked if I could provide clothes for babies, toddlers, children, milk, baby bottles, and women's and children's underwear. This would be taken on a cargo barge and given to the people of Waai who would be evacuated (this incident occurred on the first day of the disaster in Waai).

At that time, I was asked to just take whatever was available in the shops and pay for it after I had returned to our house in Belso. It turned out that they were out of stock. I told Uncle Utju that I would go and look for these items in Amplaz, Batu Merah and in the area of Waihaong. But my uncle ordered me to stay in the house and asked one of his workers to go and look for these items. 'You stay here, don't go wandering off! This is my responsibility, just give me the money and the list of things. I and some of the helpers will go and look for the items needed. They won't come home until they've got all of the items on the list'. It is only when I recall the incident that I strongly feel his aura as a marine commanding officer.

That is the story of how milk, baby bottles, biscuits, children's and infants' clothes and underwear for women and children were gathered (in limited numbers, because that is all that we could get), and were taken by the BANKOM team of volunteers on the cargo barge. I asked my brother not to say where the goods had come from, because I was frightened that if they knew, they might not want to accept them.

Another chapter that I still remember occurred in 2002, when the naval hospital in Halong ran out of anaesthetics and the wife of my friend Hendrik was about to give birth. At that time, it was impossible for me to go into the city. Again Uncle Utju and the late Dr Paeng (another Uncle) helped to obtain the anaesthetics from the Al-Fatah hospital. How the anaesthetics got to Halong wasn't important; what is important is that a humanitarian conscience cannot be eradicated when someone needs help. You only need to ask; there is no need to be afraid because the measure of love given has always been the same since life was breathed into dust and earth. To give life or to take it; it's up to the elements of dust and earth to make the decision.

Another incident took place when Uncle Utju and I had to vouch for humanitarian aid donated by Mrs Nuriah Wahid and friends in the Jakarta-Jogja network, coordinated by friends from JKRKM, which had been held by the police when it had been brought by volunteers from KontraS. Another incident happened in 2002, when aid from JKRKM was transported to the air force base in Laha. Uncle Utju bravely negotiated and strongly challenged a certain group who wanted to take a 10 per cent share of this aid for themselves.

When they said, 'This is aid for the Christians, we Muslims don't need it', he firmly stated, 'This is humanitarian aid for all the needy people of Ambon. Nobody, including you lot, has the right to ban people from obtaining aid. I am Ambonese, and my people are in need'.

These are just a few of the many incidents in my life where people around me have helped to keep me sane.

Between 1999 and 2002 there were many people in my life who also affirmed my sanity. This included my colleagues in the Baileo Ambon Network,[1] the Tujuh Lumut,[2] the Baileo Volunteers Team[3] and the Saniri Volunteers.[4] They are true humanitarians who chose to serve others without regard to their religious background. These colleagues bestowed the beautiful colour of diversity and gave meaning to the journey of whole-hearted service, with the same values that I held. Our religion is the religion of humanitarian concern. That is what we said, when we were asked, 'What is your religion?'

I still remember, at the beginning of the social disaster, colleagues at Baileo and their volunteers network tried to collect stories of how the people of Ambon protected each other during the events of January 1999. Rudi edited these stories and copied them as many times as possible, distributing them freely to all and sundry. Embong, who at that time had been given the responsibility to handle information, looked for inspiring news on the internet. This was then printed and copied and sold on A.Y. Patty Street. At that

---

1   Nus Ukru, Oni Tasik, Lina Oktoseija, Embong Salampessy, Ina Soselissa, Lely Katipana, Co Corputty and Beny.
2   Ulis Lawalata, Dalenz Utra, Samson Atapary, Dino Huliselan and Teny.
3   Ivon Silitonga, Inggrid Silitonga, Linda Holle, Dino Umahuk, Dewi Tuasikal, Rofiq, Hanafi Holle, Dur Kaplale, Vivi Marantika, Inge Reliubun, Ardath, Rudi Fofid, Cathy, Ela and Ongen.
4   Hendrik, Uncle Pe, Bosy, Jack, Rein, Boken, Nicky, Tomy, Glen, Avi, Nona, Ade Li, Sanwa and Yopi.

time hardly any national printed media was available in Ambon. Only this photocopied material was in circulation but it sold well.

This provides a realistic picture that this disaster was not a religious disaster, but a political disaster and we, the people of Maluku, were tender fodder for the unscrupulous. The people in Ambon, however, weren't interested in this news, it was defeated by 'national and local printed media' that preferred to 'sell' blood and fire.

Stories of a Muslim family that was saved by a Christian family and a Christian family that was saved by a Muslim family in Mardika, Kebun Cengkeh, Passo, Tantui, Negeri Lama, Waiheru, Waihaong, Tulehu, Liang and so on, became unimportant. A good Pela Gandong story wasn't popular at that time. Humanity was blinded by pride and by fanaticism linked to religious symbols that defeated genuine faith.

Colleagues from the Saniri volunteers were a mixed bunch from Tantui, Halong, Poka and Rumah Tiga. They chose to become volunteers just a few days after they had to be evacuated from Poka and Rumah Tiga. I simply asked them to become involved and so that they wouldn't become more deeply involved in this social disaster. At times when life was less hectic we discussed what they had learnt from this social disaster. We slowly tried to scrape away at their burning desire for revenge because they were victims and had lost their belongings and their friends. I still remember when I asked, 'What do you gain when people are removed from their homes, then retaliate by attacking a neighbouring village or join with others to attack the nearest to which they have been evacuated?'

'At least we take revenge, so that they also can go through what we have gone through', they replied.

'Then … will it return what has been lost? Will your houses be standing again? Will your acquaintances or family who have died be brought back to life? Will it make you happy?'

There was no answer at that time or during the following days. I let them digest it by themselves. They needed time to evaluate and find their own answers.

The hustle and bustle of helping the refugees without becoming exhausted, with only 2–3 hours rest a day was what I wanted to see, rather than to hear any answer. They forgot about taking revenge and became more light-hearted. I deliberately took on the ritual of cooking every Saturday and Sunday myself to help these people, whom I regarded as my new family, and to show gratitude towards those who chose to:

- lift rice and other food stuffs and commodities from the Hercules plane, load them into a truck and then arrange them in a warehouse in Passo.
- risk their lives, crossing back and forth between Nania through to Laha, which at that time was difficult to go through because they had to pass through several barricades on the road. The truck was protected by naval personnel, but they were often jarred and stopped by the mobs.
- cheerfully help refugees, helping clean up the Nania psychiatric hospital and keeping watch over the hospital at night.
- clear the jungle to pick up the people of Waai, who had evacuated from their village by travelling through the jungle near Waai. The volunteers carried milk in feeding bottles and biscuits and clothing for women and children they met on their journey, as they evacuated the people of Waai.
- help distribute medicine at night, together with the volunteer medical aides and nurses who were also evacuated from Tantui.

Thanks to colleagues from JKRKM Jakarta-Jogja who, by giving their aid, added to the opportunities of my new family to discover the meaning of life in the midst of their desolation after losing all their belongings and being forced to leave their place of birth.

My story is too long. When all the pieces of the jigsaw were collected together, I want to recall a few encouraging sentences spoken by my father. He said to me when we sitting in the yard of our house one dark night (Belso, 21 January 2001):

> San, don't ever get caught by the symbols of peace. People talk too easily about peace. They only shout about it. Although peace is not far away, it doesn't need to be shouted about, it only needs to be lived. The more we shout, the further away peace will be. Don't look for it outside ourselves, because it is inside all of us. If we allow peace to be measured physically, then everything is in vain.

> With every intake of breath, there is thanksgiving, there is a blessing, and there is a miracle. It is there that peace exists. Have you ever wondered outside formal teaching: why did God create humans on the sixth day, not the second, the third or any other day? This was because God wanted humans not to be too anxious. God didn't want humans to

have to look for their needs, all had been provided. The mandate given to humans was simple: protect, look after and love all of God's creatures on the face of the earth. God taught us to share and also be at peace with ourselves and our surroundings.

This article is dedicated to my mother, my late father, the late Mr Yusuf Elly, the late Dr. Paeng Suriaman and the late Abubakar Lakembe. Thank you, because you have given me time to grow up in a family that gives meaning to the value of diversity in peace.

Chapter 22

THE STORY OF A LITTLE CAMPAIGNER FOR PEACE IN MALUKU

Inggrid Silitonga

The Mardika and Batu Merah Incident

Ambon, 19 January 1999. The exact location of the fire was unclear. That afternoon I immediately panicked when I received the news, while I was exchanging Eid Al Fitr greetings in Galala. People started talking about the fire. They said the houses had been burned down as a result of clashes between the inhabitants of Mardika and those of Batu Merah. This information made me rush to my family home in Tantui. Tantui is not very far from Galala. People could be seen gathering in groups the whole length of the road leading to our house.

I was uneasy when I left Galala. I thought about my older sister, Ivon, who was staying with her in-laws, whose house was located precisely where this incident occurred. In the late morning she had left to exchange Eid Al Fitr greetings in Mardika. Indeed, fights often took place in that area between different groups of inhabitants. But the rumour that was spread about this time was that these were clashes between religious groups. The majority of the people living in the Mardika were Christians; while most of the people living in the Batu Merah area were Muslims.

It was true. I arrived home to find mum and dad very worried. Anxiety and fear was etched on their faces because they weren't able to contact Ivon. The situation wasn't much different to what I had seen in Galala. Neighbours were gathering together in groups close to the house, the whole length of the road leading towards Tantui. They were discussing the current situation.

Our house was located in the Provincial Government housing complex in Tantui. Our complex was wedged between the Police barracks in Tantui and Kapaha. This area is part of Pandan Kasturi in the Sirimau sub-district of Ambon. My parents had lived in official housing provided by the provincial government since 1970. My two older sisters and I had grown up in that environment.

That evening we tried to obtain information about where my sister and my brother-in-law's family were. We realised that the issue of religious conflict that was being spread would have an impact on our family. Difference in religious beliefs between our family and my brother-in-law's family would threaten the safety of our small family.

Dad tried to be calm, but he couldn't hide the expression on his face and looked very anxious. He talked seriously with my uncle who was a member of the police force. Although he had lived in Ambon since 1965, my father, who is a Batak, needed a friend in situations like this. My father especially needed my mother's relatives to understand how great the impact of the clashes would be. My dad had married my mum who has an Ambonese and Dutch background. Pluralistic values had been sown in our family for a long time. From dad's side of the family, we have relatives with Batak, Minang, Javanese and Acehnese backgrounds. Dad's family had a wide variety of beliefs because of mixed marriage.

The next day we found out that my sister Ivon, her husband Embong and my niece Inda were in the Belakang Soya area. Embong's whole family had been evacuated to the home of one of his friends, the Lakembe family. After the clashes, the roads in Ambon were blocked by members of the public. Television and radio broadcast the points where clashes occurred. This meant that this situation was becoming less conducive.

A week is a long time to wait when you are anxious. Mum and I hired a public transport minibus and brought a member of the armed forces with us to pick up Ivon, Embong and Inda. After long negotiations, we had to pay Rp. 500,000 to the member of the armed forces so that he would be prepared to accompany us. That price was more than the price of hiring the minibus. Fired by determination or, more appropriately, foolhardiness, we got through the road blocks leading to the Belakang Soya area. From Tantui we had to go through Batu Merah and then Mardika in order to reach Belakang Soya. It was very moving when we greeted each other at the

Lakembes' home. This family was a Christian family but they were prepared to protect my brother-in-law's family.

Separation

After the clashes between the people of Mardika and Batu Merah, the government seemed to be very slow in taking action. Neighbours who until then had taken no notice of the difference in religious backgrounds now began to be suspicious of each other. Rumours circulated in the community, which were provocative. The young people and community leaders in our area eventually decided to erect a guard post. This was so the residents could protect themselves and their homes from the presence of strangers, who might try to provoke people in the neighbourhood. People took it in turns to keep watch. A curfew was put in place, in anticipation of trouble. People were not free to leave their homes, let alone leave the area in which they lived.

Neighbours worked together to protect the place where they lived. The mechanism to be used and the route for evacuation if an 'attack' should take place were arranged. Really, it was a situation that was difficult to comprehend. Who would attack us? The people of Kapaha who lived next door to us? The people living in Air Kuning who also didn't live far from us? Or the people of Batu Merah who were also quite close to our neighbourhood? Then, who would we have to face? The residents keeping watch were young people and community leaders of different religious backgrounds. Our identity at that time was as residents of Tantui, not as Christians, Muslims, or of any other religious background.

Our nights were becoming very long. Every time we heard the sound of people striking the electricity poles, we ran out of our houses. The sound of the electricity poles being struck was a warning of danger. On hearing this warning, people automatically grabbed their bags containing important documents, valuables and some clothes. Our destination was the field at the Police Barracks Tantui. There we would wait until there was an instruction that it was safe to go home. It was evident that parents and children were very frightened.

We could hear the sound of shots in the distance. The longer it went on, the closer the sound of shots became. We were increasingly stunned to see flames coming up from houses higher up. According to the rumour circulating, the Laskar Jihad had been sent from Java. So what sort of war was this? Who were we really facing? This question continued to run through my head.

Clutching my rucksack, which contained my certificates and a proposal for a seminar supporting the proposal for research for my bachelor degree, I gazed at my niece and my nephew who were still very small, about six years old, with only a year's difference in their ages. Both of them looked frightened and were leaning on their mother's chest. In a situation like this, we could only hope that morning would come quickly so that we could return to the house.

There were no more lectures. There was no official announcement from Pattimura University (Unpatti) where I was studying. There was no guarantee of security in a situation like this. At that time, I was in semester VII of my studies in Forestry Management at the Agricultural Faculty of Unpatti. I couldn't carry out my practicals, complete my assignments or attend lectures. We also faced a lack of paraffin, petrol and the nine staple needs.[1]

Together with neighbours, I would buy fish from a fish factory in Galala. Tonnes of frozen fish were brought out from the factory and fish that was not fresh was sold at exorbitant prices. Shops that sold staple foods were beginning to run out of stock. In a situation like this, my mum could only prepare simple meals of instant noodles. My mum patiently helped the two young kids to understand when they whined because there was no milk available for them.

One afternoon, we were taken by surprise when we heard the electricity poles being struck. We rushed out of the house. Several women were only wearing simple house clothes and were barefoot, carrying their babies as they ran. Information came to our ears that several 'intruders' had entered our neighbourhood. Shots were heard not far from our house. In unison we rushed under the table or sought protection behind a chair. We tried to be calm until the police and the Brimob came to secure the situation. From January 1999, the sound of flying bullets, the pounding of weapons, homemade bombs, the striking of electricity poles became a daily occurrence.

Through the radio and television we learned that a number of security forces from Java and Makassar had been sent to handle the conflict. The situation started to become calmer with many security forces on the streets. The banks and offices started to open their doors again. The schools

---

1   Translator's note: Known as *sembako* (*sembilan bahan pokok*) these were the nine principle needs for the people, as defined by the Minister of Industry and Trade Decision No 115/MPP/Kep/2/1998 ofl 27 February 1998. This was during the 1998 financial crisis. The nine staple needs were: 1. rice, sago or corn; 2. sugar; 3. fruit and vegetables; 4. beef, chicken or fish; 5. frying oil or margarine; 6. milk; 7. eggs; 8. kerosene or LPG gas; and 9. iodised salt.

and universities followed suit, but there were not many people around. The people of Ambon were still worried about the security situation. I heard that Embong was active in an NGO called Baileo Maluku Network, together with colleagues who were involved in humanitarian work. This NGO was established in 1993 to empower the community. The Baileo Maluku Network then formed a team of volunteers for humanitarian causes (TRK) to respond to the situation in Ambon and surrounding areas.

Embong began to attend meetings with colleagues in the Baileo Maluku Network. Several times this foundation issued press statements calling for peace. The Baileo Maluku Network also developed a dialogue with various parties, including the government. The aim was to put pressure on the government to guarantee safety for the community, including dealing with victims of the conflict. The government appeared incapable of handling the impact of this community unrest, apart from supplying a large number of security forces.

Embong's activities in fighting for peace across religious boundaries made people suspect that he was a provocateur. Embong was the only Muslim working with Baileo Maluku Network, Ambon at that time. Attempts to bring about dialogue among students, young people and public leaders in the Muslim and Christian communities resulted in terror and death threats. Every time Embong came home, we tried to discuss this matter as well as possible. The rumour that he was a provocateur, however, even reached our neighbourhood. We saw some youths with dubious intentions wandering up and down near our house. According to a close friend, our house had become a target to be burned down, because we were hiding a provocateur. My dad read the situation and started to keep watch in front of the house. I remember him saying in a loud voice, 'Nobody can touch a child of mine, without stepping over my dead body'.

Embong's safety was threatened. He was evacuated to Wailela, to the Baileo Maluku Network office, in the middle of February 1999. Ivon and Inda were also picked up from the house and taken to safety. Baileo Maluku Network then decided to send Embong and his family to Jogjakarta.

Their leaving was very moving and my mother insisted on seeing Ivon in Wailela before they were taken to Laha to board a plane to Jakarta. My mother was very worried about my sister's little family. We took courage and made our way to Wailela. I took my mother to meet Ivon, Embong and Inda. There my mother embraced them without saying very much. I also couldn't speak. This separation might be for some time. We would not be able to communicate, because the situation in Ambon was still very tense.

When the car taking Ivon and the family left the office for Laha, I saw my mother shed some tears. My mother let go of her children so that they would be safe, not knowing if those of us left behind would also be safe. Would we meet them again?

From that time on I felt moved to do something. Deep down I knew that what Embong and his colleagues were doing was something really amazing. He fought for peace and to help his neighbours; he even put his life on the line. How could I just sit quietly doing nothing? The calling to continue Embong's work led me to go to one of TRK Baileo Maluku Network's coordination centres in Mardika. Coincidently Embong had introduced me to his colleagues. I finally became part of TRK, passing on the values that Embong had taught me, that I had often discussed with Ivon when she came home from activities.

Community Organiser (CO)

At the beginning of March 1999, I officially joined TRK Baileo Maluku Network. The TRK coordination centre used the home of Tetha Hittipeuw, one of the volunteers. She was from the same faculty as Embong and Ivon, the Fisheries Faculty, Unpatti. The majority of TRK volunteers were students or graduates of Unpatti. At the TRK I got to know several people involved in the NGO besides Embong. They included Nus Ukru, Sandra Lakembe, Jeferson Tasik, Ansye Sopacua and the 'Tujuh Lumut' (future leaders of the Baileo Maluku Network).

The initial work carried by the TRK at that time was compiling data and gathering aid from a variety of sources, starting with food, clothing and medicines. Baileo Maluku Network developed the strategy of creating organisers at the refugee camps and carrying out advocacy to restore the rights of the refugees.

The coordination centre was then moved to Galala because the work situation at the Mardika coordination centre was not conducive. The sounds of shots fired and Molotov cocktails thrown coloured our work while we were at Mardika. Sometimes we got caught in the street and couldn't get home, or we were forced to take a lift in a military vehicle so that we could return home, especially when segregation of areas based on religion became more and more common. From that time onwards we had coordination centres. The Christian volunteers were at the Galala TRK coordination centre in the former house of Linda Holle, one of the volunteers. Our Muslim colleagues were placed at the Batu Merah shophouse TRK coordination centre. From that point, we started to organise.

At the beginning of April 1999, we attended training for community organisers (COs) at the Ambon Manise Hotel. One of the speakers was a prominent leader known in NGO circles called Room Topatimasang from the Institute for Social Transformation (Insist) Jogjakarta, who was also one of the founders of the Baileo Maluku Network. After the training, we worked as COs in a variety of refugee camps. I and a member of staff from the Baileo Maluku Network, Polly Lekaneni, became the COs at the Halong naval base.

Armed with courage and a desire to help others, I went by motorbike to the coordination centre and to the refugee camp at the Halong naval base. After joining TRK, I became more courageous, even when I had to go past areas that were really 'hot', or I ran into Laskar Jihad.

Thankfully, the security situation in Ambon improved. Activities started up again on the campus and I had to do my internship. Because of safety considerations and taking steps in case an unwanted situation occurred, the locations of the Unpatti internship placements were spread throughout the city of Ambon and surrounding areas. I was placed in Galala, opposite to where we were living in Tantui but close to the Halong naval base where I carried out activities as a CO. With the locations close to each other and the internship only lasting a month, the internship didn't interrupt my voluntary activities. I could complete my internship and still be a volunteer.

It was, however, not yet a peaceful atmosphere. There were still clashes between villages with different religious backgrounds. The problem started to escalate and to spread to the small islands close to Ambon. There were many sad stories of retaliation and angry citizens. Clashes were not only between local people, and between Christian forces and Jihad forces, but also between different military establishments.

Loving and Caring for Each Other

The naval base in Halong, Ambon Bay, Baguala subdistrict, owned very extensive land. Within the naval base there is a sea port and other assets such as housing for officers, a hospital, a church, a mosque, a cinema, a primary school and a junior high school, as well as other general buildings. The housing for officers was divided into five sections. The naval base became one of the refugee camps for refugees from Hatiwe Besar, Halong, Poka and Rumah Tiga.

The refugee camp at the naval base was located near the pier, the repair workshop, at the Baruna Loka cinema, a mess and the first section of the officers' housing. The majority of those living in the house near the pier came from Hatiwe. They were peddlers and involved in the speed boat business from Hatiwe. They were of Bugis and Makassarese descent and were all Muslims. The refugees who lived in the houses near the repair workshop, right next door to the Hatiwe refugees, came from Poka and Rumah Tiga and were Christians.

The refugees who occupied the Baruna Loka cinema came from Halong and were of Ambonese, Javanese and Butonese descent. This location was even more plural in nature because the refugees came from both Christian and Muslim backgrounds. Several meters away there was another group of refugees who lived in a mess hall. The majority of refugees in this mess were from Halong, Galala and Tantui Atas and all were Christians. Not far from there, in the first section of officers' housing, there were Butonese refugees from Halong, who were Muslims.

The five clusters of refugee housing on the naval base were close to each other. There didn't seem to be any problems between the refugees living in these different locations, even though the refugees were from different religious backgrounds and had been forced to evacuate because of the problems between the different religious groups. Outside of the Halong naval base the impression was given that the conflict was a religious conflict. The refugees didn't seem to have the courage to mix between the locations, because they were still suspicious of each other. Their daily activities were carried out smoothly. Perhaps because they were living on the naval base, these refugees with different religious backgrounds remained calm.

The refugees housing was coordinated by a naval officer called Wayan. His work was reinforced by five refugee coordinators, each in their own location. Thus when we decided to become the COs of the Halong naval base, Wayan was the first person we had to meet.

Besides obtaining data about the refugees from Wayan, we also met the refugees' coordinator in each of the locations. Wayan welcomed our presence but the refugee coordinators and the refugees did not. The trauma as a result of losing their homes and their relatives made them suspicious. We needed to be patient and to seek an opportunity for dialogue, including trying to communicate with each refugee coordinator.

We spent days at the location to enable us to gather information about what was lacking. Sometimes Polly and I would eat with the refugees, lining up for food in the soup kitchen that had been provided by the naval base.

Sometimes when we grew tired, we would take a rest in one of the five refugee locations.

As time passed, Wayan gave Polly and I an office. In this office we updated the data and information that we had accumulated during our visits to the five refugee locations. Every time we came back from being with the refugees, Polly and I would record incidents and everything we came across in our daily records. We wrote full accounts noting the time of each incident, the name of the refugees and the problems that occurred, even though we were still not yet 100 per cent accepted by the refugees.

Our patience in carrying out our tasks in this situation started to bear fruit. The refugees, who initially were suspicious of us, started to be friendlier. Refugees even started to approach us if there was a problem between them. We tried to facilitate a dialogue to resolve problems that had occurred in one refugee location. When aid arrived from the local government, Wayan invited Polly and me to distribute it to the refugees. Besides being known by the refugees, the naval officers at the Halong naval base also knew our names and faces.

Every two days, we reported the results of the assistance we gave to the refugees to the TRK coordination centre of Baileo Maluku Network in Galala. At that time our work was still very limited. As yet, there was no aid given by the Baileo Maluku Network to support our activities amongst the refugees. The progress we achieved in our work at the Halong naval base meant that several volunteers and staff from Baileo Maluku were sent to Jogjakarta to discuss working together with some international humanitarian organisations. These organisations included *Médecins sans Frontières* (MSF), Oxfam GB and the Community Development Humanitarian Organisation Bethesda Jogja.

Apart from our dealings with the refugees, our relationship with Wayan also improved. Polly and I always tried to wait until he was off duty to discuss the problems of the refugees, starting from dealing with their trauma to restoring their basic rights. We organised a meeting with the head of the hospital to provide free medical treatment for the refugees. Polly and I helped a young, pregnant mother get a check-up at the naval hospital. We even borrowed an officer's car to take a refugee's child, who had been scalded by boiling water, to the Oto Quik Hospital Ambon in Tantui.

The refugees complained about many things and we discovered problems when we were among them. Polly and I discussed these matters before we finally found a solution or we asked for help from someone who had a greater capacity than we did. Even the problem of conjugal rights came up, which had never crossed our minds because neither of us was married, but we found a solution. Many quarrels occurred over minor things but they could turn into a major fight. After Polly or I talked to the refugees involved in a fight, it turned out that a problem had occurred when a husband and wife were making love. After discussing the problem with Wayan and reporting the problem to his leader, it was resolved by providing a special room.

To empower refugees, with the agreement of the commander of Halong naval base we were able to procure a piece of land where we could plant vegetables to supply the needs of the refugees. The good thing about this was that it finally facilitated interaction between the refugees of different religious backgrounds, who until then had been reluctant to mix. To begin with the women were active in the meetings held to discuss using the land to grow vegetables. Eventually the men also started to mix. It started when we tried to invite representatives from each refugee location to gather. The atmosphere was more conducive and dialogue took place between the inhabitants. Previously, they had been reluctant to greet or visit their former neighbours. Eventually they could sit in the same room and discuss their common needs as refugees.

When people were saying that our work was going really well, my colleague Polly looked unwell. Several times she complained about headaches. Eventually she could no longer be involved at the Halong naval base. Polly had fallen sick and had to take a rest from all activities. I tried to visit her, but her friends said that Polly couldn't see anyone. She had problems with her nerves.

Without Polly working with me, as I mixed with the refugees I realised that our endeavours had not really achieved very much for the refugees. Polly once complained about the slow response of aid from our colleagues at the Baileo Maluku Network. We knew about the administration work needed before aid from partners like CD Bethesda and Oxfam GB could arrive. Therefore, we were resigned to the situation we faced. Polly was sometimes disappointed with the conditions and used money from her own pockets. More than once Polly used her own money to buy sugar, milk, and mung beans. It seems that the complaints and the situation we faced had led her to drown in a deep sadness. Perhaps this was what eventually made her sick and in need of intensive medical treatment.

While Polly was being treated, she was replaced by another volunteer colleague, Econg. At that time the TRK coordination centre in Galala had been moved to Lateri, to the house of a colleague, Ansye Sopacua. Econg was a student in his final term of the Fisheries Faculty, Unpatti. Although he was able to perform the tasks left behind by Polly, it took time to introduce him to the refugees and for him to become close to them.

With Polly no longer working with me, I honestly felt that I was working on my own, even though Econg was there. This itself added to the sadness. When feelings of loneliness came over me, I usually went straight to visit the refugee children who lived in the location close to the naval base pier. When it was late afternoon, I spent time with one of the women refugees in a plot of land there. She usually gave me something to eat and a place to rest. I didn't feel awkward with them, even though they came from a different racial group and a different religious background from me. Our relationship was like mother, father, child and sister.

The medical aid from CD Bethesda finally arrived. A medical car routinely came from the TRK and medical treatment was given to the refugees. Several refugees who were medical aids and nurses were given medical equipment and a stock of medicine. Volunteer colleagues from the health section made records and reports.

Besides treatment, another regular activity we carried out with the refugees was to pray together. We tried to bring about peace through dialogue and prayer. The refugees who lived in the former Baruna Loka cinema came from different religious and racial backgrounds. They started to work together to repair the place they were living. I was moved when a female refugee gave birth in the naval base hospital in Halong. Her husband rushed around to give us the news that their first child was a girl and advised me that he and his wife agreed to name her Inggrid, after me.

The data we collated was submitted to the data section and turned out to be helpful in efforts to handle the refugees in the future. In addition to aid from TRK Baileo Maluku Network, several international organisations such as Médecins Sans Frontières (MSF), Coordinator Action Contre La Faim (ACF), Save the Children and the United Nations (UN) also channelled aid to the refugee locations.

Unfortunately, the next stage of handling of the refugees' problems was not as easy as when we dealt with them. Aid organisations gave the impression that they were competing with each other to help the refugees. There was a lack of coordination, whether it was coordination with the refugee representatives or the coordinator of all the refugee locations.

The reconciliation, which had involved the participation of all the refugees in each location, was almost destroyed. This was the fault of one of the refugees at the Baruna Loka cinema location who had a quarrel with other refugees over the distribution of aid that did not meet the needs of the refugees. Some families received more aid than others and it was given straight to them, whereas the system that we had in place was for the data concering the aid to be recorded first and the aid was held by the coordinator or local organiser, before it was distributed to refugees at each location.

Mr Piet, the coordinator for the Baruna Loka refugees, came looking for me, and he looked very pale. He told me about the incident. I tried to talk to both families involved in the spat so that there would be no sanctions from the security forces at the naval base, because one of the refugees involved in the argument had a sharp object with him. Fortunately, because I was regarded as a daughter or their younger sister, the two families were reconciled.

Becoming a Teacher to the Children of Refugees

TRK Baileo Maluku Network did not provide alternative education. The volunteers only focused on compiling data, giving assistance and medical treatment. We had limited human resources and were unable to use them for this. When I was with the refugees, however, I had the urge to teach refugee children of primary school age, who had been forced to stop going to school because of the situation. The refugees were traumatised and frightened to return to the place where they came from to organise the children's transfer to new schools.

Armed with storybooks, posters, maps, writing materials, pictures and a few primary school books, I stopped at the housing on the pier and the first section of officer's houses after the day's activities had finished. Usually I met with the children in the two locations in the late afternoon. Six children took part in the lessons in the housing near the pier, while in the other location five children took part. The ages of the children varied between five to ten years old.

After studying we usually played together. I put aside some of my allowance to buy milk for the children. Quite often parents prepared food to be eaten together. Usually we prayed together and continued our discussions about the children's problems.

One family who lived in the housing near the pier were Bugis and were very friendly towards me. I usually called the man, Bapa Daeng. He and his wife always gave me some food when I was visiting the housing near the pier. Sometimes he gave me some bananas to take home with me as a gift. His wife also cared for me as though I was a member of their family. Bapa Daeng became seriously ill. I went to visit him and helped him eat and take his medicine. They never made an issue of our differences. They pushed aside the feelings of hatred towards people of different racial or religious backgrounds. Getting to know Bapa Daeng's family helped me to learn to love, to love all the people God has created.

I Leave Ambon, the Place Where I was Born

If they didn't evacuate to houses of relatives in other areas, or to a refugee location, many Ambonese were forced to leave Ambon. There was a large exodus of people from Ambon which began at the end of January 1999. The issue of religious conflict and the expulsion of Buton-Bugis-Makassar that spread from the onset of the conflict, forced outsiders, especially those who originated from these racial groups, to return to their places of origin.

The government could not guarantee safety, although many security forces had already been deployed. The clashes, which were said to be the result of a religious 'war', were still taking place in various places across the island of Ambon. The violence receded for a few months, but broke out again between July and August 1999.

It was said that Tantui, the place where I lived, was going to be a target to be burnt down. We had no idea who was likely to burn down the houses in that area. The residents in that area were all evacuated to the Police complex close by. However, our family stayed put. Several of our Muslim neighbours had already vacated their houses. These vacated houses were damaged by people we didn't know. Then followed an issue that our area would be attacked from the direction of Kapaha and Galunggung whose residents were mainly Muslim. Although I was anxious, I chose to keep working. Sometimes I had to risk my life and the safety of my family when I went back and forth between our house and the Halong naval base.

Houses were burnt down and people died. It was said that these people were murdered. Every day I went to the naval base hospital to check on the victims of the conflict. The smell of burnt flesh and the sight of blood splattered across the floor of the hospital became a daily sight. People moaned, writhing in pain, and the victim's family wailed.

Wayan summoned me to tell me that there would be an additional number of refugees at the naval base. He had been ordered to prepare new locations for refugee housing. The sound of running gun battles could be heard outside of the complex. Naval tanks that were usually parked in their garages were placed in position. Security forces were put on standby. The naval base was tightly guarded. The situation was such that sometimes I couldn't go home to Tantui. I stayed at the naval base, sometimes in refugee housing, sometimes in the home of one of the nurses from the naval hospital, or sometimes at the guard post on the pier.

Once, when I was walking in front of the guard post in the middle of the complex, I came across Fajar, a university friend of mine. She was with her father, Mr Budi, who was a lecturer at Unpatti; they were amongst the refugees from Rumah Tiga. Fajar was born and brought up in Ambon. Her parents originated from Central Java and were Muslims. Fajar and her father's clothes looked wet. She told me that the lecturers' housing complex in Rumah Tiga had been attacked. The houses had been burnt down. Fajar and her family were forced to swim to safety from the beach at Rumah Tiga to the Halong naval base, which was quite some distance. It was so sad to see them like that.

Immediately I sped home on my motorbike. I took some clothes, food and other necessities to Fajar and her family. Fajar and her father didn't refuse my help. There was no reluctance or hatred between us, although their house had been burnt down and they had to struggle to reach the Halong naval base, because they had been driven out by a group of people who were coincidentally Christian. Occasionally I looked away from Fajar and her family, trying to hide my tears.

I carried out these activities for a long time, with the result that every day I was faced with problems; and my ammunition ran low. My weapon – enthusiasm – was beginning to wane. Every time we heard that homes of our friends had, one by one, been burnt down, our enthusiasm began to wane. It waned especially when we had to accept the fact that we who had been serving refugees would ourselves be forced to become refugees. In an emergency situation, we were summoned to the TRK coordination centre to help evacuate our friends and their families. My spirits were at low ebb. During that time, my naval officer colleagues were there for me. One of them was Hariyanto. We had become good friends during my time helping at the Halong naval base. They helped to encourage me. I was once invited to join the patrol boat in Ambon bay which escorted Pelni ships safely in and out of the naval dock. Out of the goodness of their hearts, a naval truck brought our family belongings to refugee housing in the naval base. My family was also evacuated to the naval base.

Late one afternoon I received a phone call from Embong in Jogjakarta. He was very worried about my safety. It was difficult for volunteers to travel to the refugee locations because the situation was becoming more and more tense. In this short telephone conversation, Embong asked me to come to Jogjakarta to help fellow volunteers there who were campaigning for peace for Maluku. Embong had been asked to become the coordinator of the Baileo Emergency Team (*E-Team*) in Jogjakarta.

I conveyed Embong's intention to George Coorputty, the TRK coordinator of Baileo Maluku network. He then gave me permission to go to Jogjakarta.

My parents only allowed me to go to Jogja for two weeks, to allow me to relieve my stress because of the current situation.

They were worried about my safety on board ship. We received news that there were incidents of people being murdered on board ship. Even the Pelni ships were given religious identities based on the route they served. MV Dobonsolo was known as a Christian ship, which took passengers to Manado and Papua, then returned to Ambon and afterwards headed towards Kupang, Bali, Surabaya and on to Jakarta. MV Lambelu and MV Rinjani were regarded as Muslim ships because they called at Buton and Makassar before going on to Surabaya and then to Jakarta.

Taking with me three sets of clothes, a senior high school diploma, and university papers, I headed to the pier. I took leave of Wayan, Hariyanto, Bapa Daeng and his wife. Without embracing my parents, I left. My tears flowed when MV Dobonsolo, on which I was a passenger, left the pier. My loved ones were now out of sight; I left behind Ambon, the place where I was born.

Peace from Children in Jogja to Children in Ambon

After three days aboard ship, I arrived at the Tanjung Perak docks in Surabaya. I felt different. Peace. I was met by Ivon, Embong and Inda. We hugged each other and shed tears; we were moved that we had been given a chance to meet up. We headed towards Tunjungan Plaza, to find some breakfast and to have a look round. I was introduced to Diana, a volunteer from Surabaya. Embong was organising funds to obtain humanitarian aid by establishing two Emergency Teams (E-Team): the Jogja E-Team and the Surabaya E-Team. While in Surabaya, the E-Team prepared medical, kitchen and other necessities to be sent to Ambon. This aid would be sent via a naval war ship. I helped members of the Surabaya E-Team sort out the required papers needed at the Indonesian naval base in Surabaya.

Through a few officers I knew from when they were at the naval base in Ambon and who were now stationed in Surabaya, we were able to process the requirements with ease. I had the chance to meet Lieutenant Setiawan, who used to be stationed in Ambon. He had been transferred to Surabaya. During our conversation he said that he strongly hoped that I would be able to complete my studies. We stayed for a week in a guest house in the Dharma Wangsa area. After all our work was completed we headed to Jogjakarta.

I sang softly the Kla Project song to myself. 'return to your town, there is a cup of emotions in my desires / It is still the same / Every corner greets me as a friend full of a thousand meanings / I am carried away by nostalgia of the time we spent together / Enjoying the atmosphere of Jogja together ...' the length of my journey to Jogjakarta. I felt very happy but it was mixed with sadness when I remembered Ambon. Why did Ambon have to accept this bereavement and devastation?

How could this city, which had fostered harmony between religious groups, different racial groups and traditions be destroyed? I thought of Mum and Dad and hoped that the Lord would protect them. On our arrival in Jogjakarta, we were welcomed by the Insist community. There was Saleh Abdullah, Anu Leonella, Roem Topatimasing and Mifthahudin. Several colleagues of the Baileo Maluku Network were also there. For a while we stayed at Wisma Talenta III Blimbingsari, not far from the Insist office. After that we moved into the house belonging to Saleh Abdullah in Pandega Rini, Kaliurang. While in Jogjakarta, we set up the Jogja E-Team that became an inseparable part of the TRK Baileo Maluku Network.

With the help of the Kepa Finland, Insist and CD Bethesda organisations, we carried out fund-raising and campaigned against violence in the Ambon (Maluku) human tragedy. I should really have returned to Ambon, because according to the original plan I was only to be in Jogja for two weeks. But the situation in Ambon had become increasingly tense. Commercial flights to Ambon were stopped. There were only two ways if you wanted to return home – to board a Hercules aircraft or board a naval warship to Ambon. We received information by telephone that our house in Tantui had been burnt down; all the family had been evacuated to the Halong naval base. With the help of the coordinator of officers' housing at the naval base and one of mum's friends, the family was assigned to a house in the fifth block.

While I was in Jogja, I handled a peace campaign which involved children from Jogjakarta writing to refugee children in Ambon, an idea thought up by the Jogja E-Team. We visited several primary schools, Koran recitation classes and Sunday schools to tell them about the conditions of the refugee children. We sent letters from children in Jogja through some volunteers who were returning to Ambon. We gave them replies from the refugee children after we had received them from friends who visited Jogja.

Children from Jogja also wrote poems and drew pictures. What was moving was that some of them sent instant noodles and money in envelopes to their small friends in refugee camps in Ambon. We sent the letters from Christian primary school pupils and Sunday school children to Muslim refugee children, and vice versa. This activity was reported several times in the newspaper, *Bernas Jogja*. We also organised an art performance, from children in Jogja for refugee children in Ambon. Several primary schools took part in this event, including a street children's art group and a group of young Ambonese people living in Jogja. The participation of these children, besides demonstrating their concern, also drew the attention and aid from their parents and those concerned with humanitarian causes.

We carried out several fundraising efforts in cooperation with supermarkets and a number of private banks. Friends involved in the E-Team were Anton (the uncle), Leli, Aan, Ronny, Andy, Vera and Nur. Friends from *Teater Garasi* Jogja also took part. A few of these were members of the creative team of Insist press, who printed and distributed many humanitarian posters on the corners of Jogja streets, as a form of an anti-violence campaign.

Demonstrating Peace with Love

With slow strides I entered a mosque in Jogjakarta. I took off my footwear. It felt as though my heart beat faster. The incidents of slaughter, destruction, the burning of houses and places of worship in Ambon crossed through my thoughts. Now in front of me were Muslim young people. They had been waiting for the arrival of my colleagues and me from the Jogja E-Team. I steeled myself to tell them about the humanitarian mission that was carried by the TRK Baileo Maluku Network. I told them about my experiences accompanying refugees and the children of refugees at the Halong naval base. I felt like crying when they hugged me as a sign that they were thankful that I had helped others. One campaign strategy of the Jogja E-Team was to conduct dialogues for peace with religious organisations, community leaders, school children and students.

It would be good if peace was established and we all worked for it. By retelling the situation of the community unrest in Ambon, we don't want to resurrect feelings of retaliation and rage. We want to tell the stories of helping each other and caring for each other across the racial and religious divide throughout the conflict in Maluku. Peace is only superficial without love, without dialogue, and without respecting differences. There must always be a way to maintain humanitarian and pluralistic values. All the stories that I have described are the experiences of myself, together with a number of colleagues who worked for peace from 1999 to 2000. Some parts are incomplete because it needs time to remember what happened 13 years ago. I hope this article about these limited experiences can inspire and continue to maintain peace among kin.

Chapter 23

WHY MUST RELIGION DIVIDE US?

Tiara Melinda A.S.

> *From the start all has been well ...*
> *Don't ruin it ...*
> *Oh people's traditions ...*
> *What you feel I feel too ...*
> *Happy and sad together ...*
> *Don't because of difference in race and religion ...*
> *Fight each other ...*
> *We have all sworn together to live in harmony ...*
> *Pela gandong is better oh ... oh ...*

As a student at a university in Jakarta I sometimes feel a little uneasy if I have to introduce myself in certain situations. Often when I mention that I come from Ambon, the people who asked or those who were listening then make comments that Ambon is a violent city. I have very many good memories of Ambon that are not related to the problem of violence. But, that's how it is. People always link Ambon with the conflict in 1999 which, at the time, became a daily 'consumption' for national and international media. I can easily recall the human tragedy that took place 13 years ago.

The words of the song at the beginning of this chapter, which I accidently came across when using Google but can't remember who wrote them, remind me of the tragedy 13 years ago, a time that I look on as dark and difficult.

I still remember that afternoon on 19 January 1999, relaxing with my dad, waiting for friends to come to my grandma's house in Mardika. They wanted to come and visit us on Eid Al Fitr.

However, the peace and the festivities of that afternoon suddenly turned into a huge commotion. I heard the sound of angry voices. I was five years old at that time and I was confused about what was going on. Out of curiosity, I went outside to try and see what was going on. It turned out that in front of our house there was a lot of hustle and bustle. Many people were angry and shouting loudly at each other. Others were carrying a variety of sharp weapons.

Like any small child, I felt the urge to find out. I was curious to know what was happening when the sound of gunfire came from near the house. I then ran towards the source of the gunfire. There I saw several people wearing batik shirts firing pistols in the air. I didn't understand who or what they were shooting at. Innocently, I asked, 'What's happening Uncle? Uncle, who are you shooting at?' The person in the batik shirt only replied: 'Little girl, go back into the house. Otherwise you'll be shot'. Because I was curious, however, I watched what was happening. Suddenly something hot hit my leg. I was shocked and I picked it up and held it in my fist. I started to feel afraid, because the noise of gunfire was getting more frequent. Then there was the sound of a rock landing on the roof of our house and the sound of people shouting angrily became even louder.

I didn't wait long, I became even more afraid and started to cry when I saw Mum and Granny emerge with fear and panic etched on their faces. Mum called me into the house and told me to hide in a room. All the members of the family gathered in the front room. My grandparents' bedroom was 3 x 6 metres and it became full when all of us were in the room. There was Granny and Grandad, Mum and Dad, Aunty Eca, Uncle Awin, cousin Didith and Aunty Ana, who was Dad's youngest sister. I saw that some bags had been got ready. Grandad asked us to be ready to evacuate if the situation got worse.

As the day turned into night, the situation became even more tense. The shouts of angry people became even louder. Several times we could hear the sounds of rocks falling on our roof. The sound of gunfire made the situation even tenser. Uncle Saleh, Dad's cousin, had phoned up earlier and was going to pick us up and help to evacuate us from Grandad's house. But he had not yet arrived. We stayed in the room, although the electricity had been cut from late afternoon. We were relieved when at about 10pm, Dad asked us all to get ready, because a friend had come to pick us up.

It was Aunty Sandra Lakembe, Dad's friend, an NGO activist, who came to pick us up. She was accompanied by several policemen. We left the house not knowing where we were going, because the only thing we could think about was to get out of the house and save ourselves. Apparently we were taken to Aunt Sandra's home in the Belakang Soya area, where the majority of the residents were actually Christian. At that point we still really didn't know what had happened. Angry people were shouting; occasionally someone shouted *'Allahu Akbar'*, or on the other side someone sang 'Onward Christian soldiers'.

We were warmly welcomed when we arrived at the Lakembe family home, especially by Aunt Sandra's mother who I then called 'Granny Gin'. She looked very worried and was anxiously waiting for us to arrive. 'Thank God, nothing happened to you on your way here. You all got here safely', said Granny Gin, relieved.

However, not long after we arrived at Aunt Sandra's house, we heard shots fired and the sound of a bomb exploding. Feeling uneasy, we all started to get our things together and then gathered together in one room, feeling very wary. That night we and Aunt Sandra's family didn't sleep well, being on guard because of the situation.

The next day, when we got up, I asked Mum what was happening. Mum explained in a serious tone that people were saying that community unrest based on conflict between different religions was taking place in Ambon. Everywhere people were shouting, using religious slogans. At the beginning, to be honest, we felt worried and wary staying in Aunt Sandra's home, which was in a mainly Christian area, because we were a Muslim family. But Dad, Aunt Sandra and Grandpa Man convinced us that nothing would happen to us there. Grandpa Man, who had quite an influence in the surrounding area, gave a guarantee that no one would hurt us. Aunt Sandra's family's strong belief made us feel less uneasy. They looked after us so well, as though we were their own family. Eventually we mixed with Aunt Sandra's family. Although at that time people said that a religious war was being waged, at Aunt Sandra's we respected, helped and supported each other. Our family still carried out our prayers five times a day.

After staying a week at Aunt Sandra's, Mum's sister came to take us to Mum's parents' house in Tantui. She was escorted by security forces. At that time the residents of Tantui, which was situated close to the police barracks, was a mixed community of Muslims and Christian. When we arrived at Mum's house, I remembered the object that I had been clutching in my hand for several days. I asked Mum what the thing I had been clutching was.

Mum was shocked when she saw what I was clutching. Mum explained that it was a gun cartridge. No one had realised that I had been clutching a gun cartridge since the incident in Grandma's house.

On the same day, Grandpa, Grandma, Aunt Echa, Didith and Aunt Ana were picked up by Uncle Awin, who it seems had been hiding in Grandpa's house all this time. Escorted by security forces, Grandpa and the group were taken to the Madrasah Tsanawiyah Kebun Cengkeh. They would live in the hall at the school where Grandpa had served as headmaster.

The situation became increasingly chaotic in Ambon. More people were forced to evacuate. Life in Ambon, previously harmonious and full of friendship, became disturbed. People could no longer live together in a heterogeneous area. Because of this, Dad's office, Baileo Maluku Network then established a TRK coordination centre in Ambon, located in Aunt Tetha Hittipeuw's house in Mardika. But the incident at Grandpa's house was also in my mind. This house was also in Mardika. When Dad drove away people who wanted to burn down our house, I felt afraid and I didn't want to be far from Dad. Therefore, Mum and I went with Dad to help with the activities at the coordination centre.

Evacuation

On 14 February around 8pm, Dad received a phone call from Uncle Nus Ukru, his colleague at the Baileo Maluku Network. Uncle Nus said: 'Embong, you need to get some clothes together with just your important belongings. Tomorrow you and your family must be ready to be picked up at 9am. You don't need to ask many questions, because your family's lives have been threatened.' After receiving the phone call from Uncle Nus, we started to get our things ready to take what we could with us. I was surprised and asked Dad why we were rushing to pack important belongings and our clothes. Calmly Dad explained that we were going on holiday.

The next day I was told to be ready, but I was astonished with the situation at the house that morning. Grandma, Grandpa and all the other members of the family seemed to be crying. I was confused as to what was really going on. At 9 am another of Dad's friends, Aunt Lina Oktolseja and several other people, came to pick us up. We were to be evacuated. It turned out that we were not on our own; in the car that came to pick us up was Dad's cousin, Aunt Itha, who had also been involved at TRK Ambon.

There was an interesting thing that I experienced in the car journey to Laha. On our journey we crossed several border areas; every car that went past was stopped and inspected. The strange thing was that the car we were riding was not inspected. It was as though the car was invisible. I don't know whether it was true or not. Uncle Adam, who drove the car, said that a 'spell' had been cast so that we would be invisible and would safely arrive in Laha.

Eventually we arrived in Laha and stayed in the house of the Mewar family for one night. The next day we left for Jakarta on Mandala Airlines. In Jakarta, we stayed at Aunt Itha's house in Kalimalang for a week. While in Jakarta we were taken sightseeing in order to erase the trauma that we, especially myself, had experienced. However, it was difficult to erase the trauma caused by conflict. After a week in Jakarta, we headed to Jogjakarta by train. In Jojga, we were met by Uncle Banu Soebagiyo. Uncle Banu took us to stay in his house which was next door to the Adisutjipto airport, Jogjakarta. Uncle Banu was a friend who Dad had only recently got to know as a result of the community unrest in Ambon. He was a member of staff of Oxfam, an international NGO which had helped Dad's office in handling the refugees.

Uncle Banu's house was also close to the railway line which meant that I couldn't sleep because of the trains going past in the night. The sound of trains going past woke me up, because it reminded me of the noisy disturbances during the conflict in Ambon. After a few days we moved to live with Aunt Yanti, another Oxfam worker, while we waited for our rented house to be ready. Papa started to work at the Insist Jojga NGO office.

Every day I went to work with Dad. His work was still related to handling refugees in Ambon, by coordinating humanitarian aid from various sources in Jojga that was sent to Ambon via Surabaya. This body was called the Emergency Team Baileo Maluku Network, Jogja.

Around June 1999, Dad with some other NGO friends, Uncle Piet and Aunt Sandra, went to the Netherlands to attend a conference there. The situation in Ambon was also becoming more conducive. At the same time as Dad went overseas, Mum and I returned to Ambon. We decided to board a ship from the Tanjuk Perak docks, Surabaya. We had to stay several nights in Surabaya before the ship left. While we were in Surabaya, we stayed at Uncle Cliff Marlessy's parents' home. Uncle Cliff was another of Dad's friends.

During the story of our 'exodus', I met many of Dad's friends who were good to us. They helped Mum, Dad and me, without seeking any reward, although they didn't know each other very well and had different religious beliefs. This reality made me feel a little calmer than I had previously felt.

When we arrived in Ambon the situation was becoming more conducive. Indeed, there were still many security forces guarding the streets, but I felt happy. I thought our holiday had come to an end and we were meeting up with Mum's family again in Tantui. Dad joined us back in Ambon after he returned from the Netherlands.

Then after a week in Ambon, the sound of gunfire and exploding bombs started to go off again. It was then I realised that I had not just been on holiday, but we had to be evacuated because our lives had been threatened.

Clashes started to flare up again in Ambon. Feelings of fear and stress appeared again. My cousin Merfin and I were told that if we heard the repeated striking of electricity poles then we should run towards the Police barracks, the nearest place which was regarded as safe. Merfin and I had our own rucksacks. They were filled with clothes, milk, a pillow, a blanket and other stuff. This rucksack was always by our sides. So if we heard the repeated striking of electricity poles, the two of us ran as quickly as possible towards the police barracks.

Having experienced several incidents, it was as though I had become programmed to run every time I heard the noise of electricity poles being struck. So, automatically I ran if I heard that signal. One time the family panicked because I wasn't in the group that left the house together on their way to the police barracks. It turned out that I had run to the barracks before the rest of the family.

As time passed by the situation became even more critical. The area near Mum's house was becoming more and more unsafe. Dad decided that we would evacuate to one of our acquaintances who was living at the Halong naval base. Every night in Aunt Eli's we could hear the sound of bombs exploding, gunfire and houses being burnt down.

Every time I heard these sounds I felt frightened and full of panic. As the house we were living in was close to the naval hospital, I witnessed casualties being brought to the hospital for treatment almost all the time. One day I was playing outside the house. I saw an ambulance draw up. Out of curiosity, my cousin Fadli and I summoned up our courage to go and take a closer look. We were shocked at seeing corpses in such a bad state being carried out of the ambulance. Some were in the running position while others were lying face downward. Because we were so curious, Fadli and I slipped between the other people who were going towards the place where the corpses were being laid out. Apparently there were more corpses that were in an even worse condition.

That night I couldn't sleep soundly. Not only because Mum had scolded me because of our exploits with Fadli, but because I could still visualise the victims who had died in such a sad way. They are still very vivid in my memory. Besides not being able to sleep soundly, I was also anxious and frightened of the images of the corpses that were always popping up in my mind. While I was living in Ambon, every day a house was burnt down and there were sounds of gunfire and bombs exploding here and there. Because the situation in Ambon was increasingly getting worse, Dad decided that as a family we should go on 'vacation' outside of Ambon.

Taking Refuge Again

It was August 1999. Mum, Dad and I got ready to leave by ship from the Halong naval base pier. Again we had to separate from our family and the people we loved. Tears accompanied us on our departure. We said goodbye and hurried to the pier. I was confused about the situation at the pier because it was full of passengers. They not only brought their bags and suitcases, but some also brought their fridge with them. When we tried to board the ship, we were pushed and shoved and I was hemmed in by the crowd. Because I was very annoyed, I pinched the man who was standing in front of me, carrying a large cardboard box. Eventually, after great difficulty, we managed to board the Pelni ship.

We took refuge in Surabaya for two months, staying at the Dharma Guest House. There I helped Dad, Mum, Aunt, Uncle and a friend of Dad's, Diana. Dad got to know Aunt Diana, a Buddhist, through a friend who worked in the theatre. In Surabaya we helped to send goods to the refugees in Ambon: clothes, blankets, sarongs, mats and tents. This was as a result of lobbying carried out by Dad and Aunty, who knew naval officers when dealing with the refugees at the Halong naval base. The Eastern Armada of the Navy gave permission for the goods for the refugees to be put aboard the warships heading for Ambon.

While we were in Surabaya I should have attended the first year of primary school but I was frightened. I was afraid that something might happen to Mum and Dad, because we had taken refuge for our personal safety. Eventually Mum decided to buy the text books for the first year of primary school. Mum also became my 'teacher'. When there was free time, Mum taught me the lessons from the various books she had bought.

While we were in Surabaya I also kept in touch with the developments in Ambon through TV reports and the newspapers that Dad often bought. Both sides of the family also frequently phoned to check our situation. One day, Granny, from Dad's side, phoned to tell us that their house in Mardika had been burnt down. Likewise, Mum's family no longer lived in Tantui, because it wasn't safe. They had sought refuge at the Halong naval base. They were allowed to live in official housing, which was vacant at that time. Two families shared one house. Our family in Surabaya felt relieved because all the members of our family in Ambon were in safe locations.

Dad's friends always asked about our family in Ambon, although they had only just met through the humanitarian work that they were doing together, and they were from a different religious background. They all prayed that Ambon would become safe, so that there would be no more conflict that would result in 'waves of refugees' or meaningless deaths and the loss of belongings.

Trauma

Talking about belongings, I always thought about the object that I had kept tightly in my fist for days when we were forced to evacuate. That object, a spent cartridge, changed my life. I suffered a long, drawn-out trauma. As the situation in Ambon, the city where I was born, became increasingly less conducive, my family and I were forced to evacuate. Jogjakarta became the first city where my family and I sought refuge. We had to spend our time in the student city for about a year and a half. Eventually my family and I moved to Jakarta.

During the period we were moving from one place to another, every night when it was time to sleep I was haunted by fear. I would suddenly become afraid if I heard the sound of an electricity pole being struck or the sound of firecrackers, which I took to be the sound of a bomb exploding, and I would also panic in a crowd. Even seeing people running to catch a bus made me panic and feel afraid.

This situation continued even when I went to school; Dad or Mum had to wait around the whole time for me at the school. I still remember when I was in the 3rd year of primary school, if I couldn't see either Mum or Dad from the classroom, I would panic and immediately become afraid. Seeing my condition, Mrs Novi, the headmistress of the Tegal Parang, State Primary School No. 1, discussed the problem with my parents. After Mrs Novi found about my condition she explained it to the other teachers, so that they could help me get over this trauma which I had experienced for such a long time.

Mrs Novi also suggested that Dad could become the Scout troop leader at the school. That way she hoped that I would be able to follow the lessons normally. Fortunately, Dad had been active as a scout when he was at school.

After Dad became the Scout troop leader I slowly began to adapt and start to concentrate at school. The teachers also helped me by indirectly counselling me. I was able to make good progress at school without being haunted by fear anymore. My confidence began to grow.

Not only that, Mrs Novi told Dad that I needed to be kept busy so that the trauma would not be drawn out. She said that, if it was not well-handled, children who suffered trauma due to community unrest, especially inter-religious conflict, could become angry, resentful and experience a crisis in self-confidence. There were some cases of teenagers and adults who were never able to lose the effects of their trauma.

It was hoped that with the passing of time the trauma would be reduced or totally disappear. But a trauma can also be a time-bomb, waiting to explode at any time. This trauma needed to be resolved as soon as possible, going to its roots if it was needed. Mrs Novi and the teaching staff wanted me to recover completely from this trauma. She suggested that I take classes or attend a course that was related to my hobby and talents.

Because Dad's hobby was photography, he often took me on photographing expeditions with his friends. He bought me a pocket camera to practise with. Dad said that I could channel my feelings of fear, anger and resentment through photographs. Besides going on photographing expeditions with Dad, I also took part in photograph expeditions with friends from photographic groups, for example, with Dad's friends who were alumni from the Male Emporium Photography School or the Canon School of Photography and the fotografer.net community.

I even had the opportunity to take classes at the Darwis Triadi School of Photography when I was in junior high school. Eventually, I felt that I had undergone great change. I no longer suffered nightmares, I was able to concentrate at school, and I started to gain self-confidence. One of the most important developments was that Dad no longer had to sit at school waiting while I did my lessons. It meant that Dad could go to the office during normal working hours and didn't have to leave his work at certain times to wait for me at school.

I have constantly reflected on the truth of Mrs Novi's statement that it was difficult for a trauma to disappear if the right therapy was not provided. In 2007, when our family had to return to Ambon because Dad got a job there, my trauma resurfaced. Perhaps I had not recovered 100 percent and was faced with a situation that I didn't like. Every day when it was time for me to go to school, I felt frightened. I was especially frightened of the surrounding environment. Memories of having to run to safety carrying my rucksack loomed in my mind.

Eventually I didn't want to go to school because the situation was so different from what I had experienced in Jakarta, especially the behaviour of some of the teachers, and the environment close to the house. There were teachers who slapped my classmates if they did something wrong. The teacher slapped them, even though the students had apologised for their mistakes. I was shocked by the behaviour of the teachers. When I protested to my friends about the behaviour of a teacher, they said, 'You need to understand that at the time of the community unrest, the teacher's house was burnt down. It has influenced her actions'. Didn't almost everyone in Ambon become a victim of the conflict? Luckily, the effect of the trauma didn't last long. I managed to overcome it, with help from friends and family.

When I remembered all of this, I wondered about peers who experienced the same fate during the conflict. Or about the children of Ambon, who at the time of the 1999 human tragedy actually became members of child gangs that were known as the *agas* gang or *linggis* gang. Were these children no longer traumatised? If they were still traumatised, was their trauma dealt with properly? Do they still think that diversity in Ambon is still a problem?

As time has passed, I have grown up to become a strong teenager. There is no feeling of resentment or anger because the place of my birth, full of memories, was turned upside down by the burning anger of inhumane people. I don't know who is to blame for the violence that brought chaos to Ambon. But now Ambon is beautiful again. Life is peaceful, full of friendship, love and respect for diversity, which has started to radiate from Ambon again. Hopefully Ambon will still be beautiful for all who respect and hold peace and genuine friendship in the highest regard.

Through this chapter I want to say to the government, not only must the infrastructure be rebuilt, but children's psyches also need to be restored, especially of children who are still traumatised. I, who had the opportunity to leave Ambon for a reasonable amount of time, suffered trauma. My peers who are now university students need to be encouraged and their self-confidence developed, so that each looks after the other, each watches out for the other, so that there will be no more anger and resentment between peers. Encourage the development of the Pela Gandong culture, so that it is is not just a slogan or a ceremony. Allow us to live as basudara in peace and in diversity. Why should religion separate us if we are basudara? Why must religion divide us?

I dedicate this chapter to the people who helped us during the time we were refugees without seeking any reward. I hope that all their goodness and generosity will be repaid by the all loving God.

Chapter 24

SLEEPING WITH THE ENEMY

Helena M. Rijoly

In October 2002, I could hear footsteps in the room where I was sleeping. Then a pair of hands shook my shoulders, gently but firmly.

'Helena, wake up! Where are the other Muslims? They're not here!'

The woman who shook my shoulders whispered in panic. I jumped up and looked around the room where I and seven other women slept. Besides this lady, there was only myself and the Muslim women who were asleep. After realising the seriousness of the situation, we rushed into the parlour next to the room where I slept. There were other women in the parlour. But all of them were Christians. I shuddered. My instinct told me that this was a conspiracy

I counted about 10 Christian women who looked scared, angry and suspicious. To be honest, I felt the same as they did. In the midst of the tense situation in Ambon, because of this conflict, we were in a Muslim house, in a Muslim area, but without the other Muslim participants who should have stayed together for seven days in accordance with the concept of a live-in workshop. We felt that our trust had been betrayed. They had promised to stay together. We had trusted them and had come to the enemy territory.

Several women peeked out of the windows, scared that the house that we were staying in had been surrounded and that the enemy was ready to attack and kill us in the house. Some of the other women went to the kitchen and moved the food and drink so that it would not be consumed. We were frightened that the food and drink had been poisoned. We all gathered in the living room and didn't go back to sleep.

This episode took place in Ambon during the peace-building and conflict resolution program based on the Young Ambassadors for Peace (YAP)

concept. The workshop was started with a group of women who were a pioneer movement which now uses the name 'Ambassadors for Peace'.[1]

YAP is a peace-building movement initiative, a movement that develops the culture of peace in communities whose region has been affected by conflict and violence in the Asia Pacific region. YAP has been designed to respond to conflict and tension by warding off/dealing with the negative effects of war that influences young people. YAP also helps them develop skills that could give them other choices in resolving the conflict.

Basically there is no specific formula to 'find' or 'create' peace. Its success depends on the process, sometimes it is trial and error, with hands-on activities to encourage introspection in order to recognise and deal with the source of the conflict. Usually, introspection and personal transformation has proven to be more effective and more viable in developing sustainable peace.

The YAP concept is divided into two components: a 'live-in'[2] workshop which lasts for 5-7 days and further activities in the form of an action plan. The live-in workshop is effective as training in peace-building and reconciliation with an emphasis on personal transformation and acquiring skills in resolving conflict in a peaceful manner without using violence.[3] The victims and the perpetrators of conflict/war, as well as those directly or indirectly involved in the conflict, carried anger, sadness, bitterness and hatred within themselves. They acted according to this bitterness which was made worse by the hard trials of life that struck their lives.

For youths, the opportunity to carry weapons and fight on the front lines to defend their people stirred up feelings of patriotism and courage that was contagious. For some teenagers entering adulthood, the conflict situation

---

1   The first workshop was carried out in cooperation with the Uniting International Mission from UCA, where their Executive Secretary, Ms. Joy Balazo, who founded and initiated the Young Ambassadors for Peace (YAP) movement in the Asia Pacific and Australia, together with the Concerned Women's Movement (GPP) Maluku. This workshop was called the 'Closing the GAP' workshop and the term GAP was chosen as the name of the movement because it rhymed with YAP. Henceforth, the GAP workshop target groups were adult while the YAP targetted young people. The first Closing the GAP workshop took place in October 2002 and pioneered the way to found the YAP-Maluku in 2004.

2   A 'live-in' describes a workshop comparable perhaps to a boot-camp where the particpants, committee and facilitators live together in one location for 5-7 days. The rooms are organised so that Muslims and Christian share the same room. Thus there are daily tasks and other activities which bring about cooperation, dialogue and the meeting of sides between which there is enmity.

3   Uniting International Mission – Uniting Church in Australia, 'Appeal Brochure for YAP' (October 2004).

sometimes became a rite of passage, an initiation ritual into adulthood, by proving their bravery in the battlefield. Carrying a weapon meant power and superiority. Access to weapons gave them a position where they could take control, receive recognition and be 'accepted' in the community. A variety of urges and motivations drove the young combatants to throw themselves into war – from taking revenge for the deaths of loved ones and patriotism to defending religion and God. In the heated conflict situation, they didn't see there was any other choice that they could take. They were conditioned to see everyone outside their group as an 'enemy'. This is a human instinct that is defensive and territorial.

Young people and those affected by the conflict in general should not continuously be victims of hatred and the hard challenges of life. They needed to experience personal transformation. Thus, they need a safe place where they could meet their 'enemies'. These encounters should enable them to express their anger in a controlled situation that is managed well so that they can channel their anger in a more peaceful manner. The concept behind the YAP program is one example of the provision of a safe place for those conflicting sides to meet in this way.

This is the first product of the YAP program. As someone who has taken part in this program as a participant and later became a facilitator and has helped to pioneer the YAP program in Ambon, I realise that the most important stage of the YAP concept is the personal transformation process where people discover the elements of forgiveness and reconciliation within themselves. These two elements are not only linked to the forgiveness of the 'enemy', but, more especially and primarily, forgiveness and being at peace with themselves, which in turn leads to obtaining inner peace.

This chapter is a reflective analysis of the peace-building and reconciliation process that was carried out in the Young Ambassadors for Peace and Closing the GAP programs described above. It is also an opportunity to evaluate and analyse the vision of YAP that changed 'war' and 'violence' to become 'peace' in areas of conflict, especially in Ambon. This is a reflective analysis of the peace-building program that not only taught the theory and skills in dealing with conflict, but also emphasised personal transformation, forgiveness and community-building to achieve a just peace.

An Overview of the Conflict in Ambon

The island of Ambon is located in the archipelago province in Eastern Indonesia. The island covers an area of 761 km² in the shape of two horse shoes that are linked together to create two peninsulas that are connected by an isthmus which is only one mile wide.

The Ambonese, and Moluccans in general, are famous for the pela and gandong tradition, a social system that regulates co-existence, life together, and alliance that has been handed down from their ancestors. Pela and gandong have guarded and protected the existence of harmony between Muslims and Christians for centuries. This social system came into being when our ancestors swore oaths between siblings or with those they regarded as their kin/allies to live side-by-side, protecting and respecting each other until the end of time. This oath has been guarded and preserved from generation to generation.

There have been many accounts of the historical background of each village and its pela/gandong ties which sometimes represent a sense of gratitude for aid given during war time or plague or when land was granted to newcomers. Many pela/gandong ties have come into being because of marriage or as a sign of peace after being involved in war. Pela/gandong teaches each generation to regard others as kin with ties that are binding, as though they were blood relatives without regard for their group, religion or beliefs.

One example of the pela tradition as the result of an oath sworn is the relationship between the village of Passo and the village of Batu Merah. The majority of people who live in Batu Merah are Muslims. The only road in and out of the city of Ambon is through that village. Passo is a village where the majority of the residents are Christian and it is located on the isthmus between the two peninsulas of the island of Ambon. These two villages have a pela bond. If the village of Batu Merah wishes to build or renovate the mosque in their village, then the *tiang alif*, the main pillar, has to be provided (cut down, prepared and transported) by their pela, who are Christians from Passo. On the other hand, if the church in Passo is to be built or renovated, then their pela, who are Muslims from Batu Merah, have to provide (cut down, prepare and transport) the roof for the church building.

It is a pity that in January 1999 this village which has this beautiful strong bond of brother- and sisterhood became the epicentre of the conflict in Maluku. On 19 January 1999, when Muslims all over the world were celebrating their day of victory after fasting for a full month, an incident which was commonplace in the Batu Merah area ignited the conflict which dragged Muslims and Christian in Maluku to war. The whole thing began when a young thug tried to extort money from a minibus driver and then beat him up. The minibus driver then went back to his community and urged his friends to attack the thug's community.

This incident took place on the border between Batu Merah (Muslim) and Mardika (Christian) and was like other incidents that frequently occurred between the youths of these two communities and were regarded as teenage vandalism. This time, however, the incident escalated and became a war between Muslims and Christians. As a result of the escalation, the majority of the city of Ambon and the villages in other parts of the island of Ambon and on the surrounding islands of Seram, Saparua, Manipa, Haruku and Sanana were levelled to the ground. Approximately 30,000 people had to be evacuated.[4]

The perturbing question is, how could such a systemised co-existence, which had been preserved and practised for centuries, be turned upside down in just a few hours? How could religious symbols be dragged into the type of skirmish that often happened between a minibus driver and a thug? How could this skirmish turn into what was described as a sectarian / religious conflict? How was it possible that within a few hours symbols with sectarian connotations (SARA)[5] emerged – red representing Christians, white representing Muslims – and immediately become the label that compartmentalised and segregated the community in the name of religion?

This was not a spontaneous response but rather a situation that had been orchestrated, perhaps by a third party. Those who fell into the category of the 'third party' were aware that religion was the strongest tool to create conflict because of its sensitive and radical aspects. During this time our instincts for tolerance had become inert and superficial. The diversity that was present in the community created a sense of insecurity that was easily utilised by a 'third party' to incite religious conflict.

Many theories have been proposed concerning the conflict in Ambon. However, for me personally the conflict in Ambon was a conflict that was made/conditioned into a religious conflict. We need to consider the history of tensions between Muslims and Christians during the Dutch colonial period. The favouritism shown by the Dutch to the Christians caused wounds and created an imbalance within the community. The roots of bitterness became a very effective trigger for provocation. Religion was then hijacked to compartmentalise the community and create a separating wall. When the conflict broke out in January 1999, members of the community were driven to become members of a certain 'group'.

---

4   Human Rights Watch, Indonesia/East Timor, 'The Violence in Ambon', 1 March 1999, www.unhcr.org/retworldldocidl3ae6a7i6c.html (accessed 20 April 2009).

5   Translator's note: SARA is the acronym for *Suku Agama Ras Antar Golongan*, ethnicity, religion, race and inter-group relations. These were topics that were prohibited under the New Order (President Soeharto's era).

In this situation, when reflecting on the incident of the robbery of the minibus driver, the instincts to compartmentalise was not initially based in religious difference, which had never been at the core of community groupings. The agitators followed their instincts to protect the members of their own communities (village, local environment, gang, etc.). In this chaotic situation, a third party succeeded in inserting and manipulating religious and tribal symbols. Ambonese and Moluccans then drifted in the strong current of provocation which then caused very sore wounds in the community.

A Journey towards Peace

Lao Tzu once stated in an inspiring sentence that 'a journey of thousands of miles always starts with a small step'. It is true – the long journey to forgive and rebuild peace was started with a small step. Small steps are one of the principles of YAP. Our steps (actions) should, if possible, be small, measured, and achievable. Attaining peace and forgiveness is a long process but is still possible if we continue to make small steps in that direction.

In the beginning, YAP was a peace-building pilot project that was developed by the Uniting International Mission from the Uniting Church in Australia (UCA). This program was the idea of Mrs Joy Balazo who at that time was the Executive Secretary of the Human Rights section. Joy is a Filipino who had often visited Ambon and other Asia Pacific countries in connection with her work with UCA and its link churches. She witnessed the increase in levels of violence and conflict in the Asia Pacific region at that time. As a response to the tense situation and the conflict, the idea and concept of the Young Ambassadors for Peace was conceived in 2001. YAP was started by bringing young people from conflicting groups to sit down together. YAP was designed to help young people become peace-builders and peace-makers in their own communities. The instruction and training would, in turn, help ward off the negative effects of the war and conflict and would help the young people develop the skills needed to resolve conflict.

As a pilot project, a group of young people from two conflicting groups in six countries experiencing strife were invited to take part in a workshop for two weeks in Canberra, Australia. The six countries were Indonesia (Ambon),[6] Fiji, Sri Lanka, Burma, Solomon Islands and Papua New Guinea. These countries were on the list of 'countries at risk' at the

---

6 The four representatives from Ambon were Olivia Latuconsina-Salampessy (Muslim), Muhammad Nahumarury (Muslim), John Dumatubun (Catholic) and Helena Rijoly (Christian).

Australian Embassy.[7] There were 20 participants in all and they came from different backgrounds of conflict with different root problems: religious and racial conflict in Ambon; ethnic and political conflict in Burma; tribal conflict in Papua New Guinea and the Solomon Islands, and so on. YAP tried to initiate a flexible peace project which could be applied to different kinds of conflict.

An open, safe and friendly atmosphere was provided for the parties in conflict so that they could meet each other and develop a healthy dialogue. The use of games was the main strategy used in teaching basic concepts of justice and peace, including the development of trust in each other and self-confidence.

Games were conducted so that experiences could be shared without threat. Imagine a room where everyone present harboured hatred, anger and the desire to kill one another. Through these specially-designed games participants were encouraged to work together as partners in a team and not as enemies facing each other. This was one of the main approaches used by YAP; the words 'enemy' and 'victim' were abolished. They were trained through hands-on activities to separate people from problems.

Chaiwat Satha-Anand in one of his articles, 'The Politics of Forgiveness,' once stated:

> Any situation involves victimiser and victim. The relationship of the two parties is that the former is more powerful while the latter is less so. If the victim remains passive, the power relationship remains unchanged. If the victim starts to fight back, the existing power relations become unstable.[8]

If we live in a conflict area and experience the effects of conflict, we tend to place ourselves in the position of the victim. The label of victim can be useful but it can also destroy us. When victims unite, they use their feelings of hurt and suffering as a stepping stone to create a better life for themselves and for future generations. Although this can motivate someone to improve, if the label of victim sticks to a person, it tends to make that person weak because they believe they are weak. Of course, a victim of conflict has gone through a difficult phase in life, but it is very important to prevent the conflict and the harshness of life from continuing to make us victims. Our lives are determined by the choices and decisions we make. There is power in the choices

---

7   Joy Balazo, 'Young Ambassadors for Peace,' *Freedom*, No. 1 (May 2002), p. 2.
8   Chaiwat Satha-Anand, 'The Politics of Forgiveness', in *Transforming Violence: Linking Local and Global Peacemaking*, ed. Robert Herr and Judi Zimmerman-Herr (Scottdale, PA: Herald Press, 1998), p. 72.

and decisions made, and power can transform us. We have complete power in our hands to determine whether everything will destroy us or transform us into stronger and wiser individuals who are more capable of overcoming the future challenges in life.

When a participant takes part in a workshop for the first time, we can clearly observe that they feel insecure, with thought patterns that are judgemental, full of accusations and harbouring bitterness. They will immediately sit in groups situated on the opposite side of the room. The introduction session is usually the first session of the workshop but it is not just any session in the YAP workshop. The transformation process starts right from the beginning.

This stage is very crucial and cannot be ignored. This is the process of cracking the shell of bitterness and destroying the stiltedness caused by prejudice and hatred. The YAP workshop spends two full days in this 'getting to know each other' phase. If this is done correctly, it not only lays the foundation for a successful workshop but, more importantly, lays the foundation for close friendships that will continue when participants have returned to their communities.

After 'the getting to know you' session, the participants feel 'safe' and have set the basis for trusting each other and trusting the facilitator. They are no longer objects of the program but rather part of the process, working together to ensure that the workshop is a success. They are becoming more capable of opening up and sharing their wounded and angry feelings. At that moment they are faced with their prejudice and experience, and learn to accept, respect and have empathy for the feelings of other parties. This process restores the human feelings of each party in conflict, so that they no longer see others as enemies. In this session people shed many tears, shout with annoyance, give calming embraces, and even run out of the room. This is indeed acceptable and, moveover, it is hoped that it will occur because it is part of the reconciliation process with oneself and with others.

The rules are very simple. Don't judge, analyse or object. We only need to hear what others are sharing with us. We know how satisfying and free we feel when we are given the opportunity to express the emotions, anger and sadness that we have buried for such a long time and we find that the people in front of us accept and listen, without contradicting or being judgemental. This moment is very precious, because it releases us from the position of being a victim and other parties as the victimiser; we can see the difficulties and challenges faced by other parties and understand that they also suffered like we did.

This is really liberating because it turns out that we are all victims. Geiko Müller-Fahrenholz once wrote about this process of catharsis: 'Self-cleansing must inevitably lead to turmoil of emotions. Anger, sadness, grief and shock must be allowed to surface. To face these profound emotions is the beginning of healing'.[9]

Ron Reeson, photographer and a supporter of the YAP concept from the beginning, wrote about this process:

> The workshop went really well. There was good participation and reflection was carried out wisely through role-play. All went as had been predicted, measured and calculated – like a computer program. This continued, however, to the 'burning of prejudice' stage.[10] Then all the emotions came out, and tears flowed. This was the noblest goal of this workshop: renewing the tradition of peaceful coexistence. Of course, it was very difficult to do this when the memory of your house being burned to the ground or the loss of all your possessions and your loved ones resurfaced continually. However, when tears are shed, they gradually merge and become one. Cleansing of the soul has begun and their eyes start to see everything differently. I don't know how, prayers uttered from a broken heart and the trickle of tears have been answered. The amazing power to forgive has taken place.[11]

Forgiveness

Forgiveness has been repeatedly mentioned in previous pages. This word is very popular in conflict resolution. However, this does not mean that all people comprehend and interpret 'forgiveness' in the same way. There are two sayings that we most often hear from people when we ask them about forgiveness – 'let bygones be bygones' and 'forgive and forget'. This last saying perhaps sounds very 'religious', wise and noble; however, that is not an accurate understanding. Humans cannot delete the memories from their minds by pressing a delete button on a keyboard that puts them into a recycle bin,

---

9   Geiko Müller-Fahrenholz, *The Art of Forgiveness* (Geneva: WCC Publication, 1997), p. 88.

10   'Burning Prejudice' is the title of one of the sessions of the YAP Workshop.

11   Ron Reeson, 'Tears Dissolve Prejudice,' *Live Peace*, 01 (March 2006), p.1. *Live Peace* is a YAP International newsletter published by the Uniting International Mission – Uniting Church in Australia. Ron Reeson was active in conceiving the YAP concept. He has been a member of the YAP International team since December 2001.

leaving no trace. Once again Chaiwat Satha-Anand gives a wonderful description of forgiveness:

> Forgiveness is often mistakenly assumed to relate to forgetting. But I believe the meaning of forgiveness cannot be realised unless those memories of past misery are retained. Forgiveness is not forgetting. An amnesiac loses the ability to forgive precisely because the person has lost memory. To forgive the victimiser in a conscious act of full on intentionality, a clear memory is required.[12]

Forgiveness is never easy. It needs sacrifice and courage to open oneself and return to an extremely vulnerable position. However, the process is very important for breaking the 'victim's' links with hatred and anger, so that we are able to step into the future as a better person.

Pastor Michael Lapsley, an Anglican minister who ministered in South Africa during the Apartheid era, became the target of a series of letter bombs in South Africa. He lost both hands and one of his eyes, but he then became a healer and a voice for reconciliation in the post-Apartheid period. He appealed to all people to free themselves from the 'victim' or 'survivor' labels. All people need to declare themselves as victors over evil desires, hatred and even death. After he had become handicapped, he too took a long time getting to understand the purpose of his life and the purpose and direction he should take in his mission.

In an interview after the events described above, Michael never cursed or hated the people who sent him the letter bomb. Many people expressed how much they admired his ability to forgive those evil people. What many misunderstood and misinterpreted is that he never once used the word 'forgiveness'. He is still in the long process of reaching a position where he is able to forgive. Although he is not ready to forgive, he has chosen not to curse, swear or use words of hatred. This is the beginning of a golden road that leads to 'forgiveness'.

Actually Michael is frustrated, because people hope he can forgive 'just like that' with ease, because he is a minister. However, it doesn't matter who you are and what your position is – minister, *Imam*, counsellor etc. You are just an ordinary human being who will always take different roads that will lead to 'forgiveness'. Some are short and some are long and take time. The important thing is that we take the first steps and continue towards the

---

12   Satha-Anand, 'The Politics of Forgiveness,' p. 73.

goal. Pastor Michael states, 'Forgiveness is a complex human response, to an equally complex set of circumstances'.[13]

1-2-3-4 Steps in Forgiveness and to Get on with Life

Is it possible that we can really forgive? What does it mean to forgive? How do we do it? When and where do we start? The best place to start is by carrying out changes within ourselves. Mahatma Gandhi said, 'Be the change you want to see in the world'. Only you yourself have become the greatest enemy in the world. This is why the prophet Muhammad SAW categorised jihad that involved violence and war as a lower level of jihad compared to jihad that fights against human desires and is able to control oneself.

Now, if forgiveness starts with us, then what are our first steps? The first step leading to forgiveness is the most important and most critical stage. This has a very important place in the YAP concept, especially in running a peace-building workshop.

There are many concepts and theories about the stages in forgiveness but I wish to summarise these steps or stages myself, based on my experiences when I worked with Young Ambassadors for Peace (YAP). This stage consists of five steps, which were inspired by Brian McKnight's song, 'Back at one'. The refrain of this song 'leapt out' and inspired these stages:

> One, you're like a dream come true.
> Two, just want to be with you.
> Three, girl, it's plain to see that you're the only one for me
> And four, repeat steps one through three
> Five, make you fall in love with me
> If ever I believe my work is done.
> Then I'll start back at one.[14]

Forgiveness is a process and a transformation but it is not a linear process, a straight process. This process goes in a circle, has cycles, and recycles; the process is repeated from time to time.

There are five steps leading to the ability to forgive in the peace-building program in Ambon: (1) the willingness to be vulnerable and be involved

---

13 Michael Worsnip, *Priest and Partisan: A South African Journey* (Melbourne: Ocean Press, 1996), p. 134.
14 Brian McKnight, 'Back at One'. http://www.metrolyrics.cUncle/back-at-one-lyrics-brian-mcknight.html (accessed on 25 April 2009).

and immerse oneself in an encounter; (2) sharing, listening and showing empathy; (3) cooperation; (4) evaluation; and (5) recycle.

The Willingness to be Vulnerable and be Involved

Elise Boulding wrote about the healing of the victims and perpetrators of violence and war: 'Once an individual or a community has experienced severe violence, time alone cannot bring healing and the capacity for peaceful social relationships'.[15] How is it possible for us to hope that someone who has witnessed their parents or family killed in front of their own eyes, their house levelled to the ground, or been forced to sleep on damp cold earth in an emergency refugee camp will fully participate in a peace-building process or even return to a normal life?

Mariana (not her real name) was a participant in a 'Closing the GAP' workshop, a peace-building program using the YAP concept with an adult target group. She came from a Christian village that was wedged in between two Muslim villages in the eastern part of Ambon Island. Her village was attacked and brutally destroyed and all the residents were chased out of the village. Days in the jungle and the mountains where they took refuge, then years living in a refugee camp passed with a great deal of suffering. She became hard and full of hatred after she witnessed her grandchild die when it was born on the cold mountain as they escaped and were shot at. Mariana swore that she would always hate Muslims, who attacked her village and caused her to lose everything.

People cannot always guess what God's plan will be. Mariana was chosen by her church to take part in a GAP workshop together with a friend from her village. When she arrived at the workshop location, Mariana was startled when she discovered that some of the other participants were Muslims, especially when she found out that the Muslims came from the village that attacked her village. Mariana was very angry and she grabbed her bag full of clothes, ready to go home straight away. Her friend from the same village chased her and prevented Mariana from going home.

She asked Mariana not to behave like that and said that perhaps it was the Lord's moment to liberate Mariana from her burden of bitterness. More than that, they were elders in the church who were required to initiate the transformation and become examples for the congregation. With a heavy

---

15   Elise Boulding, 'Culture of Peace and Communities of Faith,' in *Transforming Violence: Linking Local and Global Peacemaking*, ed. Robert Herr and Judi Zimmerman-Herr (Scottdale, PA: Herald Press, 1998), p. 103.

heart, Mariana returned to the workshop location but she decided to remain silent and refused to speak to any Muslim participants during the first day. Bit by bit, with the aid of games and participatory activities, Mariana eventually participated in the workshop process. On the second day, when the 'burning prejudice' session was almost over, Mariana decided to face a male participant from the neighbouring village that attacked her village. According to tradition, this man had a gandong relationship with Mariana's family. Mariana asked the questions that she had long to ask for a long time, 'Why? We never wronged you. Why did you do this to us?'

Mariana's weeping gushed in streams and smashed every bit of her heart that had hardened. The man was quiet, listening with tears glistening in his eyes. The man listened, showed empathy and gave her the opportunity so that all the anger and hurt could find a way to melt and be destroyed. At the end of this workshop, Mariana went back to her village a new person.

Being vulnerable to the 'enemy', whether towards the perpetrator or the oppressor, of course was painful. However, this was a step towards forgiveness. In the beginning Mariana stubbornly refused and shut herself off, but then she was able to channel her emotions. Mariana's action in putting the question that had been nagging her for so long resulted in the melting of her emotional burden and this was a step that was really necessary for her personal transformation. At the same time, however, this courageous action also placed Mariana in a vulnerable position because she could not predict the reaction of the other party. On the other hand, the Muslim man experienced the same process. He also allowed himself to be vulnerable, whether in acknowledging wrongdoing or in accepting that in this matter they were both victims. The Muslim man listened to and acknowledged Mariana's feelings and emotions. Expressing emotion and receiving acknowledgement are two sides of the same coin which cannot be separated from each other. This process is not complete if one of these elements is not present.

Sharing, Listening and Showing Empathy

Mariana's story is one special case when the stage of being vulnerable and then becoming involved in the process took place over a short period of time. However, there are many cases where the particular dimensions and levels of complexity were different, making the process take much more time. When they were ready to cross over and enter the first stage, however, they were ready to sit down and develop a meaningful and healthy dialogue. These dialogues involved the process of sharing experiences without interrupting, contradicting and judging every fact and detail of another person's story. This is the stage of training in listening and showing empathy.

An interesting illustration was used in this stage to explain perspective. A picture of a mountain was drawn on the sheet of paper on the flip chart and we placed three dots to represent the positions of three people and a box. Point number 1 was placed behind the mountain, point number 2 was placed at the top of the mountain and point number 3 was placed next to the box. The question asked was; from where they are standing, which of these three people has the most accurate information about the box? Of course the person who is standing next to the box. Tragically, this described one of many incidents that occurred as the result of miscommunication. A village situated on the other side of the mountain on the island of Ambon heard that the Al-Fatah Mosque was burnt down and destroyed by Christians. Immediately they grabbed their weapons and murdered the closest Christian villages, only to find out that the Mosque had not been destroyed and is still standing today.

This stage leads us to the transformation stage. Acceptance and empathy will change relationships and the balance of power. The participants are no long victim and victimiser but rather brothers and sisters. They now understand the hurt from each other's point of view and they make the past a valuable lesson. This stage doesn't only transform the two of them, but also transforms the relationship between their two communities.

> Genuine forgiveness is about unburdening the past in order to inaugurate less painful relationships in the future. Forgivingness is an intergenerational challenge and a precious opportunity to build new bonds in the place of bitter bondage.[16]

Cooperation

12 years have passed since Jodi embraced Islam. My healing took years. But now I can accept Jodi as a Muslim. Indeed, there is still a slight feeling of pain in my heart because of my disappointment every time I remember that her choice has hampered things we could do together, as a mother or as a grandmother with her grandchildren. But I respect her

---

16   Geiko Müller-Fahrenholz, *The Art of Forgiveness*, p. 30.

choice and endeavour to live a good life. Then I wanted to know about the lives of other women who had changed their religion. What was the reaction of their family? How could my story help them? I wanted to be with the parents who were saddened by the choices of their children. I wanted to help them in the process of accepting the path of life taken by their children.[17]

The story above is a small part of the book, *Daughters of Another Path*, that was given to me as additional reading in the 'Building Abrahamic Partnership' course that I took part in between 2008 to 2009. This story tells of how Carol needed 12 years to move on from stage 1 to stage 2. When she eventually crossed over to the next stage of the process, the horizons of her thinking were opened wide. She not only saw the problem as a problem between herself and her daughter but also wanted to show empathy to a group of other women like herself, who had to face the 'nightmare' she had experienced. Together with her daughter, her partner in looking for peace, she gathered together several American women who had changed their religion to share their stories. They hoped that this would be an opportunity to be vulnerable, when they invited parents and others to come into their circle of discussion.

Carol and her daughter have entered fully into a transformed relationship. From a mother who had been disappointed and broken-hearted because she felt 'betrayed' by her daughter and a daughter who felt rejected and alienated because of her choice the two of them became partners working together (a mother full of compassion and her daughter who has been liberated). Together they have created meeting points, providing places for other people to have similar experiences, to give voice to their feelings of hurt, hope and fear. They have created a support network.

YAP is a network or organisation which entered a new phase when the two co-coordinators of YAP-Maluku (Muslim and Christian) spent several weeks in Mindanao working together with YAP-international and Ranao Muslim-Christian Dialogue for Peace to train and pioneer YAP in Mindanao. One of the reasons YAP-Maluku was asked to assist was the similarity between the conflict in Mindanao and the conflict in Ambon. For YAP-Maluku, this was an honour and acknowledgment of the results of hard work until now. More than this, it was a learning process. In essence, YAP shares experiences and at the same time learns and enters a new dimension in the dynamics and the culture of other communities.

---

17 Carol L. Anway, *Daughters of Another Path: Experiences of American Women Choosing Islam* (Lee's Summit, MO: Yawna Publication, 1996), p. 1.

Evaluation

The first stage is a very important stage in laying a strong foundation or the continuity of the program. Evaluation is an integral stage to guarantee the effectiveness and success of the program in reaching its goals. As time passes, when we have gone through stages 1, 2 and 3, our focus and approach certainly changes. When YAP-Maluku assisted the setting up of YAP in Mindanao, Philippines, YAP-Maluku was retracing their endeavours and work in the beginning of pioneering YAP in Ambon. When we returned to Ambon, we realised that when the change occurred from conflict situation to post-conflict, we were not only faced with reconciliation but also trauma healing and conflict prevention.

Basically, evaluation is the same whatever we do, whether in the small projects in the schools, in organisations, in workshop and training and in peace education. The aim of the evaluation is upgrading.

Evaluation includes various components: content (target, story, theme, and topic); method (activities, games, club, discussion group etc); environment (organiser, target group, location and atmosphere); and output (whether we succeeded in achieving our target and what we had achieved). The results of this evaluation will help us to come up with new content, new methods and better ways of organising the environment to make sure that we achieve a better result.[18]

Recycle

When this has been completed, the cycle returns to the starting point. Our hope is that when we return to the starting point 'caring for each other', we will be able to overcome hatred. That forgiveness that has been given and received, it has sown the seeds of peace that are now ready to blossom. Of course this is our ideal hope. We fully realise that there has never been a shortcut to peace. Everything has to go through the door of forgiveness.

In my ear and in my heart, the Brian McKnight song 'Back at One' reflects the meaning of peace and forgiveness. One, this is like a dream come true. For someone who is trapped in anger and hatred, forgiveness and peace is only a dream. But the dream can become a reality. What is needed is hard-work and the willingness to be vulnerable and meet with the parties who caused the pain in our lives.

---

18   UNHCR, *Peace Education: Facilitator Training Manual* (Nairobi: UNHCR, 2000).

Two, just want to be with you to share my heavy burden. I need you to see the extent of the gaping wounds in my heart and I can also see and understand that you have suffered like I have: 'We need to understand how people succeed in facing their painful past. This is very complex because between feelings and the ability to overcome them, are overlapping feelings enslaved by the past.'[19]

Three, it's plain to see that you're the only one who can heal the wounds in my heart and I can do the same for you. The enemy who becomes a close friend is a model. With new experiences and new relationships, they can help others who are still struggling to reach the point which they have already reached together. In this phase, the conflict resolution that begins to blossom and develop is not only of benefit for particular groups, but for the wider community.

> Conflict resolution should not be only an ad-hoc event but rather a process which will fulfil everyone's needs, we need to transform social institutions, relationships and the procedure of allocating resources. The process empowers all the community to together constructively manage the potential conflict in the future.[20]

Four and Five, after passing through the first three stages, we carry out an evaluation and repeat the cycle of activities with improvements based on the lessons we had learnt from the previous process.

Conclusion

The Muslim women who disappeared the previous night, returned to the workshop location in the morning and found us sitting together, our faces showing our feelings of fear, anxiety and anger. They were shocked to see our expressions and they felt guilty. On the other hand, the Christian women felt angry and disappointed. The facilitator and the GPP ladies who were the committee for the workshop then invited all of us to sit down and talk. At once the women sat down in groups according to their communities and sat along the wall at opposite sides of the room. All the participants were given an opportunity to express their feelings and emotions but in a controlled manner.

---

19 Geiko Müller-Fahrenholz, *The Art of Forgiveness*, p. 50.
20 Andries Odendaal, 'Building Community Peace in South Africa,' in *Transforming Violence: Linking Local and Global Peacemaking*, ed. Robert Herr and Judi Zimmerman-Herr (Scottdale, PA: Herald Press, 1998), p. 129.

The Muslim women who had disappeared the previous night explained why they returned home that night. One had gone home to get her children ready because they were due to go away the next morning; another had to accompany her husband, who was a prominent figure in the community and who had to deal with an incident in the village; another had to meet her husband who had just returned from being at sea; and another had to return home to make cakes to be sold in the morning in order to supplement her family's income. All the excuses made sense and touched the hearts of all the participants. This is because they were all women, wives and mothers who understood these responsibilities.

All at once the atmosphere in the room changed. The Christian women expressed their feelings of relief, because it turned out the reasons were not as sinister as they had imagined. They also told of how they had felt afraid the whole night long because they were haunted by negative thoughts as a result of that incident. The Muslim women were also aware of being frightened when they had to stay somewhere that was far from their family and community, especially when a conflict situation became heated. The Muslim women then threw their arms around the Christian women and expressed their admiration at their courage to cross over the border and stay with them, to achieve peace in Ambon.

During the following days of the workshop they continued to share their stories about the struggles all women faced in life, no matter what their religious background. There were stories about their efforts to fulfil their daily needs, about the loss of a child, husband and belongings, about concerns for the future etc. With every story told, they embraced each other, they talked from the heart and dreamed that Ambon will return to its beautiful state. The incident, which had made the situation quite tense, then created solid friendships and familial relationships.

On the last day of the workshop there was an incident which made the conflict escalate. The main road was blockaded. The Christian women became tense again and couldn't wait to get back to their families, who they had left behind for a week. The Muslim women participants then accompanied them, to make sure that the Christian women could get past the barricades at every Muslim village until they safely crossed the border.

These are amazing women, they are the seeds of peace growing to become ambassadors for peace. They have experienced a hard life. They have passed through the 1-2-3-4 stages of the transformation process and returned to the beginning for perpetual peace. They are proof that the act of forgiveness from a sincere heart can take place through this process.

There is no shortcut to peace and reconciliation in a region of conflict. Forgiveness is the door that we have to pass through to head towards genuine peace and reconciliation. This is indeed difficult but not impossible. Forgiveness is a choice to be involved in the process cycle that is continually moving in a better direction. Forgiveness is not the same as forgetting. Once again, our minds are not like a computer which has a delete button to easily remove all the hurt and trauma. Memories of the past are always with us. But with forgiveness, we can look behind us and gaze at the past and no longer feel the pain.

Chapter 25

A LETTER TO A DEAR FRIEND

Nancy Souisa

Greetings!!

Dear friend ... I hope you are well when you receive this letter. Indeed, I wish you all the best. How are your mum and dad? I send greetings to them. I hope everyone is well. There is nothing more important in life than getting on with others, caring for each other and looking after each other. It's simple, but it isn't that easy to be noble in what we do with our lives.

Dear friend ... I want to share some things with you that I have kept in the depths of my heart for a long time and which have been on my mind and made my heart churn ... I feel I need to share them with you and hope you will listen ... Just hear me out ... There's no need to comment, no problem ... but if at some time you want to tell me something, I would be glad to hear it ...

It's like this ...

I've read articles, heard the news from electronic media, there are many problems and I see many things happen in day life ... some I can accept, there are some things that people say happened, although they know that the number wasn't as many as that, and I can't accept that kind of thing. Yes, people can say what they like, but don't we have the right to say what we feel is right? We're not just objects; we are also the subjects who state what in our opinion is right.

I will commence with the first thing, something that I've wanted to tell you for some time. I miss our time at school, when we were very close friends, when the differences could be put in their proper place and made us mature although we weren't yet twenty years old. Do you remember when we practised *Qasidah* to celebrate *Halal Bihalal*? It was the first time I played the tambourine ... and sang a new song ... We only experienced it together because we were friends. I personally was happy because I could join in a friend's happiness, one caring about the other. Is that too simple? I don't think so. Do you agree with me, or not? Aren't love and friendship valuable? Why are they valuable? They are valuable because they are noble. It's become more difficult to find such things in this world ... I come to realise more and more that what we did in the past was noble and right ... I still remember the song that we sang back then.

The next point – do you remember when we used to do the rounds together to celebrate Nyepi Festival at our Hindu friend's house? We thought it would be the same as doing the rounds at Eid Al Fitr and Christmas, we forgot that at the Nyepi Festival our friend must withdraw and be quiet, no fires could be lit in the house, no cooking and no rowdiness. I feel like laughing at myself when I remember the incident. We were only happy because our friend was celebrating a festival, so we went to his house to give our greetings. But do you remember how our friend didn't want to disappoint us, his family continued their seclusion but they asked the Christian granny who helped in their house to open it and let us in the house and prepare something for us to eat.

Dear friend, our friend probably broke the rules of his religion, but he happily received us to honour the effort we made to come to his house. Oh, if I think about it I get goose pimples, the whole spectrum of feelings from happiness to wanting to cry. Our friendship meant a lot to us at that time. Although we were still very young ... but I learnt a lot from those experiences. I'm certain we need to keep this friendship going. If someone doesn't agree with me and objects to what I think, I still believe that what we did is not something that needs to be changed!

Another thing, my dear friend, I want to talk about how I feel that something isn't right. It's like this, there are articles doing the rounds that are forming public opinion, which make generalisations about humankind and the conditions under one religious umbrella and suggest that everyone is in the same situation.

Some say that Ambonese Christians used to have good positions in the government in the past and so on, as though this condition was regarded as valid for every Christian. Although you know, don't you, many people don't experience these things. A great number of people don't depend on government jobs for their livelihood! Many families, parents, earn a living from the sea, in the plantations, in the forest, sell fish, living hand-to-mouth.

From a quantitative aspect, in the past and in the present I am sure that the numbers of people working in government are not so many. Why should this group represent the standard to describe Ambonese Christians as a group? I think there is, indeed, a problem of a power struggle, personal problems and others. But it's not everything is it? Are our Ambonese Christian friends who don't work in the government to be deemed non-existent, regarded as trivial or meaningless just because of stereotypes. Can people transfer the problem and ignore many other facts? And don't those facts concern the existence of many other people?! Are we not part of a group that has been ignored? It's difficult for people to go to school. Although our parents are civil servants, it doesn't mean that we are not affected by what are called 'limitations' does it?

We remember many friends who all experienced difficulties, and there were those who were worse off than us and quite a few were Ambonese Christians. I feel that it's not fair. Data has been simplified and truth has been sacrificed, based on the experiences of a number of people. It means, that we know and have a certain number of friends who have lived simply and had barely enough to live on and didn't get swept up in the prosperity just because they were Ambonese Christians, or for any other reason. I hope this honesty can still be maintained out there. There are personal and group experiences, but that doesn't mean sacrificing other people who are incorporated in the generalisation that has been made although their situation is different.

This doesn't include the many burdens of history that we have to bear. Although we weren't around at that time, we don't know why things are like this or like that. So many centuries have passed. For instance, during the Dutch period, were many Christians treated in a special way? Perhaps it's true, but a great number of people don't feel it was so. Rather I feel that we have experienced many long-term deprivations. The value gained is not as great as the so called 'special treatment' from the colonial powers.

Dear friend, colonial domination is still colonial domination. How great was the special treatment? I have heard many stories from the older generation in several of the Christian villages that they suffered and were whipped as a punishment for using regional languages. This is a very different account from the explanations that are often given, as to why someone wanted to become a Christian – it is said that they easily relinquished their use of regional languages and forgot their identity. That's definitely not true. They suffered and experienced depravation because of the colonial domination. They were controlled in such a manner, pressured and struggled in such conditions. And if I try to imagine what the situation was like not just for one year, or ten years, or 32 years, or 50 years. It continued for 300 years!! 300 years!! What a heck of a long time ... We experienced the authoritarianism of the New Order for just 32 years. After that, a great many things changed straight away, others slowly but surely. We wanted some things or tried to reject others, but eventually only a small amount could be pushed aside.

Do you remember, during the whole time we were at school, we never knew anything about Moluccan history, we didn't learn our regional language. We didn't know anything about prominent historical figures from Maluku who were involved in the history of Indonesia, even though there were quite a few who were involved in the fight for Independence. So, when we feel that, living in this independent nation, we are on a long road with no end in sight as we negotiate our own identity and life to enjoy 'freedom, equality and justice'. Why cause and judge this struggle? Was it so easy for our ancestors to shed their blood and tears shed during colonial dominion? Were they without feelings and hearts?

Dear friend ... do you know what my greatest regret is as a Moluccan? I don't know our own regional language. Shame on me! Don't laugh at me. Do you know our regional language? I don't ever remember you speaking our regional language. You can't speak it either – or are you embarrassed to speak it? Let's learn to speak our regional language, if you know it, teach me ... Then we can teach our children so they know ... Our ancestors received wisdom from God to use certain languages – that is one of the greatest inheritances to leave to our children and grandchildren.

Oh ... dear friend ... I'm sure there are also many stories from the Muslim villages ... especially amongst those who chose to maintain tribal beliefs, beliefs that have been handed down from one generation to the next, also stories of those who live in the towns and mix with people from many different backgrounds; there are bound to be many stories. I am certain that there are sad stories, happy stories, those full of reflections and those full of, a desire to be free to live in an environment where friends don't blame each other, but forgive each other, respect each other and support each other to achieve the best. One for all and all for one. What you feel is what I feel.

Dear friend ... you are still my friend aren't you? Don't discard me, don't regard me as a friend from the past ... only because you have got to know other people since. As the earth gets older, may our friendship become stronger ...

That's all I want to say ... Perhaps I've taken up too much of your time ... Thank you for taking time to read this, listen to me and feel what I have felt. When can we get together ... if we can't make it, I hope to hear from you, by letter or email, or whatever.

May the good and merciful Lord, help us to take steps forward, strengthen our hearts so that we can walk in His good paths.

Chapter 26

GANDONG'EE, LET'S SING!

Jacky Manuputty

At the beginning of March 1999, about 30 people representing the Muslim and Christian communities left for Bali. Taking different flights, the two groups arrived in Denpasar and immediately headed to one of the meeting venues up in the mountains. The British Council, together with Gajah Mada University (UGM) as its partner, deliberately placed the two groups on different flights because of the escalating religious conflict in Maluku.

The feeling that there was an in-group and an out-group was strongly evident when we met up in Bali, although a fresh mountain breeze enveloped the five-day activities around an investigation into the conflict. Tension and suspicion were etched on the faces of the participants. The organising committee was not able to eradicate this, although Balinese music and dancers were provided as an interlude at every session. It was difficult to diffuse the atmosphere, where people tended to sit groups based on their religion. Religion had split us in Ambon and it was the same in Bali.

As the third day approached, I whispered to the organising committee to get hold of a keyboard and a musician who could play songs. Moluccan instrumental music could be heard while eating lunch. In a flash the atmosphere became tense when the keyboard player played the music to the '*gandong*' song, a popular song that tells of the close familial links within the Moluccan society. Several people could be seen approaching the keyboard player and they asked him to stop playing that song. The lyrics and the melody of the song were too painful to hear because they were in direct contrast with the shattered gandong relationships in the bloody conflict at that time.

The sound of spoons clattering on plates filled the silence; all were caught up in a cold wall of silence. If anyone spoke, the majority of participants chose to whisper amongst their friends. There was no more gandong song, but a series of other Moluccan songs were played. The melodies profoundly affected the stilted 'family get-together' (*bakudapa basudara*) that afternoon. When the keyboard player invited participants to sing songs, several people went forward, took hold of the microphone and sang.

The rigidity slowly melted and a number of women's eyes became red. Tears fell one by one, a sign that the series of melodies had drawn each person into a *sangkan paran* (a realisation of one's roots), the orang basudara cosmological content lying at the heart of the music. Every beat of the melody was like a sharp bamboo blade, paring away the clump of anger and resentment, finding its way through to the place where we owned our own identity, the 'feelings of being a Moluccan', which had been long suppressed during the conflict. At least that afternoon what we were looking for happened, and then we took each other's hands and danced to the rhythm.

The music and the peaceful happy Moluccan folk songs had indeed almost been obliterated during the lengthy conflict in Maluku. With the escalation of the conflict, the songs of children as they played by the sea were silenced. The percussion sounds of *tifa totobuang* and the rhythm of *sawat* tambourine, both lying prone, had been muted, exchanged for the music of war and an orchestra of electricity poles being struck, homemade bombs or grenades being thrown, the pulling of the trigger of all types of guns. If there was any form of melody, it would certainly be a melody inspiring war. At the end of every performance there was no applause, only the groaning of sadness or weeping, while people carried away the bloody corpses.

Singing the gandong song at the time of conflict was like holding a machete against the neck. If indeed it had to be sung, the tones would echo around dark rooms, the corners of life where the gandong ran into each other, hidden from the boisterousness of war in public places. Such happenings took place as the gandong of Ouw, who are Sarane, secretly visited their gandong brothers from Zeith, who are Salam, and together they then repaired the traditional house (*rumah adat*) there.

In the same way the gandong of Ambalau Island, who are Salam, helped build a fishing boat for their gandong brothers from the island of Nusalaut, who are Sarane. There are many more unspoken gandong stories, forcibly suppressed by the screams of war. The Moluccan conflict has indeed placed the gandong into dark, hidden corners, but the conflict was never able to uproot the tones of the gandong and dash them.

Music is indeed a neutral media of dialogue for us Moluccans, because just as God does not have a religion, so too music. However, music will not always be neutral, especially if a person misuses it. In many areas of conflict, music can become an instrument in the struggle, even a weapon for each faction. Music can be used to mobilise militarism, as in Nazi Germany in the 1930s.

Before the war took place in Croatia in 1990, many songs were produced in order to increase the spirit of Croatian ultra-nationalism. It was the same in Serbia, where music was used in war to whip up the mythology of the uniqueness of Serbia. In the invasion of Iraq, American soldiers played loud recordings of rap and metal music when they were out on patrol and attacking. Songs were used to give courage to those who fought in Rwanda.

Music became a motivator for the peoples' army and volunteers during the war for the independence of the Republic of Indonesia. In the midst of the Moluccan conflict, the interpretation and contemplation of music was carried out enthusiastically as the young people screamed war against the enemy of their faith. The music was manipulated and alignments were determined, as alignments to God were arrogantly determined by the supporters of the conflict.

As the storm of the conflict began to recede, people began to sing again. Different versions of gandong songs could be heard when peace was pioneered in Maluku. The *tifa totobuang* was struck loudly, spun together in unison with the pounding of the *sawat* tambourines and the *hadrat*. We brought the *bedug* (large drum) from the Al-Fatah Mosque and struck it along with the *tifa totobuang* on the giant stage of the Eid Al Fitr joint celebrations in 2005.

The *bedug* player wore traditional white Muslim attire and pounded the *bedug* with great feeling, accompanied by the beating of the *gaba-gaba* sticks on the skin of the *tifa* that was pounded by dozens of young people from the villages up in the mountains who donned *kain berang* (red cloth). 'This is genuine reconciliation', shouted the musicians at the *sawat* and *totobuang* jam session during the *sawat* and *totobuang* festival organised by the Inter-Faith Organisation in 2006. The musicians sang out acclamations of peace through the pounding of various percussion instruments, the shrill sound of the flutes, the blowing of trumpets, or the strumming of guitar strings.

There is no doubt that music can ignite conflict. But music can also have a role in developing peace. Several music projects for peace and reconciliation can easily be found in the world.

From the start of the 90s, the use of music for peace has spread globally and quickly. The 'Resonant Community' project (1989-1992) in Norway is one example. The aim of this Project is to prevent the increase in discrimination towards immigrants, through the development of characteristic music belonging to immigrants in the schools involved in the scheme. In the Middle East, Israeli and Palestinian children have joined together in one attractive choir. In Cyprus, music and poetry have been used in the efforts of transformation of conflict.

The presentation of music and other art forms has become a new trend in almost every inter-faith dialogue event all over the world at this time. Music has become a medium for the transformation of conflict, a bridge in a dialogue; it can even be used as an instrument in therapy for many post-conflict communities.

The story of orang basudara is also a story about music. Music is always a uniting factor in the encounters of orang basudara. Music in Maluku was not born out of a need for post-conflict reconciliation; music is the very soul of the Moluccan people.

Benny Likumahuwa, a veteran jazz player from Maluku, once said that people in the past compared Maluku to the Garden of Eden, which inspired the people to sing as a way of being thankful. The natural elements of Maluku caused people to sing, said Benny. According to artist Chris Pattikawa, wind, sea and waves are the natural elements that teach the Moluccan people to sing. Daily life, surrounded by the sea, teaches Moluccan people rhythm. The knowledge of rhythm is naturally reflected in percussion music.

In Maluku, music is the medium that unites a people with peaceful nature. A great many songs are inspired by the gift of nature. The land, the sea, the swaying coconut trees, even the mist in the mountains, are often mentioned in the verses of Moluccan songs. The basudara relationship is also sung about in Moluccan songs. There are so many songs that advise how to live together as brothers. On hearing these songs, Moluccans are drawn into the holy canopy of its cosmology. This binary relationship must be maintained by the brethren and their relationship with nature, in holding account to the ancestors who wove this basudara relationship and to God who gave it to them. It is clear that through their songs Moluccans perpetuate the ethical regulations; Moluccans tend to sing with feeling, whether it is expressed in cheerful songs that are full of jokes and laughing, or songs that reach deep into the emotions and cause the shedding of tears.

Music and peaceful songs have never died out in Maluku, because music was born from the peaceful land and nature from which we came and will return. The arrogance of conflict of the people of Maluku will therefore never destroy the majestic music and songs in praise of their peaceful natural surroundings.

Now Maluku is singing again, Ambon has become the City of Music. The young people shout out loudly 'Beta Maluku' in all kinds of pounding hip-hop music. Another community of young people have chosen reggae as the music that they identify with. On the grand stage used for MTQ at the National Level in 2012 the Maluku Bamboowind Orchestra mesmerised thousands of spectators with their presenting of tambourines in unison, together with the bamboo flutes and the pounding of *tifa totobuang*. Pattimura Park now has become the stage for music concerts once a month, where people come and sing along. Annual music events in post-conflict Ambon include a jazz festival that brings together national and international jazz musicians. While in the traditional villages, Pela and Gandong communities stretch out the *kain* gandong to welcome their kin, singing songs that strengthen the gandong ties.

Music and singing has returned. Coconut leaves swaying in the breeze have produced thousands of notes. On the beach, waves ebbing and flowing string together the rhythm of love songs. Children run about on the beach carrying *tifa* and tambourines. Songs are written, songs are sung. The story of the orang basudara is the story of friends singing songs to the heavens, singing songs to the blue sea, accompanied by waves dancing along the sands, singing about the coconut, clove and nutmeg trees, singing about mother, singing about young women, and singing about the peaceful coexistence of basudara. Peace!

CONCLUSION

Positive Avoidance, Segregation and Communal Cooperation in Maluku

Rizal Panggabean

This is a rare book which needs to be read and is enjoyable. For me personally, the contributors and their stories take me back to 2000–2003, when I often visited Maluku and North Maluku working with the police, health workers and young people. It was time full of tragedy, making many people unable to 'hold onto sanity,' using Sandra Lakembe's term. Besides tragedy and insanity, there were also shocks and consternation. Why, after hundreds of years of living side by side in peace, can a society be hit by inter-community violence between the religious groups? The same consternation is still present to this day, as is evident in many of the contributions in this book. If this book was published to remember it, then there is a spirit of emancipation; what can be done so that it is never repeated? What means are provided in this diverse society so that people can work together and take steps towards the future, full of confidence?

Positive Avoidance

Gerry van Klinken commenced *Basudara Stories of Peace from Maluku* with an important and moving challenge: disclose the truth of what happened when communal violence occurred in 1999 and for several years afterwards. We have to know what happened in the past, to take a step forward. Don't let anything be regarded as taboo; everything must be talked about publicly, including that which concerns the role of the important institutions and public figures in Maluku, especially religious leaders and institutions.

This is a huge proposition and it is full of risks. There is another proposal that also could become a means in inter-faith cooperation in the future. Let's call it 'positive avoidance'.

In inter-personal relationships with friends and colleagues, including close friends, we often deliberately avoid talking about certain matters. These certain matters can vary, depending on which friends or colleagues, wages and income, domestic problems, and secrets or other personal matters are involved. Sometimes we avoid doing things. We don't hang out our underwear to dry in front of our homes but in places that cannot be seen, so that our neighbours don't see it easily. Parents do not argue in front of their children, because they are concerned that it will disturb their children's emotions.

In public life sometimes talking openly about particular matters is also avoided. There are political parties that deliberately avoid talking about internal conflict within the party, because they consider it would reduce public interest in the party. Certain parties and social organisations avoid talking about the application of *Syariat Islam*, for example, because it is thought to be divisive for the electorate and their supporters. Consider too the fact that society and the state restrict the freedom of cigarette companies to advertise products to protect people's health.

In other words, as individuals and as a group we sometimes censor ourselves when interacting in inter-personal or inter-group relationships. As is evident in the examples above, reasons and considerations vary – avoiding the emergence of unpleasant feelings with friends or neighbours, protecting that which is regarded as the greater public interest, and so on. Holmes mentions several terms that are generally used to demonstrate the same characteristic of limiting issues or agenda in social groups, including 'gag rules', 'the politics of omission', 'strategic self-censorship', 'self-denying ordinances', and 'the positive use of negative liberty'.[1] So, sometimes knowledge is a catastrophe and ignorance is bliss.

Self-censorship is within the framework and directly in the context of strategic interaction. It means that what we consider in our social interactions in the public sphere is sometimes not all that we believe and what we adhere to – like social norms, international norms about human rights and religious norms. What we will do and what will be talked about will be determined by the responses and reactions that are most likely come out of the environment and from colleagues who interact and work with us. In the context of strategic interaction, positive avoidance sometimes becomes the right choice.

If the above is true, then the people in Ambon in particular and the people in Maluku generally should avoid talking about certain topics if doing so leads to them to be divided and hurt again. In order that peace and

---

[1] Stephen Holmes, 'Gag Rules or the Politics of Omission,' in *Constitutionalism and Democracy*, ed. J. Elster and R. Slagstad (Cambridge: Cambridge University Press, 1988), pp. 19-58.

social working together on an inter-faith and inter-tribal basis can continue smoothly, serious threats to peace and coopeeration must be avoided. What are these serious threats? One of them is public debate about the role of religion (idioms, symbols, prominent figures, and organisations) in the mobilisation of militants and communal violence. In an open debate in a community that has just been divided by religion and just experienced drawn-out communal violence, the stronger arguments may not necessarily win. It is difficult to compromise, and deliberation can be filled with insults and accusations.

Quite apart from people who have just emerged uncertainly from communal violence, even for ordniary people religious issues are topics that are most frequently avoided. Religious disputes often disrupt communal co-operation; political solutions cannot resolve religious clashes; and religious controversies cannot be solved in a rational manner. Therefore, positive avoidance means the liberty of avoiding serious threats to social cooperation in a post-violence community.

Of course, restricting an agenda is not always regarded as positive. The United States of America has been criticised for restricting talks and general discussions about slavery. In the same country, speaking the truth and the 'bloody hands' in the history of the Civil War in their own country is still regarded as taboo. In the same way, Japan has been criticised because it did not inform its people about what the Japanese occupying forces did in Manchuria, Nanking, Semarang, or on Buru Island. The children were told about the Meji and Tokugawa Restoration but then history leapt forward to the atom bomb that fell on Hiroshima and Nagasaki, ignoring the militarism and barbaric behaviour of the Japanese soldiers between the two periods of history such as rape, massacre, *jugun ianfu* (comfort women), and so on.

The collection of the stories in this book, however, shows that the primary concern is peace and inter-faith cooperation. This needs to be stressed. We have not put an end to positive avoidance. At the same time, we, to borrow Hasbollah Toisuta and Abidin Wakano's term, carry out 'jihad' for peace and inter-faith and inter-tribal social cooperation.

Starting from Segregation

What is meant by segregation is spatial segregation, especially housing settlements, which are based on religious background and, to a certain extent, tribal background. Traditionally, the people of Maluku have been spatially segregated. Christian communities live in one village and Muslim communities live in a different village. Some of the villages are separated by quite a distance, while others are only separated by a main road. In certain villages the two communities tend to live in their own clusters, so that, although Christians and Muslims live in the same village, in practice the two communities live in different neighbourhoods.

These clusters based on religious background and the resulting spatial segregation are due to several basic mechanisms. The first is the desire to feel secure when there is uncertainty, tension and communal violence. The second is the high intensity of intra-faith interaction through a calendar of frequent social-religious activities, which Robert Putnam calls 'bonding'.[2] The conflict, especially in Ambon and generally in Maluku, had a tendency to increase the level of spatial segregation. Housing settlements that were integrated and initiated in new housing areas are on the decrease.

The pela gandong institution and other similar activities linked to this institution assume that village segregation is based on religious background. Although it seems ironic, communal harmony is preserved more easily when the citizens are divided on religious lines and perhaps also tribal lines. If the pela gandong has been belittled and ignored because of social changes due, for example, to the spread of Islam and Christianity, then the capacity of the people to live side by side will be diminished. On the whole, the contributions in this book accept spatial segregation based on religious background.

For example, M. Noor Tawainela, in 'When the Conscience Speaks,' explains about the village of Tulehu which is Muslim and has a pela gandong relationship with Waai, which is Christian. He remembers the wonderful meeting involving the two villages:

> The atmosphere was lively, serene, and full of kinship and friendship nuances. There were songs – *cakalele*, *tifa* and *totobuang*, *pantun* and *lania* – that were sung in a language I found difficult to understand and sung in rhyming choruses calling back and forth. There were *pasaware* that told of the history of the relationship of their descendants, the history of the traditional villages and how they came into being, before the West set foot on the land of their birth, whether it is Honimoa, or Lataela, or Harua or Lataenu.

Pela gandong makes it possible for inter-faith encounters, especially among the indigenous Moluccan population that is differentiated from newcomers

---

2   Robert D. Putnam, *Bowling Alone: The Collapse and Revival of American Community* (New York: Simon & Schuster, 2000).

such as the Bugis, Butonese, and people from Makassar. As emphasised in several contributions (like those by Jacky Manuputty, M. Azis Tunny and Weslly Johannes), it is hoped that encounters will bring about an atmosphere of trusting and understanding each other. But, after the encounters and festivities are over, each returns to their own groups, to their own cultural worlds, and to organise in their own communities. Calhoun explains that this is one way to interpret and utilise differences.[3]

In the context of spatial segregation, communal peace and social cooperation can still be developed. One of the important mechanisms here is an increase in daily interaction in the villages, markets, and schools, whether for social or religious events. This was strongly practised in the past, and the contributors to this book wish that it would increase in the present and in the future. Direct inter-faith and inter-tribal communications and mixing in various domains of daily interaction will reinforce peace.

Collective cooperation in various associations whose members come from different religious backgrounds will reinforce peace. These associations could be inter-faith organisations, but other associations such as those in the arts, sports, trade, industry and party politics, are no less important. Varshney mentioned that inter-faith interaction in everyday life associations plays an important role in preserving peace, including when there is tension and disharmony.[4]

Creating an Opportunity

Sometimes, the agenda of public deliberations needs to be limited in the interests of the common good; inter-faith social cooperation in a community has, with great difficulty, come out of communal violence. The limitations can be carried out based on the joint will of the communities that have been involved in the violence, rather than because of pressure and force.

In addition, everyday encounters and inter-communal associations need to be revived and increased. Local institutions and traditions that make it possible for people of different religious backgrounds to work together need to be supported to reduce conflict. Pela gandong institutions, which are often mentioned in this book, are the initial capital. But new innovations also need to be carried out in the form of modern inter-communal associations that are active in various areas of life.

---

3   Craig Calhoun, 'Social Theory and the Politics of Identity,' in Craig Calhoun (ed.), *Social Theory and the Politics of Identity* (Cambridge, Mass.: Blackwell Publishers, 1994), 9-35.
4   Ashutosh Varshney, *Ethnic Conflict and Civil Life: Hindus and Muslims in India* (New Haven: Yale University Press, 2002).

EPILOGUE

Stories with a Million Dimensions

Aholiab Watloly

We are all brothers is a wise view about a self-identity based on a depth of thinking. This cannot be achieved by only relying on limited reasoning, but with an open heart and a depth of feelings. The life journey of the orang basudara is important for the educational curriculum of the orang basudara at this present time.

The story of the *orang basudara* (people with a brother- and sisterhood relationship) marks a million dimensions of the Moluccan people who live on a critical frontier. It's true we almost lost the direction of our lives, we almost lost our lasting heritage, the human heritage of the people of Maluku, the heritage of the lives of the orang basudara!!! They (the contributors to this book) speak from their consciences, from myriad cultural, religious, humanitarian, artistic and nationalist dimensions, from dimensions of instinctive journalism and a million dimensions of the daily lives of the orang basudara. They tell their stories with a high level of intellect, occasionally with feelings of indignation, emotion, tears, sadness, regret and a million other feelings. They tell their stories in the *baileo* belonging to the orang basudara while sitting on wooden seats, and then occasionally they dive into the deep ocean heart of the Moluccan seas and then paddle home on a traditional canoe from a tempest in another place, which was very tiring and moving. Occasionally they shed tears when telling their stories from the depths of their hearts. Occasionally they pour out their thoughts with a brilliant and shrewd analysis. They use riddles, throw in jokes, or, occasionally, use the logic of René Descartes, even tell stories using metaphors from Friedrich Nietzsche and Richard Rorty in the conflict. The contributors tell of the mystery of a visiting conflict, controlled by Mr X. They tell their stories as the orang basudara's 'mission statement', that is inscribed in their hearts and expressed in the local dialect and in universal languages, communicating a million dimensions of the orang basudara.

Indeed, from times past until the present day, every Moluccan is used to living in the genuine habitat of the Moluccan people, that is, the environment of living together as brethren. Moluccans were created with a blueprint that they are brothers and sisters with an understanding of themselves, that being brethren is a joint identity and orientation, now and for always. Each has merged into one to become 'we are all brothers and sisters' in a million dimensions with a variety of personal features, languages, traditions, traditional regulations and the aroma of fruit and food, without omitting anyone. They have been brought up with the original Moluccan character, that is, the character of living side by side as brethren; protecting their relationships with each other; caring for each other; sharing with each other; being forbidden to fight, hate or kill each other. Their flesh and blood are the flesh and blood of the orang basudara. The flesh and blood of the orang basudara are also their own flesh and blood, culturally and genealogically. They all merge into a million dimensions and are always preserved and protected, so that they are all safe and healthy in their joint historical tasks. They have been brought up and honed by the Moluccan wise thoughts, the philosophy of living together as brethren as taught through the verses of songs, the rhythm of the music, rhyming couplets, wise sayings, appeals and pela gandong covenants. They were born and brought up in a cosmos known as the homeland of the orang basudara.

For Moluccans, being basudara is a specific description of their joint identity. Being basudara is not an empty idea on an intellectual agenda, but more a hope that inspires them, influences their thinking and strengthens them in the totality of limitless dimensions. It has become the foundation, like a cornerstone (not a grave stone) that has been erected for a sturdy Moluccan socio-cultural building. It has also become a 'touchstone' for them, to shrewdly test and respond to the various current offers or spoils that flow in front of them with a misleading fervour. The orang basudara's hope becomes the breath that is closely bound to the pounding of the pulse and the blood, forming a stream of perpetual life of which there is no comparison. It is embedded deep in their souls, assimilated into their brains, and flows in their actions, forming an atmosphere (conditions and performance), radiating an aura of a million dimensions and the characteristic smile of the Moluccans. The basudara's hope and the sense of the orang basudara's daily lives is not a current that sweeps away, but rather a current that pours into the course of life of those who head towards eternity, in the silence of their spirituality (Salam-Sarane).

As a terminology of life that indicates a philosophy and wisdom of life, the orang basudara's habitat and character contain philosophical values that are rich, vast and deep. These are available to become the agenda of the tasks that need to be understood and implemented with complete reason, morality and ethics. These are not historical fossils from the past, but an actual enchantment in the spectrum of reality in this age and in the history of life. They are not just something that has existed, but something that co-exists, that continues to exist: their existence is real, objective, actual and functional. More than that, they bring the subjectivity of rational and inner instincts and the social mechanism of the Moluccans into a collective consciousness that is intact and dynamic and forms an actual objectivity.

The orang basudara become the reference of identity with eternal values and excellence that always refreshes the Moluccan heart and conscience of each Moluccan from one generation to the next, crossing the horizon of time with a spectrum of meaningful incidents. It becomes the strength of enlightenment, the dawn of reason, the renaissance, and the cultural task that will guide, direct, and return of the Moluccans' spirits to their cultural base in their endeavours to live peacefully together and for their welfare. Basudara terminology integrates two types of reasoning that are dialectic, that are logical and have social reasoning, as a source of joint wisdom. It not only guides linear logical reasoning but also inner thinking and self-reflection.

The hopes of the orang basudara are in the million dimensions of the life of the orang basudara in the land of the orang basudara. The hopes do not forbid differences and diversity in that land: the land of a thousand islands with thousands of clans, traditional regulations, traditions, with its types of trees and the produce of the plantations of a million dimensions in that fertile archipelago. Difference and diversity is not just a nutritious menu that triggers an appetite of a million flavours. It produces a generation in the ocean of the islands of Maluku that works together and is tough, adroit, shrewd, courageous and artistic. More than that, it can take them to the golden peak – the peak of satisfaction and enjoyment, the warmth and passion of love that is full of incomparable satisfaction – sharing each other's feelings. If the orang basudara is the foundation for the 'home for the orang basudara', then the differences and diversity of tradition, language and traditional regulations in the lives of the orang basudara are the pillars; the differences in the different villages are the rooms in the building of the world of the orang basudara. They are always served in a dining room that is full of the nutritious diversity of a menu of a million flavours. They joke in the living room in the home of the orang basudara with a variety of rhythms and languages including traditions, religions and cultures. With the polite demeanour characteristic of the traditional ways of the orang basudara, they usually receive guests in the parlour of the esteemed basudara house. They always show great respect to their guests – that is part of the traditional customs of the basudara.

The orang basudara's hopes and the million dimensions in the lives of the basudara are not a flawless deity for eternity. It, in the original philosophy of the Moluccans (the orang basudara philosophy), becomes a surgeon's knife to use in operations in an action of restoration, individually and communally, extracting all seeds of disease, viruses of hell, and deviant spirits that seem to be living in them, poisoning the personal and social body. It purifies, cleanses and exalts their lives from the variety of pollutant of civilisation that have haunted them. The hopes and sentiments of a million dimensions of the basudara have proved to be a giant weapon to implant the heroism of love, to say, 'We are all brothers', in a joint opposition movement to put an end to the conflict and chase it from the homeland of the basudara. The hopes and sentiments of a million dimensions of the basudara have become like the spines of the traditional broom bound together in the grasp of the lives of the basudara, to clean their bedrooms, the living room, the parlour, verandah and the front gardens of the land of the basudara. When gathered together it becomes a joint strength to clean out the pollution of civilisation and the garbage of evil that has soiled individuals and their social, political and religious lives.

How Could the Orang Basudara Kill Each Other and Burn Down Each Other's Houses???

The orang basudara's hope and the character of their lives have to become a shrewd cultural ideology. *Basudara Stories of Peace from Maluku* wants to say, 'Never … never … and never allow a degrading[1] ideology with the tricks of the silver-tongued[2] and betraying lips that use religious or humanitaian symbols, to make us dance out of control to the sound of the *tifa* from outside of

---

1   Translator's note: The word used here is *lata*, which can also be a form of *latah*, a psychological disorder caused by sudden shock. In a state of *latah*, a person can only imitate what he/she sees, often using vulgar language. The condition may last for a number of hours until the victim drops exhausted and recovers normal consciousness.
2   The term used here, *mulu baminya* is a specific Moluccan term, similar to the Indonesian term. *mulut berminyak*, which describes speech that gives the impression of being fluent, smart and polite but is, in reality, full of intrigue, flattery, temptations and deceit.

Maluku in the world of those willing to do anything to achieve their wicked ends.' Various ironic incidents indicate that the orang basudara's hopes and the million dimensions of their lives were often deceived and dragged into the deceptive tricks of the losers with their lying discourses. Many contributions in *Basudara Stories of Peace from Maluku* highlight the case of Mr. X, ex-pseudo-militia and ex-Katapang Ambonese thugs and their controllers who cloned newborn brethren in a counterfeit womb outside of Maluku. Being aware or unaware, on purpose or not on purpose, this premature newborn baby of the basudara, of this female controller who was clever at hiding (X) behind the symbols of the counterfeit basudara, religious symbols and symbols of the state. She underwent a caesarean section carried out with the blade belonging to her hypocritical controller, then honed with a two-faced basudara ideology. One face had a mission to slaughter and to set on fire the orang basudara's descendants, who were officially born from the real womb and the flesh and blood of the ancestors and their noble cultural fanaticism. The other face sharpened extremism that expanded the grip of the controllers, scooping profit from political, economic and power out of the rich, natural resources of the orang basudara's land.

Ironically, the birth of the orang basudara's premature baby was celebrated on the day when the basudara were starting to get together, greeting each other with greetings of peace and joy at the victory of their dear Salam friends for attaining their true religion on that glorious day. The artists and actors of the celebration, returning to their home villages, started to set up billboards celebrating the festival with the orang basudara's symbols versus BBM, Salam versus Sarane, red versus white. The nerve of extremism was given some firm-footing by thugs from the capital city that collaborated with local thugs. Welcome to the guests of the conflict in Ambon, to the orang basudara's peaceful land. Was that the sign of the presence and the orang basudara's beautiful gifts from outside of Maluku? Only God knows! The rites of conflict began to be carried out with the regular striking of electricity poles, relayed from place to place, through red and white uniforms, and through red and white coordination centres, using military type organisations, field commanders, generals, colonels, generals for life and adjutants on left and right.

The rites of conflict, with those who were willing to do anything at the command of Mr X, went alongside the rites of holy celebrations of divine nature from the radiance of the Divine, full of peace and the true essence in the victory of His forgiveness. The media and the journalists were also prepared to publish provocative news, arouse indignation, inflame even greater emotions and ask for the presence of militia and the troops under operational command. That was the sign of the gift of the second presence from the premature controller from outside of Maluku. The conflict was carried out with the ignition of fire, which became the trigger point. Did the two brothers, Yopi and Nursalim, really become the victims or the trigger which took hold of the orang basudara's extremism versus the BBM, Salam versus Sarane, white versus red? The location for the trigger was surveyed and selected. The location was chosen as the demarcation point and the embarkation point for the guests of the conflict, the place where local conflict usually took place almost every crazy season. The traditional rites of visiting each other were hijacked by the right to burn each other down, when the time came to visit each other on this holy day; when boiled rice wrapped in coconut leaves, chicken, baked fish, *salak* fruit, Ambonese bananas and other delicacies were waiting for the arrival of the kin; when eyes were shining with pure light, ready to greet the arrival of the brethren with open hands, ready to embrace the orang basudara; and a sincere heart to forgive and receive forgiveness from the orang basudara.

The orang basudara's hopes turned into 'false basudara', full of mystery and questions because they were recorded with misleading contents, blown up and expressed by a misleading and unclear network of the powerful. This was also evident in the politicising of religion and the symbols of religion of the Moluccan people, known to be fanatical about their tribes, religion and villages. This silver-tongued discourse always insulted and oppressed the orang basudara's consciences with a mixture of prejudice, cynicism and pessimism, which has always accompanied the reality of the historical journey. Sometimes (like when conflict struck Maluku) people were led to double standards and thinking in their responses (to doubt or certainty, falseness or genuineness, eternity or pretence, myths or facts). Pessimistic questions were often asked in this silver-tongued discourse, such as: Are the orang basudara, who are fluent in expressing a fake conscience, able to guarantee peace and prosperity in their lives together? Are the orang basudara able to guarantee sustainability or perpetuation of the Moluccan lives to continue through the course of history, amidst the dynamics of upheaval, whether local, national, or global? Can the basudara be held up as the human heritage of the Moluccans, which is always stable and solid in their personal and community commitment to face the struggles of life as they are continuously changing and developing? Or, is it possible that the basudara in the construction of fake hearts only become a 'stumbling block' in the religious lives and autonomy of beliefs of the multicultural Moluccans and in the archipelago state that professes unity in diversity?

Will the Basudara Continue to Kill Each Other and Burn Down Each Other's Houses Indefinitely?

The species of evil genius, descendants of the 'counterfeit brethren' still kept an eye on things from the rear, when the generation of basudara increasingly lost their inner strength in the vast spiritual ocean. They were always ready at any time to transform people with friendly dispositions, misleading them with evil heroic ideas, to become rioters; people with spiritual dispositions in a place of worship could be changed into people with militant tendencies who don't balk at slaughtering people with a gandong or pela relationship with them. Listen, *Basudara Stories of Peace from Maluku* wants to say if cleptocratic and hypocritical urges are still arrogantly residing in the orang basudara's hearts, then the basudara's hopes will still be shaken from within or from outside. If the basudara's socio-cultural tenacity becomes increasingly fragile and is dragged into the games for power that have no conscience; if tenacity of mind and spiritual intelligence is increasingly infiltrated by the current of material pleasure and momentary intoxication, and they allow themselves to be subjugated by the addictions to pleasure at the unconscious level, then this new species of the descendants of the 'counterfeit brethren' will continue to roam in this sad, joint history. The motivating force of the descendants of the 'counterfeit brethren' will always emerge as a virus of the age that will present the orang basudara's discourse as a commodity for transactions in the dark and dirty rooms. The descendants of the 'counterfeit brethren' will continue to wet the fertile land with the orang basudara's blood and tears. They only play with unreal or inconsistent, smarting discourses and proverbs about the principles and actions of daily life. Have the orang basudara's hopes only become word games? Do the basudara's hopes have to be enslaved in unclear, metaphorical language? Perhaps there is a truth that needs to be scrutinised: that the behaviour of the 'counterfeit brethren' is a shadow reality that has exploded the rhetoric and riddles of the Moluccans. The descendants of the 'counterfeit brethren' will continue to be a counter-productive force in certain hands to 'steal and plunder the palace' of the Moluccans by inciting and playing Moluccans against each other for political, economic or other reasons. The 'counterfeit brethren' could become a means of politicisation that drags the Moluccan people into a systemic conflict, whether it is secret, latent or even manifest. The behaviour of the 'counterfeit brethren' will continue to collaborate with the new, premature controllers to damage the orang basudara's inheritance, dragging its noble reality into a frightening use of terminology.

Basudara Stories of Peace from Maluku states that the genuine pioneers of RMS accused the creative imagination of 'the general' as the embodiment of misleading the people's opinion, that the perception that the 'test tube baby RMS', induced prematurely by the hands of the controller – the counterfeit mother who possessed no flesh and blood relationship to it – as though the genuine ex-RMS had been deserted. The doctor was charged with being the counterfeit midwife, who aided the birth of the counterfeit RMS, which had been created by the shadowy imagination that only functioned as a tool in the hands of the step-mother controller to keep a hold on extremism, to invite the guest militias to a duel in the land of the kings. *Basudara Stories of Peace from Maluku* wants to say, the shadowy imagination of the age still continues to threaten every moment as a latent danger. It will try to use all its energy to manipulate the orang basudara's habitat and character to become the unknown enemy. It will always be ready to manipulate the orang basudara's conscience and the orang basudara's understanding of life as a shallow and irrational humanitarian understanding; becoming a taunt, 'an evil smelling humanism' with gossip and a new discourse that is more tragic. *Basudara Stories of Peace from Maluku* wants to say that the unknown enemy will continue to drag the peaceful land of the orang basudara into bloody cycles full of greed. This species of descendants of the 'counterfeit basudara' can be recruited from the grassroots through to the elite, from those who use the crowbar to those who use the pen, from those who sit on the side of the road to those who sit in luxurious air-conditioned rooms; from patient to doctor; from pupil to teacher. This was a shameful point in history and has even become a sad story in the collective memory of Moluccans to which we need to pay intelligent attention.

Mother Aga and Uncle Maku Say Don't Do That, Uncle Nan Says Stop ... No More!

Listen, the *marinyo* announced the proclamation of the village chief. Attention all people of the village, tomorrow morning we will all meet in the *baileo*, we are going to restore the traditional values; the way we are living is not right, we are totally disorganised, we no longer know the traditional rulings of how to live as basudara. If we are not careful, we will continue to be uncivilised and are in danger of becoming an uncivilised generation in a world that is becoming more and more uncivilised. Swearing at our brothers, being jealous of our brothers and sisters, burning down our siblings' houses, burning the mosques and the churches that our ancestors built together, shedding the blood of our gandong who had been protected by a sacred oath to live together and look after each other. The shedding of blood will make its demands until the seventh generation, or tenth and much longer. Stop ... Take notice ... Listen to the voice from the Moluccan natural world. Restore the habitat of living together as basudara, restore the characteristics of living together as basudara in a movement of the true spirit and cultural conscience of the people of the village. The orang basudara's hope is not the result of premature cloning outside Maluku, definitely not ... The hope did not come from the womb of the female controller who subjugated the pure consciousness of the Moluccans with money, promised positions, dreams of an angel at the gates of heaven. The orang basudara's hope is the original habitat from the cosmological womb of the orang basudara's world, from the noble character of the ancestors.

Stop, this is not just a respite, but a point of repentance, a turning point in the astuteness of faith and culture. When the greed is stopped and overpowered with clever awareness that shines from the outpouring of the Divine spirit, reflected in the hearts and thoughts of humankind, there is an awakening of the hopes that have slumbered in the obsession of the greed of the age. Coming together in the *baileo* signifies a return, which is guided by the current of cultural awareness, where the increasingly fragile heart of tradition is being dragged by the predators of the age. The termites gnaw into its centre, they are two-faced and have lost the energy of sincerity and love of the fellow humans; and have become hypocritical. In the *baileo*, the orang basudara's hopes have been built up by the world of the orang basudara's micro-cosmos. In the *baileo* they started to sit together, listening intently to the whispers of the voice of the orang basudara's macro-cosmos. Where are the pela, where are the gandong? Where is the *bongso*, where is the *kakal*, where is the fish hook and where is the river? Perhaps there are victims who have gone to the hereafter with the ancestors? Perhaps there are people who will be disabled for the rest of their lives?

In the *baileo*, the basudara's hope begins to be restored, spreading through the encounter of carrying on the traditions together; having started with confusion, ending in wisdom. The orang basudara's hope begins to be dug out of the ruins of destruction, from the smell of rubbish, gun powder and dust. It seems the orang basudara's hope can still be found there and it is not an accessory in a house that was burnt down. It has been strongly embedded as a principle and inner light that shines out from Maluku. The orang basudara's hope has been woven into a genuine self-narration. The orang basudara's hope is not just the external cover of the dictionary of the indigenous kin, but really constructs their existence. It gives meaning to the self-concept and the true, special, perpetual reality of the people of Maluku. It perpetuates humanitarian values and the humanitarian charm of the orang basudara in a special and unique humanitarian understanding. It exceeds all perceptual constructions and forms a philosophy of life and an authentic cultural ideology for them. It asserts an outlook on life that is based on the orang basudara themselves and forms a specific and objective humanitarian understanding for the next generation of Moluccan people. Living together side by side as basudara gives meaning to the atmosphere of life that embraces, caresses and guides the Moluccans' way of seeing things and their way of life within the framework of strong traditions or culture.

It is Time to Rise Up from Colonisation!

Being aware or not, being in agreement or not, is not a problem. The tempest of the conflict has caused a number of research themes to emerge, whether in discourses concerning the orang basudara's culture, religiosity or nationality. The orang basudara's cultural or religious positions or even nationality is still a sensational instrument that can be used from time to time to drag this generation of the basudara into a colonial pattern and into a narrow oppressive exclusiveness. The historical facts show that orang basudara's traditional, cultural and religious reasoning and their sense of national identity demonstrate a shrewd reasoning that led many generations in their eras to guarantee the belief in the establishment of the great Indonesian Archipelago. Indeed, the state's honesty towards the basudara should be challenged because there are still a number of mysteries, like a thorn in the flesh, in the state's handling of the conflict. However, the orang basudara's honesty has to be guaranteed, so that they will never again be attracted by the clamour of misleading, irresponsible ambition.

Traditional, cultural and religious reasoning and the sense of the orang basudara's national identity demonstrate that the basudara's understanding of life is not simply a religious, cultural or nationalistic term that has been hijacked by a narrow exclusiveness. The orang basudara's understanding is a genius that penetrates genealogical space through to the geo-socio-cultural space to address universal humanity with their own, modest, intact book. The portrait of the orang basudara's authentic meaning has to be read from the point of view of a Moluccan conscience and not from misleading political doctrine or shallow religious doctrine. Although the inner book of the basudara has not been included in various works of literature in public libraries or schools, it can be enjoyed and read about in the tracing of the history and track record of the lives of the orang basudara. All of this can be enjoyed and experienced as a joint historical task.

The resurrection of the orang basudara's hope is the sign of a new dawn of life in the midst of turmoil and the chaotic thinking of this age. It is not just a myth or legend, but an authentic fact of life. It is not something that is believed simply as a thought or comprehended fully in the soul, but it is experienced and actualised as a special personal narration and its ultimate value is on the historic stage of civilisation. The portrait of the basudara relationships of the Salam with the Sarane is a fact and is a living library. The orang basudara's genuine hope signifies a spectrum of life that synergises the inner strength of the Moluccans who have a variety of religions, languages, traditional villages, islands, coasts, interiors, even periods of life. The inner synergy causes noble seeds to grow in the womb of culture in order to process the species of superior descendants in the actual existence and habitat of a life of total friendship.

As a consequence, people must trace the essence and the veiled meaning of the orang basudara's hope, not by using straight-forward logical terms, but by using dialectic terms (greeting each other) to reflect the complete inner spirit. The basudara's hope is a logical construction from a logical discourse (a lesson in logic) that always takes place in the reasoning of the orang basudara's lives. It combines pure rational logic with social and cultural logic and the reflection of the generation in the context of each era. The orang basudara's logical discourse signifies the productivity of the Moluccans over the ages, as a manifestation of the perfect presence of togetherness (we are all kin). Perhaps classes on the history of the orang basudara's lives are now important in the basudara's educational curriculum.

Revive the Orang Basudara's Hope with a Clear Self-Concept

The orang basudara's hope is entirely framed in a clear and distinct self-concept, as can be traced in the basudara's humanitarian philosophy. It is not a blind imagination or fantasy, but can be understood, demonstrated, thought out, researched and formulated in a definitive manner in representing thought, reason, pure reasoning and special logical reasoning. In this way, it can be relied on as proof and a reference to truth, whether it is general knowledge or even scientific knowledge. All of this can be revealed in the orang basudara's humanitarian philosophy.

We are all brothers and sisters becomes a humanitarian philosophical term, within a standard self-concept. The standard is a threshold of satisfaction in the intellectual adventure in finding the essence and the authentic meaning of life. The adventure in the quest for the authentic meaning of life penetrates the limits of narrow reasoning, and breaks through and enters the vast and deep horizons of learning and wisdom. In this adventure there are many struggles with a variety of interests: you-me, you-us, eventually arriving at a specific zenith that is truly beautiful and cannot be refuted: we are all brothers and sisters.

At the epicentre – we are all brothers and sisters – I discover the foundation and essence of my life that is authentic and fundamental, a point in the ocean of adventure in a search that was so ambitious, only to discover a standard of truth and consideration in perpetuating living together side by side in an authentic manner. So, we are all brothers and sisters possesses a depth of thinking that cannot be achieved by only relying on limited reasoning, but with an open heart. The orang basudara's humanitarian philosophy asserts a 'collective humanism' concept that leads to the wisdom of living together side-by-side, as has been evident in their collective behaviour. All share the same; all have the same experiences, *potong di kuku rasa di daging, sagu salempeng di pata dua, hiti hiti hala hala, Ain ni Ain, ita rua Kai-Wai, Sita kena sita Eka, Etu, Kalwedo.*

The 'collective humanism' concept of the orang basudara is not emotive-temporary behaviour, because it contains clever, natural reasoning with organised logical principles. A constructed 'collective humanism' in a building with an open ontological base encourages feelings of awe, curiosity and critical examination. This ontological building of the orang basudara's 'collective humanism' contains an inner awareness, a beautiful mind and rays of the soul that are full, compact, solid and complete. Thus, people have to reason with the totality of their minds, hearts and lives. Every person who faces it has to be immediately aware that he or she is temporarily facing a world of understanding, with connotations and denotations full of rational arguments. It is so full of social-cultural arguments, psychological arguments, and arguments about life convictions that are solid, full, complete and total in a synergy of terminology.

As a rational term, the orang basudara's collective humanism wants to advance codes for thought and the meaning of life. Therefore, it is interesting for us to research, criticise, examine, dissect and expose it with a healthy mind to produce formulations of thought and honest ideas about it. Thus, people have an epistemological guarantee (the basis of authentic and objective knowledge and science) in the course of continually developing and changing science and thinking. The basudara's claims to truth in its 'collective humanism' are legitimate, valid, objective and undisputed. This is an unequalled truth, believed, held and kept as an objective value in the teachings of a humanitarian philosophy. These claims of truth are not just an opinion but have been proved and validated in the history of living side by side for all time. When they built a mosque and a church, when they were in conflict, when disaster fell, when there was a wedding performed according to traditional requirements and so on, everyone came together and resolved issues together: that is the traditional requirement for the basudara. Truth and conviction then become a cultural value system, belief system, moral system and social system. They are institutionalised in various existing regulations and social institutions. Truth and conviction unite their souls and bodies; they even bring happiness, tranquillity in life and welfare for them. Therefore, their personal identity is that they are orang basudara and their character, living together side by side, has to be maintained with a humanitarian grip, as the combined human heritage of the Moluccan people. Every process and all results of research, revelations or rational formulations, which are hypotheses, correlate with the dynamics of the age and a culture that continues to give meaning to the orang basudara's hope, in the context of open discussions of thought and knowledge.

According to social-cultural terminology, the orang basudara's authentic truth radiates from the orang basudara's inner light, like the mind radiating a beautifully shining light. 'We are all siblings' does not just put forward a beautiful way of thinking, but a beautiful system of reasoning, which is difficult to refute within the social cultural concept of the Moluccan people. It becomes an enchanting self that shines in the glowing words, languages, thoughts and actions of the orang basudara. Everything is built on a civilised community system (social existence) with life values that are believed and held strongly as a beautiful heritage and eternity together. The beauty of the orang basudara's souls does not only 'become the brains' – the knowledge or thinking of their generation – but, more than that, it 'forms the character' of their lives completely and perpetually, as a philosophy and an authentic sanctity of life. It is therefore not just handed down to the next generations as a way of thinking (mainstreaming) but as a special way of life (life streaming).

Examining the Validity of the Collective Humanism of the Orang Basudara

The principle of epistemology adhered to in the concept of 'collective humanism' of the orang basudara is evident in the constancy of the pattern of their thought system. The constancy of their thought system is not just informative but the principles of critical thinking reveal reality and dissect it in a series of rebuttals and examinations, with both a foundation of coherence as well as correspondence and pragmatics. The test of coherence is to obtain a level of conformity between the orang basudara's concept of living together side by side with the contents of the orang basudara's thinking, so that fatal misleading patterns of thought do not occur while living together. Through a coherence test a satisfactory conclusion is reached, if there is a local system of knowledge that can be handed on to the next generation to help them avoid any attempts to mislead them, whether by an evil genius, in the name of goodness and truth, or by eternity in the afterlife. My Moluccan-ness is my identity because I, with my basudara, have been constructed into a system of reasoning and a system of cultural values.

The testing of correspondence, on the other hand, tries to discover a level of conformity of thinking that is contained in the orang basudara's concepts and the local teachings in the reality of everyday life. Are the arguments of truth and the validity of this reasoning only held in memories and in empty words or is there obedient conformity in the practice of everyday living? A system of reasoning has to form the real world of everyday life, in the power of love and openness. The essence is 'know that all your fellow Moluccans are your brothers and sisters and live together side by side as orang basudara'. The basudara's hope has created a house to live in together. Seeing myself inside the 'traditional home' of basudara forms the pattern of my thinking and my way of life, which always has a sense of belonging among the basudara, that senses all the aura and the aroma of the life of my orang basudara and the sense of perpetual belonging in thought, feeling, heart, soul, even in my prayers and hopes. A pragmatic test to discover the purpose of meaning of the orang basudara's 'collective humanism' is a task of building the sustainability of the orang basudara.

The epistemological construction above positions an individual and all his/her actions in a complete system of understanding, we are all brothers and sisters. The term 'basudara' therefore shows the meaning of the self in a sea of knowledge and a depth of social-cultural meaning, and in the need to think with critical and holistic social-cultural nerves, because embracing a variety of autonomous plurality in a holistic system of understanding (connotations) and meaning (denotations). The structure of the connotations and denotations becomes perfect by embracing every special historical event in society and every characteristic in the culture that continue to supply inner strength to the Moluccan people in the womb of the Moluccan realm (Moluccan cosmos) and the womb of the kin – Moluccan flesh and blood. An epistemological construction that gives meaning to the true self-concept of the orang basudara also puts forward an authentic personality, which also becomes the 'moral fortress' and the orang basudara's 'anchor of self-defence'. Thus, it is capable of building an historical consistency as well as a generational consistency in developing the orang basudara's human drama through enculturation and the transformation of the characteristic culture, and the strengthening of self-confidence, to continue to appear as an actor on the world stage in the constellation of global civilisations. His/her existence as a member of the basudara is a clever, intellectual work and an awesome cultural achievement in a noble civilisation. He/she is not only received as a gift of normal natural reasoning, but experienced, understood, processed and reasoned in a social reasoning (that is rich, dynamic, open, and complex). The epistemological construction of the orang basudara's 'collective humanism' is not just a humble terminology that fills the flat intellectual sphere, but an authentic and fundamental fact of existence. It possesses a number of rich mysteries and aromas of life with a level of vastness and depth of meaning, which is difficult to reveal simply by limited reasoning in the temporality of time and age.

The axiological principles that are adhered to in the orang basudara's concept of 'collective humanism' are marked by the constancy of behaviour, which is regarded as noble and cultured. My ideals as an autonomous individual, happily united in the loving embrace of my orang basudara, form axiological principles that we ought to carry out as moral and ethical principles. As a moral principle, the basudara's 'collective humanism' concept explains moral commands, which should be obeyed as a manifestation of virtuous obedience: to acknowledge each other, guard each other, protect each other, care for each other, and live side by side together. Social virtue is not just ethical advice and virtuous teaching to be remembered, but moral instruction that demands obedience and forms characteristic spiritual values for traditional regulations. As an ethical principle, the orang basudara's 'collective humanism' affirms a shrewd attitude in using the term 'orang basudara living together side by side' as a touchstone to test, consider and decide various concrete actions, to maintain and continue to develop an authentic, sustainable orang basudara life as instructed in the task and historical responsibility.

The Basudara as a Manifestation of their True Selves

As a psychological term, the basudara wish to put forward a 'vision of the vastness and depth of the inner soul' that is full of meaning in a manifestation of their true selves. A manifestation that is very strongly embedded in full and total comprehension of the inner self. It affirms a self-existence that is very real, that is enveloped by an ambience: *gandong hati tuang*; *potong di kuku rasa di daging*; *sagu salempeng dipata dua*; that gives meaning to the values of solidarity, kinship, friendship; and an attitude of being prepared to sacrifice for the sake of the basudara. This is the main concept behind the basudara's concept of 'collective humanism', which has to read the depths of reasoning and authentic inner being; not just the formality of language; not just rhetoric but the actuality. The Moluccans in their daily interactions with each other always have to prove, demonstrate and carry out by the manifestation of basudara. They have to carry out this historical task from one era to the next, directly from within an authentic, real self. 'Not loving one's basudara is the same as not knowing or not understanding' the meaning of the basudara life. It is the principle of reasoning, understanding, or meaning of life that is taken from and inherited from the lexicon of the tradition of the daily lives of the Moluccan people. The term is not just indicative, but it is an imperative. It is an inheritance of knowledge and a study of traditional regulations which must be obeyed. If there are people among us, who hurt or deliberately forget their brethren by manifesting improper behaviour towards their orang basudara, then that person will be ridiculed as someone who does not know the traditions or someone who is uncivilised.

The true self will greet the reality that continues to become history. It exceeds hypothetic formulae in the treasury of a life that is open and dynamic. This terminology is always created in the inheritance of real tradition and culture. The main meaning of orang basudara is organised in the basudara's humanitarian 'collective humanism' and life wisdom, which affirms rational logic, social logic (the structure of social reasoning) and cultural logic (value structure). It affirms that the natural habitat of the Moluccan people is as an orang basudara. Every Moluccan, whether living in Maluku against a background of a variety of islands, religions, languages, traditional regulations or living outside Maluku, always defines him/herself as 'orang basudara'. The orang basudara becomes a constant reference to identity that triggers an awareness of the true self, causes reasoning to develop, produces creative imagination about one's self and the personalities of fellow orang basudara, and creates 'pride in themselves' as orang basudara on life's stage.

The manifestation of the orang basudara's self becomes an objective reality, not because of interpretation or political acknowledgement of an individual or a nation. It is not because of reasoning and academic studies about it. It preceded these as the dawn of reason in a primary reality. The manifestation of the orang basudara's true self is autonomous, because it is embedded and part of themselves and their personalities. It is available at the heart of their lives as the conscience to the actual source, which continues to make history in ever-changing time and space. It is available as a basis of reality for various rational approaches and formulae that have been established about it. It exists as a pure and authentic truth that comes before, and exceeds the rational truths based on studies or speculative-hypothetic formulae. The manifestation of the self of the orang basudara is essential in nature, because it is not dependent on the merit of words or the formulation of sentences, which are attributive and temporary in nature. The truth of words, sentences, or rational, scientific, attributive arguments will perhaps become obsolete, disappear, or be frequently changed, according to the taste in language and the intellectual level of the age, but the reality of the orang basudara's true self will remain within themselves and in their daily lives through the ages.

The orang basudara's true self is substantial in nature, because it is not only psychologically experienced to obtain emotional satisfaction. More than that, it is studied and analysed and organised in an epistemological manner to produce healthy thinking that is clean, distinct and honest. The orang basudara's habitat and their character in living together side by side possess the means for self-verification, which is authentic and objective-rational and is argumentative and conceptual in meaning. This means of verification, whether based on valid sources of reasoning or the scope of reasoning, is an objective way to consider organising and constructing thinking into rational and theoretic argumentation. Thus, the existence of the basudara as a species can be seen from a scientific perspective as a valid, scientific concept.

The orang basudara's true self is universally objective, because it gives meaning to values of life that are universal, to perpetuate peace, love, honesty, faithfulness, sincerity, solidarity, the spirit of sacrifice, caring for each other and being responsible. It is present and develops broadly as the spirit of a specific culture that constructs an order of life that is pro-self-existence side by side and pro-life, which revitalises the order of a peaceful universe. At the local level, the basudara give meaning to an entire existence, rich in the diversity of traditional values for organising the social productivity of a traditional community in developing intensive encounters with fellow humans from different tribes and language groups in the constellation of life in this modern world.

Strengthening the Orang Basudara's Dramatic Imagination in the Global Constellation and the Strong Misleading Currents

The orang basudara's true self gives meaning to a dramatic imagination (the orang basudara's dramatic imagination) in virtual activities which transform the orang basudara's self-capacity in the vast public sphere. The orang basudara's dramatic imagination is a cultural medium to help the orang basudara represent themselves clearly and distinctly in the context of the age, so that they are not confined to their self-portrait of the past, but are able to produce critically-innovative ideas, to revitalise and actualise themselves in criticising various distortions or corrosions of themselves or provocation that undermines the orang basudara in the confines of misleading logic. The orang basudara's dramatic imagination becomes a genuine endeavour, not a hallucinatory deception. It not only relies on good principles based on moral commands from the past, but also principles of truth, development and support for progress, based on shrewd reasoning, imagination and transformation.

The orang basudara's dramatic imagination wishes to reaffirm the orang basudara's noble character, by continually creating and authenticating themselves in the midst of the changing times and advances in the world. Individuals and cultural, traditional, religious, academic, political, state and economic institutions, including the press and humanitarian activists, are involved in developing advocacy for the orang basudara. The orang basudara are capable of playing the role of the prophet (as a genius of the times), with a vision and systematic assistance, that is effective in the history of saving this generation of the orang basudara. Because of this, they must possess personal integrity and not become disintegrated or two-faced in their thinking and attitudes to life. As part of this, they must also have a noble cultural commitment, so that they do not become the destructive variable in the hands of the aggressor, to annihilate the essence of their own lives. In short, the orang basudara's dramatic imagination is a socio-cultural source that is capable of providing the generation of the ever-changing age with creativity of thinking and language, to assist the orang basudara's creativity to develop in every arena of upheaval.

On the other hand, the orang basudara's dramatic imagination gives meaning to a survival strategy, to constantly affirm the orang basudara's existence in the vast multi-cultural constellation. The orang basudara's dramatic imagination becomes a creative means to affirm their identity in the midst of modern human generic construction, which tends to interpret local wisdom as something that is irrational. The conflict that raged in Maluku over that time and with so many casualties shows the arrogance of the modern actors in rationalising their despicable actions outside the code of conduct of the Moluccan civilisation, and destroying the orang basudara's intertwined lives. Ironically, all of it was carried out in the name of religion, religious symbols and religious interpretations being so strong for the Moluccan people.

Thankfully, in this situation, public officials, local institutions, government, religion and press, which were managed by orang basudara in playing the role of dramatic imagination; by offering what religious leaders referred to as the themes of 'the pro-life theology of the orang basudara' and the 'theology of anti-violence', constructed the strong theological and orang basudara's cultural imagination. The same dramatic imagination was also used by intellectuals, government, traditional leaders and leaders in the orang basudara's community with what is referred to as 'the orang basudara's call for peace'. The orang basudara journalists carried this out in what is called 'peace journalism'.

They played their role in the orang basudara's dramatic imagination in various books, media, *dakwa*, and lectures that went against the 'mainstream' enslavement of stupidity, to restore the hearts of the orang basudara and the diversity in the orang basudara's hearts. They transformed their own imagination as bringers of peace and love. In this context the orang basudara's dramatic imagination has been thought through and instigated in various meetings, dialogues and discussions together. The Bakubae Movement, or the Maluku Baku Dapat Movement, continues to be systematically disseminated at all levels of society through worship services, sermons, *dakwa* about peace, lectures, teaching and guidance. This has been carried out to turn back 'mainstream', dualistic and triumphalistic theology, in the face of extreme pressure from militia and threats in disturbing situations. This orang basudara's dramatic imagination is like the critical analysis in *Basudara Stories of Peace from Maluku* that attempts to respond to the mysteries of the conflict in Maluku, in mapping political conflict. According to *Basudara Stories of Peace from Maluku*, the orang basudara's involvement in the conflict was because they were snared by the political strategy of the conflict, without themselves being aware that they were just the objects. This had been the position from colonial times to the present day.

The role of the orang basudara's imagination is the endeavour to strengthen and evenly spread 'love' and '*ukhuwah*' (solidarity) in the orang basudara's lives. This dramatic imagination has been represented through various themes in this book including, 'When The Conscience Speaks', 'The New Maluku', 'Peaceful Maluku', 'The Collapse of the Baileo', 'The Rise of the Existence of the Indigenous People', 'I Covered the Story, I Told the Story, I Wept', 'We are all kin', 'Thousands of Headlines Without Deadlines', 'The Little Campaigner for Peace', 'Love and Caring for Each Other Exists', 'Tracks Leading to Encounters', 'Making An Escape While Harbouring An Inner Trauma', 'Experiencing the Same Fate', 'We Have Always Got on Together', 'Don't Destroy Anything Else', 'What's Happened to the Traditions of the Moluccans?', 'What You Feel is What I Feel', 'Together We Go Through Good Times and Bad Times' and 'Maluku Belongs to Us, Our Future is in Maluku'.

In this context, dramatic imagination is needed as a means and a strategy to reinforce the orang basudara's lives with a basis of faith, culture, politics and civics at all levels. According to *Basudara Stories of Peace from Maluku*, the human tragedy that struck the orang basudara has to be faced with the wide role of imagination and the backing of the press. The aim was to obtain effective advocacy for the orang basudara. The orang basudara's dramatic imagination should be disseminated, whether through intellectual, academic, press or humanitarian channels, so that the world community can urge the government of Indonesia to be more serious in solving the problem of the conflict in Maluku. The orang basudara's dramatic imagination has been clearly demonstrated in the 'Masariku' mailing list as a forum for discussion, exchange of ideas and points of view, to fight against the large wave of violence that has raged in Maluku. This process has led to the conception of a work produced by the *Satu Nama Community* (One Name Community) with the title *Nasionalisme Kaum Pinggiran* (The Nationalism of the Marginalised). This proves that every Moluccan can take an adventure with the orang basudara's dramatic imagination on the stage of global competition. They have to be passionate in struggling to obtain prestige and advancement for themselves and their people. Their dramatic imagination will always reinforce their humanitarian heritage.

This dramatic imagination demonstrates the roles of the agents of peace who have become characteristic of the orang basudara. They are so optimistic about the orang basudara's psychological vocation, which authentically sees the difference or diversity in life as God's gift. Thus they will always be open to developing dialogue on an equal platform. They will always carry it out in order to manifest perpetual and authentic peace in Maluku as a humane homeland and the most peaceful and beautiful palace.

GLOSSARY

AIN NI AIN	We come from the same egg
AGAS	Teenage gangs involved in the violence of the community unrest
ALE	You (polite form)
ALE RASA, BETA RASA	Literally, 'What you feel, I feel'. Having the same feelings
ALIFURU	Name of a clan in Central Maluku
ALHAMDULILAH	Praise be to God
APIONG	Spinning top
ASEN	A children's game
BAILEO; BAILEU	The traditional building where meetings of the community are held
BAHASA TANAH	Local languages used in different villages mainly in the past
BAKU BAE	To make amends, to do good to each other
BAKU DAPA SUDARA	Family get-together
BASUDARA	Kith and kin, family and friends showing love and solidarity and being willing to help one another
BEDUG	A large drum used to call the faithful to prayer at the Mosque
BETA	I
BETA MALUKU	I am Moluccan
BHINEKA TUNGGAL IKA	Unity in diversity
BONSO	Youngest brother or sister
CAKALANG	A tuna-like fish
CAKALELE	War dance
CAPEU	Hat

DAENG	A title for a man from South Sulawesi. A respectful term of address for pedicab drivers
DAKWA	Religious teaching, usually taken from place to place
DANGDUT	A type of music
EID AL FITR	Festival marking the end of the fasting month for Muslims
EID AL ADHA	Muslim festival of sacrifice
EMBAL	Food made from cassava
GABA-GABA	Dried sago stems
GANDONG	Kinship relationship between two or more traditional villages based on a blood relationship
HADRAT	Music, which is a combination of Middle East and Moluccan rhythm
HAINUWELE	The daughter of a village chief in the mythology from Seram Island
HAJJ AL –WADA'	The last and only pilgrimage of the prophet Muhammad
HALAL BI HALAL	A get-together after the end of the fast month, when mutual forgiveness is given
HATUHAHA	The name for the region of the five neighbouring villages on Haruku Island: Hulaliu, Pelauw, Kabauw, Rohomoni and Kailolo
HENA MASA WAYA	A folk song in a regional language, the title literally means 'the village above the water'
HIO HIO	The title of another folk song about the past, sung in a regional language
HITI HITI HALA HALA	Enjoying the good things together and facing difficulties together
IMAM	The leader of prayer in a mosque
ITA RUA KAI-WAI	The two of us are siblings

Glossary

JIHAD	Holy war
JILBAB	Muslim women's headcovering
KAIN BERANG	Red cloth that can be a head band, tied around the neck or around the wrist. It is a sign of bravery and can only be worn after an initiation ceremony.
KAIN GANDONG	A white cloth several metres in length which is wrapped around visitors from a clan that has kinship ties in traditional welcome ceremonies. It symbolises that they are all from the same womb.
KAKA	Older brother or sister
KALWEDO	Peace to us all
KAPATA	A traditional rhyme
KATONG	We
KATONG DENG KATANG	Us and them
KYAI	A title for a venerated scholar in Islam
LAENG TONGKA-TONGKA LAENG	Supporting one another
LANIA	A poem
LARVUL NGABAL	Traditional or customary law in the Southeast Maluku
LASKAR JIHAD	An Islamist vigilante group founded in 2000, literally 'Soldiers of the Holy War'
LINGGIS	Gangs of teenagers, who looted houses during the community unrest
MALOKO KIE RAHA	The brother- and sisterhood of four mountains in the North Maluku (Tidore, Ternate, Bacan and Jailolo)
MARYINO	A town crier or public announcer
MASOHI	Mutual cooperation/working together to share the load

MUHAMMADIYAH	A Muslim mass organisation, founded by Achmad Dahlan in Jogjakarta, Central Java in 1912. Its modernist theology brought more scripturally-oriented views of Islam to Indonesia, and it criticised such practices as amulets and adoration of saints, which had been a part of many Indonesians' Islamic practices.
NUNUSAKU	A place in the mountains on the Island of Seram
NYEPI	Seclusion Day: a Hindu holy day when people refrain from work and any type of activity
OHOI	Village
ORANG BASUDARA	The close relationship between fellow Moluccans
PANCASILA	'Five principles', the Indonesian national ideology: 1. belief in an almighty God, 2. humanitarianism, 3. Indonesian unity, 4. representative democracy and 5. social justice.
PANTUN	A song with verses of four lines, often sung with one person responding to another
PAPARISA	A small shack in the forest
PAPEDA	A local dish made from sago flour and boiling water
PASAWARE	A prayer according to traditional beliefs using a traditional language
PELA	A pact of brother- and sisterhood made between two villages
POTONG DI KUKU	Moluccan saying 'tearing the fingernail is felt in the body'
RASA DI DAGING	experiencing the same fate
RASULULLAH SAW	The messenger of God, peace be upon him

Glossary

RATSKAP MAUR OHOI	A traditional council representing a group of villages in a particular area in Southeast Maluku
REFORMASI	Reformation, the term used for the period after President Soeharto resigned
RUMAH ADAT	A traditional house, see also 'Baileo'
QASIDAH	Muslim music
SAHUR	The meal taken before dawn during the fast month by Muslims before the day's fasting begins
SALAM	The local name for Muslims
SARANE	The local name for Christians
SAUREKA –REKA	A traditional dance involving dancers dancing between poles made from sago stems
SAWAT	The name of a Muslim dance
SITA KENA SITA EKA, ETU	Saying: 'We are the same and we are united'
SAGU SALEMPENG DIPATA DUA	Saying: 'Sharing slices of sago, divided in two'; a life style of sharing with one another. *Sagu salempeng* is a sweet made from sago, coconut milk and red sugar
TAUHID	The unity of God
TIFA	Traditional drum used in Maluku
TUANG HATI JANTONG	My dearest
UKHUWAH	solidarity
ULAMA	Islamic scholar
USTAZ	Term of address for Islamic teacher
UWA	Aunt, the sister of my father
WATE	Uncle

ACRONYMS AND ABBREVIATIONS

AJI	Aliansi Jurnalis Independen, Alliance of Independent Journalists
AMGPM	Angkatan Muda Gereja Protestan Maluku, The Youth Wing of the Protestant Church of Maluku
ARHANUD	Artileri Pertahanan Udara, Artillery Air Defence Corps
ARMC	Ambon Reconciliation and Mediation Centre
ASMIL	*Asrama militer*, Military barracks
BANKOM	*Bantuan Komunikasi*, Communication Forum
BBM	Buton Bugis Makassar, also the acronym for *Bahan Bakar Minyak*, refined fuel oil
BRIMOB	*Brigade Mobil*, mobile brigade, special operations police force
COB	*Carita Orang Basudara*, The Basudara's Stories or 'stories of kith and kin'
DPRD	Dewan Permusyawaratan Rakyat Daerah, Regional People's Representative Council
FKM	Front Kedaulatan Maluku, Maluku Sovereignty Front, a secessionist movement established on 15 June 2000 on Ambon Island, with the aim of restoring the Republic of the South Maluku
FORLOG Sul Sel	Forum Dialog Antarkita Sulawesi Selatan, South Sulawesi Dialogue Forum
GPM	Gereja Protestan Maluku, Protestant Church of Maluku
HMI	Himpunan Mahasiswa Islam, Muslim Students' Association
IAIN	Institut Agama Islam Negeri, Government Institute for Islamic Studies
ICMI	Ikatan Cendekiawan Muslim Indonesia, Indonesian Association of Muslim Intellectual
IMM	Ikatan Muslim Muhammadiyah, Muhammadiyah Student Association, founded in Jogjakarta on 14 March 1964

KAHMI	Korpus Alumni Himpunan Mahasiswa Islam, Islamic Students Alumni Association
KONTRAS	Komisi Untuk Orang Hilang dan Korban Tindak Kekerasan, Commission for Missing Persons and Victims of Violence
LAIM	Lembaga Antar-Iman, Inter-Faith Organisation in Maluku
LKDM	Lembaga Kebudayaan Daerah Maluku, Regional Cultural Organisation
LPJ-GPM	Lembaga Pembinaan Jemaat Gereja Protestan Maluku, Congregational Advisory Board- Protestant Church of Maluku
MMC	Maluku Media Centre
MPC	Maluku Photo Club
MPRK UGM	Magister Perdamaian dan Resolusi Konflik Universitas Gajah Mada, Magister Peace and Resolution of conflict Gadjah Mada University
MTQ	Musabaqah Tilawatil Quran, contest of Koranic Recitation
MUI	Majelis Ulama Indonesia, Indonesian Council of Religious Scholars
MV	Motorised Vessel
NGO	Non-Governmental Organisation
NKRI	Negara Kesatuan Republik Indonesia, Unitary State of the Indonesian Republic
NU	Nahdlatul Ulama, literally, 'Awakening of Ulama' (ulama are Mulim religious teachers or leaders), a large, Indonesian Islamic organisation
OSM	Opleiding School of Maritime; a maritime training school
PELNI	Pelayaran Nasional Indonesia, Indonesian National Shipping Line
PERSETIA	Perhimpunan Sekolah-sekolah Teologi di Indonesia, Indonesian Association of Theological Colleges

PII	Pelajar Islam Indonesia, Indonesian Islamic Pupils
PMII	Pergerakan Mahasiswa Islam Indonesia, Muslim Student Union, founded on 17 April 1960 in Surabaya.
PSKP UGM	Pusat Studi Keamanan dan Perdamaian Universitas Gajah Mada, Centre for the Study of Security and Peace, Gadjah Mada University
PUSAD	Pusat Studi Agama dan Demokrasi, Yayasan Paramadina, The Centre for the Study of Religion and Democracy, Paramadina Foundation
PWI	Persatuan Wartawan Indonesia, Union of Indonesian Journalists
RINDAM	Resimen Induk Daerah Militer, Military Training Centre
RMS	Republik Maluku Selatan, South Moluccan Republic
RRI	Radio Republik Indonesia, Indonesian National Radio Station
RST	Rumah Sakit Tentara, Military Hospital
SARA	*Suku Agama Ras Antar Golongan*, ethnicity, religion, race and inter-group relations, topics that were prohibited under the New Order
SD (N)	Sekolah Dasar (Negeri), Primary School (State)
SMA(N)	Sekolah Menengah Atas (Negeri), Senior High School (State)
SMK(N)	Sekolah Menengah Kejuruan (Negeri), Vocational College (State)
SMP(N)	Sekolah Menengah Pertama (Negeri), Junior High School (State)
SPN	Sekolah Polisi Negara, State Police Training Collgee
STIKOM	Sekolah Tinggi Manajemen Informatika & Teknik Komputer, College of Computer Studies
STT	Sekolah Tinggi Teologi, Theological College
TAPAK	Tim Advokasi untuk Penyelesaian Kasus (Ambon), Advocacy team for Resolving Cases (Ambon)
TIRUS	Tim Relawan untuk Kemanusiaan, Team of Volunteers for Humanitarian Causes

Acronyms and Abbreviations

TNI	Tentara Negara Indonesia, Indonesian Armed Forces
TPG	Tim Pengacara Gereja, Church Lawyer Team
TRK BAILEO	Tim Relawan Kemanusiaan Baileo, Baileo Team of Volunteers for Humanitarian Causes
TPIN	Tim Penyelidikan Independen Nasional (untuk Maluku), National Independent Team of Investigators
TVRI	Televisi Republik Indonesia, Indonesian State Television
UGM	Universitas Gadjah Mada, Gadjah Mada University
UIN	Universitas Islam Negeri, Islamic State University
UKIM	Universitas Kristen Indonesia-Maluku, Indonesian Christian University in Maluku
UKSW	Universitas Kristen Satya Wacana, Satya Wacana Christian University
UNMER	Universitas Merdeka, Merdeka University
UNDP	United Nations Development Program
UNIDAR	Universitas Darussalam, Darussalam University
UNPATTI	Universitas Pattimura, Pattimura University
VOC	Verenigde Oost-Indische Compagnie, United East Indies Company
YAP	Young Ambassador for Peace

ABOUT THE CONTRIBUTORS

Abidin Wakano was born in Kairatu, West Seram regency. He completed his doctorate in the Postgraduate program of Sunan Kalijaga Muslim State University Jogjakarta. He is now teaching as a lecturer at the State Islamic Institute (IAIN) Ambon and a guest lecturer in the postgraduate Theology program of the Indonesian Christian University in Maluku (UKIM) and the bachelor program of the Theology Faculty UKIM. He was previously a member of staff at Dian/Interfidei Jogjakarta (2002–2007) and General Secretary of KAHMI Maluku Province (2007–2011). He is currently deputy chairman of Tanfidz NU Maluku Region (2007–present) and Director of Ambon Reconciliation and Mediation (ARMC) IAIN Ambon (2010–present).

Aholiab Watloly was born in Ilih, Damer, Southwest Maluku. He completed his first degree at the Theology Faculty of the Indonesian Christian University in Maluku (1981). He gained his Master's and Doctorate degrees in Philosophy from Gadjah Mada University, Jogjakarta. He is a lecturer in the Social and Political Science Faculty, UNPATTI, Ambon. His books include *Tanggungjawab Pengetahuan* [Responsibility of Knowledge] (Kanisius, Jogjakarta, 2001) and *Baru, Bangkitnya Eksistensi Anak Negeri* [The Indigenous People are Rising Just Now] (Kanisius, Jogjakarta, 2005). His previous positions include Head of the Sociology Graduate Program of Study, UNPATTI Ambon (2005–2007) and Chairman of the Quality Assurance Board, UNPATTI, Ambon (2009–2012).

Almudatsir Z. Sangadji completed his first degree in the Faculty of Law of the Muslim University of Indonesia (UMI) Makassar (2005). He started his journalistic career as the Chief Editor of the daily newspaper, *Info Baru* in Ambon in 2007. He is also involved in a number of advocacy activities at the Maluku Media Centre (MMC). Since 2009, he has become a news contributor to the daily, *Bisnis Indonesia*. He is currently managing editor of the weekly newspaper, *Spektrum*. As well as writing for several local newspapers, he lectures in the Constitutional Law Study Program, the Law Faculty, Darussalam University (Unidar) Ambon.

Dian Pesiwarissa, who was born in Ambon, is a staff member of a private company. When the conflict in Ambon broke, she had just started Senior Vocational High School No. 6 in Ambon. After graduating in 2001, she continued her education at the Economics Faculty, Pattimura University, where eventually she could mix again with Muslim friends. Until 2007 she worked as a journalist for the news website, www.radio bakubae.com. There she wrote many articles from a humanitarian viewpoint, an aspect that was often ignored during the upheaval of the conflict.

Dino Umahuk was born in Capalulum, North Maluku. He completed his first degree at the Faculty of Mechanical Engineering, Darussalam University, Ambon, 1998. He also obtained training at both national and international level on environmental issues, peace journalism, advocacy journalism and conflict resolution. In addition to working as a journalist for various media in Ambon, such as the tabloid *Kabaresi* (1998–1999) and the daily *Ambon Ekspres* (1999–2000), he also became a local correspondent for a number of media such as *detik.com* (2002–2004), *Voice of Human Rights Radio Program*, Jakarta (2001), and *Southeast Asian Press Alliance* (2002–2004). His experience in the Team of Volunteers for Humanitarian Causes Ambon (1999–2000) and the Investigative Division of KontraS, Jakarta (2000–2001) meant that he was given responsibility as coordinator and program officer in a number of organisations, including Maluku Media Centre (2002–2004), TPIN-Maluku (2003) and Tifa Foundation (2006). He was Liaison Officer and consultant for Sustainable Peace Development Program, UNDP and PSKP UGM, Ambon (2004). He is currently teaching Communication Science in the Faculty of Social and Political Sciences, Muhammadiyah University, North Maluku. He also works as an expert for the Parliamentary Reform Faction, City Area in Ternate.

Elifax T. Maspaitella was born in Rutong. He spent his childhood until the age of 13 in this village, which is in South Leitimor, on the edge of Mount Horioril. He then continued his education at Junior State High school No. 1 and Senior State High School No. 1 in Ambon. He then studied Theology at the Indonesian Christian University in Maluku (UKIM) fulfilling his childhood ambition to become a minister. Having completed his first degree at the Alake campus in 1998, he then continued his Master's degree in the Gospel & Tradition Study Program, UKIM, at the same campus. Because of the community unrest in 1999, he continued his master's degree in Sociology of Religion, at Satya Wacana Christian University (UKSW), Salatiga. He worked as a curate in the Protestant Church in Maluku (GPM) in 2005 and he was consecrated as a GPM minister on 11 March 2007. He is currently the minister of the Rumahtiga congregation, Ambon Island GPM diocese, and he is also chairman of AMGPM (2010–2015).

Gerry van Klinken is a Professor of Social History and Economy of South East Asia at Amsterdam University, and senior researcher for the Royal Netherlands Institute of South East Asian and Caribbean Studies (Koninklijk Instituut voor Taal-, Land- en Volkenkunde, KITLV), both in the Netherlands. Between 2006 and 2012, he coordinated a Dutch-Indonesian research project with the theme 'In Search of Middle Indonesia', that studied the middle classes in the provincial cities. Two of his works concerning conflict in Indonesia are *The Wars: Bringing Society Back* (2001) and *Communal Violence and Democratization in Indonesia: Small Town Wars* (2007).

Hasbullah Toisuta was born in Siri Sori Islam, Central Maluku. He gained his Master's degree at the State Islamic Institute (IAIN) Alauddin Makassar, and completed his doctoral program (S3) at the Sunan Kalijaga State Islamic University (UIN) Jogjakarta. He is the Rector of IAIN Ambon; a researcher in religion, social science and culture; and a peace activist. He was involved in the Muslim Students Association (HMI) Ambon branch, and became a declarator of the Moluccan Agreement in Malino. In addition to being active in writing for a number of media and journals in Maluku, he is also involved in social activities in the community.

Helena M. Rijoli completed her first degree in the Teaching and Educational Science Faculty of Pattimura University in 2005. She took a long course at Hartford Seminary in 2009, then continued her studies with a master's degree in Educational Science at Sussex University, UK, and completed her studies in 2012. She was the coordinator for Young Ambassador for Peace (1999–2002) and became Information and Documentation Manager at the Inter-Faith Organisation in Maluku (LAIM).

Hilary Syaranamual has a degree in religious education from Warwick University, UK, and an MA in Church Religion and Society from Trinity College, Bristol, UK. She is one of the founders of Amansplus Ministry, which is involved in humanitarian activities. APM started in Malang, East Java, in October 1999, and has continued in Maluku from July 2005 until the present. Having lived in Indonesia since 1983, she moved to Ambon in 1993 and has visited a number of the areas in Maluku. Her previous positions have included being a member of the editorial team of *Kacupeng* magazine (a magazine for Moluccan children in the Moluccan dialect) and also a member of the Ambon-Vlissingen Sister City Steering Committee. She is also active in art and cultural activities, including the Maluku Photo Club.

About the Contributors

I.W.J. Hendriks was the Chair of the Protestant Church in Maluku Synod 2001–2005 and member of the delegation to the Malino Agreement. He completed his doctorate at Jakarta Theological School (STT). He was head of the Postgraduate Program at the Indonesian Christian University in Maluku (UKIM) until 2013.

Ihsan Ali-Fauzi is the Director of the Centre for Studies in Religion and Democracy (PUSAD), Paramadina Foundation and a lecturer at Paramadina Graduate School, Jakarta. He studied history and political science at Ohio University, Athens, and the Ohio State University (OSU), Columbus, both in the US. He writes for a number of national mass media, including *Kompas*, *Koran Tempo*, *Majalah Tempo*, *The Jakarta Post* and journals such as *Studia Islamika* and *Asian Survey*. As part of the PUSAD Paramadina team, he published *Disputed Churches in Jakarta* (2011) and *Pemolisian Konflik Agama di Indonesia* [The Policing of Religious Conflict in Indonesia] (2014).

Inggrid Silitonga completed her degree in Forestry Management at Pattimura University Ambon in 2002. In order to complete her studies, she studied in the Forestry Faculty UGM, because of the conflict that beset Ambon. The conflict in Ambon also led her to be involved in humanitarian work, starting with TRK Baileo Maluku (1999), as a Community Organiser at the refugee camp at the Halong naval base, Ambon, and as a member of the Emergency Team Jogjakarta. These experiences led her to work for the Canadian Human Rights Foundation (2000–2005), and an NGO called Demos (2005) as Finance Staff and Office Manager. She has also been invited as a speaker at training in human rights and democracy in Indonesia, carried out by UNDP, AEC and DG BRIDGE. Since 2009, she has been the Executive Secretary of Demos and continues to write her blog, http://tunjuksatubintangku.wordpress.com/.

Irsyad Rafsadi is a junior researcher at the Centre for Study in Religion and Democracy (PUSAD), Paramadina Foundation, Jakarta. He is responsible for the Ahmad Wahib Award Program in the same foundation (2013–2014). Irsyad is a graduate of the Syariah Faculty, of the State Islamic University (UIN) Syarif Hidayatullah, Jakarta, and attended Summer School in India, on Human Rights and Development, conducted jointly by Hivos (Netherlands), The Centre for the Study of Culture and Society (CSCS, Bangalore, India), and Centre for Religious and Cross-Cultural Studies (CRCS-UGM, Indonesia). In addition to writing for *Koran Tempo*, *Majalah*

Tempo and *Jakarta Globe*, he has, as part of the PUSAD Paramadina team, published *Pemolisian Konflik Agama di Indonesia* (2014).

Jacky Manuputty is a minister in the Protestant Church in Maluku. He is also Director of the Research and Development Agency (Balitbang) of the Protestant Church in Maluku (GPM). He is the Founder and Director of the Inter-Faith Organisation in Maluku (LAIM). He is a graduate of Jakarta Theological College (1989), Driyarkara School of Philosophy, Jakarta (2003) and has an MA in the graduate program on Pluralism & Inter-religious Dialogue at Hartford Seminary, Hartford, CT-USA (2010). He was born in Haruku, Central Maluku Regency in July 1965. He has been awarded the Ma'arif Award 2005 in the category of peace worker and the Tanenbaum Award, New York, USA in 2012 for the category of Peacemakers in Action. He is often invited as a speaker at national and international seminars and discussions on the theme of peace and inter-faith relationships.

M. Azis Tunny is a journalist who was born in Ambon. When the community unrest erupted in Ambon in 1999, he was still at senior high school. While at university, he was involved in a students' outdoor pursuits group, while he sharpened his journalistic skills. He has held the positions of general secretary of the Young People's Outdoor Pursuits Association – The Creativity of Nature's Young People (PPSWPA-KANAL) Ambon (2002-2004). In 2005, he won a feature-writing competition on Peace journalism for journalists in Ambon. He has worked for the daily *Info* (2002), *The Jakarta Post* (2003), and is a contributor to *Radio CVC Australia* (2006). In 2007, he was invited to lead the Maluku Media Centre (MMC). He also held the position of deputy chairman of Maluku Regional Broadcasting Commission (KPID) in 2009. In addition to articles in the Ambon mass media, his articles have been published in a number of books, such as *Antara Kriminalitas dan Ketidakpahaman (Kasus Jurnalis Maluku)* [Between Criminality and Misunderstanding (The Case of Moluccan Journalists)], and *Potret Jurnalis Ambon (Survey Kesejahteraan Jurnalis Ambon)* [A Portrait of Ambonese Journalists (A survey on the Welfare of Ambonese Journalists)].

M. Noor Tawainela completed his first degree in Social and Political Science at Pattimura University in 1978. He was involved in PII, HMI, Muhammadiyah Youth, KAHMI, ICMI, HSBI, and the Regional Cultural Organisation (LKDM). He worked at WI LB, Papua and Papua Barat. He currently works as a lecturer at IAIN Ambon and Darussalam University, Ambon. He has also been invited to speak at local, regional and national seminars, and is active writing about poetry, history and culture in the *Panji Masyarakat* newspaper.

M.J. Papilaja completed his first degree in Accountancy at Hasanuddin University, Makassar in 1982, his Masters in Accountancy at Gadjah Mada University, Jogjakarta, November 2000, and his Doctorate in System & Provision of Capital for Catching Fish, at the Agricultural Institute Bogor, June 2012. His previous positions included Dean of the Economics faculty UKIM, (1985–1988), lecturer in the Economics faculty, Pattimura University Ambon (1982–2010), and Head of the Extension Program of the Economics Faculty of Unpatti (1990–1999). He is currently a lecturer at the Business School of Pelita Harapan University, Jakarta. In addition to his work in education, he has been involved in government. After becoming Chairman of DPRD Ambon, 1999–2001, he was Mayor of Ambon, from 2001–2011. He was also a member of the Team of Mediators in the Malino Agreement, February 2002, which was chaired by Jusuf Kalla and Susilo Bambang Yudhoyono.

Nancy Souisa is a minister in the Protestant Church of Maluku and a lecturer in the Theology Faculty UKIM Ambon. She completed her theological studies in the Theology Faculty of UKIM and studied for her Master's degree in the Sociology of Religion master's Program, UKSW Salatiga and the Pacific School of Religion (PSR) in Berkeley, California, USA. She has twice worked as the Managing Director Association of Theological Colleges in Indonesia (PERSETIA) and since 2012 has been studying for her doctorate in the Sociology of Religion in the Doctoral Program, UKSW.

Novi Pinontoan is a journalist who graduated from the School of Social and Political Sciences, Pattimura University, Ambon. His experience in taking part in various professional workshops for journalists, peace journalism and advocacy of the media and conflict, has made him a trusted speaker for various workshops for new journalists or for NGOs. He was a member of the Indonesian Delegation representing the press from Eastern Indonesia (KTI) at the Asia Europe Meeting (ASEM) at Nusa Dua Bali, 2005 and Intercultural and Faith in Jogjakarta, 2006. He is now editor-in-chief of the daily newspaper, *Suara Maluku*.

Rizal Panggabean is a lecturer in the International Relations Department and the Master's Program in Peace and Conflict Resolution (MPRK), Gadjah Mada University (UGM), Jogjakarta. He is a senior researcher of The Centre for Study in Religion and Democracy (PUSAD), Paramadina

Foundation. He studied for his master's degree at the Institute for Conflict Analysis and Resolution (ICAR), George Mason University, United States of America. The results of his research have been published in various journals including *World Development*, *Asian Survey*, and the *Journal of East Asian Studies*. Together with the PUSAD Team Paramadina, he published the book *Pemolisian Konflik Agama di Indonesia* (2014).

Rudi Fofid is a senior journalist who was born in Langgur. His journalistic career started with the school press at Xaverius Senior High School, Ambon. When he was chairman of the Presidium of Catholic Students Association of the Republic of Indonesia (PMKRI) Ambon Branch, he also published the *Sintesa* bulletin. His journalistic tutor, Pastor Jan van de Made MSC, mentored him in the *Pastoral Newsletter*, Amboina Diocese (1987–1990). On campus, he also became a journalist with *Media Unpatti* (1987–1988). He then worked as a reporter for the *Union of Catholic Asian News* (UCAN), Hongkong (1990–1991), an editor of *Suara Maluku*, Ambon (1993–1995), correspondent for *Suara Pembaruan*, Jakarta (1995–1997), deputy chief editor of the tabloid *Tabaos*, Ambon (1998–1999), daily editor of *Patroli Manado* (2000–2001), editor of www.mediacentre.net (2003–2004), and returned to *Suara Maluku* first as a senior editor and now is deputy chief editor. In press circles in Maluku, he is more than just a senior journalist, he has become an elder brother and mentor. For more than ten years he has been a facilitator in journalistic training.

Sandra Lakembe completed her studies in the Fisheries Faculty of Unpatti in 1995. She became a consultant for WWF on conservation in Aru in 1998 and coordinator for TIRUS 1999–2002. She was also involved in the Consortium for Assistance and Recovery towards Development in Indonesia (CARDI) in Maluku, Aceh and Papua.

Steve Gaspersz completed his primary and secondary education in Malang, East Java. He went on to study theology in the Theology Faculty, Indonesian Christian University (UKIM). His masters in Theology was obtained from the International Reformed Theological Institute (IRTI) Vrije Universiteit, Amsterdam. He took short courses at the Global Institute of Theology (GIT), Calvin College, Grand Rapids, Michigan, United States (2010) and at the Institute for Advanced Study of Asian Cultures and Theologies (IASACT), Chinese University, Hong Kong (2013). Since 2011, he has been studying for his doctorate at the Indonesian Consortium for Religious Studies (ICRS), a consortium of three universities – UGM, UIN Sunan

Kalijaga and UKDW – all in Jogjakarta. Several of his articles have been published in national and international journals, including a few anthologies. He also wrote the book *Iman Tidak Pernah Amin: menjadi Kristen dan Menjadi Indonesia* [Faith Never Says Amen: Becoming Christian and Becoming Indonesian] (BPK Gunung Mulia, Jakarta 2009). He is now working as a minister in the Protestant Church of Maluku (GPM) and is a lecturer in the Theology Faculty, UKIM Ambon.

Thamrin Ely completed his education at the University of California, Berkeley (non-degree) in 2002. He was a member of the Regional Consultative Assembly of Maluku 1999–2004, and an expert working for the Civil Emergency Authority in Maluku 2000–2003. At the time of the conflict in Maluku, he was active at the MUI Coordination Centre in Maluku and was Head of the Muslim Delegation at the Malino meetings (Malino II) 2001.

Theofransius Litaay is a lecturer in the Law Faculty, Satya Wacana Christian University Salatiga. He was involved in establishing the Satya Wacana Peace Centre. At present he is the Co-Chairperson of the Anticorruption and Good Governance Study Centre, UKSW Salatiga.

Tiara Melinda A.S. is a student in journalistic communication in the Institute of Social and Political Science (IISIP), Jakarta. She has been involved in journalism and photography from an early age through various courses and non-formal education, including the Darwis Triady School of Photography (2007). She has been a photographer at the *Mimbar Maluku* daily newspaper (2008–2009) and *Kacupeng* magazine, Ambon (2008–2010). She has won several awards: Photographer of the Editor's choice at the website fotografer.net (2007); 2nd place of the Ambon City Anniversary Photography Competition – for Photography Associations, Ambon (2007); 3rd place in the 'Building' Photography Competition – PWI, Ambon (2008); and 3rd place 'Ambon My City' Photography Competition – Maluku Photo Club, Ambon (2009).

Weslly Johannes was born and grew up in Namlea, Buru Island and now lives in Ambon. He completed his studies at the Theology Faculty, Indonesian Christian University in Maluku. He is busy studying and playing with the kids of the Gunung Mimpi (Mountain of Dreams) community; he writes poetry and is involved with several communities of young people, as well as the peace movement in Ambon. Weslly is active using social media, his Twitter account: @wslly and Facebook page: Weslly Johannes. His writings can be found at https://wesllyjohannes.wordpress.com/

Zainal Arifin Sandia completed his first degree in Arabic in the Tarbiyah Faculty IAIN, Alauddin Makassar in 1999. He was the chairman of the training section of the Coordinating Body of HMI South Sulawesi from 1995 to 1997 and became an activist in the South Sulawesi Dialogue Forum.

Zairin Salampessy, usually known as 'Embong', is a graduate of the Fisheries Faculty, Unpatti. He was known as a pavement artist in Ambon from 1987 to 1992. In 1994, *Suara Maluku* newspaper asked him to draw caricatures and so he became a journalist, an assistant editor and then senior editor until 1998. He then joined the Baileo Maluku Network NGO in Ambon. When the conflict struck Ambon in 1999, he, together with a number of colleagues, immediately formed a team of Muslim and Christian volunteers, who worked to handle the victims of the conflict. He continued doing this until he moved to Jakarta, where he was involved in advocacy at a national and international level through the Advocacy Team for Case Solving in Ambon (TAPAK). While at TAPAK Ambon, he was on several occasions, part of the Indonesian NGO delegation to the Assembly of the UN Human Rights Commission in Geneva, Switzerland. He has now returned to Ambon and has become a freelance photographer for the *Antara* Photographic Bureau and a volunteer in the Inter-Faith organisation in Maluku. He also leads the Maluku Photo Club that has a mission to photograph communities as a way of being 'peace provocateurs'.

ABOUT THE HERB FEITH TRANSLATION SERIES

The Herb Feith Translation Series publishes high-quality non-fiction manuscripts not previously available in English, which enhance scholarship and teaching about Indonesia. Published by the Herb Feith Foundation in conjunction with Monash University, the books are available in print and online.

The Herb Feith Foundation was established in 2003 to commemorate the life and work of Herb Feith (1930–2001), volunteer, scholar, teacher and peace activist. Its mission is to promote and support work of the kind to which Feith devoted his life, including the study of Indonesia, through a range of educational activities including research and teaching and in the publication and promotion of such work.

This current title, *Basudara Stories of Peace from Maluku*, is the first in a mini-series of translated publications 'Healing and reconciliation after conflict'. The first mini-series of publications, co-ordinated by Dr Kate McGregor and Dr Jemma Purdey, focused on the mass violence in Indonesia in 1965–66. Until recently there have been very few accounts available in Indonesian or English of the mass violence as told by witnesses, survivors or perpetrators. Today, an increasing number of memoirs and short testimony collections are available in Indonesian; however, very few are yet available in English. This has prevented a greater understanding outside Indonesia of how this violence continues to impact on Indonesians and of how they now understand this traumatic period in their nation's history.

These translated works are valuable resources for all who seek to understand Indonesia today, and especially for undergraduate students of Asian history and the history of mass violence and genocide.

Breaking the Silence
Survivors Speak about 1965–66 Violence in Indonesia

Edited by Putu Oka Sukanta | Translated by Jennifer Lindsay

Edited by former political prisoner Putu Oka Sukanta, this is a collection of accounts from people around the archipelago who experienced the 1965 violence in Indonesia. Fifteen witnesses from Medan, Palu, Kendari, Yogyakarta, Jakarta, Bali, Kupang and Sabu Island share their stories of how they navigated this horrifying period of Indonesian history and how they have lived with this past. The book is based on life history interviews with ordinary people who worked as teachers, artists, women's activists and policemen, whose lives were turned upside down when the attack on those considered to be supporters of the Indonesian Communist Party began. These accounts, including one from a perpetrator who is now tormented by guilt, and survivors who still feel isolated and rejected by society, show how the violence continues to influence Indonesian society. The book will be a valuable resource for students of history, of Indonesia and for people wanting to understand the impact of this violence.

For more information see
http://www.publishing.monash.edu/books/bs-9781922235121.html

Forbidden Memories
Women's Experiences of 1965 in Eastern Indonesia

Edited by Mery Kolimon, Liliya Wetangterah and Karen Campbell-Nelson | Translated by Karen Campbell-Nelson

This is the first book to consider the experiences of women survivors of 1965 anti-communist violence in the majority Christian province Eastern Indonesia. So far, most studies of the 1965 violence have focused on the Muslim majority population of Java and Hindu majority population of Bali. The book presents stories from across the regions of Sumba, Sabu, Alor, Kupang and other parts of West Timor of women who were imprisoned and tortured or whose husbands were murdered. The book is a critical examination of the role of the Protestant Church at the time of the violence and in its aftermath, including ongoing sanctions and political purges against those considered to be supporters of the Indonesian Communist Party. Themes include the impact of the violence on women teachers, members of the women's organisation Gerwani and the fracturing of social and religious communities. The writers critique the role of religious and state institutions for failing to care for this vulnerable community in the face of state terrorism and a culture of fear. The editors and research team hope this publication will create a safe and peaceful environment for survivors to tell their stories and for society to acknowledge their suffering and to struggle with them to restore their rights.

For more information see
http://www.publishing.monash.edu/books/fm-9781922235909.html

About the Herb Feith Translation Series

Truth Will Out
Indonesian Accounts of the 1965 Mass Violence

Edited by Dr. Baskara T. Wardaya SJ | Translated by Jennifer Lindsay

This striking compilation of essays surveys a variety of views about the 1965 mass violence in Indonesia and current efforts to understand it. The book is the product of an oral history project involving senior and young researchers from Yogyakarta. The accounts it presents include a military man who continues to see the violence as justified and refuses survivors the status of victim; two Muslims who believe that the Communist were and continue to remain a threat to society; and a Catholic activist who reflects on how they were manipulated to support the violence. These accounts are complemented by the views of survivors of the violence, some of whom see this as a national problem that goes far beyond individual suffering. This book provides a valuable window into why this past remains contested today and some of the obstacles to reconciliation and full rehabilitation of survivors.

For more information see
http://www.publishing.monash.edu/books/two-9781922235145.html

CPSIA information can be obtained
at www.ICGtesting.com
Printed in the USA
JSHW040815170920
7993JS00004B/236